An Introduction to
Educational Research

An Introduction to

Third Edition

This third edition is designed for a wider audience of students than earlier editions. It has been thoroughly rewritten and the more technical aspects of the field have been de-emphasized. Considerable new material has been included to update the volume.

Robert M. W. Travers

WESTERN MICHIGAN UNIVERSITY

Educational Research

THE MACMILLAN COMPANY, NEW YORK

COLLIER-MACMILLAN LIMITED, LONDON

Preface

I<small>N</small> <small>PREPARING THE</small> present edition, the author has taken considerable care to simplify the language used without losing the central message that the entire volume has been designed to convey. The theme that only educational research based on theory is likely to have solid payoff over the years still remains. This position does not deny the possibility that a direct attack on a local problem may be effective, for obviously it often is, but the solving of one local problem is likely to help little in solving other local problems in other communities. In contrast, research based on a scientific tradition has had a long history of providing a means of solving a wide range of problems and that is the kind of research this book attempts to promote.

The earlier editions of this book were directed primarily at the well-read doctoral student with some background in measurement and statistics and with some sophistication in reading research literature. This edition is directed at a wider audience, to include those education students who are embarking on a master's degree. The expansion of the research activities of the United States Office of Education into schools makes it imperative for teachers to acquire some insight into the nature of scientific research and the ways in which it differs from finding stopgap remedies for local problems. Although there often is expediency in distributing Federal funds to local communities so that some politically visible effort can be made to improve education, the kind of research thus engendered is likely to have mainly politically useful outcomes. On the other hand, research on problems of education that is founded on the scientific tradition is likely to have great impact when measured over decades, but perhaps little utility in an immediate major election. A major hope underlying the writing of this book is that research on problems of education will become, in the future, less politically oriented and more scientifically oriented. The wider audi-

v

ence that the present edition seeks to reach may well have great power in bringing educational research nearer to the scientific tradition.

This edition also brings with it some new features that reflect changes in the research scene. The chapter on computers is an acknowledgement of the impact that these devices are now having both on school systems and on research related to learning. Although only a few years ago many prominent schools of education did not even have a supply of desk calculators, today most graduate students of education have access to a computer. Those graduate students who plan to enter the administrative field should have some broad knowledge of computers because these are becoming major record-keeping devices. The author hopes that the chapter on computers presented here will whet the intellectual appetite of the reader to learn more about these important components of our modern civilization.

Another innovation in this volume is a chapter on devices developed for the purpose of recording and analyzing events in the classroom. There has been a considerable proliferation of these devices, which are already forming a basis for a large research literature. The selection of such devices for research is often made on the same basis as a popularity contest. The intent of the chapter is to promote critical evaluation of them.

Another new chapter in this edition covers the area of content analysis. Some of this material appeared in scattered locations in the previous edition, but a considerable amount of new material has been added. Summarized in the chapter are some of the attempts that have been made and are being made to make a content analysis of research studies and to code the results of the analysis in a form that permits a computer to search the studies and identify those that include particular kinds of information. This is an innovation both in content analysis and in research that will soon have widespread impact and influence on the work of the graduate student. The time-consuming work of searching libraries for information relevant to the conduct of a particular study will soon be replaced by much more efficient electronic procedures. Teachers should also be aware of these new methods of handling human knowledge because within, perhaps, a decade they may become available to schools.

In this edition considerably more space is devoted to a review of the areas in which educational research is being conducted, reflecting the fact that expansion of inquiry into new areas has been one of the important developments of the last decade. To some extent this expansion reflects the fact that behavioral sciences other than psychology are now becoming interested in educational phenomena. The present extraordinary diversity of research related to education is clearly evident from the recent programs of the annual meetings of the American Educational Research Association. These programs include scheduled sessions on such varied matters as laboratory experimentation on concept learning; new statistical techniques; computer analysis of written materials; comparative studies of systems for analyzing classroom interaction; dynamics of the school board; and a host of other topics that would not have appeared on the program even a decade earlier. The great diversity of the events that are studied and the increasing sophistication of research workers in handling theoretical issues represent some of the healthy aspects of the development of the field.

I must express my appreciation to many who have offered suggestions that helped in the revision, but I am particularly indebted to Dr. William D. Coats, who gave substantial help with the chapter on computers; to Dr. Jason Millman, who kept careful notes while reading the previous edition when it first appeared and who sent me these notes; and also Prof. William Rabinowitz and Prof. Gordon Fifer, who reviewed the draft of the present edition at two different stages and who made many very significant suggestions.

R. M. W. T.

Contents

CHAPTER **1**

A Conception of Research

CHAPTER **2**

Conducting Research Within a Framework of Theory

CHAPTER 3

Areas of Educational Research

CHAPTER 4

The Planning Stage of Educational Research

CHAPTER 5

Measurement in Research

CHAPTER 6

Problems of Observation

CHAPTER 7

The Use of Multiple Observations in Measurement

CHAPTER 8

Instrumentation of Classroom Observation

CHAPTER **9**

Survey Methods

CHAPTER **10**

Analysis of the Content of Verbal Materials

CHAPTER 11

Prediction Studies

CHAPTER 12

Experimentation in Education

CHAPTER 13

Problems of Research Design

CHAPTER 14

Studies of Development

chapter 15

Data-Processing and Reporting

chapter 16

Some Problems of
Conducting Historical Research

CHAPTER 17

Applications of Computers to Education

CHAPTER 18

Some Final Considerations

List of Figures

List of Tables

An Introduction to
Educational Research

CHAPTER 1

A Conception of Research

INTRODUCTION

The Impact of the Scientist on the Problems of Education

PROBLEMS in education did not attract the interest of scientists until very recent times. A few descriptive studies were undertaken in the field of education in the nineteenth century, but not until the twentieth century did educators recognize the impact that research could have on educational progress. Clearly, both educational practice and thought have been influenced by research, but there is not much agreement on the procedures the scientist should adopt if he is to contribute to educational progress.

In the nineteenth century many philosophers attempted to describe in general terms how the scientist went about his work, perhaps in the hope that pointers might be found that could be used to guide men in the pursuit of knowledge. The most notable of the nineteenth-century philosophers to pursue this problem was John Stuart Mill. He believed that he had succeeded in identifying the essential processes leading to the making of a scientific discovery. Mill wrote with a certain finality about how the scientist proceeds, but this is still a matter of controversy. The working scientist often disagrees strongly with the descriptions of his procedures written by philosophers.

B. F. Skinner (1956), the famous experimental psychologist, has written about this matter, comparing his personal experience of how discoveries are made with textbook accounts of the procedure. The following quotation well reflects the gap between the person who teaches *about* research and the practicing scientist: "The laboratory scientist is puzzled and often dismayed when he discovers how his

1

behavior has been reconstructed in the formal analyses of scientific method. He is likely to protest that this is not at all a fair representation of what he does."

The usual formula for conducting educational research is based on the idea that there is such a procedure as "the" scientific method. This is a notion that has had to be discarded, simply because scientific knowledge is arrived at by a variety of procedures and methods. Scientists vary greatly in this respect. A few say they follow "the" scientific method. Some, once they have even a vague idea of what they want to do, like to collect small samples of data and conduct rather rough-and-ready experiments; in this way, further clues are derived that may help to sharpen up a hypothesis. Still others may begin their explorations by reading widely in related fields, without too much concern about what they are looking for or what they may find. Some rely tremendously on personal hunches, whereas others reject anything that savors of intuition. *Techniques of arriving at knowledge, as they are manifested in the behavior of scientists, are highly personal and individualized. "The" simple scientific formula that all well-behaved scientists use simply does not exist.*

Those who read research, but do not carry it out, often derive from research literature a false impression of how research is undertaken. The published report of a piece of research is presented in an orderly way. It generally begins with a statement of the problem and the review of related literature. Then there follows a description of the procedures used to investigate the problem, a table containing the results, and a discussion of the implications of the results. What the published article hides is the fact that the scientist may not have proceeded in this order at all. His starting point may have been an interest in a particular laboratory technique that he saw had applications in solving a wide range of problems. Then, perhaps, the scientist may have thought through the possibility of using it for solving first one problem and then another. Finally, he may have become intrigued with the possibility of exploring the application of the technique to a particular problem that had long defied solution. On the other hand, the scientist might have started with a statement of problem or he might have started with some doubts about the validity of a particular theory. From the published report of his research one cannot tell where he started, but the chances are that his thinking did not proceed in the order in which it is reported in the published account.

This book attempts to help the graduate student avoid some of the traps that experienced research workers have learned to avoid. Some of the material presented is based on the fact that much can be learned by studying some of the pitfalls into which mature scientists have, at times, fallen. Even the most experienced research workers make errors, stumble down deadend alleys, make unwarranted generalizations, and mistake artifacts for real effects. This book cannot provide a recipe for finding scientific solutions to educational problems. No such recipe is possible.

Levels of Research

Research includes many different kinds of activities: some simple, others highly complex. The reader who has had little experience in research may jump to the unwarranted conclusion that basic research and complex research are the same, and that applied research is simple research. This is not necessarily the case. Although much of what is commonly classified as basic research is very complex, many studies conducted within the scope of basic research programs are relatively simple and easily executed; for example, studies that reproduce important experiments to determine whether the results will hold. In the field of applied research some studies are very complex but some are very simple. Basic and applied research do not differ in the level of complexity involved, but rather are differentiated by the goals they help to achieve. Basic research is designed to add to an organized body of scientific knowledge and does not necessarily produce results of immediate practical use. Applied research is undertaken to solve an immediate practical problem and the goal of adding to scientific knowledge is secondary. Some applied research is very complex and can be undertaken only with the backing of a large organization. For example, the study by J. K. Hemphill, D. E. Griffiths and N. Frederiksen (1962), on the behavior of elementary school principals in handling day-to-day problems, required the development of elaborate techniques both for observing the behavior of the principals and for analyzing the data thus derived. The book, reporting the results of the study, is both long and technical and suitable only for the well-trained reader. Yet the study represents applied research—a direct attack on the problem of selecting elementary school principals. Good applied research may require as much technical skill as good basic research, but simple problems calling for only the skill of the apprentice are found in both areas.

Applied research does not generally add to the organized body of scientific knowledge, but occasionally it may. In applied research one problem is solved at a time and the results are not likely to have any general application. On the other hand, research that contributes to scientific knowledge leads to understandings that have application in a wide range of situations. This is why basic scientific research leads, in the long run, to a greater payoff than applied research. For example, research on what pupils learn from a particular textbook produces results that cease to be of interest once the textbook vanishes from the market. In contrast, research on the characteristics of documents and other displays that facilitate the acquisition of information by the pupil may provide results that will remain of value at least as long as pupils have to acquire information from documents.

Although skill in research is an important factor in the choice of the level at which to start, there are other considerations in making this decision—one is the amount of time involved. Research at complex levels generally involves an ongoing program pursued over many years. The graduate student of education could hardly be expected to commit himself for such a long time. On the other hand, he is also not expected to engage in an inquiry that involves little more than the routine collection and tabulation of data. The thesis or dissertation should be at a level requiring him to master new and useful research skills.

Educational Research: The Present Scene

The term *research* has come to be applied to such a wide range of activities within the field of education that it has ceased to have a single identifiable meaning. Within some school systems there are research departments that serve only the function of maintaining records of pupil enrollment and attendance and related data pertaining to the operation of the system. There are educational research organizations that devote their energies to the tabulation of data pertaining to such matters as the expenditures of the different states on education or the teacher-selection practices of different communities. Other educational research organizations administer tests, develop norms, prepare distributions of scores, and engage in routine testing programs.

Somewhat different are the activities of a few educational research institutes that conduct studies of variables related to and affecting the efficiency of learning, or studies of problems related to the development of personality. Such activities perform a function that goes far beyond that of data gathering, because the data are collected for the purpose of deriving scientific generalizations that can be applied

to the solution of a wide range of problems. This is the meaning of
the term *scientific research* that will be employed throughout this
book.

Educational research, as it is conceived here, represents an activity
directed toward the development of an organized body of scientific
knowledge about the events with which educators are concerned. Of
central importance are the behavior patterns of pupils, and particularly those to be learned through the educational process. A scientific
body of knowledge about education should enable the educator to
determine which teaching and other learning conditions to provide
in order to produce desirable aspects of learned behavior among
young people who attend school. Presumably, learning conditions will
also have to be suited to the aptitudes and other characteristics of
the learner. Where the researcher can most advantageously begin to
develop such an organized body of knowledge about educational
events is still a matter of conjecture. Wherever he does begin, however, the assumption is made that the phenomena studied, in the ultimate analysis, affect the pupils in the schools.

The scientific goal of educational research is to discover laws or
generalizations about behavior that can be used to make predictions
and control events within educational situations. For example, the
early studies of transfer of training undertaken by E. L. Thorndike
indicated that a curriculum based on the doctrine of formal discipline
was unlikely to achieve broad educational goals. Later research on
transfer of training, although embracing a more complex and sophisticated theory of transfer than that proposed by Thorndike, has generally supported his conclusions and has had important implications
for educational planning. The goal of educational research workers
is to produce a body of knowledge consisting of generalizations about
behavior that can be used to predict behavior in educational situations and to plan educational procedures and practices. Such a body
of knowledge would, of course, include knowledge about the physical
environment and its relation to the behavior of pupils and teachers.
Enough has been said at this point concerning the author's conception
of the scientific objectives of educational research, but something
remains to be said concerning the scope of its applications.

In order to clarify this point, consider some of the areas of education where a mature science of behavior in educational situations
could be applied. It could be applied to the selection and training
of teachers, to ensure that their behavior in the classroom was as
effective as possible in promoting specific kinds of pupil change. It
could be applied to the design of textbooks and other learning aids,

to insure effective use. It could be applied to the design of classrooms, not only to provide good physical conditions for personal comfort but to insure that the social organization of the class is optimal.
It could be applied to helping the pupil make long-range plans by
forecasting what he could and could not accomplish. It could provide
the principal with a sound basis for organizing the faculty and could
guide him in providing conditions that would permit teachers to
develop fully their potential as professional persons. It could provide
the foundation for the development of a technology of education.
Thus one can continue. There is not a single phase of the educational
process that a mature science of behavior in educational situations
could not render more effective.

Despite the emphasis today on finding quick solutions to pressing
educational problems, even a superficial survey shows that this latter
kind of research has had little impact on education or on educational
thought in the past. One can, however, point to a number of impacts
that research has had on both thought and practice in education: the
work of B. F. Skinner on learning; Jean Piaget on conceptual development; and D. O. Hebb on the role of early learning. The impact of
all of these stems from the power of the ideas developed, but the
powerful ideas were a product of almost a lifetime of research. History appears to show that a long period of scientific effort is needed
before ideas emerge that have the capability of producing extensive
change. One also suspects that there are not very many individuals
capable of producing research that over the years has the capability
of leading to educational change.

Research and Value Judgments

Many of the most persistent problems of education are ethical and
moral and cannot be solved by the procedures that the scientist
typically pursues. Whether greater emphasis should be given in schools
to the development of social values or to work skills represents one
such broad issue that cannot be settled by turning to empirical science.
Any solution that can be found must be derived from moral philosophy. All questions pertaining to the selection of educational objectives involve issues of ethics—issues of what is worthwhile, or virtuous,
or desirable. The scientist working on educational problems cannot
entirely escape such questions even though he is in no position to
provide answers.

Research on educational problems often involves implicit assumptions concerning what *should* be the goals of education—assumptions that involve ultimate questions about the values that *should* be achieved by our society. Consider, for example, the scientist who devotes his life to the development of mechanically equipped classrooms designed for the effective teaching of spelling, computation, history, geography, and vocabulary. An assumption underlying the work of this scientist is that these are the important areas of human development. After an examination of his equipment which, let us assume is impeccably efficient, one might conclude that he viewed the central and only goal of education as being "preparation for life." This scientist may well not have recognized the hidden values guiding his work and, for this reason, may come into conflict with a teacher in whose classroom he may wish to install his teaching machines. The teacher may well reject the scientist's program of innovation, claiming with John Dewey that education is much more than preparation for life, but that it is life itself; hence, each experience a child has in a classroom must be a worthwhile experience in living. The teacher might claim that the scientist's equipment was worthless because it failed to achieve one of the most important objectives of the classroom—a set of experiences of immediate worth.

In this instance the teacher and the scientist were concerned with different educational goals and different sets of values. Much of the conflict that occurs between research workers and teachers stems from the scientist's failure to recognize the value judgments implicit in his research.

There is no doubt in the author's mind that the usefulness of educational research would be greatly enhanced if the researcher were sensitive more often to the central ethical and moral problems of education. There is little worth in developing research on problems unrelated to these central issues.

The Nature of Scientific Data

The product that the scientist seeks to develop as the outcome of a particular study is not a table of "facts," but a generalization. This point is sometimes lost in educational literature because there are many so-called educational research agencies that direct their energies to the accumulation of "facts." Educational practitioners need facts to solve local problems, but the scientist collects facts only to provide a basis for discovering generalizations that have wide applicability.

Although scientists engage in fact collecting, they generally undertake this task in a rather different way from the layman or the information-seeking administrator. The facts collected by the scientist are generally referred to as *data*, to distinguish them from the day-to-day collection of information in which everyone engages. Data represent a very special class of information. When a person says "I have noticed that thin people are ill-tempered," he is not providing data in a scientific sense for a number of reasons. First, nothing is indicated about the conditions under which the information was collected. From the statement one cannot tell whether the observer went out and located thin people or whether he is referring to a particular thin person he knows. Secondly, no information is provided concerning the number of people on whom the observation is based. Thirdly, there is no indication about the way in which it was determined how any particular thin person came to be classified as ill-tempered. Fourthly, the statement implies that there are no negative instances, that is, there were no thin people who were not ill-tempered—a very unlikely state of affairs unless only a very few thin people were observed.

The term *data*, used in a scientific sense, refers to clearly identifiable information collected under conditions that are precisely specified. If a study were to be undertaken of the acquisition of skill in spelling, the data presenting the measures of initial and final skill in spelling would be meaningless unless a clear statement were available concerning the instrument used for measuring spelling skill. Certain other aspects of the data-collection conditions would also have to be known. One of these would be whether the testing task emphasized or did not emphasize speed. Others would be the procedures used for selecting those whose spelling ability was tested. The conditions have to be sufficiently well described so that another experimenter can actually reproduce the experiment and expect to obtain similar data.

A teacher says "I know that my children spell well. Why, one only has to look at their compositions to see that this is so." He does not have data in a scientific sense. He has information of a kind, perhaps, but not data. A superintendent visits two groups of classes, one taught by what we may call Method X and the other by Method Y. He rates each of the classes for the amount he judges the children are learning and concludes that the one method is superior to the other. Even though he could tabulate his ratings, the resulting table would not even remotely resemble scientific data, for it would be virtually impossible for the superintendent to describe with any precision how the ratings were arrived at. Although the superintendent reached the generalization that one method was better than the other, the generalization is worth no more than the information on which it was based. In this case, as a scientific generalization it is worth precisely nothing.

On the other hand, when a scientific research worker prepares a table of the frequency with which children have been reinforced, one can be sure to find in the accompanying text information concerning what was used as a reinforcement, the nature of the contingency that resulted in the reinforcement, how the reinforcement was administered, over what period of time the reinforcing events occurred, how the children were selected, and so forth. A basic requirement of scientific research is that there must be absolutely no question about what the procedures and conditions related to the collection of the data were.

Scientific data also have another important characteristic. It is not just any set of observations, but a particular set with relevance for developing further the ideas that man has already evolved about related phenomena. Data have meaning only in relation to particular problems.

THE ORGANIZATION OF IDEAS

From Data to Generalizations

No research worker worth his salt is interested merely in the collection of data, for he will want to derive statements that are true for situations other than those in which the data were collected. If a teacher of educable mentally retarded children were to develop a method for teaching them reading, and were to demonstrate that a group of such children learned to read substantially and significantly more rapidly than a group of similar children exposed to more typical reading instruction, the teacher would then be concerned with asking whether similar results would be found if the method were used with other groups. The teacher wants to draw a generalization from his data, because his study is of little import if the method is effective only with the groups studied and not with other groups. We are assuming here that the teacher is of a scientific disposition, for, if he were not, he might be content with having discovered the fact that the new method was an effective one for his particular class and leave the matter at that. The scientist never stops with data, he is always concerned with deriving generalizations that can be applied to other situations.

A valid generalization derived from data is sometimes referred to as a law, although the term *law* is more commonly used in the physical sciences than in the behavioral sciences, perhaps because behavioral scientists have difficulty in determining what is and what is not a valid generalization. Generalizations or laws must be such that they can be used to predict events. A generalization that applies only to past events is not a particularly useful one, although many of the generalizations derived from history are of this type. Generalizations that can be used only for accounting for events in the past provide what are called *postdictive* systems; the generalizations developed by the scientist must be *predictive*.

The generalizations and laws of science are always based on considerable quantities of data. Nevertheless, it is not enough for the researcher to have voluminous facts if he is to discover laws. Many students have arrived at graduate schools of education with files of data collected in their school systems and have found that those vast quantities of facts could not be used to form the basis of a doctoral dissertation. Masses of data should not represent the starting place of most behavioral research. Data should be collected only after the problem to be investigated has been well defined. Hypotheses that form the basis for a major research project are not derived from masses of unorganized facts but from the available body of organized knowledge.

A theory consists of a group of generalizations that together account for particular classes of phenomena. For example, the atomic theory of matter that revolutionized chemistry during the last century consists of a set of generalizations such as (1) all matter consists of atoms; (2) an atom of a particular element is the smallest quantity of matter that can enter into a chemical reaction; (3) elements differ in the mass of their atoms; and so forth. Educational theory does not generally consist of such clear-cut and concise generalizations. The statements or generalizations that form the body of a theory are sometimes referred to as the *postulates* of that theory.

Theories and Laws

Theory has a place in educational research as in all other types of research. The place of theory is not usually adequately recognized or identified. Too often it is mentioned in terms of a gulf between theory and practice, and frequently with some ridicule concerning the theory side of this gulf. A distinction is made between the practical people who deal with facts (and who are alleged to "get things done") and the researcher who deals with theories. Such distinctions and discriminations serve only to produce confusion, because they are based on misunderstandings concerning the function and nature of theories.

All actions of a practical nature in educational situations are based to some extent on a theory of behavior. The teacher who attempts to enrich the curriculum with field trips and demonstrations is basing actions on a theory that learning is most efficient if the experiences provided for learning occur in a variety of different milieus. The principal who institutes a series of staff conferences in order to install a new experimental curriculum is basing his action on a theory of social behavior insofar as his approach to the faculty is concerned, and a theory of learning insofar as the new experimental curriculum is concerned. The actions of practical people who operate educational programs nearly always are based on some kind of theory of behavior. In this respect they differ from the researcher in that the researcher must state explicitly the nature of the theory underlying his work, whereas the practical educator does not have to do this. They differ also in the characteristics of the theories involved.

N. Campbell (1952), who has written at some length on this phenomenon, points out that the practical man always seems to be willing to discuss his theories, which he has in abundance, but which differ from those of the scientist in both the way they are derived and the way they are used. The practical man's theories are formulations of what he has observed, but his observations always tend to refer to whatever events he *wanted* to see. A principal we know advocated teaching reading in kindergarten. He perhaps had arrived at this point of view by observing just one or two teachers who were particularly effective in teaching reading to a young group of very bright children. From that point on, he probably responded like most persons who have formulated or initiated a theory—he remembered only those subsequent instances that fitted his theory and forgot or disregarded the instances that did not.

One does not have to wander far in educational circles to find theories pertaining to every type and aspect of learning. Many of these theories go back to such notable thinkers as Aristotle and Thomas Aquinas; some are local in origin. Most, however, are based only on the type of observation that the scientist considers as merely a beginning for his activity, whereas to the lay person they are a sound basis for theorizing.

A theory as developed by a scientist is, like the theory of the layman, a set of generalizations believed to have some value in predicting important events. But the scientist and the layman differ in the way in which they derive their theories—the theory of the scientist is derived from well-established knowledge and is formulated in as precise terms as he can find; that of the layman is rooted in casual observation. A theory may be formulated in a set of carefully worded statements or, if the state of knowledge is far enough advanced, in a set of mathematical equations. From the theory he has formulated, the scientist derives _hypotheses_, which are simply statements of some of the consequences that can be expected of the theory if it is true. He can then investigate these hypotheses in order to determine whether the theory he has formulated continues to apply when it is used for making predictions.

There are certain real difficulties in bridging the gap between the theories of the "practical" educator and those of the researcher. The theories of the former are couched in the language of the layman and are relatively easily communicated. Those of the researcher are stated in a technical language derived from the behavioral sciences and often are of a type that few scientists and far fewer laymen understand. Thus the practical educator, because he does not understand them, may often feel that the theories of the researcher have little application to actual educational problems. The ultimate interpretation of these theories in terms that the educator understands presents difficulties that have not yet been solved.

On Becoming Involved in Research Based on Scientific Theory

The hope is expressed here that an increasing number of students of education will become involved in research that extends scientific knowledge and is based on scientific theory. Such students, many of whom have never previously conducted any research, may have difficulty in knowing where to begin such an enterprise. A part of his difficulty is a result of the fact that theory-oriented research is generally undertaken through long sequences of studies. The graduate student wishing to undertake such research would do well to attach himself to some such program through which he can participate in problem solving and theory development. If he wants this kind of experience, he would do well to avoid investigating some isolated problem in which he has some deep and personal interest, because such personal ventures restrict greatly the intellectual experiences that his research can provide.

Most research of consequence today involves groups of studies undertaken over a period of years. Such research is said to be programmatic and is necessarily theory oriented. It is to be contrasted with the kind of research that is undertaken through an isolated study here and an isolated study there that are not tied to a common thread of theory. Studies of the latter type are, fortunately, slowly disappearing from the scene, largely because they have been unproductive. Thus the student of education must come to realize that, however much he may want to attack some problem of special interest to him, unless the problem is related to the systematic development of a set of theoretical ideas, and unless it extends work already undertaken, his efforts are likely to be wasted.

Constructs and Theories

In the behavioral sciences, it is common practice for the scientist to develop theories that postulate underlying mechanisms to account for behavior as it is observed. In a sense, these ideas concerning underlying mechanisms can be considered to be products of the scientist's imagination, but they help him immensely in thinking about the phenomena he is studying. These imagined mechanisms are known as *constructs*. Sometimes they are referred to as *hypothetical constructs*, to indicate that they are not considered real objects or events. Most theories of behavior involve constructs. Words such as intelligence, motivation, memory trace, inhibition, mediation, and set all refer to constructs. Constructs are the abstract elements of a theory, and the words used to represent them are called theoretical terms.

It is almost impossible to discuss behavior in terms of modern psychological theory without introducing constructs; even much ordinary speech involves their use. Unfortunately, in common speech there is a tendency to reify hypothetical constructs; that is to say, to refer to them as if they were real and observable entities. An important part of the research worker's training is to learn to discriminate between hypothetical constructs and observable events, a distinction to which the scientist strictly adheres. We may speak of a person as having a "liberal" attitude, although we cannot observe his attitude directly; all we can ever observe is the result of this attitude as it is manifested in behavior. The attitude itself is a hypothetical construct introduced by the observer to explain consistency in behavior as it is seen. Abilities such as verbal ability, mechanical ability and numerical ability are hypothetical constructs. The abilities themselves cannot be observed, for only behavior that *results* from these abilities is observable.

Hypothetical constructs may be derived from many sources. First, there are those derived from neurology. Although relatively little is known about the functioning of the nervous system, something is known about the location of specific tracts and nuclei and about the transmission of impulses along these tracts. With this limited knowledge, it is possible to postulate the existence of certain mechanisms to account for behavior as it is observed. For example, the student who has read elementary textbooks on psychology usually is familiar with the diagrams of the supposed nerve mechanism that underlies the conditioned reflex. Now in actual fact, no person has ever directly observed such a mechanism. It is postulated on the basis of general knowledge of the nervous system. It is, in fact, a hypothetical construct introduced to account for behavior. A further example of neurological constructs is seen in the type of associationist psychology with which the name of E. L. Thorndike is connected. In this sort of theory, it has been common to think of the development of connections between stimuli and responses as representing changes in the synapses, the areas of tissue that separate one nerve cell from another. In more recent times, D. O. Hebb has introduced many constructs derived from neurology to account for behavior. Hebb makes it clear in his writings that nobody has ever directly observed the mechanisms he postulates, and he drives home this point by distinguishing between a conceptual nervous system and the real nervous system.

A second source of hypothetical construct is the scientist's own field of consciousness, or his *phenomenal field,* as it is called. Many constructs are derived from this source. When we speak of associations among ideas, perceptual structuring, and purposes, we are using constructs derived from our personal experience. Some modern psychologists have doubts about the usefulness of such constructs. Nevertheless, such theories have a strong group of supporters who work mainly in the clinical field. Carl Rogers, for instance, has exercised leadership within this group for many years, and a number of his students have written extensively concerning this type of construct and the theories that result from its use.

A third source of constructs is physics. The research worker may take the position that the inner, unobservable mechanisms underlying the behavior of the pupil in the classroom can be described in terms of *forces, fields of force, movements,* and similar terms derived from physics. Gestalt psychologists used such terms extensively in discussing behavior and considered that they presented useful and convenient ways of describing the roots of behavior internal to the organism. The late K. Lewin also made extensive use of such ideas derived from the physical sciences and would draw diagrams showing the operation of psychological forces analogous to the physical forces of attraction and repulsion exerted by electrically charged particles. These and other analogies from physics are considered to be merely convenient ways of representing underlying phenomena that cannot be directly observed. The system of constructs they involve are introduced as convenient crutches for thinking about behavior. Constructs are discarded as soon as they are found to be of little value or as soon as they are replaced by constructs of greater utility for research.

Definitive advice cannot be given at this time concerning the relative utility of the three main sources of constructs discussed. The author is under the impression that constructs derived from neurological and physical analogies are preferred by most contemporary theory-builders who distrust the type of theory that derives its constructs from the content of conscious personal experience. But the fact that a construct is derived from a particular area does not guarantee its utility. Each construct should satisfy at least one important condition, which must now be discussed.

In the development of constructs, the essential condition, as C. L. Hull (1943) has pointed out, is the avoidance of circularity of argument. This common defect may be clarified by means of an example. In the study of problem-solving behavior, the custom in the past has been to explain such behavior in terms of a construct called intelligence. This procedure involves circular argument, for specific problem-solving behaviors are used as a basis for postulating an underlying ability referred to as intelligence, and then this underlying ability is used to explain the problem-solving behavior on the basis of which it was originally derived. In such a situation, the invention of a construct serves no useful purpose.

Consider another example in which the introduction of a hypothetical construct can be justified. Teachers commonly state that children have a need for approval. This statement means only that the behavior of children can be modified and shaped by comments demonstrating the approval of the adult. There is no need to introduce the concept of an inner need for approval, if this is the only data we have, for the introduction of the concept adds nothing to what is already included in the statement that approval can be used to modify behavior. However, J. L. Gewirtz and D. M. Baer (1958a, 1958b) have shown that, after children are deprived of approval for a short period, approval becomes a stronger reinforcer of their behavior. Such data are more readily understood when they are interpreted to imply that depriving a child of approving comments increases an inner need for approval which, in turn, makes the child more sensitive and responsive to approval. In such a case, a need for approval is introduced as a construct that links the effects of deprivation with the resulting heightened effect of approval. A useful construct always links an antecedent condition (deprivation of approval) with a consequent condition (increased effect of approval).

Models

The student cannot long pursue graduate studies without encountering the term *model*, an expression used very freely with many differing meanings. The treatment of models in this chapter follows closely that of A. Chapanis (1961).

A model is an analogy, a way of representing a particular phenomenon. Models are widely used by teachers for helping pupils understand phenomena. One of the models most commonly found in the classroom is the globe, which should not be construed as being merely a miniature of the earth. Although the shape of the globe represents the earth in miniature form, other features of the earth are not represented realistically; for example, the color of a country on the globe has nothing to do with the color of the actual terrain of that country. The surface of the earth is generally represented as smooth, but if mountains are represented they have to be grossly exaggerated in size otherwise they would not be visible to the student. The lines of latitude and longitude are drawn on the globe, but of course they are imaginary lines on the planet. The globe is merely a convenient way of representing the earth. It is not designed to be a realistic miniature in all respects, but despite this lack of realism its value as a teaching device has been recognized by generations of teachers. Other examples of models are found in the administrative offices of the school system. The table of organization found in the superintendent's office is a model of the administrative machinery of the school's system. The architect's plans for a new school building provide yet another example of a model.

Models are analogies. Chapanis states the matter in this way: "Scientific or engineering models are representations, or likenesses, of certain aspects of complex events, structures, or systems, made by using symbols or objects which in some way resemble the thing being modeled." No clear-cut line can be drawn between models and constructs. Some scientists have adopted the custom of limiting the use of the term *model* to concrete representations of objects or phenomena, while *constructs* are left to refer to more abstract representations of unobservable aspects of phenomena. However, no widely accepted distinction has been adopted. The reader might as well recognize that in reviewing research literature he will come across what are called models, developed for the purpose of representing behavior with its underlying mechanisms, but other research workers using the same framework of ideas will refer to them as constructs.

Chapanis, in following through on his definition, classifies models as *replica models* and *symbolic models*. A replica model looks like the object or phenomenon that is represented. A globe is roughly a replica model of the earth, although it does incorporate many symbolic features—the little circles representing cities, for instance. Symbolic models, on the other hand, use abstract symbols to represent either parts of an object or the relationship among phenomena. A symbolic model of perception and communication provided by D. E. Broadbent, shown in Figure 1, is an example of a symbolic model. This model is

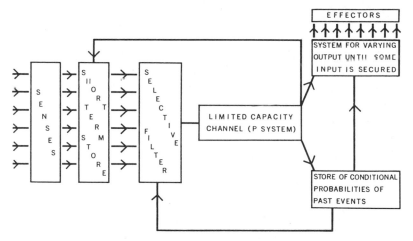

FIGURE 1. Symbolic model of the processing of information received by the human organism. (From Broadbent, 1958.)

able to represent some of the events that have been observed in experimental studies of perception. It has also been used to suggest a number of experiments which have actually been undertaken.

The Broadbent model shows information about the world around us entering the senses. The information is then held in a short-term storage system, but most of the information held in storage is held there for only a matter of a few seconds and is never used. In order for information to be remembered fairly permanently, or used for making a response to the situation in the environment, it has to enter the perceptual system (represented by the Limited Capacity Channel). Only a small amount of the information held in short-term storage can enter the perceptual system. The selective filter has the function of determining what information will enter the perceptual system and what information will be allowed to fade away in the short-term memory. The model also shows that the perceptual system leads to a permanent memory (Store of Conditional Probabilities of Past Events) and also to actions. In fairness to the model one must also say that it represents a set of scientific ideas, much more sophisticated than those reflected in this brief description.

Models representing generalized forms of administrative relationships have also been produced. Of the latter, one developed by J. W. Getzels and E. G. Guba (1957) has had a long history of influencing thought about administrative problems and has been reproduced in many variations. One variation presented by Guba (1960) is reproduced in Figure 2. The latter model is an interpretation of administrative behavior derived from sociology and psychology. It shows that administrative influence can be exerted in two kinds of ways: through delegating roles and tasks to those supervised and through personal influence. The model also indicates that there are both integrating forces and conflicts in any organization with which all members have to cope. Once again, it must be said here that this popular account of the model does not do justice to its scientific sophistication.

Although a distinction has been made between constructs and models, the scientist may start with a highly abstract set of constructs and then build a model to clarify aspects of them. Niels Bohr's highly mathematical conception of the atom has been presented to generations of students in the form of a simple mechanical model in which an atom is represented as a miniature solar system with the nucleus at the center and electrons spinning around the nucleus at varying distances from it. The scientist passes from the constructs to models and back again as it is convenient for the development of his thinking.

The widespread use of models in scientific work derives largely from their value in suggesting experiments and studies and their long history as a means of achieving important knowledge. They have an additional value: sometimes it is possible to experiment first with the model itself and then with the real phenomena. An example of this is found in the study of thinking processes in which computers have been made to simulate the thinking involved in, say, the derivation of a proof of a theorem of Euclid. The computer can be programmed to

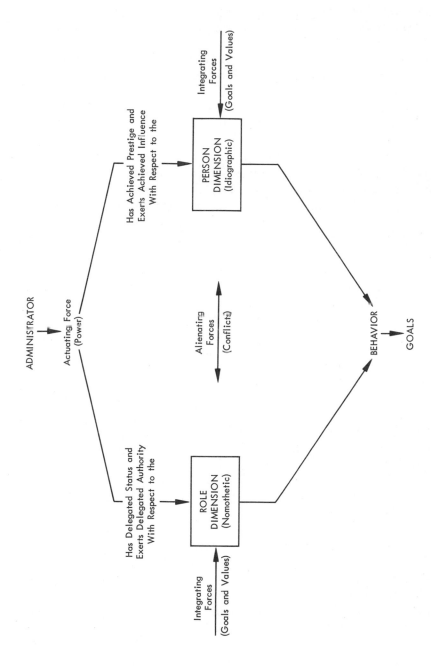

FIGURE 2. *Model of internal administrative relationships.* (From Guba, 1960.)

19

generate the proof. The false moves it makes in undertaking this task can be studied. Once such false moves have been identified, studies can be conducted on human subjects to determine whether similar false moves are also made by human problem solvers. The experimenter can then go on to find ways of preventing such false moves in thinking from taking place. In this case the computer's operation is used as a model of the thinking process.

Models are invaluable assets to the pursuit of scientific research, but a poor model can be as much a hindrance as a good one is a help. The usefulness of a model is shown in the quality and value of the research it stimulates. However, a scientist can often cling to a useless model because it presents a plausible and convincing picture of the phenomenon under investigation. One can do well to reflect on the fact that for thousands of years men used as a model of the earth a flat disc, a model that confused thinking for generations. Another example of a faulty model was the idea held by early chemists that the phenomenon of burning involved the giving up of a substance called *phlogiston*. The firm hold this model had on the thinking of chemists not only prevented them from embracing alternative conceptions of combustion but also resulted in a state of stagnation of the field of chemistry for more than a century.

Models are *not* theories, but they may represent a stage in thinking that often has to take place before a theory can be stated. Theories have to be based on a great amount of firmly established evidence and are generalizations based on the evidence. Scientific models tend to be much more speculative than theories. They are the product of the scientist who says, "Suppose we look at things in this kind of way and see whether it helps us." They are clever conjectures that can be immensely helpful in thinking, but they are not claimed to be truthful representations.

A Conception of the Role of Theory in Research

When the scientist states that he knows a law that will serve the purpose of making a particular prediction or some other purpose, one can be sure that the law has been verified by determining that it is capable of making the predictions that its alleged to be able to make. All laws have their limitations; and because these limits are rarely, if ever, precisely known, there is often a question as to whether a law can be relied on as a basis for a particular prediction. The theories that are used in educational research are usually represented by a series of generalizations about some aspect of education. These generalizations are based on information and are often substantiated by research, but they do not yet have the certainty, usefulness, or status of laws.

An example from a field outside education may perhaps clarify this point more easily than one from education itself. From the chemical theory that burning represents a compounding of a substance with oxygen, it can be deduced that the products of burning must weigh more than the object that is ignited. Thus, in one of the classical experiments of chemistry, it was demonstrated that mercuric oxide resulting from the burning of mercury weighs more than the mercury from which it was derived. This and similar evidence was collected to support the oxidation theory. Later, as chemistry grew to be a quantitative science, it became possible to predict from a more general theory just what would be the amount of oxygen that would combine with a particular substance.

The basic generalizations or laws that constitute the very core of a theory are commonly referred to as the postulates. In its early stage of development, the theory that burning is oxidation, involved, like any other theory, one or more basic postulates from which deductions were made; or, to say the same thing but in different words, from which hypotheses were derived. In this simple chemical theory there are two basic postulates or generalizations:

Postulate 1: When elements combine chemically they give up energy.
Postulate 2: Combustion is the chemical combination of a substance with oxygen.

One deduction from this theory of burning is that the product of burning mercury will weigh more than the original weight of the mercury. The latter deduction was the central hypothesis in a classical experiment by Lavoisier that was designed to test whether the chemical combination theory or the phlogiston theory of burning should be accepted.

Whereas in the physical sciences a theory consists of a system of laws, that is to say statements that are highly valid, theories used in behavioral and educational research are based on generalizations that are much more open to question. An example nearer to education may now be cited that illustrates this point. A. Bandura and R. A. Walters (1963) have reviewed research related to the appearance of aggressive behavior in children. The following four generalizations emerge from this review:

1. Aggressive responses, if reinforced, increased in frequency.
2. Aggressive responses learned in one situation generalize to other situations.
3. Punishment by an authority figure inhibits direct aggression in the presence of the punitive agent.
4. Punishment by an authority figure for aggression toward a particular target increases aggression toward other targets.

These generalizations form a *primitive* theory. Unfortunately, the generalizations are not sufficiently well established for one to be able to refer to them as laws, which is why the theory is described here as primitive. As a test of the utility of the theory for understanding and managing classroom aggression of children, one might make the deduction from the theory that children who were praised by their parents for aggression toward other children would show more aggressive acts in school than those whose parents ignored such acts. A research undertaken to test this hypothesis would provide information concerning the applicability of the theory to the handling of certain problems of the classroom. Such a research probes the boundaries of the theory, asking just how far from the experimental research one can go and still find the theory valid.

The primitive theory presented here also shows rather clearly that such a theory is a summary of the state of knowledge. It brings together, in a concise form, what is known. Because research should build on what is known, theory forms a starting point for most research. Not even the development of applied research can escape entirely the need to have theory as a starting point.

Even though theory-based educational research will often involve testing whether a particular theoretical position can be applied to the solution of a particular category of classroom problems, such research may also serve other purposes. A related problem is that of discovering whether knowledge acquired through experiments on subhuman species can be applied to the solution of human problems. Research on reinforcement learning has undergone this kind of development. Most of the work on reinforcement learning until midcentury was undertaken in animal laboratories; however, because interest developed in applying the results to the planning of human learning, the research has had to be extended to the human species. There it has been found that, within certain limited boundaries, the results of animal studies apply rather well.

A more ambitious attempt to develop research within the framework of theory is involved when the researcher seeks to extend the theory to include new variables. For example, early theories of reading emphasized such factors as frequency of exposure to particular words, use of pictorial cues, the frequency of feedback and reinforcement, the discriminability of words, and level of maturation. However, evidence from a great many different sources indicates that a very important variable is the extent to which the children have been previously exposed to perceptual learning in their preschool environment. This introduces into a theory of reading a new and, probably, a very important variable. The introduction of new variables into a theory, which in turn refines the theory, has always been a very important function of the scientist and one that leads to significant advances.

The most ambitious function of all research undertaken in a framework of theory is the execution of a series of studies that result in the reformulation of the entire theory. Such ventures are rare in science and even more rarely successful. Kepler's analysis of astronomical data, which led him to the theory that the sun, and not the earth, was the center of the solar system, would be an example of one such successful venture. Modern physical science offers many less well-known programs of research that have led to a reorganization theory. Sometimes, of course, as in the case of Einstein, new theoretical formulations are produced without further empirical research through a reexamination of all the available data and through an attempt to fit into the new theory facts that did not fit the earlier one.

Summary

1. There is no simple formula called the scientific method that can be applied to solve complicated problems. Scientists differ from one another in the procedures they follow.

2. Research is sometimes divided into the categories of basic and applied. Work in both of these areas may require extensive technical skill. The central aim of an applied research project is to discover a solution for some pressing practical problem. Basic research, on the other hand, is directed toward finding knowledge that has a broad base of application and that adds to the already existing organized body of scientific knowledge.

3. The term *research* is applied by people in education to a wide range of activities, from the informal collection of data for the purpose of solving administrative problems to work undertaken by scientists over a lifetime. This volume is concerned more with the latter type of research than with the former. Most of the research

that has had impact on educational practice has come from the laboratories of scientists who have devoted a lifetime to a program of discovery.

4. Although many of the central problems of education are those related to the making of value judgments, the scientist is involved only indirectly with such issues. However, he must remain sensitive to problems of value so that he recognizes those values his research may help to achieve.

5. The scientist collects data, a special form of information. The data of the scientist are always collected under very carefully defined conditions. They never represent either hearsay or casual observation. In addition, data are collected because they have relevance for the solution of particular problems. Only very rarely does a scientist start with data and then find a problem that he can use the data to solve. He generally starts with a problem.

6. The scientist is interested in data insofar as he can draw generalizations. In advanced sciences, the generalizations drawn are called laws. Useful laws permit predictions to be made. The generalizations that form the body of a theory are sometimes called the postulates of the theory.

7. The essential differences between the theories of the scientist and the theories of the practical man reside both in the kinds of information on which they are based and on the rigor with which generalizations are drawn from the information.

8. The statement of a theory generally involves the introduction of constructs. These refer to imagined mechanisms that cannot be observed but that help to explain phenomena. The idea that much of behavior has to be understood in terms of the underlying attitudes of the person behaving, involves the introduction of the construct *attitude*. Constructs can be derived from all kinds of different sources including our own mental life, neurology and physiology, and even the physical sciences. However, too often educational writers will introduce constructs when little purpose is served by doing so.

9. Scientists use models in thinking about problems. A model is nothing more than a convenient analogy that serves as a crutch to thought. A model is involved when one thinks of an atom as something like a very small billiard ball, or when one thinks of the eye as a communication system, as is involved in a television camera and transmitter. These analogies provide simple ways of thinking about very complex phenomena. Teachers and learners as well as scientists find models of great help in thinking.

10. The statement of a theory summarizes concisely the knowledge available and, hence, provides a starting point for research. A particular research may test the applicability of a theory to a particular situation, or it may extend the theory to new fields, or it may result in the restatement and reformulation of that theory.

||||||||||||||||||||||||||||||||

CHAPTER 2

Conducting Research Within a Framework of Theory

Precision in the Statement of Theory: The Problem of Language

Common language lacks the precision necessary for the stating of scientific theories. Much of the difficulty of producing clearly stated educational theories derives from the fact that they are generally formulated in common language. In contrast, the most highly developed examples of theory in science all involve a technical language. The failure of professional educators to evolve a respectable technical language accounts for the vagueness and ambiguity of much pedagogical literature and is the source of endless educational debate. Confusion has been further confounded by borrowing languages from other areas without first considering carefully what properties a borrowed language should possess if it is to help rather than hinder. An example of an ill-chosen language borrowed by educators is the language of clinical psychology. This language has been commonly adopted by teachers because they are concerned with problems of mental health and the language appears to permit the discussion of such problems. But it is an ill-chosen language because the clinical psychologists themselves have found that it involves much ambiguity and leads to poor communication. If a technical language is to be borrowed, it should be one that is well recognized as permitting clear communication, or at least clearer communication than is possible with common language.

The basic terms of such a language must be ones that can be operationally defined. For example, the term *reinforcement* is acceptable as a term in a technical language because there are well-identified experimental situations in which the term is consistently applied. In all of these situations a living creature makes a response, an event follows the response, and the event has the property of increasing the probability that the response will occur when, on future occasions, the same living creature is confronted with the same or similar situations. The event is the reinforcer. We can give indisputable examples of reinforcers for childhood behavior such as saying, "That's right" or "Very good!" and there is excellent agreement on the situations to which this term applies.

If the terms used in educational theory were as well defined as, say, reinforcement, the problem we are considering here would not arise; but many of the key terms in large areas of educational theory lack the kind of definition we have been considering. In which situations is a child demonstrating self-actualization or self-fulfillment? These situations can be described only in the vaguest terms. In fact, there might be strong disagreement among those concerned in the practical business of education concerning the situations in which either of these terms could, or could not, be appropriately used. The basic terms of an educational theory have to be ones that can be unambiguously defined by pointing to the situations to which they apply. This is what is meant by an operational definition. If one is not sure of the situations or events to which a term is to be applied, then the term lacks an adequate operational definition. A theory has to have some terms that are operationally defined. If an attempt is being made to derive from research a theory of reading, then care must be taken to define operationally what is meant by *reading*. If this is not done, different interpretations will be given to the theory of reading. One might define reading, for example, as a controlled form of talking in which the words said are controlled by the nature of the written symbols. This definition does not include any concept of meaning. If the latter concept is to be included then further definitions would be required.

The lack of operational definitions is a notorious deficiency of educational literature. It is a deficiency stemming from the fact that most producers of educational literature are not research workers. Because a research worker is engaged in conducting research in real situations, it is easy for him to define his terms clearly and unambiguously with reference to what happens in those situations. A research worker interested in the effects of teacher-administered reinforcements can define these in terms of certain easily observed acts of teachers. The speculative writer in the field of education, on the other hand, is remote from concrete and observable situations that could be used to define his terms. This leads him to seek definitions in a world of words in which vague terms are defined through other vague terms.

A major function of research in any area is to develop a technical language, the basic terms of which refer to events that can be readily identified by every competent person who utilizes it. Chemists can communicate clearly and unambiguously because chemistry has a well-developed technical language. When a chemist talks about sodium, he means a particular element with a particular atomic weight and no other substance. He can also make meaningful statements involving not only the term *sodium*, but also other technical terms in the vocabulary of chemistry. He can make such statements as "Sodium has many chemical properties similar to potassium." This brings out an important point in the development of technical languages, namely, that the terms of a technical language form a system. This is a point we must return to, so keep it in mind.

Those engaged in research for the purpose of completing a master's thesis have long had impressed on them by their thesis committees the importance of defining in operational terms the key words used. What has not been emphasized, although it should have been, is that a set of operationally defined terms may be useless. Suppose that a measure of dominance in a superintendent is defined operationally as the sum of his height in inches, plus the loudness of his voice in decibels measured in a standardized interview. Enough is already known about problems of measurement in this area to say that the proposed measure of dominance would be worthless, and the fact that it was operationally defined can bestow on it no value. The basic defect in the procedure is that of inventing a particular concept of dominance in isolation from established knowledge. If the research worker had turned to social psychology, he might have found a set of terms that could have been used for discussing dominative behavior of superintendents and he might have found that this characteristic could be measured in ways that other research had shown to be useful. The language of social psychology would have provided him with a set of terms that identified important and related characteristics of social situations.

The language used by Skinner in describing learning phenomena has been widely used by research workers in education because it is a language that has emerged in a research context, because it has terms that connote phenomena of significance, and because the terms represent a related system of concepts. Terms such as reinforcement, aversive stimuli, shaping behavior, inhibition, stimulus control, extinction, all represent part of a system of concepts of how learning takes place. A statement about learning such as "Reinforcement shapes behavior," is an example of how two of the terms are related in a basic generalization about learning. Although one may criticize the language of reinforcement approaches to learning as representing too limited phenomena to be of concern to the teacher who must think of the whole child, one achieves more by being able to discuss limited phenomena with precision than by indulging in exchanges of vague generalities where each interprets a statement to mean what he wants it to mean.

Operationally defined terms are not the only ones that are necessary for the development of a technical language, theoretical terms are also necessary. Examples of theoretical terms are *motivation* and *attitude,* both of which refer to conditions that underlie behavior, but which do not refer to directly observable events. One can observe the consequences of motivation, but not motivation itself. Such theoretical terms appear to be essential for the development of a technical language, but they have to be used sparingly and they must also be closely tied to observables. Theoretical terms refer to abstract ideas called constructs. The theoretical term motivation is generally related to the construct that behavior is energized and directed in some way. Theoretical terms also have to be tied in closely with terms that can be operationally defined. A theoretical term such as *motivation* does not become a useful theoretical term unless statements can be made about how motivation can be heightened or lowered and statements about the changes in behavior that occur as motivation is thus changed. Even though theoretical terms are abstract, they do have to be tied down at some place to the real world. They are of no use if they just float in a vacuum. Educational theory that is vacuum packed is useless for any purpose. Perhaps a good rule to follow is to use a minimum number of theoretical terms if one has to introduce any at all.

In addition, there are some terms within any theory that are neither operationally defined nor theoretical terms. These are words that are intuitively understood. In geometry, the word *point*, represents an important concept that falls into this category. In education, some examples are experience, phenomenal self, and words with meanings closely tied to personal experience. These elements in a theory are commonly referred to as primitive terms. Well-constructed theories contain a minimum number of terms that fall into this category; but it is impossible to exclude them completely.

Statement of a Theory As a Starting Point of Research

Because scientific research involves building organized knowledge, and not collecting miscellaneous items of information, a very desirable place to begin developing an enquiry is a theory. A study that starts with a theoretical position and then extends knowledge is, inevitably, a contribution to organized knowledge. Some of the ways in which this extension can take place have already been considered here.

A limited theory that deals with relatively few major variables, all of which can be measured, can be a much more productive enterprise than one that deals with a larger number of variables, most of which cannot be measured. It is important in this respect, as in others, to prevent oneself from becoming mentally suffocated under a mass of detail. Relatively simple and incomplete theories have had a history of usefulness in the behavioral sciences and an unexpected degree of success in terms of what was anticipated fifty years ago.

Although ten years ago there might have been difficulty in locating statements of limited theories in areas that might interest the educational research worker, there is today a wealth of material from which he may draw. H. Fowler (1965), for example, has presented a theory of curiosity and exploratory behavior based on a very careful review of accumulated knowledge. C. E. Noble (1966) has presented a theory of selective learning that finds its roots in a vast quantity of laboratory research extending back to the early studies of E. L. Thorndike. D. P. Ausubel (1963) has brought together research on meaningful verbal learning and has organized the findings into a theory. Bandura and Walters (1963) have presented a theory of social learning involving situations similar to those encountered in the lower elementary grades. G. A. Scherer and M. Wertheimer (1964) have summarized a number of different theories that attempt to organize knowledge in the area of foreign-language learning. Numerous other examples could be cited from the areas of perception, motor-skill learning, and emotional behavior.

The presentation of these theoretical positions is not always as precise as they could profitably be. Indeed, the central propositions of the theory presented are sometimes difficult to tease out from the remaining material. A good exercise for the reader is to select a major research contribution in an area in which he is interested, and in which the essence of a theory is stated, and then attempt to write out the propositions that represent the essential core of the theory. As an illustration of how this may be done, the author has worked over an article concerned with the early stage of learning to read and has produced a statement of the theory implicit in it. The theory derived from the article is presented in Table 1.

Note should be taken of the fact that the statement of the theory involves a set of definitions and a set of statements that constitute the postulates of the theory. The deductions simply represent hypotheses that could be tested through research for the purpose of providing further validation of the theory. In general, it is desirable to expand the statement of the theory to include the sources of evidence from which the theory is inductively derived. The reader of the theory, thus presented in an expanded form, can evaluate the evidence and decide whether the postulates really do follow from the evidence presented.

TABLE 1. *A theory of the early stages of learning to read*

DEFINITIONS

1. *Reading* is defined as a controlled form of talking in which the words that are said are controlled by the nature of the written symbols presented.
2. A *correct reading response* is defined as the act of saying the agreed-on response for the written symbol presented.
3. *Accuracy of response* to a word is defined as the percentage of correct attempts to say the word.

POSTULATES

1. When reading is learned by means of the sequence: written-word presentation, vocal response by the teacher, vocal response by the pupil, the frequency of occurrence of this sequence is related to the accuracy of response of the pupil. (This method of learning to read is commonly referred to as the *look-and-say method* and will be so referred to here.)
2. The effectiveness of the look-and-say method in producing correct reading responses in the pupil is related to the ability of the pupil to discriminate form and shape. Pupils must have a minimum of the latter ability if the method is to produce learning. Additional increments of the ability beyond the minimum result in increased rates of learning.
3. Words are identified by the reader through the use of specific cues such as a distinctive letter appearing in a particular location, the word being unusually long or short, the same letter appearing twice in succession, and so forth.

DEDUCTIONS

1. Tests of form discrimination will predict the ability of first-grade children to read.
2. The selection of words for reading material that provide distinctive cues will facilitate the acquisition of the reading skill in young children.
3. Procedures that help the child recognize cues by which words can be identified will facilitate the acquisition of the reading skill. (For example, the double letters in *look* and *hello*).
4. Some children unable to learn to read in the first grade may be helped by providing specific training in form discrimination.

The deductions in Table 1 represent ideas that might be explored in research related to the theory. Another kind of research that would extend the theory might investigate the training conditions necessary for developing the ability to discriminate one word from another. The researcher might hypothesize that those given systematic training in form discrimination prior to beginning reading might learn to read more rapidly than those who did not have this kind of systematic training. If the research showed that such training produced positive results, then a new variable would have to be added to the theory—namely, amount of previous experience with form discrimination.

In contrast with theory-oriented research, let us consider a few examples *not to follow* of research projects that represent the exploration of isolated ideas without any tie-in with organized knowledge. Consider, for example, the problem of the student who decided to make a study of the spelling errors of fourth-grade pupils by counting the frequency with which each error was made. This problem, if it has any virtue at all, might provide information useful to the teacher, but it is a problem that could be investigated by a competent secretary given a little professional supervision. It avoids the central educational problem in the spelling area about which much is known—namely, how to teach spelling more effectively. There are many other problems related to the *learning* of spelling that might be studied productively with a resulting contribution to the organized knowledge of the problem. As a part of the study of the learning process, note might be made of the spelling errors observed, and new methods of arranging learning might be tried out in order to reduce the number of error responses. However, a study that focused on error responses alone would be as unproductive as the study of crime in terms of the objects stolen from department stores.

Another example of a research that fails to build on any recognized significant body of knowledge is found in a dissertation on what sixth-grade children know about India. That they know very little and have many misconceptions is almost a foregone conclusion, yet this is all the writer of the dissertation found. The dissertation adds nothing to what is already known about how children acquire stereotyped conceptions of peoples of other lands. Neither does it indicate what can be done to prevent erroneous stereotypes from emerging. Much is already known about the development of stereotypes and related attitudes and their relation to the student's knowledge, but the study contributed nothing in this respect. The study is a structure built on sand into which it will sink and disappear, when it should have been built on a solid foundation.

Formalizing a Theory

The concept of a formal theory has been used with a great diversity of connotations, and often these two words are uttered as if they had some special magical power. The implication is that all one has to do is state a theory in formal terms and great scientific achievements will result. But what is meant by a formal theory? The author has a preference for the meaning used by Gustav Bergmann (1957), who regards the formal statement of a theory as one in which all of the words have been translated into abstract symbols such as are used by mathematicians. A theory stated in the form of a series of mathematical equations is a formalized theory. The science of behavior in educational situations is not advanced to the point where a formal theory of this type is feasible. Perhaps we may ultimately aspire to the statement of educational theory in such terms. At the present time it is not known whether this is even possible.

Causal and Functional Relationships

The educational research specialist should seek to establish organized systems of relationships among events and among variables. Such relationships can be stated without introducing the notion that some events cause other events. For example, from the data collected in the past concerning the motions of the planets in the solar system, positions of the planets at some future time can be predicted. The lawfulness of planetary behavior is neither increased nor decreased by introducing the notion that the state of the planetary system at one point in time is a consequence of prior conditions. The concept of cause is irrelevant to the statement of the laws of the planetary system and is unnecessary for making predictions from the laws. The reader may here jump to the conclusion that the concept of cause has no role to play in the development of a science, but this conclusion is not justified. Even though the concept of cause may not enter into the statement of the laws that are the final products of the work of the scientist, it does nevertheless play an important role in his thinking and may help him in the discovery of laws. Even scientists in advanced fields of knowledge admit to *thinking* in terms of cause and effect. For example, biographical accounts of Einstein's early thinking illustrate this point vividly. A personal concept of the nature of the universe seems necessarily to involve some concept of the causation of events, and this way of thinking plays an integral part in the process of scientific discovery.

A brief discussion of the origin of the concept of cause may make this point clear.

Personal experience leads one to believe that all events are the products or results of other events, which are referred to as their causes. The product of these causes is referred to as the effect. The origin of the belief in the existence of causal relationships is found in personal experience, in that each of us performs at least certain acts for the purpose of producing certain effects. In addition, we have the experience of other events producing certain effects on us. This has led ultimately to a concept of a universe in which every event has a cause and in which there is thus a continuity and order among events.

Although it is desirable to avoid the projections of one's personal experiences onto the universe at large, there still seems to be merit in retaining a conservative conception of cause in thinking about natural phenomena. Indeed, it is almost impossible to conduct thinking without the concept of causal relationships. This conception retains the idea that in order for a particular event to be produced it is necessary for certain conditions to exist; the necessary conditions are referred to collectively as a cause.

Consider, for example, the problem that agricultural research workers have long studied, namely, that of determining the conditions favorable for plant growth. Among the well-established conditions are those of a suitable air temperature, sufficient soil moisture, and adequate amounts of available nitrogen and phosphorous. Now one cannot say that any one of these factors *causes* growth, for any one alone is not sufficient to produce growth. If the temperature of the air is right, but if the soil is dry, no growth can occur. All of the factors mentioned, and others too, interact in a complex way to produce an increase in size of a plant. The factors are said to be *functionally related* to growth, but one cannot say that each causes growth.

There is perhaps a certain safety in using the term *functional relationship* rather than the term *causal relationship*. When we demonstrate that rewarding a child for performing certain acts increases the probability that the child will perform those acts in the future, we may say that we have established a functional relationship. In doing this, we avoid stating that there is a direct causal relationship between the reward and the heightened tendency to perform the rewarded behavior. Nevertheless, the implication is that the relationships are more than just coincidental, but are a necessary part of the phenomena studied. We can be almost certain that the relationship between the reward and the changed response probability is an extremely complex one, not one that is well described in terms of a simple and straightforward causal relationship. Some philosophers would even go so far as to say that almost any relationship that appears on the surface to be a simple causal relationship is, in fact, a matter of great complexity. For this reason, throughout this book we propose to use the term *functional relationship* rather than the term *causal relationship*. Of course, we will not quarrel with those who prefer to use the term *causal relationship* from time to time.

Knowledge Can Be Acquired at All Levels of Precision

There has been a tendency in psychology as it has developed within the American culture to emphasize the need for expressing theories in terms of variables that can be measured. For the most part this emphasis has been a healthy one, for it has led psychology away from the field of philosophy in which it had its beginnings and developed it as one of the biological and social sciences. In this matter, however, one can carry the emphasis on measurement too far. There are those who would prefer to quantify the trivial rather than to study the significant with qualitative methods that fall far short of the precision to which modern sciences aspire. It is perhaps worth reflecting on the fact that most of the generalizations of science began as qualitative statements, that is to say observations that did not involve measurement, and only later developed more fully into a quantitative form. On the contemporary scene one can point to the work of Piaget, involving no measurement, which has stimulated extensive quantitative research. History is full of similar examples. The basic principles of thermodynamics were first stated in a qualitative form. Harvey's discovery of the circulation of the blood, together with the other qualitative discoveries of the great school of medicine at Padua, laid the foundation for what became ultimately the quantitative science of physiology. The important discoveries that represent the very cornerstones of a quantitative science are almost invariably of a qualitative nature.

The author is not advising the graduate student of education to plan qualitative studies for his master's thesis. Major qualitative contributions in research are made by the few, rather than by the many who make substantial but not brilliant contributions. It is almost essential that the graduate student build his research on the qualitative contributions and generalizations of others. He should appreciate the great importance of these qualitative generalizations and realize that the quantitative studies that follow build on the foundation they have laid. Our present emphasis on quantification should not prevent us from perceiving its merits in their true light.

Types of Laws

The scientist is able to make predictions when it has become possible to state a generalization, or law as it is commonly called. Laws may be either highly limited or broad in the range of events that they include. In this connection, the reader should note that two classes of laws have commonly been considered in the behavioral sciences, and these must now be considered here.

The traditional goal of a science of behavior has been the discovery of laws that apply to all individuals; that is to say, laws that have wide applicability. Some psychologists have suggested that such laws may not be the only type of law that can be used in the development of a science of behavior. Indeed, some have even suggested that such laws may have only the most limited value. An alternative position, particularly favored by those who work in the clinical field, is that there are laws that pertain to the behavior of one individual but do not apply to the behavior of other individuals. Thus it is claimed that the sequences and orderlinesses of behavior manifested by one person may be entirely different from those manifested by another under similar circumstances. The orderlinesses of individual behavior that are unique to that individual are referred to as *ideographic* laws, a term that distinguishes them from *nomothetic* laws applying to all individuals.

Just as an individual may manifest lawfulness applicable only to him and to none other, so too may institutions also show unique individuality in their pattern of development and ways of conducting business. There are, for example, school systems that have shown a rare capacity for innovation in the area of science curricula; other systems are notable for high teacher morale; others have had a long history of pioneer work in the field of guidance; and so forth. These distinguishing characteristics of school systems are analogous to attributes characterizing an individual but not necessarily characterizing other individuals.

Because there are great difficulties involved in conducting research on characteristics that are unique to a particular person or institution, or that are relatively rare attributes, most research in education is likely to involve attributes characterizing in some degree all pupils, or all teachers, or all school systems, or all sixth-grade classrooms, and so on. The educational researcher, and particularly the beginning educational research worker, would do well to avoid projects that attempt to develop ideographic laws. Research that seeks to establish nomothetic laws is more readily undertaken and also derives knowledge with much wider applicability.

SUMMARY

1. Theories vary in the level of sophistication that they represent and in the scope of the events that they encompass. Educational theories of the past have suffered from being both vague and all-inclusive. Often they have been so vague that one cannot determine what kind of evidence would support them and what kind of evidence would go against them.

2. The present trend in theory construction in the behavioral sciences is away from the development of broad theories because attempts to develop the latter kind of theory have resulted in products with little utility. A limited theory that includes a few well-defined variables is likely to have much greater value both for predicting behavior and as a basis for developing research.

3. A theory is generally stated in a technical language in which most of the essential terms have been operationally defined. The terms of a suitable technical language should form a system of related terms. However, not all terms can be operationally defined and most theories use what are referred to as *theoretical* terms. For example, the word *motivation* represents a theoretical term because there is no direct way of observing motivation. What one observes is the result of motivation.

4. The statement of a theory is a starting point for research. Contemporary research literature in the behavioral sciences provides many instances of the use of theory as a basis for research.

5. A theory consists of statements of definitions, postulates, and sometimes also of deductions made from the postulates.

6. In an advanced stage of theory development all the terms of a theory are translated into abstract symbols. Educational theory is not likely to reach such a stage of formal development for a long time.

7. The terms *cause* and *effect* should be used with the greatest caution. The use of the term *functional relationship* has tended to take the place of the term *causal relationship*.

8. The distinction has been made between ideographic laws that apply to individual histories and nomothetic laws that apply to all individuals or to individuals in a particular category. Techniques for the discovery of ideographic laws have not been well developed largely because the scientist is interested in making discoveries that apply to more than one individual.

||||||||||||||||||||||||||||||

CHAPTER 3

Areas of Educational Research

THE selection of a problem suitable for a study or dissertation requires the student to take stock of himself and to identify the area of educational research in which his knowledge, talents, and abilities will permit him to make the most successful contribution. Too often this is not done—the student jumps ahead with enthusiasm to tackle a problem that intrigues him but that he is hardly prepared to study. Ideally, the student should have had good training and have already undertaken intensive reading in the area in which he plans to undertake research.

Before considering the task involved in the selection of the problem, a brief review will be presented of the different areas in which educational research has often been undertaken. Certain of these areas are discussed in greater detail in subsequent chapters for the purpose of illustrating some of the technical problems the research worker may face.

Educational Research Related to Development

Early studies of development, undertaken in the first third of this century, emphasized the internal factors that controlled development. Such studies were particularly concerned with the description of the pattern of development and in identifying the sequence with which particular behaviors emerged. Such studies had only limited implications for educational planning, for they had little to do with the environmental conditions that influence development. Because education attempts to influence development through control of certain aspects of the environment, the knowledge of internal factors that cannot be controlled has only meager value for educational planning. Recently research has moved to the study of the external factors that influence development, with results that have greater significance for educational practice.

Studies of external conditions in relation to development may involve the study of changes over a short period of but a few months, or long-term changes over periods that may last many years. Short-term studies are generally concerned with those conditions in the environment that can be expected to exert fairly immediate influences on behavior. The effect of education on child development has been the central theme for such studies. Long-term studies of development over periods of years have more often been concerned with those environmental conditions that may be expected to have a slow but cumulative effect. The various influences that home, neighborhood, peer relationships, and church affiliations may exert fall into this general category.

Interest in the study of development at particular age levels has varied from time to time. During the thirties, concomitant with the emphasis then found on expanding adult education facilities, many studies were made of development during the years of maturity and the problems adults encountered in learning new skills. More recently, interest has been shown in the study of development during the pre-school years, for evidence has been accumulating that much closer attention must be paid to providing effective learning conditions during these early years.

Explorations of the usefulness of various theories of learning for designing conditions that produce effective learning in schools have also formed the core of many significant researches. Although much of learning theory emerges from laboratory research, studies need to be conducted under conditions more similar to those existing in classrooms. Such studies need not be undertaken in actual classrooms but may involve groups of children in classroom-like situations.

Of great interest in recent years has been the study of the influence of the environment during the first few years of life on subsequent intellectual performance. Even though the overwhelming weight of the evidence is that level of intellectual functioning of the individual is highly dependent on what happens to him in his early environment, much still has to be learned about how to design that environment so that it has maximum impact on intellectual development. Studies in this area are quite feasible for dissertations and theses because suitable stimulation over as short a period as six months may sometimes produce striking intellectual growth.

Much of what is known about development has had to be derived, in the first place, from comparative studies involving different cultures and even different species. For example, much of Hebb's striking work on the impact that the early environment may have on the very young organism was undertaken with subhuman species. Yet the results have been successful in providing a basis for understanding many aspects of learning in young humans. The new John F. Kennedy Center for Research on Education and Human Development at George Peabody College, an outstanding center for the study of mental retardation, has a primate laboratory attached to it. In such a laboratory problems that cannot be attacked directly can be studied indirectly. For example, the effect of deprivation of oxygen at birth on subsequent mental retardation can be studied experimentally with primates and the extent of oxygen deprivation can be carefully controlled. In contrast, data on human births provides only very rough guesses whether oxygen deprivation did or did not occur. Also, by the time that mental retardation is recognized, there may be no data at all on record concerning the extent of oxygen deprivation at birth. The use of subhuman primates permits the collection of very good data on such problems, even though caution must be exercised in extending the results to human subjects.

Curriculum Research

The term *curriculum research* covers a multitude of very diverse activities. This is partly because the concept denoted by the word *curriculum* has had an evolving and expanding meaning and curriculum research has shown a corresponding evolution and expansion. A century ago, the concept of a curriculum was that of a body of subject matter to which the pupil was exposed. Today the concept is different, although the old-time meaning has not entirely vanished.

In Carter V. Good's *Dictionary of Education*, second edition, published in 1959, the following three distinct meanings of the word *curriculum* are noted:

1. A systematic group of courses or sequence of subjects required for graduation or certification in a major field of study, for example, social studies, physical education curriculum.

2. A general over-all plan of the content or specific materials of instruc-

tion that the school should offer the student by way of qualifying him for graduation or certification or for entrance into a professional or a vocational field.

3. A body of prescribed educative experiences under school supervision, designed to provide an individual with the best possible training and experience to fit him for the society of which he is a part and to qualify him for a trade or profession.

The first and third of these definitions involve the notion of a body of content; the second introduces the idea that an *over-all plan* is also an essential feature of a curriculum.

Further light is thrown on the development of the concept of a curriculum in the *Review of Educational Research*,[1] prepared on the occasion of the twenty-fifth anniversary of the founding of the *Review*. This particular issue traces the development of curriculum research, pointing up some of the changes that have taken place in the educator's concept of a curriculum. It is implied, in this review, that the tendency in the past was to think of the curriculum as consisting of all the *experiences* that a pupil had during schooling. The emphasis, according to this outlook was on the experience aspect; hence the curriculum was considered important insofar as it represented an element in the pupil's conscious experience. This was, in fact, a very narrow conception of the curriculum, for surely there are important factors in the pupil's environment that have powerful influences on his behavior but of which he is never aware. Any useful conception of the environmental influences that play a role in the development of the child must not be limited to those to which he consciously responds. For this reason, the emerging concept of the curriculum held by research workers and others is that it consists of all the planned conditions and events to which the pupil is exposed for the purpose of promoting learning, plus the framework of theory that gives these conditions and events a certain coherence. Recognition that a framework of theory is needed to give meaning to the happenings in the school is an important step forward. Modern writers on this subject stress that a curriculum can have no real meaning unless it is part of a theory of education.

Techniques for the study of curriculum problems exist to some extent; these must be wedded to a body of theory. For example, there are already many methods for measuring important characteristics of textbooks. Readability is one of the best explored of these characteristics. Much needs to be done to improve readability formulae, but

[1] Vol. XXVI, No. 3, 1956.

those available at present are valuable research tools. There is a need for techniques that will measure the complexity of written materials. An excellent beginning has been made in the development of techniques of content analysis, and enough has been accomplished to inspire research workers to apply these techniques to the study of curriculum problems.

An aspect of curriculum research that shows signs of developing is that concerned with the structure of subject matter. Mathematics has a logical structure and the order in which mathematical concepts are taught is based on this structure. Other subject-matter areas do not show such a simple and well-defined structure that can be used as a guide for instruction. History, for example, involves many different structures. One of these is time. Although teachers have commonly emphasized time relationships in history, and have expected students to remember the order in which events occurred, young children have difficulty in mastering such concepts. However, history also involves other structures: The study of feudalism involves the understanding of a social structure. An appreciation of the history of religions involves an understanding of the structure of philosophical ideas. Many other additional structures could be named. There are many educational problems to be studied that involve deciding how to teach history at particular age levels and the structures that such teaching should involve.

The last decade has also seen the emergence of techniques for making an analysis of the psychological demands placed on the learner by various learning experiences. For example, R. M. Gagné (1965) has proposed a system for analyzing learning tasks into components such as discrimination learning, signal learning, problem solving, and so forth. Gagné's position is that when a task involves various psychological components the simpler components have to be mastered first. If learning to read requires both visual form discrimination and also associative learning, then the form discrimination must be mastered first, because it is at a simpler and more basic level than associative learning.

A research area that falls mainly within the curriculum domain is that of audiovisual communication. The problem of how to design audiovisual materials so that they will instruct with maximum effectiveness represents an important area of inquiry requiring the research worker to bring together knowledge of perception, learning, and subject matter. Important though the area is for education, almost nothing is known about how to design an illustration for various age levels, and even less is known about how to design a sound-motion picture. Even such a simple problem as the relative effectiveness of simple sketches in comparison with detailed photographs has not yet been properly investigated.

Research on Teaching

The major focus of educational research in the past has been on problems of teaching. Common sense suggests that the classroom is a good place to begin educational research and, even though common sense is often wrong, the availability of schools, teachers, and pupils, makes them attractive objects for study. In fairness to those engaged in such enquiry one must add that these research workers have generally voiced the opinion that most problems of teaching will be solved through research conducted in school settings. Indeed, the view was commonly expressed in the period before World War II that, once sufficient research had been undertaken on the events of the classroom, the reform of education would rapidly follow. Much of the early research of this nature involved the study of the relationship between rated teacher personality traits and rated teacher effectiveness. The results of such studies were of little consequence because the ratings of teacher effectiveness are obviously influenced by the raters' personal views concerning which traits are important for teaching. In later studies this problem was handled by using measures of achievement as a means of assessing teacher effectiveness, but this improvement did not overcome the weakness of ratings of personality as a source of data. Further innovation was obviously necessary if classroom research were to become the panacea that it had been widely claimed to be. Then attempts were made to substitute personality inventories and other measuring devices for ratings. Although these changes were technical improvements that overcame the major criticisms directed against the earlier studies, the yield of knowledge was of microscopic proportions in relation to the effort expended.

The next step in the development of classroom research was to collect samples of verbal behavior in the classroom. The verbal behavior could then be subjected to an analysis based on a psychological theory of teaching. Research on what is referred to as interaction analysis is of this nature. Verbal transactions in the classrooms are either immediately analyzed by an observer or they are recorded and later analyzed at leisure. The assumption made by most of those who engage in research on interaction analysis is that the key to good teaching is to be found through a study of the verbal behavior of those in the classroom.

Even the refinements introduced into classroom research through the various methods of interaction analysis, ingenious though they are, have not yet produced hopeful signs that methods for the successful attack on problems of teaching have at last been found. Indeed, the data so far produced when examined coldly and critically, and not through the rosy writings of some of those who have produced it, seems to add little to the knowledge already available concerning the conditions that produce effective learning. The disappointing results thus far achieved have led some to puzzle over the reasons why such an apparently promising approach has produced so little, and reflections on this problem have led to explorations of new approaches to the problem of discovering the conditions that provide effective teaching.

Perhaps the greatest obstacle in the way of critically examining classroom research as an approach to the improvement of teaching is our prejudice that direct attacks on problems of education are likely to be more fruitful than indirect attacks. The argument that the best way to improve teaching is to study teaching, appears to be both logical and persuasive, but the history of science is full of examples of the obvious approach to a problem being a useless approach. The direct study of what the Greeks believed to be the four essential elements of earth, air, fire, and water, did nothing to develop the sciences of physics and chemistry. Major advances in the control of virus diseases have come, not through the study of sick people, but through an understanding of how the virus molecule reproduces itself. Examples could be listed almost endlessly. The evidence is overwhelming that, in research, one should always be on one's guard in assuming that the common sense approach is the right approach. Perhaps the best way to improve teaching is *not* through the direct study of teaching. Perhaps teaching, as it occurs, never presents the observer with data about good teaching. Perhaps such observations are useful for understanding teaching as it is, but what is needed is an understanding of teaching as it should be. These are cogent criticisms of current classroom research, but there are others too. In studying the intact classroom the effect of one category of the teaching event cannot generally be determined because it is but a tiny fragment of the total teaching process. It is like trying to determine the effect of a small grain of salt on the taste of a large cauldron of soup.

An alternative approach is to set up classroom-like groups in situations in which careful control can be exercised over the teaching conditions. Schools will commonly permit research workers to conduct experimental teaching sessions on selected groups of pupils who are released from their regular classrooms for this purpose. R. L. R. Overing and Travers (1966), for example, conducted experiments on teaching the principle of refraction by four different methods. Small groups of pupils were selected from regular classes for this purpose and the teaching occurred under well-controlled conditions with the main part of the instruction delivered through a tape recorder. The use of a tape recorder permitted the spoken part of the instruction to remain the same for all pupils, but four different methods of presenting visual materials were employed. In addition, the experiment permitted an evaluation of the effect of instruction on the ability of the pupil to transfer what he had learned to the solution of a novel problem. The data from such an experiment may permit the collection of information about teaching that no amount of observation of a regular class of pupils could ever provide.

Another alternative is to study teaching through the use of computer-assisted instruction. One of the research advantages of computer-controlled teaching situations is that they permit very precise regulation of some aspects of instruction. Indeed, many research workers in the area claim that the chief value of such teaching situations is that they provide excellent research situations in which instruction can be carefully and systematically studied in highly controlled situations.

At the present time, the indirect approaches to the study of teaching through the use of constructed experimental teaching situations offer more promise than their predecessors, but knowledge about optimum conditions for teaching is going to be very difficult to acquire.

If work is undertaken on a problem of teaching, the researcher cannot escape considering the nature of theory of teaching. The author has expanded on this matter in other writings (1966). For him a theory of teaching expresses a set of relationships between teaching conditions, including the curriculum as broadly defined here, and outcomes defined in terms of measured changes in pupils. A theory of teaching would thus indicate how the conditions of learning would have to be arranged in order to produce particular changes and states in the pupils. A theory of teaching, as any other theory, would have to be closely tied to data that had established the relationships expressed by the theory. This conception of theory of teaching is to be contrasted with vague speculations and writings, primarily inspirational in nature, that commonly claim to present theories of teaching.

The latter kinds of documents represent theory in a popular sense of the term and not theory in a scientific sense.

Research Related to Sociological and Economic Conditions Affecting Education

Many of the conditions external to the classroom that affect education are investigated by educational research workers interested in studying the sociological conditions that ultimately influence the educational process. Political pressures that influence the educational philosophy of a school system in one direction or another, the financial aspects of the system, and the sociological conditions that result in increased or decreased support for education may be studied. But answers to the questions, "What philosophy of education is implied in the curriculum of the school?" "What kinds of individuals constitute school boards?" "What barriers exist to the raising of funds in communities of certain specified types?" supply information that can be applied only indirectly to improvement in the effectiveness of learning in schools. Many such studies attempt to answer questions of local significance only, and the results cannot be applied to other communities.

Although the central topic of educational research is the development of a science of behavior in educational situations, peripheral studies pertaining to sociological and anthropological problems are of considerable importance. Just as classroom behavior may be described at various levels—from those that involve the movement of the constituent elements or muscle twitches of the body to descriptions of the over-all behavior of the individual—so, too, can studies be conducted either at the level of individual behavior or at a level where the unit studied is a group. Sociological and economic studies of educational problems are concerned more with group than individual phenomena.

A sociological concept that has had great importance on both educational thought and practice is that of social class. Although this concept has long been used by sociologists, its signifiance to the field of education came largely through the work of W. L. Warner. He provided the stimulus for much of the early work by showing that experiences associated with life in a particular social class influenced the pupil's responses to learning in school. At least some of the present research on the problems of the disadvantaged shows the influence of Warner and his associates, although with the passing of time there have been considerable changes and improvements in the devices used for the identification and assessment of background factors. Whoever should wish to engage in research on the education of the disadvantaged should become familiar with modern research literature on the relationship of behavior to social-class background and class affiliation. An area of considerable interest in this connection is the relationship of the class origin of the teacher to what he does in schools and how he reacts to children who come from other classes. The outcomes of research on such problems have important implications for teacher education.

Problems related to the integration of schools fall largely within the area of study of the sociologist. Indeed, if educational organizations had sponsored sociological research over the last few decades, much could have been done to reduce the tensions associated with school integration.

The academic discipline of economics has not yet had the impact on educational research that it should have had, although there are many problems of education that the economist must be the one to solve. For example, studies can be undertaken of the effect of salary policies on the retention of teachers in a school system. Such very narrow problems are likely to provide more profitable studies if they are broadened so that this particular study becomes an investigation of the conditions affecting the job stability of teachers. There are also many other economic problems that can be studied. At least one generation of students of educational administration has devoted its efforts to the development of measures of educational requirements of communities. These measures must be such that they are comparable in some way from community to community. At first sight one might be tempted to take the pupil as the unit of need, but it soon becomes evident that this is not a satisfactory procedure. If the pupils are widely scattered, schools tend to be small and the unit cost greater than when schools are large. Scattered pupils also increase the cost of transportation to the school, and then the pupil unit has to be adjusted for such factors if it is to represent a unit of educational service to be provided. These complexities have resulted in the development of an extensive technical literature, which has attempted to derive a useful measure of educational need that could be used in subsequent research. Studies of the economics of education often provide useful data for the solution of immediate problems, but rarely do they provide generalizations useful for the solution of a great range of problems. The generalizations that can be derived are qualitative and usually lack any property that might be described as precision. The late Paul Mort, who thought through this matter at great length, pointed out that these generalizations are not scientific laws but categories under which can be classified a multitude of rule-of-thumb canons widely accepted as the major lessons that have been learned through studies in this area. One of these is the equalization principle, which states that financial disbursements should be such that poorer districts are helped more than wealthy districts. Another is the reward-for-effort principle, which posits that funds should be disbursed in ways that encourage other bodies also to release funds for education. An example of the operation of the latter principle is the case in which states provide educational funds for local communities on condition that the local communities expand their education expenditures by a certain amount. When one considers the limited degree to which this area of educational research has developed quantitative methods, it is gratifying to note the order that such principles have apparently introduced.

Another area of research related to educational administration is the study of population changes. Its importance to education is substantial from many points of view. First, if the supply of teachers is to be related to need, then it is necessary to predict several years in advance the number of classes of a given size that will have to be staffed. These long-term predictions are required for adequate educational planning because it may take four or five years to train a teacher, and perhaps another two years to recruit him. In addition, some experience on the job under qualified supervisors also seems to be most desirable. Thus, if there is to be an increased number of teachers available in 1980, it will be necessary to start an active recruiting campaign possibly as early as 1970.

In demographic studies, there are no great difficulties in estimating pupil enrollment five or six years ahead because the future pupils already have been born by the time the estimate is made. Death rates and immigration and emigration rates can be estimated with considerable accuracy. On the other hand, real difficulties are encountered when estimates are to be made ten or more years in advance, for the birth rate may show sudden changes in response to a great complexity of causes. Hardly more than a beginning has been made in establishing scientific laws of population change. Just as the prediction of pupil enrollment is an area fraught with difficulties, so, too, does the problem of estimating the future teacher supply present numerous unsolved problems that may challenge the student of education.

Research on Problems of Educational Administration

There has long been a need for the development of research related to problems of educational administration but, until recently, most departments giving instruction in that field had almost no capability for conducting or supervising research. The need to stimulate research has long been recognized by professors of educational administration and one important step taken by them to meet this need was the formation of the University Council for Educational Administration. The latter organization has done much to stimulate interest in research. In addition, some university centers have been established in association with the Council. The most notable of these is the Midwest Center for the Study of Educational Administration at the University of Chicago.

The promotion of research on problems of educational administration is a far larger problem than that of finding competent research workers willing to do research in the area; for even among research workers considerable controversy exists concerning how one should go about conducting such research. The present decade has been characterized by a flow of literature taking the position that much more precisely formulated theories of educational administration are needed before useful research can be conducted in this area. An example of a plea for greater effort in the development of theory of administration as a prerequisite for research is found in a volume by A. W. Halpin (1966). Models, which can be considered simple ways of presenting ideas before they reach the stage of theory, have begun to have had an influence on the field of educational administration. An example of such a model has already been presented on page 19. Another model of administration is found in the work of Halpin. Such models indicate where to look for research problems and also what kinds of variables seem to be important to measure.

Theories have to be based on the kind of substantial knowledge that is derived from research. Although one cannot expect to derive a theory of administration from the kind of research that has typically been pursued in departments of educational administration, largely because it has tended to be focused on specific and local problems, there is still the possibility that the ideas on which a theory of administration may be based can be derived from research in social psychology and sociology. Certainly business management has long drawn from knowledge derived from such fields in order to develop theories of management. The impact of social psychology and sociology on business management has been far greater than on school administration, perhaps because business has been so highly dependent on research for many aspects of its development.

Experimental studies of leadership in small groups began with the work of Kurt Lewin and his associates before World War II. Through varying some of the characteristics of the leader, the resulting effect on the performance of the group could be studied. The aim of such research has been to determine the leadership conditions that are effective for producing a high work output, or high morale, or sustained effort, or some other performance characteristic. A common criticism of such work is that it involves *ad hoc* groups, assembled for the purpose of the experiment, and that behavior may be rather different in such groups from that in groups having a long history of working together. Because research workers are inclined to believe that the conclusions concerning leadership, administration, and management, derived from such groups, are of limited value, psychologists and sociologists have extended their work to the study of conditions affecting performance in established groups. Much of the research has been undertaken in military settings, partly because the military has been interested in problems of leadership, and partly because a high degree of control can be exercised in military groups. One can, for example, set up small military groups with leaders having specified characteristics and study the effect of these characteristics on group performance.

Problems of leadership and administration can also be conducted in natural settings in which little control can be exercised over the situation. Such a study is that by Halpin and Croft (see Halpin 1966). The Halpin and Croft study begins, where such studies have to begin, with the development of an instrument for assessing the organizational climate in schools. The usefulness of such an instrument for developing administrative research still has to be determined, but it is a beginning. The production of a measuring instrument may well be the place where administrative research has to start, but such a step is still a long way from developing substantive knowledge about administration. The area is also in need of alternative instruments for studying administrative behavior.

Research on the Development of a Technology of Education

A technology is a highly developed and complex procedure that makes possible the use of raw materials for the production of highly useful products. Thus one refers to the technology involved in the production of metals from natural ores, one of the first technologies that man developed. Early man, who found lumps of quite pure copper and hammered them into useful shapes, could not be said to have developed a technology; but his descendants, who had learned that copper could be produced by heating ore with charcoal in clay-lined holes in rocks, had developed a rudimentary technology. From the first use of naturally occurring pure copper to the development of small furnaces for smelting copper ores required about 2500 years, but once the rudiments of the process had been developed the door was opened for the smelting of ferrous metals and the iron age had begun. Then thousands of years had to pass until man learned to control the carbon content of iron so that he could produce cast iron or steel at will. The development of technology in the absence of a science on which to base it is desperately slow and tedious. Consider, in contrast, the modern manufacturing drug industry that has developed within the memory of many who are still living. The rapid development of this industry was possible only because there existed, and grew alongside the industry, the basic scientific disciplines on which the production processes have been based. A technology that has a scientific foundation may develop to an advanced stage in far less than a century, but most technologies that have slowly emerged through the efforts of skilled men in the arts and trades have taken thousands of years to develop.

Today there is much enthusiasm expressed about the possibility of developing a technology of education. The thought seems to be that just as the production of material goods has been revolutionized by technical developments, so too may education be made efficient beyond our present dreams through the development of an appropriate technology. The thinking in this matter tends to be rather loose, for many speak and write about the development of an educational technology as though education were analogous to a production-line process in an industrial plant. Indeed, much educational literature draws from this analogy. Educational objectives have a similarity to industrial product specifications, the school program can be seen as having more than a passing resemblance to production processes, and pupil evaluation is like the industrial inspection process that takes place during the various manufacturing phases. The concept that education must be designed to turn out a product, the specifications of which have been precisely identified, is quite objectionable to many. The latter individuals cannot endorse a technology developing to improve the industrial efficiency of the classroom for the production of specified pupil products. Those who protest the industrial production model of education take the position that there can be no technology of education in the sense that there is a technology of glass manufacture, even though they believe that the pupil may choose to take advantage of technological developments as he does when he consults a printed book. Humanists who assume this position concede that there may be technological developments that pupils and teachers may choose to use, but there can be no technology of education in the sense in which there are industrial technologies. The difference between these two viewpoints cannot be underestimated.

The impact of various aspects of technology on education is, of course, nothing new. No single aspect of technology has had greater impact than the development of both the printing press and the advanced technology that has developed related to printing. One also cannot disregard the impact on education of the mass production of material articles including pens, typewriters, and all kinds of other equipment. Attempts have also been made to apply knowledge of human development to the design of familiar school equipment such as tables, chairs, and desks. A study by R. D. Tuddenham and M. M. Synder (1954) attempted to provide a sound basis for the design of such equipment.

In recent years, technological developments related to the school have found new roots in the movement that has attempted to find ways to provide instruction through mechanical devices. The roots of this movement are found in the work of Sidney Pressey of half a century ago, but the movement did not derive substantial impetus until Skinner entered the field at midcentury. Pressey emphasized in the development of his machines the importance of providing the pupil with immediate knowledge of results. Skinner also emphasized this factor in learning but stressed other factors such as the breaking down of the knowledge to be learned into elements to be acquired and the proper sequencing of the elements. For Skinner, the task was to shape human behavior, but behavior had to be shaped a small step at a time. For the followers of Skinner, the central problem of education was that of deciding how to organize subject matter and how to present it in such a way that the student could be effectively and efficiently reinforced for the manifestation of the acquisition of knowledge. Because Skinner believed that behavior had to be shaped slowly, only very small amounts of information were provided in each *frame* of the instructional program. In addition, because he emphasized that the actual behavior reinforced was the behavior learned, the instructional program dispensed by Skinner's teaching machines required the student to perform the responses that he was learning to make.

Students did not just *choose* answers, they had to produce answers. No substitutes for real answers were acceptable.

Teaching machines and programmed learning were heralded by many as the great advances of all time in the educational field. Indeed, one can read articles written near to midcentury promising that with these devices pupils would learn many times as fast as they had learned with traditional methods. The great educational revolution was believed to be at hand; and while engineers were developing the new teaching hardware, curriculum and subject-matter experts were arranging subject matter into suitable programs for presentation to the students through the newly designed machines. But, as with many revolutions, the dawn of the new era did not come with the anticipated rosy hue.

The immediate impact of the ideas of both Pressey and Skinner were not on school practices but on educational research. The revolution in educational practice did not occur largely because teaching machines and programmed instruction, born of the first flush of enthusiasm, fulfilled few of the promises that came with them. About all that could be said of the new devices is that they did teach and, over short periods, with no more and no less success than more traditional methods; but, in terms of the theory on which they were based, things should have been different. Why the machines did not transform education became a matter for research.

Research from the early teaching-machine era has shown a number of separate and distinct directions. One direction has been the further analysis of the content of the curriculum, a matter that is discussed in Chapter 10, "Analysis of the Content of Verbal Materials." If content is to be presented to the student in a systematic manner, then much has to be learned about the manner in which knowledge is structured. The development of programmed textbooks represented one kind of innovation that emerged from the work of Skinner, but there have been others.

A second area of research has been the further development of mechanical and electrical equipment for performing various teaching tasks. These pieces of equipment include some equipment for helping children to learn to read such as the *Language Master,* a device that says a word printed in large letters on a card; the talking typewriter; and various machines that present the task of matching a word with a picture of an object. In the case of some of these pieces of equipment the claims of what they can accomplish have already far outstripped the evidence, but at least some sober research is being carried on to establish their usefulness. That such devices teach can hardly be doubted, but the real issue is whether their use is more effective than other less-expensive and widely endorsed procedures.

A third area of research involves the development of computer systems for use in instruction. The main effort in this area has been an exploration of the problems this involves and both the modification of available equipment and the development of new. auxiliary equipment. Many who embarked on research in this area in the mid-fifties anticipated that within a few years schools would be equipped with computer-controlled teaching systems, but the deeper the research workers probed the area the more distant appeared to be the day of practical application. Of course, there have been demonstrations of computer-controlled instruction at Stanford University, Pennsylvania State University, Florida State University, the University of Illinois, and also at other places, but these demonstrations have been impressive more because of their novelty than because they reflected excellence in teaching. The area is one that must be regarded as immensely interesting to the research worker and the main danger is that attempts to make practical applications at too early a stage of the art may give the entire approach a bad name before it has been given a chance to develop fully. The enthusiasm of manufacturers cannot be blamed entirely for pushing applications of computer-assisted instruction even when the state of the art is primitive, for academicians have been equally guilty. Indeed, one would not be hard pressed to find a suitable recipient for an annual award of "Promising more and delivering less." There would be many well-qualified recipients. Nevertheless, a particularly encouraging aspect of the entire area is that most of those engaged in research on computer-assisted instruction and related problems are not only content to pursue research without much thought of immediate applications, but with the realization that a long road lies ahead before extensive applications are likely to be feasible. Among the major developments that need to be undertaken are those of inventing suitable means by which the learner can communicate with the computer. In an academic area such as mathematics the problem of communication is much less acute than in other subject-matter fields. Some have regarded this as a problem of developing a new language, perhaps a simplified form of English, that both the machine and the student might use in their interactions. Substantial effort is being devoted to this whole problem of developing simple means whereby the student can ask a computer questions and receive back straightforward answers, but the solution still seems to be quite distant. The dialogue that can be undertaken between student and computer with the present equipment is dull, uninspired, and very restricted in content, but developments in technology may ultimately remove these limitations. As the reader knows, computers have been programmed to play chess, but the game they play is unimaginative even if it is respectable. They never make obvious mistakes, but they also never display a brilliant move. In order to graduate as teachers, computers will have to overcome some of these gross and obvious deficiencies. A major objective of research is to do just that.

The aim of much of this research is to develop teaching equipment that will be *adaptive* to the behavior of the student. The hope is that as the student encounters difficulties, the teaching device will adapt to the student's predicament and provide the help that he needs. More complicated adaptive behavior would be required if the student suddenly were to have an idea that he wanted to explore further. Some formulate this problem as that of developing a *responsive* environment.

Intensive work on the development of a computer technology for the classroom has led to a few demonstrations in schools. Such demonstrations have often been misunderstood and have been taken to show that computer-assisted learning has already developed to the point where it can provide improvements in classroom instruction. However, no evidence has been provided to show that these demonstrations are anything more than the exhibiting of an infant who can perform only a few tricks but who has potential for growth. The future of a kicking infant is a little difficult to predict.

Research on Problems of Individual Differences

No area of educational research has had a longer history than that of attempting to identify individual differences among pupils, teachers, and supervisors that have significance for them in their respective roles in the educational system. There is almost universal acceptance of the idea that individual differences among pupils should be taken into account in planning educational programs, but clear-cut answers have not been forthcoming. The idea that teachers and supervisors should be selected in terms of suitable characteristics is also generally accepted; but, here again, little agreement can be found on what these characteristics should be and how they should be measured.

Numerous studies have been undertaken on the value of various methods of grouping children according to their abilities and achievements in order to facilitate learning. No method so far studied has produced any very notable improvements in pupil achievement. The latest of these kinds of studies attempts to use computer records of individual achievements so that individualized assignments can be made in terms of past accomplishments. The procedure looks promising, but so have many others that have later turned out to have negligible value. Individualized programs of instruction that attempt to adapt to individual differences fall into two broad categories: The one type of program adjusts the speed with which all pupils pass through the same program of instruction with the same content; the second type adjusts the content of the program to each individual program. Only the first of these two types of programs have been studied to any extent.

Studies of teacher characteristics designed for the purpose of selecting teacher personnel were common at midcentury but have become increasingly fewer in numbers. The decline in interest in this area derives partly from our inability to develop useful measures of teacher effectiveness that can be used as the criteria against which the measures of teacher characteristics can be evaluated. Of what avail is it to measure twenty teacher characteristics that may be important for teacher selection if one cannot find out which of these characteristics are really important. Another basic difficulty in the development of research in this area is that the instruments available for measuring teacher characteristics, particularly in the area of personality, are of very limited value as measuring devices. Research related to the selection of administrators is also plagued by the problems of inadequate criteria for determining who are the best administrators and unsatisfactory instruments for measuring the characteristics of applicants.

Historical Research

Every area of human endeavor can benefit from the study of its own history, but historical studies probably have special value in education where the latest innovation is all too often only the revival of a long-discarded idea. For example, the recent interest in initial teaching alphabets represents a revival of an idea that had considerable popular vogue during the last century. The historian can often tell us whether our ideas really are new and whether there are earlier and related efforts with which we should be familiar. The history of an idea in the educational scene is often the most neglected part of its development. Other aspects of history of the greatest importance are those having to do with the sources of innovation and the forces in society that promote or discourage educational change and progress.

Basic Research

The reader should not derive the impression from preceding sections that educational research cannot be basic research. All of the areas of research discussed provide opportunities to undertake very basic research, that is to say research leading to important scientific generalizations. Some of the most important contemporary research in psychology is taking place in the field of development, and educational-research workers are participating in this work. Research on teaching, if conducted in carefully controlled experimental situations, may provide us not only with information of great practical utility on how to arrange teaching conditions for maximum effectiveness, but may also contribute to fundamental knowledge of learning. Research on administration may involve basic research in social psychology, sociology, and economics. Educational research does not have to be the dull, unenterprising pursuit that it appears to be from a study of Doctor of Education dissertations. It can be an exciting quest for knowledge leading to both important scientific developments and significant educational change.

Although the present pressures are forcing educational research into applied channels, the important ideas that have had impact on education have come from scientists renowned for their basic contributions to knowledge. All the applied-research workers in education taken together have had little influence compared with the forceful impression of the ideas of such men as Thorndike, Binet, Piaget, Lewin, and Skinner. The lesson is clear. Some schools of education and other education-connected research organizations are making some provision for basic research, but it is the rare administrator of an educational enterprise who has had sufficient contact with scientific research to know its potential for educational progress.

The relationship between the research of the scientist in the laboratory and the conduct of education has long been controversial. Although in the physical sciences there are well-developed links between, say, the laboratory physicist and the manufacturer of useful products, similar links do not exist in the case of the behavioral sciences. The latter do not have groups of workers comparable to the engineers who convert laboratory discoveries into products and services that the community needs. Indeed, even if groups of educational technologists were to emerge and attempt to convert laboratory knowledge about learning to useful purposes, there is some doubt whether these technologists could fill a useful role. Because groups of educational technologists are now emerging, the next decade may provide some answer to this question.

A recent report of government-sponsored research by R. R. Mackie and P. R. Christensen (1967) has attempted to explore the problem of finding ways of developing a closer relationship between psychological research conducted in the laboratory and the conduct of practical enterprises such as education. According to Mackie and Christensen, the major difficulty in the application of laboratory research to situations beyond the laboratory is that the laboratory variables cannot be readily identified in the real-life setting. In the case of physics, the problem does not seem to exist to the same extent. The effects of gravitation can be readily identified in many practical situations, as can the effect of the expansion of substances as a result of increases in temperature. In contrast, how obscure are the reinforcements of behavior operating in the classroom in contrast with the reinforcements of the laboratory. Indeed, most laboratory scientists would be willing to admit that the reinforcing events of the classroom have not been identified and, probably, cannot be identified at this time.

The same report goes on to emphasize the need for validating any planned applications of laboratory-derived knowledge about learning before actual applications are made. However, there are obvious difficulties in conducting studies in classroom situations that are designed to test the extension of laboratory generalizations to real-life situations.

SUMMARY

1. A central area for educational research is that of development. Of particular interest are those studies designed to determine the effect of particular kinds of stimulation on intellectual growth. Some studies in this area may be undertaken profitably and may have to be undertaken on subhuman subjects.

2. Curriculum research is a quite ill-defined activity in an ill-defined area. Although it has been an area lacking research techniques, these are now beginning to develop, particularly in the field of content analysis and in the analysis of the structure of subject matter. Many of the traditional areas of research for the curriculum

specialist, such as the study of the needs of children, still lack research techniques suitable for their investigation.

3. Research on teaching has been the traditional focus of interest for the educational-research worker; but, despite all the effort that has been invested in such research, the results have been meager and disappointing. The observation of teaching as it exists may not provide useful information about how teaching should be. One alternative to the study of teaching in classroom settings is the study of teaching in carefully constructed experimental situations in which substantial control can be exercised over many important conditions. Another approach is to study teaching through the use of the well-controlled teaching situations provided by computer-controlled instruction.

4. The study of sociological and economic conditions influencing education is an area of expanding interest to the research worker. A sociological concept of importance that has had great influence on educational thought and practice is that of social class. Challenging opportunities exist for the study of the effect of background conditions on the achievement of educational objectives.

5. Research on problems of educational administration covers a wide range of problems ranging from direct studies of the behavior of administrators to laboratory studies of leadership in small groups. A growing emphasis in the field is the development of models and theories of administrative behavior. Although some influential models of administration have appeared in recent years, research has been handicapped by a lack of measuring instruments and devices for conducting research on administration.

6. Considerable research is now in progress with the aim of developing applications of technology to problems of education. Although many reject the idea that education is something like a production line in industry with its own specialized technology, these same critics would still want to adapt technological developments for classroom use. One can reject the notion that the pupil is a piece of raw material moving down a production line where he is shaped step by step, but still see him as an autonomous being who may choose to be helped by the tools of technology. Most of the research involving the adaptation of technological advances to education would claim to have little application at this time, but many of the products have important research applications. A central difficulty in providing equipment, fully adaptive to the student's progress, is that of developing a means by which the student can communicate with the com-

puter. Various approaches to this problem are being explored including that of developing simplified languages.

7. Problems related to individual differences and personnel selection have long been studied by educational-research workers. Major difficulties in the personnel selection area derive from the limitation of present measuring techniques.

8. Schools of education and some educational-research organizations are showing a revived interest in undertaking basic research. This interest reflects to some degree a disillusionment with the little that applied research has accomplished and it also demonstrates a better understanding of how a scientific foundation for educational practice has to be built.

‖‖‖‖‖‖‖‖‖‖‖‖‖‖‖‖‖‖‖‖‖‖‖‖‖‖‖

CHAPTER 4

The Planning Stage of Educational Research

THE SEARCH FOR A PROBLEM

THE planning of research is commonly thought of by the novice as an initial stage that is quickly passed, to be followed by the more elaborate and prolonged stage of collecting data. Many of the weaknesses in current educational research are attributable to this fundamentally unsound viewpoint. The fact is that the major effort in the undertaking of research should be devoted to the planning stage, which may include not only a careful formulation of the problem, but also some preliminary data-collecting activities. Once a research has been well planned and the techniques have been given a preliminary trial to make sure that they are feasible methods of attacking the problem at hand, the actual execution of the research is a simple and mechanical matter, which requires more patience than brilliance. Weeks may go into planning an experiment that may be completed in a single day. The difficult part of all research is the planning stage, which is the thinking stage.

Conant (1946) has pointed out that there is no simple formula to help the researcher in the most crucial stage of the development of research—the stage of developing hypotheses. The would-be researcher must recognize that much brilliant work owes its brilliance to the significance of the hypothesis that is tested. Some researches, of course, are brilliant because of the unusual and ingenious way in which the hypotheses are tested. The unfortunate fact is that most research conducted in education is nothing short of drab in both conception

62

and development. If this chapter can do anything to reduce even a little of the drabness in research in education, it will have done much.

There can be no doubt that individual researchers differ greatly in their sensitivity to problems. Research administrators know that some researchers are quite unable to locate and identify problems even though they may do a workmanlike job in solving problems assigned to them. Experience is an important factor. Intensive reading is essential for identifying important problems in an area. The student thoroughly familiar with the technical literature of his field of interest cannot fail to become conscious of the problems other research workers consider to be important. Attendance at and participation in research seminars may help to sharpen the student's ability to discriminate between researchable and nonresearchable problems. Seminars may also bring the student into contact with researchers who are highly sensitive to the existence of researchable problems, and this experience may help him in developing his ability. Even though it is possible in this chapter to offer the student some help in identifying problems, little is likely to be achieved in the direction of making the student more sensitive to those that are researchable.

The student of educational phenomena should embark on research with full respect for the complexity of the phenomena with which he is faced. In this regard, much educational research lacks the humility that is essential if matters of importance are to be discovered. The author can recall instances where persons who should have known better have approached educational problems as if they were of the complexity of a party game. On one occasion, a professor in charge of an educational research project remarked to him, "This year we are going to settle the problem of measuring teacher personality so that next year we can move on to other matters." From our present perspective, it is quite clear that a hundred years from now scientists will still be attempting to measure some aspects of teacher personality. The student may reflect that even in an area where problems seem so simple, relatively speaking, as in rote learning, investigation soon reveals that the phenomena studied are of enormous complexity. How much more complex must be the phenomena that take place in the classroom, or even those occurring in miniature educational situations set up for research purposes. Herein lies the central difficulty in identifying researchable problems.

Much of the deceptive simplicity of educational phenomena stems from the fact that considerable progress has been made in predicting success and failure in different types of curricula. The fact that persons with little research experience have been able to develop tests for accomplishing just this adds to the deception. Such straightforward relationships are fortuitous, not typical, circumstances. The discovery of clear relationships beyond this point is a much more difficult matter. Sometimes even years of research on a single problem may yield but small returns.

Acceptability of a Research Project in Relation to the Social Milieu in Which It Is Undertaken

It is a mistake for the researcher to orient his work in relation to some social issue about which he has deep personal convictions. Even though such convictions may stem from the most desirable and highly esteemed values, there are reasons why they form an unsound basis for research. In the first place, they usually lead the graduate student to attempt to solve a problem that is beyond his capabilities, and often beyond the scope of available techniques to solve. The common trait of overambitiousness seen in so many doctoral studies is most often an outgrowth of the individual's own personal values, and this leads the researcher to seek evidence that will support some private belief. Much wiser would such an individual be to develop a research project as an outgrowth of another's systematically developed program.

When the student of education embarks on finding a research problem, he must recognize that he is not free to pursue his own whims and fancies. He must also see that he has much to gain by attaching himself to a professor in whose research he may have an opportunity to participate. This participation may lead to the development of a thesis or dissertation. The advantages that accrue from selecting a problem in this way far outweigh the disadvantages of exercising his own complete freedom of choice. In short, the student has to give up some freedom of choice in the selection of a problem if he wants to receive an education. But the student is not the only one who works under restrictions; many, if not most, scientists do. Even the academic laboratory scientist may be limited in what he can study by the funds available. The industrial scientist needs to recognize the goals of the concern for which he works, and at least to some small extent he must modify his own goals to make them compatible with those of his organization. In government service, it is necessary to realize that only certain types of research projects can survive over the years, and if a scientist embarks on a long-range program he should also have other short-term programs that will yield more immediate results of practical value.

This problem is an old one. Leonardo da Vinci found it necessary to spend much of his time devising instruments of war so that his patron would permit him to engage in scientific research. The system of patronage of the last century always required the scientist to modify at least a part of his pursuits to conform to the desires of his sponsors.

There is, of course, much evil in the fact that in most situations the scientist must take cognizance of outside forces that can influence the acceptance or rejection of his work. It might even be argued that many notable discoveries have been made in flagrant opposition to current ideas. The work Galileo pursued in the face of social opposition is familiar to every reader. Although the older scientist who is well established can perhaps afford to be insensitive to the social milieu within which his work takes place, the younger scientist has need of this sensitivity, if only to reach the point where he can afford to present highly novel ideas that oppose current concepts. Here the author is not endorsing the idea that the graduate student should pursue a line of thought thoroughly acceptable to his elders. He is only pointing out that the faculty of a school of education represents what might be called a subculture, and that, as in other subcultures, some ideas will be much more easily accepted than others. A graduate student would do well to select a school where his ideas and those of the faculty display some degree of harmony.

Finding Problems

It is difficult to supply definitive ideas concerning how the student should obtain ideas for his research. Part of the trouble arises from the fact that we know little, as yet, about the usefulness of various techniques for this purpose, and the scientist who is asked to say how he finds his ideas is usually quite unable to give a definitive answer. Certain procedures that the student may possibly find useful can be suggested, but these have not been validated. One method, already considered, is to have the student attach himself to a professor who is already engaged in research.

A second method of deriving research ideas is to read articles published in the current literature and to consider how the techniques and ideas discussed therein might be applied to the solution of other problems. The adaptation of techniques to the solution of new problems is a profitable and worthwhile enterprise in which many scientists engage. Indeed, many such enterprises can be judged to have high originality.

A third approach is to identify in the literature studies that would have had merit except for some central defect that makes it impossible to draw conclusions from the findings. This is not to be looked down on as an activity, for it often yields results of great importance.

A fourth procedure is to refer to the discussion section of technical papers (usually it is the final paragraph), wherein the author presents reflections concerning the significance of the results and what type of investigation should be undertaken as a follow-up. Such suggestions appear in considerable numbers in the concluding sections of technical reports. Many, of course, present only ideas rather than practical suggestions, and many are beyond the realms of usability at the present. Nevertheless, fruitful ideas may still be found in quantity.

All of these procedures involve a review of the literature. Because the latter is not the simple matter it may seem to be, some comment on this activity must now be made. Locating published material requires well-developed techniques for using a library, and this book assumes that the student has those skills. If he does not, he is referred to an excellent book by A. J. Burke (1966) designed specifically to provide that type of training. It is limited to the mechanical aspects of using a library; it does not concern itself with the more subtle subject of how information derived from a library should be used. A person may locate all relevant references but fail to derive from them relevant information.

The identification of the research literature pertaining to a field may begin in any of several different places. The *Education Index* is one place to start, but the student should avoid accumulating a massive bibliography before reading a few important articles of recent vintage. The *Encyclopedia of Educational Research* should be consulted for major references. Some of the articles in it provide outstanding overviews of particular areas of inquiry.

Unfortunately, a tradition has grown up that a "review of the literature" is a low-level task undertaken by the student who is not very advanced. Many, of course, would disagree with this view, as is evident in the fact that the chapters in each *Review of Educational Research* are usually written by the senior members of the profession. In a similiar spirit, the *Annual Review of Psychology* is, for the most part, written by persons who have had considerable experience in the fields they cover. A first-class review of the literature requires the maturity of viewpoint that comes from years of study and research. The student of education who has had a brief experience in graduate school cannot be expected to have the intellectual maturity to prepare a thoroughgoing review of research in an area of education in which he is interested; but the experience of making the review can be a worthwhile one, and with a few precautions much can be done to give it a professional and polished appearance.

Advice commonly given in making a review is to start by preparing a fairly complete list of references, but this is poor counsel, and any person who has engaged extensively in such work will know it. The first thing that a would-be reviewer must do is familiarize himself with the issues and problems of the field. Until he has done this, he cannot possibly know what are and what are not relevant contributions.

Critical review articles serve the purpose of indicating to the student the central issues to be taken into account in his own reading and review of the literature. He would also do well to discuss his early impressions of the literature with some professional person thoroughly familiar with the area. He will then be ready to begin work on his own review.

Through his preliminary reading, the student will have located some of the major references. These should be consulted next. At this stage a good plan is to enter the title of each reference at the top of a five-by-eight-inch card and to use the remainder of the card for summarizing the article with particular reference to the light it throws on major issues. A small section at the bottom of the card may be reserved for critical comments and further hypotheses suggested by the author of the study.

Additional references will be found in each article reviewed, and thus most of the significant sources will be obtained. At this point, the reader may ask why it has not been suggested that he prepare a comprehensive list of references from a source such as the *Education Index*, which lists every article and publication that has any relevance at all to educational problems. The answer is that in such a source the classification of references is necessarily very crude and often depends more on the title of the article than on its content. Such comprehensive lists of publications may supply a rough check on what is available, but they cannot provide a basis for a critical review. However, such lists do permit a superficial independent check of the completeness of the references obtained from published articles.

In the development of his review of the chosen field, the student will have opportunity to discover a problem that he can use as a basis for his research. Once such a problem has been found, the review can be written in terms of the relevance of the various studies to it. Until such a problem is found, it may be well to postpone the final integration of the material into a single review, which will usually constitute the first chapter of the thesis or dissertation.

The reader should pause at this point to link up what has been said here with the previous discussion of the need for conducting research within a framework of theory. The review of the literature, if conducted with thoroughness, should lead the reviewer to summarize the state of knowledge in the area in terms of a few generalizations. Such a set of generalizations constitutes the essence of a theory. Very often the reviewer will find that one of the articles or books in the area under study will already have presented such a list of generalizations based on the findings. In the area of administration, for example, a number of different attempts have been made to state a theory of administration based on the research that has been undertaken.

The prospective research worker may also find that the results of different studies in a field are so conflicting that no generalizations can be derived from them. Such a state of chaos is not uncommon in the behavioral sciences, but when it is encountered the student should realize that such a field is no place for a beginner.

The theory derived from the review of the literature summarizes the essential core of what research has discovered. This is the essence of a theory. The student in search of a problem should then ask himself what some of the consequences of the theory are, or what he can expect to predict from the theory, or how the theory can be applied to the solution of a particular problem. Questions such as these form the essence of what we have termed hypotheses.

Research Designed to Choose Among Theoretical Positions

The fact that a research hypothesis is clearly stated does not mean that it enables one to choose between alternative theoretical positions, but the more important scientific hypotheses enable one to make such a choice. In the field of educational research at this time, the most one can probably expect from researchers is that they will state clearly just what they want to find out.

J. R. Platt, in a well-known article on scientific inference (1964) has suggested that a rapidly developing science is one in which hypotheses are precisely stated and in which the data from the resulting experiments clearly reject one theoretical position and support another. Many experiments, Platt argues, do not result in clear-cut decisions concerning the direction in which the advancement of knowledge should move next, and such experiments, he suggests, have little value. He also states that those sciences showing rapid advances are those in which experiments are being used to draw unambiguous conclusions about what is a sound theoretical position and what is not.

The Platt article sounds very convincing, but many have doubts about its soundness. Although Platt argues that a science advances rapidly when experiments can be conducted that clearly reject one theoretical position and accept another, one should not conclude, as he does, that the application of this method to any area of enquiry will immediately produce results. A much more plausible argument is that once a science has developed to the point where it is ready for great advances, it is possible to design experiments that give precise answers rejecting one theoretical position and accepting another. Many areas of science have not reached the point where such experiments can be conducted. In such areas, the scientists are often still attempting to find out how to ask precisely stated questions. The behavioral sciences are still to a large degree attempting to formulate clearly stated questions, the answers to which will add to knowledge without settling any great theoretical issue. The rare experiment that does the latter is of supreme importance, but those who perform such experiments are few in number. For most of us, the aim of research has to be much less ambitious, and useful research can be conducted that serves the more modest purpose of determining whether a theory can be applied in a particular situation, or even of finding out whether a simple prediction made from a theory can be validated. Only a very small fraction of the research in the behavioral sciences yields clear knowledge supporting one theoretical position and rejecting another. All this is a far cry from an advanced science making rapid advances where critical experiments can be carried out.

DESIRABLE CHARACTERISTICS OF THE PROBLEM

The problem that is eventually isolated can be stated in terms of a question for which the proposed research is designed to obtain an answer. Sometimes the question to be answered is referred to as a hypothesis. Sometimes in this book it has been called a deduction from a postulate. Certain criteria may be suggested for judging the merits of hypotheses, and these need to be discussed further at this point. It will be assumed in this discussion that the hypothesis is firmly rooted in a framework of theory, hence this particular criterion will not be discussed here at further length.

Hypotheses should be clearly and precisely stated. When hypotheses are clearly stated they usually avoid the use of common expressions such as good teaching, personality, favorable climate for learning, and others in the common vocabulary of education. On the other hand one may refer to "personality as measured by the Minnesota Multiphasic Personality Inventory," or to "the climate of teaching defined as the number of positive reinforcing or encouraging statements made by the teacher during a given time period." The clear statement of a problem generally involves the use of a technical language that provides terms better defined than those in common language.

Hypotheses should be testable. One of the commonest sources of difficulty for the graduate student who embarks on a dissertation is the selection of a hypothesis that is not really testable. The same difficulty is also apparent in the researches of some of the more mature members of the educational profession. For example, one educator selected for his research the hypothesis that secondary school teachers did not know enough algebra to teach pupils competently. This is not a scientific problem; nonetheless it was one of some interest. He proceeded to test this untestable hypothesis by administering an algebra examination he had devised to a group of secondary school teachers. Because the questions in his test gave the appearance of having been devised to confuse, it is hardly surprising that most of the teachers achieved a very low score. His conclusion was that the teachers did not know enough algebra to teach with competency, which was just a reiteration of the opinion he had held in the first place. The data provided no genuine information to endorse or reject the conclusion. He wanted to "prove" a point. What was needed in order to make his hypothesis a testable one was a prior study establishing what mathematical knowledge was and what mathematical knowledge was not essential or desirable in an algebra teacher.

This point should be emphasized because some of the most interesting and important hypotheses are quite untestable at this time. It is important to learn this lesson, because a common way of attempting to select problems for a program of educational research is to start by listing the problems that are in most urgent need of attack from the practical standpoint. The author has been associated with several projects set up in this way and has invariably protested the use of this procedure, but the result has always been the same. The research program has bogged down in a swamp of untestable hypotheses. Although the researcher may begin his thinking with some focal point in education where answers are urgently needed to important questions, he should start by struggling to find a contact point between available organized knowledge and the problem with which he is confronted. If such a contact point does not exist, the researcher must assume that he is attempting to operate in an area that, because of its isolation from organized knowledge, is likely to yield untestable hypotheses.

Hypotheses should state relationships between variables. A well-developed hypothesis that meets satisfactory standards should state an expected relationship between variables. Unless hypotheses can be stated in this form, they have not reached the point where they are appropriate as a basis for research. A hypothesis such as "Children who attend Sunday school show greater moral growth than children who do not" is not testable, because the term *greater moral growth* does not refer to a variable that is measurable at the present time, or likely to be measured in the near future. On the other hand, a hypothesis such as "Teachers who manifest aggression in the classroom have pupils who also manifest aggression" refers to a variable, aggression, than can be measured through such procedures as counting the number of specific types of aggressive incidents that occur. However, the reader should recognize the fact that it is often necessary to use quite indirect means of measurement. This is true of all sciences. The physicist measures the amount of various elements in the sun by studying the spectrum of its light. The psychologist may attempt to measure emotional disturbance through the response of the individual to an ink-blot. Although hypotheses should state relationships between variables, it does not mean that these variables have to be measured by any direct method, although any indirect measurement should be based on a clear-cut rationale.

Hypotheses should be limited in scope. A common error of the graduate student of education in planning research is to develop hypotheses of global significance. It is perhaps natural for the beginning research worker to be overambitious in his initial efforts, partly because of his earnestness and partly because it takes maturity of viewpoint to realize how little can be accomplished in a lifetime. The more mature research worker is likely to choose hypotheses narrower in scope and therefore more testable. The student should seek hypotheses that are relatively simple to test yet highly significant. He should try to bring order into a very limited corner of the universe—but it should be an important corner.

Hypoheses should be consistent with most known facts. Any hypothesis formulated as a basis for research must be consistent with a substantial body of established fact. It is too much to expect that it be consistent with *all* established facts because in so many areas the facts themselves appear to be inconsistent with one another. For example, in the area of vision, no theory has been able to resolve all of the apparently inconsistent facts, and almost any hypothesis formulated is likely to be consistent with some of the facts and inconsistent with others.

Hypotheses should be stated as far as possible in simple terms. This is desirable in part to permit the meaning to become clear to others, but it is also desirable because, in order for a hypothesis to be testable, it must be stated in relatively simple terms. The simplicity of the statement has nothing to do with its significance. Some of the most important hypotheses ever tested have been such as could be explained to an average child in junior high school. It is the simple truths tentatively formulated as hypotheses that form the fundamental cornerstones of science. For example, Pasteur's hypothesis that life would not be spontaneously generated from organic matter if all living matter were first destroyed is an easily understood concept, yet it is one that deals with an idea of fundamental importance. Newton's hypothesis that a body continues in uniform motion until acted on by a force is a simple one, yet it became a cornerstone of physics.

Hypotheses should be simple from another point of view. They should avoid the use of vague constructs, however popular these may happen to be in current educational thought. It is quite useless to formulate a hypothesis such as, "The adjustment of the pupil to the classroom situation will depend on the total classroom situation." Such a hypothesis includes several vague concepts, one of which is *the total classroom situation.* To say that an event depends on everything else that is happening fails to do what the scientist has to do—namely, isolate a few aspects of his environment that have special relevance as factors in the production of the phenomenon in which he is interested. The specification of these characteristics must be undertaken in the formulation of a clear and simple and important hypothesis.

The hypothesis selected should be amenable to testing within a reasonable time. The student of education is too often excessively ambitious when he first seeks to undertake research. This is usually a result of the fact that he is in close contact with the pressing problems of education. He is frustrated by being perpetually confronted with problems that must be solved before major advances can be made, and to overcome his feeling of personal frustration he sets himself the goal of solving one of the major problems. Yet the fact is that nearly all such problems cannot be solved for a long time to come. They are mainly problems of immense difficulty that cannot be profitably studied because the essential techniques for attacking them are not available. This is well illustrated by the numerous graduate students of education who suggest each year that they develop a doctoral dissertation in the field of teacher effectiveness. The common proposal is that a study be made of personality traits as related to teacher effectiveness. Such studies assume that measures of relevant teacher traits are available—and of course they are not. These studies also assume that the effectiveness of the teacher in achieving various kinds of significant objectives is known, and that the growth of the pupils with respect to these objectives can be measured. It is almost certainly true that most of such achievements cannot be measured at the present time and that no means will be found to measure them for a long time to come. Most studies of teacher effectiveness that the graduate student is likely to consider are impractical because the techniques for carrying them out simply are not available and cannot be developed rapidly.

The student should be warned against doing what is commonly done when the would-be researcher finds that techniques are not available for the study of a particular problem—that is, using what are often hopelessly inadequate techniques. For example, many who have wished to study personality characteristics of teachers related to their effectiveness have ultimately settled for studies involving the correlation of ratings of teacher effectiveness with ratings of personality characteristics. Such activity can be described only as pseudo research. It bears a relation to well-conducted research in that it involves the statement of a hypothesis and the collection of data, but the data have only a superficial relationship to the testing of the hypothesis. The serious research worker would find it hard to accept the belief that actual teacher effectiveness in achieving a particular objective is related, except to a slight extent, to ratings of effectiveness produced by an observer, for the judgments of an observer are likely to be very erroneous. Similar doubts may be expressed about the validity of ratings of the teacher's personality characteristics. Educational literature is full of examples of studies in which a student's enthusiasm for a problem has blinded him to the weaknesses of the techniques through which he has tried to study it.

SOME ADDITIONAL CONSIDERATIONS IN SELECTING A PROBLEM

Some Practical Matters Related to Research

Before the final selection of a problem is undertaken, the student should ask himself a number of quite practical questions which only he can answer. The first of these is whether he is well equipped in terms of his background to carry out the research. A student in school administration may be fascinated with the idea of exploring faculty-principal relationships, or some phase of these phenomena. However, if he has never undertaken work in social psychology he will rapidly find himself out of his depth. The would-be research worker must ask himself whether he has sufficient mastery of the area to undertake an attempt to advance knowledge. The advancement of knowledge can be undertaken only by those who have already covered all of the territory up to the frontier of knowledge.

A second question, somewhat mundane but important nonetheless, is whether the study falls within the budget the student can afford. For this reason, a careful estimate must be made of the cost of apparatus, tests and other printed devices, and other equipment called for by the study. In addition, the cost of computational work must be considered. Sometimes a study cannot be undertaken because adequate space is not available. In recent years the matter of space has become an acute problem, for enlarged enrollments have stretched university facilities to the limit.

A third very practical consideration is whether the necessary cooperation can be obtained from those who must participate in research as subjects. Many studies require the cooperation of schools, and although they will generally cooperate with faculty on major research projects, school districts are becoming increasingly unwilling to work with graduate students on research projects.

Indirect Versus Direct Approaches

A common error in educational research results from attempting to direct an attack on problems. For example, research on the development of improved professional training programs for teachers may not be a feasible enterprise until certain other problems are first solved. For example, we probably know far too little about how children learn to be able to train teachers effectively at this time. Research on learning in children might lead more rapidly to better methods of teacher education than would direct experimentation with teacher-training programs. In addition, the improvement in these programs may require that knowledge be first obtained on the difficulties that teachers have in communicating with children and the conditions that interfere with effective communication. The direct approach to the improvement of teacher education is likely to be much less successful than an approach that will develop bodies of knowledge about learning to be taught to students of education. Undoubtedly some improvements can be made in teacher education, but the major improvements will have to wait until more basic research has given us better insight into the conditions that make for effective learning in schools.

Another good example of an important problem that probably cannot be successfully studied directly is that of the high school dropout. Evidence suggests that such youngsters are dropouts, not because of immediate circumstances confronting them in school, but because of conditions in their background that go far back into their childhood. An understanding of the problem is to be found in research on early childhood development and the cultural factors that produce achievement motivation and life goals. A direct attack on the dropout problem does not permit the research worker to study the important conditions that lead to this problem.

Indirect approaches to problems are typical of all branches of science. The realization that the laws of falling bodies could be studied best by studying not free-falling bodies but such artificial situations as objects moving down inclined planes, opened an entirely new era in physical experimentation. The study of human genetics has been made possible through studies of the microscopic structure of plant cells. The development of radioactive materials has made it possible to investigate human metabolic processes that have defied any direct approach. Much scientific knowledge has to be acquired by indirect methods. Even the practical problem of measuring the diameter of the earth does not lend itself to the direct approach, which would involve the stretching of a measuring tape around its circumference. All knowledge about the atom and its structure is acquired by extremely indirect methods, where the measurements made are connected only remotely with atomic phenomena and where the conclusions involve a long chain of supposed events.

The directness of approach of many who work in educational research is not too different from the approach of the physical scientist of the Middle Ages who wished to solve the problem of converting lead to gold by simple and direct means. Part of the reason for this is that our ingenuity has not led us yet to useful indirect methods of attack, and thus we tend to keep hammering away with direct approaches, which mostly have no value at all. However, we can take a few steps in the right direction. Even an opinion survey at times can avoid to advantage a direct question concerning a problem. For example, a person may be unwilling to admit what he pays his servant, but he may be quite willing to state, without embarrassment, what he believes to be the prevailing wage in the community for that kind of work.

Sometimes the indirect approach to problems involves the conduct of a study in a laboratory situation rather than in a real-life setting. Many problems of reading have been attacked successfully in this way, and subsequent classroom studies have validated the results. There are advantages in a direct approach whenever it is likely to yield results, but the student who finds that only an indirect avenue is open to him should not feel discouraged. He should remember that some of the most important discoveries of science were made by a similar means.

Research in administration is an area in which a direct approach is often not feasible but in which indirect attacks on the problem may be highly productive. The author can recall the suggestion of a student interested in the question of how information was passed around in a large board of education building. The suggestion was the simple one of keeping a record of who called who on the telephone within the building. There was no intention of keeping a record of what was said, for the purpose was only to draw up a diagram rather like a sociogram that would indicate the channels through which information passed during the course of daily business. Of course, there has also been much laboratory work conducted on the effect of various administrative practices on the morale of groups, and these studies are being slowly extended into the field of real administration. The choice of level of reality of a study, its directness or indirectness, is determined by a multiplicity of factors, including the amount that is already known about the phenomena.

Data Language

An earlier chapter pointed out that the development of research in an area is highly dependent on the development of an appropriate technical language. That part of the technical language referring to the scientists' data is referred to as the data language. Because the behavioral sciences use many different languages, sometimes the same data may be described in different languages. For example, suppose that a research worker collected data on children learning the definition of a number of words. In terms of Skinner's model of learning the data would provide information concerning the occurrence of *verbal operants.* Other psychologists might say that the data showed the occurrence of particular *verbal associates* or *verbal habits.*

The phenomena of education can be discussed in many different ways using many different vocabularies. Consider the case of the researcher studying some aspect of the behavior of the teacher. Much of the data of any such study must be derived in some way from the movements of the teacher in the classroom or from disturbances that he produces in his physical surroundings, as when his vocal cords cause vibrations in the atmosphere. Now an educational researcher who described all of the movements of a teacher and all of the physical disturbances produced by his behavior in the physical environment during a one-hour period would not have a description of events that would be in the slightest respect meaningful to another research worker. A graph showing the decibel level of noise produced by the teacher's larynx would not convey to most of those who inspected it just what had happened in this respect in the classroom. A language that described teacher behavior in terms of the physical properties of movement, direction, force, pitch, and the like, would at the present time be an entirely inappropriate data language for any researcher who wished to study the classroom behavior of teachers.

A much more appropriate language for discussing teacher behavior would be that derived from the psychology of learning. In terms of such a language one might describe the behaviors of the teacher that were directed toward the *reinforcement* of pupil behavior and the *aversive* characteristics of the teacher's behavior; or one might record the extent to which pupils *modeled* particular aspects of the teacher's behavior. However, many other technical languages might be used for describing the behavior of the teacher. One can, as B. O. Smith and his associates (1965) have done, describe the discourse of the teacher and pupil in the classroom in terms of its logical properties.

A data language should avoid references to unobservables. For example, a researcher recorded the statement, "The teacher felt frustrated because he was unable to maintain order." This statement referred to the teacher's feeling of frustration, which could not be observed but only inferred from observables. The kind of inference that is implied in the researcher's statement should never be included in the data language; the data language should refer to the events on which the inference is based.

The development of a suitable data language for any program of research in the behavioral sciences must take cognizance of three facts: First, it must be based on the recognition that all behavioral events that occur during a data-gathering procedure cannot be recorded as part of the data, for much more occurs than can ever be recorded. Secondly, what is recorded constitutes only certain aspects of behavior, and terms must be employed that are scientifically recognized as referring to the particular aspects of behavior that are abstracted. Thirdly, the terms used must refer to objectively identifiable events; that is to say, events that independent observers can identify.

The Advantage of Breadth and Narrowness in Defining Problems

There are disadvantages in the definition of a problem in narrow terms, particularly in the early stages of exploration. Narrowness hampers the possibilities of an imaginative approach. This can be appreciated by presenting a concrete problem from a field other than education. The example here is one developed by the late John Arnold, who, in his classes on creative engineering, stressed the importance of defining problems at first in broad terms. He points out that in one of his classes some students embarked on the engineering problem of designing an improved automatic toaster. By stating the problem in this way, the possible ideas that could be incorporated in a plan of action were restricted. If the problem had been defined as that of *developing new methods of providing the consumer with toasted bread,* a wide range of new ideas would have become available for exploration. For example, one can conceive of the possibility of providing the consumer with ready-packaged toast. Industrial methods of large-scale toast making could then be considered. There was also the possibility that some commercial substitute for toast might be developed. So long as the problem was that of *developing a better toaster,* these latter possibilities could not receive consideration. Now there is no question that ultimately a problem has to be narrowed before it can be worked on, but this should not happen until opportunity has been provided to explore the problem on a wide base with the full play of imagination.

There are similar disadvantages attached to the early narrow definition of problems in the field of education. Thus, in the search for a problem to work on in the field of mathematics education, the researcher might well start by asking himself the question, "In what ways is it possible to improve the teaching of number operations?" rather than the question, "In what ways is it possible to improve the teaching of long division?" When the student begins to think in terms of the broad problem, he is free to identify some crucial aspect of the teaching of arithmetic, the improvement of which would result in the improvement of the teaching of arithmetic in general. On the other hand, if the student thinks only in terms of teaching long division, the outcome of the resulting research is likely to be applicable only to the teaching of long division. The student should direct his thinking in such a way that the ultimate product of the research envisaged is a principle that has at least the possibility of being widely applicable.

It should be pointed out here that we are referring in this section to the early stages of developing research. As thinking progresses, it is necessary to consider more and more specific aspects of the problem.

Preliminary Explorations of the Problem

The selection of a problem for study is not usually undertaken in a single step, for it is commonly necessary to run a preliminary study before the decision is finally made. The need for such a preliminary study does not arise when the problem requires the conduct of a research closely similar to one that has already been done, for it is then known that the research can be undertaken. However, when the field of inquiry is relatively new and does not have available a set of well-developed techniques, a brief feasibility study must almost always be run. Such brief trial runs demonstrate whether it is practical to undertake the research, whether the available techniques are sufficiently sensitive to measure differences that it is desired to measure, and whether one can obtain the necessary cooperation of others involved in the study. Negative results in any one of these directions may be sufficient to cause the researcher to change his problem.

A preliminary trial or pilot study also provides some indications of the availability of subjects, if human subjects are used, or of other needed materials. Certain studies may require specific population characteristics, and it is necessary to determine whether populations having these characteristics actually exist. For example, one study required a comparison of the performance of children who did not like their teachers with that of children who did, and each one of these categories of children had to be divided into a bright group and a dull group. A preliminary study was needed to determine whether enough children existed who would admit not liking their teachers to make the study possible.

Preliminary trial runs involve not only the selection of a problem, but also the selection of some kind of design for the study. In practice the design of the trial run may be much simpler and less sophisticated than the design that is finally adopted. The trial run may provide much information that is needed for the final design.

Research on Individuals and the Infringement of Their Rights

Research with people introduces problems that are not involved when the material for research consists only of things. People have rights and many kinds of research cannot be undertaken because the collection of the data, and perhaps even the reporting of the data, might infringe on those rights. The ambitious novice in research has to be particularly careful to select a problem that does not involve such difficulties, because his enthusiasm may lead him to choose one of the many attractive problems that should not be studied because of such considerations.

Until midcentury few ethical issues were raised in the matter of the collection of data, but in recent times considerable attention has been focused on such issues, partly because many questions related to them have been raised both in Congressional committees and in state legislatures. The major issues that have been raised pertain to certain distinct areas, but any answers given here can represent only the moral judgments of the author.

Issues related to the questions that can be asked legitimately of captive audiences. This matter was brought to a head some years ago when wrath was expressed in state legislatures because children were being asked questions on personality tests that were believed to invade their privacy. Considerable public irritation was caused by the fact that some of the questions were concerned with the relationship of the child to his parents, and such matters were considered to be strictly the concern only of the child and his parents except where a court had reason to believe that a child was being mistreated. An important point to note in the whole controversy is that the children who were given such tests in schools generally had no say as to their willingness to answer the questions. The children were captive in the situation and were not free to walk out. The situation involving the wholesale administration of personality tests in schools is entirely different from that of administering tests in clinics where children might be sent for treatment. In the clinic there is some guarantee that the relationship between the child and the therapist is one involving privacy. In the school there is no such guarantee. Renewed interest in the rights of children has been partly responsible for bringing this matter to the forefront, and the trend in both public sentiment and in the decisions of the Supreme Court has been to establish the position that children have essentially the same rights in many areas as have adults.

Any research worker who wishes to obtain personal information from others, whether they are children or adults, must ask himself whether his questions will or will not invade their privacy. He must also ask whether he is taking advantage of the fact that he is dealing with a captive group that cannot readily escape from the situation. Sometimes the privacy of the individual can be protected by a guarantee of anonymity, but such a guarantee, if given, must be given with complete honesty. There have been too many cases in which anonymity has been guaranteed, but the experimenter has then gone on to establish the names of the respondents through some devious device. The latter is very easy to do, but should not be done under any circumstances.

The ethical problems posed by the administration of personality tests are also raised when data are collected through individual interviews. Under the latter conditions, the research worker does not have the right to enquire into the personal lives of individuals to the same extent that the therapist does.

The panel on Privacy and Behavioral Research appointed in 1966 by the President's Office of Science and Technology defines the right to privacy as the right of the individual to decide the extent to which he will share with others his thoughts and feelings and the happenings in his personal life. The essence of the right to privacy is freedom enjoyed in making a choice of what parts of himself he will or will not share with others. The research worker must behave in such a way that he upholds this right of the individual.

The use of deception in orienting subjects in experiments. A related ethical issue is that concerning the deception of subjects in experimentation. In most psychological experiments, the subject has to be given some orientation concerning the nature of the experiment and how he is expected to behave. If a subject is given a difficult task and is told that it is readily mastered by most first-grade children, his behavior in relation to the task is likely to be different than if he is told that the task is considered difficult by most adults. In most experiments, the experimenter cannot tell those involved in the experiment exactly what it is about. Most experimenters take the position that such deceptions are justified provided the subject is told, before he leaves, whatever information is needed to relieve his anxieties or feelings of inadequacy that the experiment has generated. Here again limits are set if the subjects are captive that do not have to be set if the subjects can walk out. The author once used electric shock in an experiment with children, but all of the children were volunteers in a residential area during summer vacation and knew that they would receive a dollar if they stayed through to the end of the experiment. In addition, the children were all free to walk out through the open door at any time. They were told that they were free to leave but that if they did so before the end, they would not receive the dollar. The use of the dollar, as an incentive for staying may have seriously disturbed the results of the experiment, but no other ethical means was available for restraining the subjects from walking through the door. An additional point to note in connection with this experiment is that the children were informed that the electric shock was harmless and the apparatus was constructed in such a way that no subject could receive more than a very small electrical charge. The reader is warned to keep away from such experiments unless he has substantial knowledge of electronics so that the subjects can be properly protected.

When college students are the subjects for an experiment, the research worker may feel obligated to reward the students for their efforts by making the experiment into a teaching situation. After the data have been collected, the research worker may send each subject a report of the experiment giving the true purpose of the study and the results that were found. This procedure, or its equivalent, should be followed whenever students participate in an experiment as a course requirement. An honest course requirement has to involve learning.

Developing a Research Plan

A stage arrives in the development of every research at which it becomes desirable for the worker to arrange his ideas in order and write them down in the form of an experimental plan. A few experienced and sophisticated research workers may never actually write out such a plan, just as most experienced writers do not start by making an outline, but most research workers need a formal plan just as most writers need to make an outline. The student of education who is embarking on his first research enterprise will certainly need to develop a research plan that will serve a number of different purposes.

First, the research plan helps him to organize his ideas in a form whereby it will be possible for him to look for flaws and inadequacies. Many research studies appear to offer excellent promise until the details are laid out in black and white. Only then do the difficulties of executing the study become apparent.

Secondly, the research plan provides an inventory of what must be done and which materials have to be collected as a preliminary step to undertaking the study.

Thirdly, the research plan is a document that can be given to others for comment and criticism. Without such a plan it is difficult for the critic to provide a comprehensive review of the proposed study. Word of mouth methods of communicating the proposed study are more time-consuming and less efficient than that provided by a written plan.

A research plan should cover at least the items discussed in the paragraphs that follow. Only a brief discussion is presented here, because many of the points are treated at greater length in the chapters that follow.

1. The problem. The plan should include a clear statement of the question or questions that the research is designed to answer These are the hypotheses. The plan should also provide a concise account of the background of the problem and the theory on which it is based. The questions must be clearly and precisely stated. The statement of the problem must be complete, and it must be presented in a form that makes absolutely clear just what information must be obtained in order to solve the problem.

2. The method to be used in solving the problem. This section of the plan provides an over-all description of the approach that offers an avenue to the solution of the problem. Sometimes it is necessary to adopt methods that make special assumptions, and these should be explicitly stated in this section of the plan. For example, if the method involves the measurement of attitudes by means of verbal attitude scales, then it may be necessary to assume that verbal expressions of attitude are related to other expressions of attitude. In the latter case it might not be desirable to continue with the research unless evidence can be marshaled showing that the assumption was justified. Usually it is necessary to introduce assumptions about methods simply because direct attacks on the problem are not possible and the indirect nature of the approach that must be taken introduces the need for assumptions.

3. Procedures and techniques. Whereas the previous section describes the over-all approach to the problem, this part of the plan is concerned with the details of the techniques to be adopted. If inter-

view methods are to be used, an account of the nature of the con-
templated interview procedures should be given here, as well as
whether the interview is to be structured and if so in what way, and
the characteristics that the interviewer should possess for the purposes
of the study. If tests are to be given, the conditions under which they
are to be administered should be specified, as well as the nature of
the instruments that are to be used. This section is an appropriate
place for describing apparatus to be used or to be built. If public
records are to be consulted as sources of data, the fact should be
recorded here.

4. *The population to be studied.* The population to be studied will
depend on the population to which the results of the study are to be
generalized. If the results are to be generalized to all seventh-grade
pupils in a certain school system, the research plan should state this
fact. Because it probably will not be possible to include all seventh-
grade pupils in the study, but only a sample, the research plan should
state how the sample is to be identified. The method of identifying
the sample should be such that generalization from the sample to the
original population is feasible. If textbooks are the subject of the
research, the population of textbooks to which the results are to be
generalized must be specified as must the method of identifying the
sample of textbooks to be studied.

5. *Methods to be used in processing data.* A research plan should
indicate the statistical and other methods that are to be used for
processing data. Such methods should not be left until the data have
been collected. Many students have completed considerable work on
a study, only to find that statistical techniques did not exist for answering the questions that were asked. This part of the plan should
be reviewed by a person expert in the field of statistics, because such
a specialist can often suggest changes that result in substantial savings
of time and effort.

SUMMARY

1. The critical stage of educational research is the planning stage.
Often it is the most time consuming and may extend over a longer
span of time than the research.

2. There is no simple formula for finding research problems, but
a good first move is for the student to become thoroughly familiar with
the technical literature related to the area in which he wishes to
work. Problems selected by graduate students are rarely too simple.

They are often too complex and reflect excessive ambition. The identification of simple, solvable, and significant problems is one of the most difficult tasks of the scientist. The selection of a problem because it is related to an important social issue is generally a mistake. The student may gain considerable advantages by selecting a problem closely related to the research of a major professor with whom he wishes to work.

3. Many methods have been suggested for finding a research problem if one cannot be located through personal contact with a professor. Most of these involve a search of the technical literature. Techniques described in articles can be applied to the solution of novel problems, or the student can consider repeating a study after remedying certain basic defects in the original design. Sometimes the student may find in the conclusions of published studies some suggestions for further research. In any case, the student should be sufficiently familiar with the literature that he can identify a theoretical position to serve as a guide in his work.

4. The most powerful of all studies are those that produce results giving a clear-cut endorsement of one theoretical position and the rejection of another. Most research workers cannot hope to produce research of such importance but can expect to make some more modest contribution to knowledge.

5. The statement of the problem and the problem itself have to meet certain standards. The problem must be clearly and precisely stated. The hypothesis has to be testable, but the fact is that most of the significant hypotheses one can state about educational phenomena are quite untestable. The most suitable form for the statement of hypotheses is a relationship among variables that can be measured. Hypotheses should be limited in scope and should be simple rather than complex. Finally, there are many excellent hypotheses that should be rejected by the graduate student because he cannot spend a lifetime collecting data to test them.

6. The student must also consider some quite mundane and practical matters in selecting a problem, such as whether he has the funds necessary for carrying out the project and whether he can obtain the time and cooperation from those who will be the subjects for study.

7. The scientist commonly attacks problems indirectly mainly because a direct attack is rarely feasible. This is a lesson that many engaged in educational research still have to learn. The head-on attack still remains seductively attractive in education, despite the fact that it has not been particularly productive.

8. That aspect of the technical language of an area used to describe the data collected is referred to as the data language. Because the data all refer to observable events, the data language refers only to observables. The choice of a data language depends mainly on the theoretical position of the research worker. The data language of a person with a background in clinical psychology is likely to be quite different from the data language of a person grounded in sociology or experimental psychology. The use of common language from everyday speech for describing data generally indicates a lack of background and sophistication.

9. Sometimes there are advantages in first considering problems in broad terms and then narrowing down the problem later.

10. Many researches should not be undertaken until a preliminary study has shown that the proposed attack on the problem is likely to be useful.

11. The beginner in research should be sure to develop a research plan in which he details exactly what he is going to do.

5

‖‖‖‖‖‖‖‖‖‖‖‖‖‖‖‖‖‖‖‖‖‖‖‖

Measurement in Research

MEASUREMENT, OBSERVATION AND DESCRIPTION

Measurement and Science

IT IS difficult to conceive of a scientific approach to problems that does not involve the use of measurement. When measurement is involved, it is usual to say that *quantitative* methods are being used, as contrasted with *qualitative* methods, which do not involve the use of measurements. Quite obviously, much of importance can be learned by the use of qualitative methods, but the organized body of knowledge that is called a science seems to require measurement techniques for its development. The histories of most areas of knowledge show that, in the early stages of development, knowledge is acquired by qualitative methods, without resort to measurement. Such knowledge is usually lacking in precision and often hopelessly vague, but the kernel of truth that it contains opens the way to the development of progressively more precise knowledge.

Sometimes these early qualitative observations are of immense importance. For example, the observations of Freud formed the basis for the development of much of clinical psychology, although many years had to elapse before the development of measuring techniques and experimental methods permitted the systematic testing of aspects of his theories. Qualitative observations seem to be essential for the development of any branch of science, at least in its early stages, but it is ultimately careful work involving measurement that builds a science of real value. At a rudimentary level, even qualitative concepts can show some organization, as did Freud's; but the ultimate test of the validity of such concepts is whether or not they facilitate prediction. Tests of the accuracy and validity of prediction almost inevitably involve measurement.

The statement that measurement is central to the development of a science is justified more by history than by logic. Each field that has become a science has shown a dreary period of slow advance prior to the introduction of methods of measurement.

Perhaps it would be well to pause here and reflect briefly on the role that measurement has played in science. Consider, for example, the well-known studies of Gregor Mendel. He started out with the observation, familiar to most farmers, that crosses of different types of the same plant produce a new generation in which the characteristics of the parent plants may be distributed in various ways. Mendel was able to count the frequency with which each of the characteristics appeared in the offspring, and on the basis of these counts he was able to lay the foundation for a science of genetics. It is quite inconceivable that a mechanism underlying the inheritance of attributes would ever have been discovered without the use of such measurements. The crucial fact was one that involved quantity; namely, that approximately 75 per cent of the offspring of a cross between dwarf peas and tall peas were tall.

Numerous other examples could be given of the dramatic role played by measurement in the founding of other areas of science. A science of mechanics came into being when Galileo was first able to introduce a simple way of measuring the rate at which bodies fell. Much of the work that Newton had begun came to a standstill for nearly one hundred years until that great experimentalist Cavendish was able to measure the gravitational constant. Lavoisier's careful measurement of the weight of the products of combustion demonstrated that the phenomenon of burning involved a combination of a substance with a component of the air, and this in turn revolutionized chemistry. Later the measurement of atomic weights supplied the basis for laws of the combination of the elements. Almost every major advance in science has been closely allied to the development of new methods of measuring or handling quantities.

Much of the same seems to have been true in the behavioral sciences, of which research in education constitutes a part. Binet's attempts to measure intellectual power advanced immensely the possibilities of making predictions of behavior in ways that the earlier qualitative methods had been unable to do. When J. M. Rice first developed methods of measuring certain outcomes of the educational process, he made it possible to compare systematically one classroom procedure with another. E. L. Thorndike made it possible to exercise control over certain aspects of the curriculum by providing measures of the relative difficulty of various words, which in turn made it possible at a later stage to measure the difficulty of reading materials. Further development of evaluation techniques has made it possible to conduct research in education that simply would not have been possible fifty years ago. Even though the measurement techniques that have been introduced in education are crude, they have permitted a great expansion in our knowledge of the educational process.

Measurement involves the assignment of numbers to events according to some rule. The scale used at the post office for weighing packages assigns to a package a number that indicates its weight. The scale has been built to assign numbers to packages according to a rule prescribed by the National Bureau of Standards. A much simpler type of measurement is illustrated by the assignment of numbers to baseball players in order to label them. In the technical meaning of the term, the latter also involves measurement because it involves the assignment of numbers to objects or events according to a rule. Measurement, as the term is used in this book, is hence rather broadly defined.

Levels of Description

It used to be said, not so many years ago, that only insofar as the observer was describing specific acts was he describing behavior with any precision. Actually this is not true, for behavior can be described in a whole range of terms, from those that refer to the minutest detail to those that refer to gross total units of action. This concept is better understood by illustration. It is possible to describe behavior in terms of large units, such as, "The teacher showed the class how to carry out long division by working several simple examples on the blackboard." It is also possible to describe the same situation in terms of smaller units of behavior, such as, "The teacher (1) entered the class, (2) said, 'Good morning, children. Today we are going to learn long division,' and (3) explained the general idea of long division and why it was useful to learn it . . .". Still further details could be given by describing the movements of each part of the teacher's body in space and in time, and by providing a record of the sound vibrations produced by her larynx. Such a detailed level of description of behavior probably could not be used because of the vast quantity of data it provides and the immense difficulty involved in handling such massive quantities of fact. On the other hand, the broad descriptions provided by observation of the gross over-all type provide too little data for the purposes of most research. All levels of description refer to behavior, and both stimuli and responses can be described in terms of a great range of complexity. What the scientist has to do is choose the level of description that will ultimately permit him to make useful predictions.

In this connection it is common to distinguish between *molar* and *molecular* approaches to research in education. This distinction comes from the field of chemistry, where the term *molar* refers to a rather large mass of material in contrast to *molecular,* which refers to a small particle. When research in the behavioral sciences is said to be undertaken at a molar level, it means that it is concerned with gross aspects of behavior rather than with minute details. Research can involve the minute aspects of behavior, but this is not generally considered to be profitable. Hence, most educational research is molar.[1]

The choice of the proper level of description is important in all aspects of educational research. If one is concerned with school plant and facilities, it is probable that he will not be concerned with the size of the brick used, but the classroom may be a convenient unit with which to deal. Then, again, all of the buildings in a school system would probably compose much too large a unit with which to be concerned. Much the same is true of behavior. A unit of behavior must be selected that is neither too large nor too small for the particular purposes that the researcher has in mind.

If a study is being conducted in which pupils are required to read

---

[1] When Hull originally considered his molar theory of behavior, he was inclined to think that all of the response dimensions, such as speed of response, forcefulness of response, and others, would be related and indeed positively correlated dimensions. Empirical research has shown that this is not the case. It seems far more correct to assume that measures of two response dimensions will be correlated only when they are learned (reinforced) together. The Hull theory of the interrelationship of response dimensions, which has become known as the micromolar theory, avoided the need of measuring any other than the gross consequences of behavior. Considerable question has been raised in recent years concerning the soundness of the assumptions on which it is based, and some have advocated a micromolar approach that admits the necessity of the study of behavior in greater detail and that recognizes each aspect of a gross response as a separate response in itself, to be studied in its own right. Little advice can be given the student concerning the degree to which he should plan his studies on a macromolar or a micromolar level. Nevertheless it may be pointed out that, as research proceeds to a more detailed level of behavior, there is increasing difficulty in measuring the characteristics that it is desired to measure, and more and more complex laboratory instruments are needed. There are strictly experimental advantages in the study of molar behavior rather than molecular, and these exist quite apart from any theoretical advantages. From the point of view of the educator, it is molar behavior rather than molecular behavior that is of interest.

as quickly as possible words that are flashed on a screen, it is likely that the experiments will be concerned only with whether the words are or are not correctly read, and not with all the variations that may occur in how the word is said. The response involved in saying a particular word is an involved constellation of events, and the word may be said softly or loudly, almost immediately on presentation of the stimulus word or after considerable delay; it may be spoken clearly or slurred; it may be said in a monotone voice or it may be said with fluctuations in pitch; and so forth. In addition, the reading of the word on the screen may involve a variety of processes. Sometimes the word may be recognized immediately, and sometimes its pronunciation is elucidated by means of the application of phonetic principles. In the molar approach we are not concerned with the myriad variations that may be related to the making of a particular response. It is evident that when this is done, a certain amount of information is lost.

CLASSES OF VARIABLES IN EDUCATIONAL RESEARCH

In order to test hypotheses in ways that determine whether they should be rejected or accepted, it is almost always necessary to use concepts that permit measurement. It has been found convenient to classify variables on three rather distinct bases, with which the reader should be familiar.

First, it is common to classify variables into the categories of *dependent variables* and *independent variables*. In experimental studies the condition that is varied is referred to as the *independent variable*. If the amount of time devoted to drill in spelling is varied in a study, then this is the *independent variable*. If the effect of drill is measured by means of a spelling test, then the score on the spelling test is referred to as the *dependent variable*. These terms have second meanings, commonly used by statisticians: the variable that is being predicted is called the *dependent variable*, whereas the variable from which predictions are made is called the *independent variable*.

Secondly, one may classify variables in terms of the phenomena to which they relate. Thus it is common to distinguish between variables related to the stimuli that impinge on the individual and those that are related to his responses.

Thirdly, one may classify and consider variables from the point of view of their mathematical properties. Even though a very large literature has been written on this last type of classification, it will be touched on only briefly in this chapter because up to the present it has had only limited consequences for research methodology.

Each one of these three classifications of variables must now be considered.

DEPENDENT AND INDEPENDENT VARIABLES

Consideration must first be given the primary meaning of the distinction between these two classes of variables, which derives from experimental psychology. The experimenter, whether in education or elsewhere, varies certain conditions in order to determine how variations in these conditions produce certain consequences. In most educational experiments, the experimenter varies some condition in the environment of the child, such as some aspect of the teacher's behavior. He then seeks to determine how this affects achievement as measured by a test or some other device. The variation in the teacher's behavior is the independent variable, whereas the achievement score constitutes the dependent variable.

The second and broader meaning of these terms seems to have been derived from statistics rather than from any other source. In most scientific research, events are considered to occur in a time continuum, and certain events precede and are considered to be necessary antecedents of other events. The researcher usually measures certain characteristics of a situation as it exists at a particular time and tries to relate his findings in this respect to measures of previously existing conditions. It has become customary to refer to the variable to be predicted as the dependent variable, because it is viewed as being dependent on previously existing conditions.

The type of event that it is sought to predict is occasionally an all-or-none affair, such as whether a person will or will not graduate from high school, will or will not commit a crime. More often it is desired to predict some aspect of behavior that can have a range of values—as, for example, the grade a pupil will achieve in a particular course; or the liking a student will express for specific curricular materials; or the change in the absentee rate when a new building is provided. In such cases, and in most cases in educational research, the research worker desires to predict the value that a variable will assume under given conditions.

The variables that educational research is ultimately concerned with predicting are response variables, characteristics of the way in which the person responds to his environment. This may not be apparent to many educational researchers, so further comment is necessary. Much curriculum research, for example, appears to have as its main goal the development of a curriculum. The curriculum developed exists only because the researcher believes it will have a better effect on the child's behavior than other existing curricula. In a similar way, research on problems of school plant are justified only because it is believed that the type of plant provided affects the behavior of pupils. Much research is based on the assumption that certain educational events affect behavior, and ultimately such assumptions must be tested even though this cannot be done at the present time.

The variables that are used for making predictions are commonly referred to as the independent variables of research. It is not the nature of the variables that makes them dependent or independent but the way in which they are used. Indeed, it frequently happens that the dependent variables in one study become the independent variables of another study.

In a study of predicting reading skill resulting from training in a foreign language, a measure of skill at the end of the period of training would probably be the dependent variable. The independent variables would be chosen according to the nature of the inquiry. They might include various aspects of the way in which teaching could be varied and aptitude tests given prior to training. The independent variables might also include earlier conditions related to the ability to learn the particular language, such as exposure to related languages in childhood. They might also refer to such matters as the rewards, incentives, or reinforcements provided by the learning situation, or to any other condition related to the learning process.

The dependent variables of educational research, which ultimately are response variables, may refer to the frequency with which certain types of behavior occur or to qualities of behavior in particular situations. Often they represent verbal behavior, which, in a civilized society, is one of the more important aspects of behavior. The ways in which response variables are derived from the vast number of events that constitute the flow of behavior are discussed elsewhere in this book. It is sufficient to say at this point that many unsolved problems are involved.

The ultimate purpose of a science is to permit both the prediction and the control of events. Some sciences must be content with only the prediction of events, as is the case of astronomy, where control appears to present insuperable difficulties. The educational researcher is relatively fortunate in this respect, because not only can he expect to be able to predict events—such as who will succeed in college—but also he can aspire to exercise control over events—as when he seeks to develop a curriculum that will achieve a particular goal with maximum efficiency. At the present time, it is probable that the educational researcher knows much more about predicting events than he does about controlling the educational process to achieve particular ends. Prediction alone fulfills an extremely important function in education, and the capacity provided by research to do this has had a very significant influence on educational practice. If it is possible to predict who will succeed in medical school and who will not, it may then be possible to prevent many from experiencing the frustrations of failure. If it is possible to predict who will become delinquent unless remedial action is taken, there is a possibility of making a radical change in certain aspects of our culture. If one could predict which students of education will become highly neurotic, if not psychotic, teachers, a major problem of educational administration would be solved.

Although prediction performs an extremely important function in education, an even greater contribution could be made by educational research if it could tell the educator how to arrange conditions in order to produce specific results. Some progress has been achieved in this direction. A little is known about the types of classroom conditions that are effective for particular purposes. Some knowledge is available about the effects of particular types of classroom organization. But knowledge concerning the control of educational conditions is still fragmentary because it is hard to acquire. The reader will note, in subsequent chapters, that it is generally much easier to conduct studies that lead to prediction than to conduct those that lead to control.

The conditions that produce effective learning in one pupil will not necessarily produce effective learning in another. When it is said that the function of the educational research worker is to discover the conditions related to effective learning, it is assumed that these will be such that they can be modified as required by individual differences. The fact that children come to the classroom from different backgrounds and with different abilities results in their responding to the learning situation in different ways. Our knowledge of conditions related to effective learning should make us flexible in prescribing for particular pupils; it does not imply any rigidity of educational practice. In addition, teachers vary in the conditions they themselves are capable of producing. For example, some who may be otherwise capable are unable to generate a warm, friendly atmosphere. Such teachers will probably have to use somewhat different teaching techniques from those of teachers who have sympathetic dispositions. All such differences among persons, whether pupils, teachers, or others, must be included among the variables with which educational research is concerned.

STIMULUS RESPONSE, AND INTERVENING VARIABLES

Stimulus Variables

An important classification of variables that has had great influence on the language of current theories of behavior is that of stimulus variables, response variables, and intervening variables. Thirty years ago this classification could have been glossed over in a few lines and summarily dismissed, but its current importance is such that it cannot be treated so briefly today. Over the years it has become necessary to specify with increasing precision what is meant by these classes, and although full agreement has not been reached, it is important that tentative definitions be given here.

The term *stimulus* was taken into the behavioral sciences from physiology where it referred to a very simple environmental event that produced a response in a receptor organ. In the context of physiology, a stimulus was a stimulus only when it produced a response in a receptor. However, when the psychologists acquired the term, they used it in a rather different meaning, generally implying that it produced an *experience* rather than a receptor response. This is an entirely different usage for, clearly, there are many events that produce receptor response that are not recorded in experience. For example, much that goes on at the outer edge of vision produces receptor responses in the retina and yet persons report that they are unaware of what occurs. Thus a second meaning for the term stimulus was introduced. This second usage was found to be unsatisfactory to those psychologists who found the concept of experience an unnecessary one to introduce into a science. For this latter group, the term stimulus was given a third and different meaning: namely, an environmental event or condition that could be demonstrated in some way to produce a change in behavior. Thus a stimulus variable became, essentially, what others call an independent variable, that is to say, a condition influencing subsequent behavior. The latter term has tended to displace the term stimulus in much of modern psychology.

Those concerned with verbal stimuli have tended to discard the term stimulus in some of their recent writings. The new trend is to refer to *information inputs,* rather than to the term stimulus. The term *information* is derived from the highly technical area known as information theory. Thus, environmental factors influencing behavior have been designated by different names depending on the particular viewpoint of the user.

Any measurable aspect of the pupil's environment that in some way may be expected to affect his behavior is considered here to be a stimulus variable. These aspects include not only the characteristics of the buildings, textbooks, visual aids, and other features of the physical environment, but also the behavior of teachers, counselors, parents, principals, and others with whom the person seeking education comes into contact. So far, relatively little effort has been devoted to the isolation and measurement of stimulus variables related to the educational environment, but a few may be mentioned by way of illustration. A first example is presented by measures of reading difficulty such as those provided by the Lorge index or the Flesch index. These measure an important property of printed verbal material.

A second example is found in measures of the amount of behavior in various categories emitted by the teacher. For example, N. Wallen, *et al.* (1961) systematically recorded samples of verbal behavior emitted by teachers during the pursuit of their classroom duties. These statements were later classified in order to obtain measures of various aspects of the teaching performance. One of the categories used in the classification scheme was *controlling behavior.* The measure of controlling behavior was the number of controlling statements made by the teacher in the sample of verbal behavior studied. Such a measure represents one characteristic of the environment of the child exposed to the particular teacher.

Relatively little is known about the relevance of physical aspects of the surroundings of the child, and most relevant stimulus dimensions that have been defined refer to the behavior of persons with whom he comes into contact. It is hardly surprising that this is so, because the major influences in a person's life result from contacts with other persons rather than from contact with physical events as such. This may be the result, to a very great extent, of the fact that educators have not yet learned to arrange physical conditions to maximum advantage. Recent studies in the teaching of foreign languages have shown that much is to be gained by isolating students in booths where they are instructed by tape recorders. In this learning situation, not only is the student isolated from distracting stimuli, but also it is possible for him to repeat parts of the lesson on the tape recorder as many times as he wishes. Although research in the past has emphasized the importance of the role of the teacher and the resulting interpersonal relations, educational research may become more preoccupied with the physical conditions related to learning.

Many studies of classroom learning are concerned with a whole range of stimulus variables represented by conditions other than teacher behavior. Of particular interest at the present time are so-called visual and auditory aids, which are extensively used although there is little evidence to justify their use.

The growth of the use of visual and auditory aids unfortunately has been influenced by factors other than those derived from rational planning. Because visual aids are an easily observable but probably superficial aspect of the classroom environment, there is always a temptation for the teacher to cover the walls of the room with charts and other devices, for these may be the basis on which parents, school board members, and even supervisors may judge the merit of the teacher's performance. This basis for judging a classroom is seen frequently enough in civilian schools, but it is probably the most common way of judging teaching effectiveness in military establishments, where the inspection system is such that major emphasis is placed on superficial detail. This emphasis on the importance of what can be easily observed has stimulated not only the worst features of the current use of visual aids but also some of the best features.

Research on the use of visual and auditory aids has had a long history. Slide projectors came in for their quota of educational research forty or more years ago. In the early thirties substantial research was undertaken on the use of the film as a teaching device. Some of this research was undertaken by well-known scientists, among them L. L. Thurstone of the University of Chicago who conducted extensive studies of the use of the moving picture for the changing of attitudes. The use of sound pictures by the armed services for training purposes also stimulated substantial research within the military establishment.

In the late forties extensive research was undertaken on audio-visual materials through a project developed at Pennsylvania State University under the direction of C. R. Carpenter. This project involved the evaluation of training films that had been developed and the effect of modifying various aspects of these films. For example, one study presented the same film in both a colored version and a black-and-white version in order to determine the usefulness of color for promoting learning. The study showed that color contributed little to learning except where color discriminations were to be learned. Although the project did provide many interesting and useful findings, it did not yield a set of principles to follow in the design of audiovisual aids. A major difficulty that limited the outcome of the research was the extraordinary complexity of the materials that were studied, most of which had been designed for classroom instruction.

In a later series of studies Travers, *et al.* (1966) abandoned the use of instructional films for the purpose of studying problems of audiovisual design and used, instead, simplified materials developed in the laboratory. With these materials it became possible to demonstrate that many of the basic concepts concerning the use of audiovisual materials, which have been widely publicized in textbooks, are fundamentally unsound. For example, the notion has been taught for generations that, when the same information is transmitted simultaneously through two senses, more is learned than when a single sense is used. Under most learning conditions this is simply not the case. What has been taught in this respect as a principle of learning is simply a figment of the imagination. The series of studies under consideration attempted to develop a model of how students learn from audiovisual materials from which inferences could be made concerning the manner in which these materials should be designed.

Visual and auditory aids have been considered manipulable aspects of the pupil's environment. In this sense, the total curriculum can be considered an extended program of this type, because the visual and auditory senses are the main channels through which curricular materials have an impact on behavior. In view of what has been said, the best possibility of obtaining differences in pupil behavior as a result of differences in educational treatment would be when two matched groups of students are exposed to fundamentally different curricula. However, there are difficulties in this approach, which need brief consideration.

First, there is the difficulty of locating curricula that differ in any fundamental and permeating respects. Social pressures are such that most curricula contain a common core of material required by society if not by school boards. Few bodies that control education permit much deviation from the social norm in the design of curricula.

Secondly, it is often difficult to determine just how curricula do differ. We must not be fooled by names and assume that, just because they differ in name they differ in significant characteristics as far as the pupil is concerned. The results of much research on curricula in the past have had little validity because the differences in curricula have been differences only in name. What are needed are measures of various properties of the curricula. This is feasible in many cases; for example, when measurements are made of the amount of time spent in various activities such as lectures by the teacher, class recitations, group activity, individual study, and so forth.

The difficulty of quantifying differences between curricula stems from the fact that quantification must depend partly, if not largely, on judgment. Detailed analysis of recordings of what happens in the classroom is a complex venture because of the vast amount of material that it entails. Various approaches to this problem, including inter-action analysis in its many forms, have had periods of fashionableness, but none of these seem to have produced variables with significant and consistent relationships to learning.

In summary, although a science of education requires that measures of important characteristics of the environment, believed to have relevance to the educational process, should be available, there are as yet few aspects that can be measured satisfactorily. At least a part of this difficulty stems from the fact that most branches of the behavioral sciences have devoted little of their effort toward the measurement of environmental conditions related to behavior.

Response Variables

The ultimate purposes of education are defined in terms of desirable ways of responding to life situations. It is clearly not enough for the educator just to believe that he has produced certain internal changes in those who have passed through his educational program. It is generally conceded that the success of any educational program lies in its effect on behavior in those situations that the program has been designed to help the pupil face. If a program has among its objectives that of developing a critical attitude toward political propaganda, it is a failure unless in later years the person who has passed through that program shows through his behavior a critical attitude toward political propaganda. It is always through responses that the success or failure of an educational program can be established.

The common approach to the measurement of the way in which a person responds to his environment is best understood by turning to some of the classroom responses that are commonly accepted as evidence of achievement. A useful illustration is provided by the teaching of reading, in which it is common in the early stages to build up a recognition of fifty to one hundred everyday words. The pupil becomes able to recognize these words although he has no knowledge of phonetics, and this recognition enables him, with a little help, to read simple books designed around them. The pupil's recognition ability for these words can be measured in terms of the number he recognizes and speaks correctly. His learning in this respect is measured in terms of the frequency with which he makes a correct response in a standardized situation. Frequency of response is one of the commonest types of response variables that the educator is likely to encounter. Many personality variables are measured in terms of frequency of occurrence of a particular response. Frequency of occurrence of a particular class of behavior is used as a major method of measuring response characteristics. Aspects of the pupil's personality development can be measured by counting the number of antisocial acts shown toward other pupils, or the number of acts of hostility shown toward the teacher. The frequency of occurrence of many kinds of maladjustment is often used by counselors as an important item of information to be used in helping the pupil.

In research in education there are many frequency-of-response variables of great significance. In the early stages of reading, the frequency with which particular words are recognized represents an important class of variables. The frequency of errors in written compositions in English or in foreign languages is one of the commonest variables measured by teachers in those areas. They are not concerned with the level of seriousness of these errors, but with the number of times they occur within a given range of opportunity. Computational errors are also of this type. The arithmetical operation 9×9 is performed perhaps one hundred times by a child, and on 95 per cent of the occasions he performs the operation correctly; but from time to time, even though the response is highly overlearned, an error occurs. One might say that the probability of a correct response in such a case is 0.95. In other children the correct response probability is perhaps 0.75 or 0.42. There are differences at any given time in the response probability for groups with exposure to equal amounts of training. In practice, we are likely to be interested in predicting a sum of such response probabilities, as when we administer a test of one hundred simple computational problems from the multiplication tables and count the number of errors that are made. In measuring computational skill, this procedure is more likely to be adopted than is the procedure involved in preparing a set of problems of graded difficulty—which, in this case, would be problems graded in terms of complexity.

Although frequency of response is a very common measure used both by the practicing teacher and the research worker, there are other response characteristics that are also commonly recorded. Latency of response or speed of response is often measured for the appraisal of certain skills. For example, the level of skill achieved in typing and shorthand is commonly measured by determining the speed with which the pupil can perform the skill. This amounts to measuring the speed of response to either the words on the page, from which typed copy is being prepared, or the spoken words, which are being taken down in shorthand. In some cases the vigor of response may be measured, as in the case of a speech teacher whose pupils give speeches in almost inaudible timid tones at the beginning of the year but six months later hold forth in a vigorous and dynamic manner. The athletics coach also attempts to develop vigor of response, among other characteristics.

The response variables that have been considered up to this point provide convenient scales of measurement. For example, the frequency with which a particular spelling error occurs forms a scale with equal intervals. Speed of response is also conveniently scaled along a time dimension. However, many aspects of behavior are not so readily scaled. When the teacher asks herself the question, "How much arithmetic does Johnny know?" she is trying to find a general answer. She does not expect to be able to answer the problem by preparing a list of all the different kinds of arithmetical problems that Johnny can solve and another list of all those kinds that he cannot solve. Rather, she expects an answer such as that he is at the level of a beginning fourth-grader. This answer assumes that arithmetical skills can be assigned to a position along a scale and that one position on the scale can represent the knowledge and skill of the beginning fourth-grader. A scale position summarizes conveniently Johnny's arithmetic skills and is far more convenient than a complete inventory of what he can and cannot do in the area of arithmetic.

The production of a scale of arithmetic skills requires that the tasks can be arranged in some kind of order. This is the order in which the various tasks are learned. Because arithmetic skills are generally learned in one particular order, there is little difficulty in arranging them in an order that forms a scale. Much more difficulty is encountered in ordering the knowledge and skills acquired in, say, social studies, in which there is considerably less agreement on the order in which the student should be confronted with various materials. However, even in such an area some ordering is possible. Pupils learn a few stories about George Washington before they ever hear of Grover Cleveland, and they learn that there was a Civil War before they learn about carpetbaggers. Social studies problems can be arranged in order and scaled in a rough way, but the scale involved is not as clear and definitive as that representing achievement in arithmetic. What this means is that achievement cannot be conveniently summarized by stating a scale value that represents the pupil's level of achievement.

Research related to achievement generally requires that the tasks through which achievement is to be measured can be arranged in some form on a scale so that level of achievement can be represented by a single score summarizing extensive information about the pupil. If tasks cannot be arranged along a scale in this way, then achievement can be described only by listing all the tasks that the pupil can successfully undertake and those that he cannot undertake. Voluminous descriptions of the latter kind are almost worthless for research purposes because they are bulky and unmanageable.

Intervening Variables

A few psychologists have taken the view that a science of behavior can be built simply by studying the relationship of stimulus variables to response variables. Such psychologists assume that response variables are direct functions of stimulus variables. If this were the case, education would simply be a matter of arranging and scheduling stimuli so that the desired responses would be elicited. The teacher of reading would only have to arrange an efficient set of conditions for practicing the component skills of reading, and all children would learn to read.

Every schoolteacher in the first and second grade can testify to the inadequacy of such a theory and can show why it is wrong. Pupil after pupil in the first grade shows no improvement at all in recognizing words, even though extensive practice is given. Some pupils in the first grade are not capable of reading, hence a theory of reading that has at least minimum adequacy must include the concept of capability, an internal condition that is not directly observable and that accounts for individual differences in the responses of children to equal amounts of word-recognition practice.

Even in the simplest cases, it is not possible to describe events merely in terms of the relationship between environmental conditions and responses. Consider, for example, the case of the eyelid reflex produced by a slight puff of air on the cornea. If the puff is very light, the response may or may not occur, depending on the condition of the individual. Responsiveness varies according to internal conditions such as fatigue, attentiveness, the degree to which certain chemicals are present, and so forth. In the case of more complex behavior, the intervening conditions cannot be identified with any known chemical condition or identifiable neural structure. The intervening conditions that must be considered to exist therefore are said to be hypothetical. Whatever varies when these intervening conditions vary is referred to as an *intervening variable*.[2] Aptitude for reading or reading readiness is not a property that can be observed with any directness in a child. All that can be observed are the results of this variable as they are manifested in the task of learning to read. Hence, aptitude for reading is an intervening variable.

The reader should be warned against the introduction of intervening variables by circular argument. The fact that children differ in the rates at which they learn to read is not a sufficient basis for inferring a variable referred to as reading aptitude. It helps little to postulate the existence of an intervening variable and then to use this variable to explain the differences on the basis of which it was postulated. Such circularity serves little purpose. On the other hand, if it can be shown that equal conditions of learning still result in individual differences in reading skill, the investigator is on rather firmer ground in postulating such a variable. Indeed, some variable must be postulated to account for the lack of relationship between the stimulus variable and the response variable. The theory would be on still firmer ground if it could be established that a variable measured by a certain specific test (other than a reading test) could be used as if it were a measure of this aptitude. If, for example, a measure of physiological maturity were to account for individual differences in reading skill after exposure to equal training conditions, it might be said that this variable operated as the intervening variable that must be introduced to account for reading behavior.

Intervening variables may refer to a wide range of conditions. Sometimes they may have a clear relationship to tissue functions, as when a condition of hunger is produced by food deprivations over a period of hours. Studies of changes in behavior in pupils at various

---

[2] The terms *intervening variable* and *hypothetical construct* (*or construct*) are used by many writers almost interchangeably. At one time an attempt was made by P. E. Meehl and K. MacCorquodale (1948) to draw a clear distinction between these two concepts, but objections were raised to the distinction they proposed. The suggested distinction was that a *hypothetical construct* involved ideas over and above those included in an *intervening variable*. Much of what is referred to as a hypothetical construct in current psychological theory represents mechanisms that are postulated to mediate between stimulus and response. These mechanisms are not observable and should really be considered as imaginary mechanisms. The utility of such devices for guiding the thoughts of the scientist will depend on the extent to which they lead to variables that have predictive value.

stages of food deprivation have been conducted that have shown that behavior changes as food deprivation is increased. The condition of deprivation can be considered to be a measure of an intervening variable in such experiments. An experimenter might, for convenience, refer to the condition of food deprivation as a condition of hunger, but by doing this he is likely to confuse the issue. Although children deprived of food for a period of four hours might refer to themselves as "hungry," it is quite possible that the vague inner state of discomfort of which they were aware might be of only minor importance in modifying behavior in comparison with the effects of deprivation of which they were not aware. For this reason, the wise experimenter would do well to refer to this variable as deprivation rather than hunger. He would also do well to measure deprivation by the number of hours without food rather than by any subjective estimation of how hungry the children felt. It is not suggested that research on food deprivation in children is likely to be particularly profitable. It is merely a convenient example of an intervening variable that illustrates many of the problems of defining such variables.

A major class of intervening variables includes the so-called aptitude variables. These are presumed to measure conditions that facilitate learning, and there is substantial evidence that many of them measure facilitations produced by previous learning. It is possible that some measure rather permanent conditions in the nervous system, which have been influenced only to a small degree by learning. Relatively little is known at this time about the way aptitudes are developed, but the fact that they can be measured and that these measures have predictive value have given them a position of the greatest importance in educational research. One of the rather surprising facts about this class of variables is that relatively few aptitudes have definite predictive value in learning situations.

Motives also represent intervening variables, as they do variables that are commonly but erroneously postulated on the basis of direct observation of behavior. Strictly speaking, motives are unobservable. If two persons perform the same task but at different rates, there is no value in stating that the one is better motivated than the other, for by this is meant only that one worked more rapidly than the other. A beginning has been made in the measurement of motives by independent techniques, and a start has been made in a useful classification of human motives. At one time it was thought that interests might constitute powerful measures of human motivation, but these promises have not been fulfilled.

CLASSIFICATION OF VARIABLES IN TERMS
OF THEIR MATHEMATICAL PROPERTIES

An earlier section of this chapter pointed out that scales of measurement are necessary if very clumsy descriptions of pupil behavior are to be avoided. Scales of measurement can also be considered in terms of their mathematical properties, which tell us something about the utility of scales of various kinds. Some kinds of scales are much more useful than others. The classification given by S. S. Stevens (1946) will be given here together with some later modifications of the classification provided by C. H. Coombs (1964).

At the least powerful level of measurement is the *nominal scale*, which is simply a system of assigning number symbols to events in order to label them. The usual example of this is the assignment of numbers to baseball players in order to identify them. If these players were arranged in order of the numbers on their shirts, the order would have no meaning. Thus the numbers cannot be considered to be associated with an ordered scale, for their order is of no consequence. In educational research, it is quite common to identify events by numbers. All hostile gestures of the teacher could be recorded by placing a check mark against the number 11, whereas words of praise administered by the teacher would be indicated by checks against the number 15. The numbers are just convenient labels for the particular class of events. In these scales, the numbers refer to events that cannot meaningfully be placed in some order. Nominal scales provide convenient ways of keeping track of people, objects, and events. One cannot do much with the numbers involved. One cannot, for example, usefully average the numbers on the backs of a group of football players and come up with a meaningful value. The average social security number of a group in an office has no meaning. Neither can one usefully compare the numbers assigned to one group with the numbers assigned to another. The numbers used in a nominal scale are just convenient labels. Chinese letters would do almost as well, but they would not be as convenient or recognizable to inhabitants of the western world.

The lowest level of the *ordered scale* that is commonly used or discussed is the ordinal scale.[3] The *ordinal scale* places events in order, but there is no attempt to make the intervals of the scale equal in

[3] Coombs introduces an intermediate category, *partially ordered scales*, in order to cover certain psychometric measuring devices that fall between nominal scales and ordered scales.

terms of some rule. *Rank orders* represent ordinal scales and are the commonest used in educational research. A student's rank in his graduating class involves the use of an *ordinal scale*. One has to be very careful in making statements about scores based on ordinal scales. If John's position in his graduating class is 10 and Peter's position is 50, it *cannot* be said that John's position is five times as good as that of Peter. The statement would make no sense at all. All that can be said is that one person is higher or lower on the scale than another, but more precise comparisons cannot be made.

Stevens distinguishes two types of scales in which the intervals can be said to be equal in some way. These are *interval scales* and *ratio scales*.[4]

In the case of the interval scale, the intervals are adjusted in terms of some rule that has been established as a basis for making the units equal. The units are equal only insofar as one accepts the assumptions on which the rule is based. For example, in psychophysics it is common to accept as a unit the smallest difference that can be perceived. This unit is referred to as the differential threshold. Interval scales can have an arbitrary zero, but it is not possible to determine for them what may be called an absolute zero.

Interval scales are commonly used in educational research. Most standardized achievement tests are built on the basis of assumptions that, if accepted, lead one to consider the scores as representing interval scales. If one can consider the scores of a test to represent an interval scale, then one can reasonably compare the gain made by one student with the gain made by another during a semester or during some other period of time. However, one cannot regard Ivan's score of 50 and say that it is twice as good as Pedro's score of 25. The Fahrenheit scale is an example of an interval scale and shows similarities in what one can and cannot do with it. One can say that an increase in temperature from 30 degrees to 35 degrees involves the same increase in temperature as an increase from 60 degrees to 65 degrees. One *cannot* say that a temperature of 60 degrees is twice as warm as a temperature of 30 degrees, because both numbers are dependent on the fact that the zero on the scale is set arbitrarily at the temperature of the freezing point of water. If the zero had been set at the freezing point of alcohol, the two temperatures would have had an entirely different ratio. The ratio of the two temperatures, 30 degrees and 60 degrees, means nothing because the zero is an arbitrary point.

Ratio scales have an absolute zero of measurement. The term

[4] Coombs also distinguishes *ordered metric scales*, which might be considered a class between ordinal scales and interval scales.

absolute zero is not as precise as it was once believed to be. We can conceive of an absolute zero of length, and similarily we can conceive of an absolute zero of time. Nevertheless, an absolute zero of temperature is theoretically unobtainable, and it remains a concept existing only in the scientist's mind. The number of minor traffic-rule violations and the number of incorrect letters or spaces in a page of typescript represent scores on ratio scales. Both these scales have absolute zeros and all minor traffic violations and all typing errors can be assumed to be equal in significance. Because these measures involve close approximations to ratio scales, one can make statements such as, "Jane's typing performance was twice as bad as Mary's." In this case, the ratio of two measures does have significance and a comparison can be made of a kind that could not be made in the case of an interval scale.

If one were to make some unacceptable assumptions, it would be possible to establish a scale of intelligence that would have an absolute zero, but there would be many who would balk at the assumptions. Indeed, so many would reject them that the enterprise would not be considered worthwhile. It is of interest to note that E. L. Thorndike suggested at one time the establishment of a scale of intelligence that would have something approximating an absolute zero.

The purpose of our discussion here has been to point out that the kinds of comparisons one can reasonably make between two measures depends largely on the kind of scale involved. One has to be particularly cautious in taking the ratio of two scores and thinking that it has some particular significance. Only in the case of ratio scales does this have any meaning at all, but ratio scales are found rarely in educational research.

Some Problems of Scaling

Certain aspects of scaling that have not ordinarily been considered in the past have appreciable consequence for educational research. Attention was first drawn to this matter by L. G. Humphreys (1956) in an address to the annual testing conference sponsored by the Educational Testing Service. He pointed out that Cattell many years previously had noted that scales could be divided into two categories, *normative* and *ipsative*.[5]

Normative scales are represented by intelligence tests and tests of

[5] Coombs had drawn a similar distinction between relative and irrelative measurement.

achievement, and generally by tests in which a scale consists of a distinct set of items where the total score represents some function of the number of correct and incorrect answers. Scores on normative scales are usually interpreted with respect to the performance of persons collectively described as a norm group. On a set of normative scales, such as are represented by an achievement test battery, a person may have all high scores or all low scores, and we are interested in considering each score separately and independently of all other scores.

In contrast, *ipsative scales* are illustrated by those derived from the *Study of Values*. This instrument attempts to provide measures of the extent to which each of six values influences a person's life. These six value systems are the economic, the religious, the social, the theoretical, the political, and the aesthetic. The test is set up so that the person taking it must express a number of preferences for one or the other of these values. Where he is asked to make a choice between a decision based on religious values and a choice based on economic values, he must choose one or the other; he cannot choose both. The result is that if he tends to choose religious values, scores on the other scales of value tend to be depressed. The scores are derived in such a way that the average scores are the same for all persons. A person scoring high on some scales must necessarily be low on others. The scores can thus be used for ranking the values for a single person. They compare the strength of one value with another *within that person*. They do not permit comparisons of one individual with another. This fact has certain important consequences when these scores are correlated with other variables that it may be desired to predict—this is a particularly significant point to notice when tests of interest are used in an attempt to predict performance in some activity.

When ipsative scales are used, they should be used for predicting ipsative characteristics. A test designed to provide ipsative measures of interest in school subjects should be used for predicting an ipsative criterion, such as the rank order of the success achieved by pupils in these subjects. The rankings on the interest scales and the rankings on the achievement scales would be compared for each person included in the study. It is possible that the interest rankings might predict the achievement rankings for some persons and not for others.

Another aspect of scaling that has particular importance for educational research is the difference between altitude and breadth. The distinction is important in building achievement tests, and it can be explained fairly easily in terms of the problem of building an achievement test in American history to be given to college freshmen. Such a test might call for information concerning the major facts of American history from the days of the early settlers up to modern times. It would not call for any of the more obscure facts of history but would measure the breadth of a person's knowledge of the important facts.

A different test in American history could also be made covering the same period. The latter could be divided into sections, such as the Colonial period, the Revolutionary period, and so on. Within each of these periods, questions could vary from those that call for commonly known facts to those that pertain to relatively obscure events. A person answering the questions within any one of these sections would tend to answer questions up to a certain point, failing items beyond that point. Such a test would measure something different from breadth of information; what it measures might perhaps be termed "altitude."

Oddly enough, those who construct tests do not seem to be too concerned over whether they are measuring breadth or altitude. Usually no mention is made of this in test manuals, and it is necessary to examine the test in order to determine whether the emphasis is on the one or the other. As a result, relatively little is known about the relationship of breadth scores to altitude scores.

Does the Research Worker Predict Behavior?

An ambiguity commonly occurs in referring to behavioral measurement. Current usage is to say that we measure behavior. What in actual fact we do measure is *some property of behavior*. When the researcher states that he is measuring the behavior of the teacher in the classroom, he is really measuring only certain properties of behavior. To state that the behavior of the teacher is being measured carries with it the implication that the measurement supplies a complete description of behavior. In actual fact, the researcher is likely to measure, and that only rather roughly, certain limited aspects of behavior. From the measures themselves, it is possible to reconstruct to only a very limited degree what happened at the time the measurement was made. We are never likely to be able to perform the literal function of predicting teacher behavior in the classroom. Nevertheless, this should not discourage us, for what is important is to predict, not teacher behavior as a whole, but those aspects of it that have some crucial effect on pupil behavior.

Even if it were possible to predict accurately every aspect of teacher behavior, there would be no particular purpose in doing so. Much of what can be observed represents a great range and variety of events that have little bearing on what is accomplished. A teacher who is restless and moves around the classroom may be displaying merely the consequences of a long period of sedentary work. The activity may function only as a means of restoring the circulation in the muscles of the legs. It is clearly a phase of behavior that there appears to be no particular use in predicting. The same is true of pupil behavior. We are not concerned with predicting the numerous isolated actions that the pupil may perform after he leaves school, for most of these are specific responses to incidental situations and have only immediate consequences. On the other hand, we are very much concerned with the prediction of trends in behavior and characteristics of behavior that appear in a wide range of situations.

SUMMARY

1. The development of most sciences has usually been accompanied by the introduction of quantitative methods.

2. The scientist must decide the extent to which he is to study details or gross events. He chooses a level of detail that is convenient and appropriate. In educational research it is molar behavior that is likely to be examined.

3. It has become customary to refer to the variable that is predicted as the *dependent variable* and the variable that is manipulated or used for making predictions as the *independent variable*.

4. Variables that are predicted in educational research are usually responses to the environment—either the frequency with which certain responses occur or the characteristics of the responses.

5. A stimulus is defined, for the purposes of this volume, as a condition existing in the environment, which is hypothesized to produce a response in an individual. Educational research restricts its interest to those environmental conditions that are hypothesized to affect behavior. Studies in the field of curriculum are studies of environmental conditions and their relationship to the learning process. Studies of visual aids are studies of the manipulation of certain of these conditions.

6. Studies in the audiovisual area should lead to the statement of principles that permit the more effective design of teaching materials.

7. Differences produced in learning by differences in curricula are more likely to produce positive findings than are studies of the effect of specific learning devices. However, curriculum studies are difficult to undertake, and differences between curricula are difficult to measure.

8. The central difficulty in the conduct of curriculum studies, apart

from administrative difficulties, is the measurement of differences between curricula. Curricula may differ in rather complex ways, and their characteristics cannot usually be measured in a simple manner.

9. The child's and the adult's responses to his environment are commonly measured in terms of the frequency with which a particular response is made. This is generally the simplest type of measurement procedure.

10. A more sophisticated procedure for measuring responses is the use of an ordered scale. Achievement is commonly measured by tests that approximate such scales.

11. Intervening variables represent characteristics of the person that influence behavior. Most of these characteristics cannot be observed directly and hence have been referred to as *hidden variables*. Such variables are used to predict individual differences in performance to learning situations, and they include intellectual aptitudes as well as motivational characteristics.

12. Scales of measurement may also be classified in terms of their mathematical properties. These properties determine the extent to which various operations, such as subtraction and addition, can be performed meaningfully, with scores derived from them.

13. Normative scales are used for comparing the performance of one's person with that of another. Ipsative scales compare a person's performance in one area with his performance in another area. Normative scales should be used for predicting normative characteristics. It is not meaningful to predict normative characteristics with ipsative scales.

||||||||||||||||||||||||||||||

CHAPTER 6

Problems of Observation

D
ISCUSSION up to this point has been focused on some of the factors involved in the way in which the scientist thinks and on the general characteristics of the tools he uses in his work. This introduction should not distract the reader from the fact that the scientist does not work in a vacuum: that his research is deeply rooted in events in the real world. The educational-research worker cannot sit in an ivory tower. He must, at some time in his work, go out and collect data that has relevance for the building of scientific knowledge about educational events. This chapter and the next are especially concerned with the data-collection phase of the educational-research enterprise.

What Is an Observation?

The term *observation* is used by the scientist in a somewhat different sense from that in which it is generally used. The data that form the central core of a scientific study and from which the results and conclusions are ultimately derived consist of observations. Indeed, an item of data may be referred to as an observation even if it was derived from a machine that recorded how individuals in a particular situation behaved, and if it involved the scientific observer only indirectly. The subjects of the inquiry may not have been directly observed at all, but the resulting record is referred to as an observation or as a series of observations, even if never recorded by a human observer.

In the behavioral sciences, observations may be made in two distinct areas. They may be made concerning the situations to which individuals are exposed. They may also be made concerning the responses of persons to those situations.

From a research point of view, the nature of conditions to which individuals are exposed must be determined directly. Hearsay such as the clinical psychologist or the psychiatrist is forced to consider cannot possibly form a basis for research that is at all satisfactory. Conditions existing in the classroom should be established independently of what pupils say about them. Insofar as feasible, they should not be described in terms of what a human observer believes them to be, because the process of interpreting events introduces distortion in an unknown direction and by unknown amounts. If mechanical instrumentation can possibly be used for recording relevant conditions, it should be used—not only because of its objectivity, but also because of the permanence of the records that such instrumentation provides.

The Observer's Frame of Reference

Faith in the value of observing behavior would appear to be a cornerstone of teacher education. Some teacher-education programs emphasize the need for sending the teacher-in-training out into schools to observe at the earliest stages of professional study. Observation as such is considered a useful activity. Some, however, question this procedure, saying that unless a person knows what to observe the activity may be quite pointless and useless, and that the mere activity of looking and seeing serves little purpose unless certain other conditions have been established previously.

Much the same is true of scientific observation. It would be almost universally agreed that observation is an activity of central importance to the scientist, but it is not just a looking-and-seeing activity. This is a fact that is not always properly appreciated by the person who embarks on his first scientific inquiry. The writer can recall an educator who was starting on one of his first researches, which he decided should be in the general area of teacher effectiveness. He decided that the best way of starting research in this area was to undertake an extensive program of classroom observation. After many hours of this activity, he found that it did not seem to be leading anywhere. Because he felt that his technique of observation might be at fault, he invited some of his graduate students to participate with him in these observation sessions. Much to his surprise, this did not seem to improve matters, and the project was abandoned because it did not produce results.

The error in this approach lies in the assumption that the mere process of looking at phenomena will reveal what is relevant in them for particular purposes. This concept is derived from a fallacious psychology, which equates the data of sensory experience with what is perceived. Perception is, in contrast, necessarily an interpretative process. In observing a classroom, the sensory data consist of movements of physical objects and vibrations in the atmosphere that are referred to as sounds, but what is perceived is vastly different from this conglomeration of changes in physical energy. What is perceived is an organized, continuing activity; but the concepts and ideas in terms of which the activity is perceived depend on the experience and training of the observer.

The latter point can be clarified by describing an experience that happened to the author some years ago, when he was invited to participate in classroom observation as a part of a program of research. One of his fellow observers was a clinical psychologist with strong leanings toward the psychoanalytic point of view. The other was an educator with substantial experience in the training of teachers but with only a meager background in current psychological theory. Indeed, the interests of the latter individual were more in the realm of developing specific classroom skills, and were little inclined toward the interpretation of teacher behavior in terms of personality traits and mechanisms that were products of the individual's own background and personal history. These two observers gave entirely different descriptions of what went on in a particular classroom. In his description, the clinical psychologist referred to the extensive oral aggression of the teacher whenever it appeared that the classroom situation was getting out of control. He also pointed out that such oral aggression (raised voice) was also followed by feelings of guilt, which made her inclined to offer the children various minor rewards, consisting mainly of mild praise. The educator, on the other hand, described the teacher's raised voice merely as disorganized behavior resulting from the fact that she had not acquired genuine facility in using the skills needed for the control of a class of children. What the clinician described as behavior reflecting guilt feelings, the educator described as a return to skillful methods of exercising control over a classroom.

The point here is that any useful description of the tremendous complexities of events in the classroom must be made in terms of a system of interpretation, commonly referred to as a frame of reference. It is necessary for the observer to do more than describe the objectively occurring events, for these are mere movements of conglomerations of matter. What is needed is the abstraction of various classes of these events, in terms of what are believed to be certain relevant determinants of behavior or to have certain important consequences. The situation is considerably different from that encountered by physicists in observing the moving needle of a galvanometer. The physicist would be able to stay closely with the task of describing strictly what he observed in terms of a simple motion in space. No complex interpretations need be introduced. The situation to be observed does not involve the vast complexities of a classroom, which, because of the immense number of simultaneously occurring events, can be described only by reducing these events to certain broad but meaningful categories.

The reader may well ask at this point, "Would not the observer be performing an observation process comparable to that performed by a physicist when he enters a classroom and notes the frequency of such well-described events as yawning among pupils?" However, even when such well-defined phenomena are involved, judgment is not entirely eliminated. The observer must decide whether a student who opens his mouth just slightly and then closes it is yawning. Human activity of even the simplest sort shows a wide range of variation. It is for this reason that the student of behavior must be concerned with the reliability of observation, whereas the physicist does not have this problem except under very rare circumstances. If human behavior were more stereotyped, the psychologist would not be faced with this problem to the same degree.

What has been said does not lead to the conclusion that observation without clearly defining what has to be observed is always a pointless activity; for the fact is that under certain circumstances it may be useful, particularly in the early stages of an inquiry, but only if it is properly carried out. Suppose that an investigator held the theory that hostile acts on the part of the teacher tended to result in hostile acts on the part of the pupil. He might start by sitting down in his office and listing pupil acts and teacher acts that could be considered as hostile, but his own memory might turn out to be a poor source of materials for this purpose. At this point, he might feel that a better source of information would be the classroom itself. On this basis, the investigator might well visit several classrooms for the purpose of obtaining lists of behaviors that might be considered symptomatic of hostility. At the same time, he could obtain some estimate of the frequency of each one of these behaviors. Clearly it would not be useful to include in such a list of behaviors those that occur only very rarely, because the investigation might not include a sample of sufficient size to include a single observation in this category.

General classroom observation of the type discussed in the previous paragraph also serves the purpose of indicating the extent to which hostile behaviors are identifiable. Although careful reliability studies must be undertaken later, it is important to obtain at an early stage a rough estimate of the extent to which observers can agree on the presence or absence of particular aspects of behavior. Items that are not easily identified may then be removed from the list at an early stage. Sometimes items of behavior that one may expect to be easily recognized do not appear so when an attempt is made to identify them in a classroom situation.

Once this initial stage has been completed, the investigator will have in his possession knowledge of what can and cannot be done in the way of collecting in the classroom data that are relevant to the solution of his problem. It then becomes important to systematize the observation process. This is usually accomplished by preparing a schedule that is to be used by observers in subsequent phases of the investigation. Such a schedule both serves the function of indicating what is to be observed and provides a means of recording the observations.

Distortion in Observation

Real differences exist in the ability of individuals to observe and to report what they have observed. J. H. McPherson (1954) studied this problem with the object of developing means of identifying high distorters. His primary attempt to do this involved a situation in which his subjects were exposed to paragraphs of material and were later presented with a series of questions about each paragraph. The materials were presented in group situations in which time was allowed for the discussion of the content. McPherson came to the conclusion that the high distorters and the low distorters were distinguished by the following characteristics:

Low Distorters	*High Distorters*
1. Able to integrate the content with their own ideas and the ideas of others.	1. Parrot the content and give little evidence of understanding the material they are trying to present.
2. Tend to relate the ideas introduced by group members to the content and to each other. Will clarify errors and misin-	2. Tend to avoid questions about content and accept misinterpretations without attempting to correct them.

| *Low Distorters* | *High Distorters* |

terpretations made by group members.

3. Demonstrate a freedom with material by using it as a basis for introducing relevant ideas that serve to broaden or extend the range of ideas.

4. Restate comments of others in an attempt to clarify contributions and relate them to the general trend of the discussion.

5. Maintain a high level of work orientation. Initiate work and join others in the task.

6. Show a greater facility for maintaining an objective point of view in situations that are emotionally laden.

7. Are able to make decisions about alternatives that contain emotional elements.

3. Escape the material by using it as a springboard for introducing highly personal experiences that do not forward an understanding of the content.

4. Restate comments from members of the group but show no evidence of an ability to tie member contributions together in meaningful relationships.

5. Tend to avoid the work task of the group and engage in frequent "flight" behaviors.

6. Are more inclined to be influenced by emotionality in such a way that they cannot view material objectively.

7. Become indecisive in certain instances where the alternatives contain emotional elements.

This study provides some clues about the factors that lead to distortion when persons engage in observation in quite complex social situations. However, in most scientific work the observer is much more detached from the situation about which observations are later to be recorded, and this detachment may provide a better condition for objective observation than the one that McPherson studied.

Training Observers

There is much talk in the literature about the need for using trained observers in research, but just how an observer is trained or what this involves is usually left to the imagination of the reader. The problem of training observers can perhaps be introduced by discussing a familiar situation—that provided by a baseball game. The radio commentator observing such a game describes the nature of each pitch, whether it is fast or slow, curved or straight, inside, outside, or down the middle, and so forth. In contrast, the occasional onlooker, the author among them, finds it quite impossible to make these discriminations, for all balls look much the same to him and differ only in what happens to them in the subsequent play. The commentator also notices and remarks on many other events that pass unnoticed by the amateur. He notices movement in the outfield as different batters come up to the plate as well as other responses of the players to the changing situation. The commentator has, in fact, learned to do two things that the inexperienced observer has not yet learned: First, he has learned to make discriminations that the inexperienced observer has not learned to make. Secondly, he has learned to respond to more cues, as when he responds to movements in the outfield that few others even notice.

A professional psychologist is sometimes referred to as a trained observer, but this does not mean that he is trained in all situations. One who has spent his life working with rats may be called a trained observer of those rodents, but he may not necessarily be considered trained for conducting an experiment with children. Observation of a particular situation may require special experience that is not provided in ordinary professional training.

In conducting studies that require extensive observations, it is usually necessary for economic reasons to employ observers who have had little training as psychologists. Often graduate students in their early stages of training are selected for this purpose. Under such conditions, it is desirable to follow a few simple rules in the establishment of observational procedures.

The observers should participate in the development of the system to be used for recording observations. They should be in on the procedure from the beginning of its development. If this is not possible, then they should be in on the tryout of the tentative schedule. During this process they can be of help in determining what they can learn to observe and what they cannot. They can also acquire facility in the mechanics of recording their observations, and at the same time help in the development of a convenient recording schedule. Through the use of such tentative schedules, observers can compare their records after a period of observation, and, when there are differences attributable to misunderstandings of particular words, come to some agreement on the definition of the terms to be used. The categories of behavior used must be as specific as possible; one might possibly suggest the rule that the more naïve the observer, the more specific they should be. Categories that involve a considerable amount of interpretation should be avoided. Untrained observers may show little agreement with one another concerning what they consider to be aggressive behavior. Trained observers may ultimately agree on this classification as they learn a common system of interpretation.

The observers should be informed of the purpose of the experiment except insofar as this may prejudice the outcome of the study. If the groups or persons to be observed have been exposed to two different treatments and if differences between treatments are studied, it is not desirable to inform the observers of this, lest even a slight prejudice result in a tendency for the observations to come out in one way rather than another.

Finally, one suspects that if there are great cultural differences in the backgrounds of the observer and the observed, the significance of much that happens may pass unnoticed. This cultural factor is one that scientists are only just beginning to understand.

The Effect of the Research Worker's Intrusion on the Situation He Wishes to Observe

Sociologists and social psychologists have long recognized that when the research worker goes out to collect data, he often influences the situation he observes to an extent sufficient to produce marked changes in it. A book by E. J. Webb, *et al.* (1966) has made an excellent summary of these *reactive effects*, as they have become called, and classifies them under the following categories:

1. *The guinea pig effect.* People who recognize that they are guinea pigs behave differently from the way they ordinarily behave. The typical response is for the guinea pig to be on his best behavior, but sometimes hostile responses may occur. Children in schools who come under observation show an undue amount of cooperation with the teacher, and the use of television or film recording in the absence of the experimenter does not overcome this effect. One may attempt to solve this problem by returning to visit the classroom, day after day, until the children cease to be inhibited by the experimenter's presence. However, this procedure introduces other problems. When the author visited a first-grade class on repeated occasions, he found that the children began to acquire new behaviors toward him. Although on the first few visits the children kept their distance from him, after a few visits they began to interact with him. Some brought books to him and asked how to read certain words, and others began to ask him

questions about why he was there. The classroom became a different place because of his presence and nothing he could do would alter that fact.

2. *Role selection.* Each person's repertoire of behavior permits him to play a number of different roles and the role he chooses depends on the social cues that are present. A superintendent, for example, may play a very different role at a school board meeting than at a meeting of his principals. In the one situation he might appear as a docile, submissive person, and in the other as authoritarian, controlling and severe. The role that he might turn on when interviewing a research worker in his office might depend on such irrelevant cues as whether the research worker reminded him of a board member or of one of his principals. Again, a pupil may have to choose whether to react to the research worker as he would to his father or as he would to his teacher.

3. *Learning effects initiated by the research worker.* The encounter with the research worker may initiate learning and upset the validity of subsequent observations. Ask a student on a state university campus "Should students run their own Union without interference from the faculty?" The student may never have thought about this matter before, but your question may start him thinking. Before your encounter has developed much further, the student may be on his way toward becoming a campus activist.

4. *Response sets.* The best known of these is for a respondent to tend to agree with the questioner. This latter phenomenon is known as acquiscence set. Another well-established response set is for the respondent to give the more socially desirable response.

In addition there are a number of interviewer effects that are more appropriately discussed in later pages.

The book by Webb, *et al.* has some interesting suggestions concerning how the effect of the intrusion of the research worker may be often removed through the use of what they term *unobtrusive measures.* A simple and commonly cited unobtrusive measure is that used in determining which of the many exhibits in a museum are the most interesting to those that pass through its halls. One could, of course, ask the visitors as they leave, but such an intrusion into the life of the visitor begins to raise the problems that have just been discussed. An unobtrusive measurement of visitor interest might be derived by measuring how much the floor was worn away in front of each exhibit. At least such a measure might not be influenced by the presence of the research worker, although it might be influenced by other sources of error.

Webb, *et al.* reviewed a number of different "erosion" measures. They suggest that the extent to which particular books in the library are actually read could be determined by measuring the wear on the corners where the pages are turned. Although the number of times that a book is withdrawn may provide some indication of the extent to which the book is read, there is always the possibility that a book may be withdrawn, but not read. Also, books may be read but not withdrawn. The erosion measure would appear to provide a much better measure of use than would those derived from circulation records. Other suggestions for erosion methods include the proposal that the activity of children be measured by the rate at which they wear away their shoes. The writing and scribbling activity could be measured by the wear on uniformly sharpened pencils.

Human behavior not only wears away selectively certain parts of the environment, but it also leaves positive traces behind. Webb, *et al.* refer to the use of these positive traces as *accretion methods* of data gathering. One example they give is that of studying the attractiveness of an advertisement by determining the number of different fingerprints found on the page. Examples of accretions nearer to educational research are the doodles and notes left by school board members, the materials in the wastebaskets of classrooms, school newspapers, and the exhibits prepared by children on display in classrooms. Inscriptions on the desks of the pupils represent another accretion that might be used as a source of data in some research. The use of accretion methods has had a long history of successful use in archeology, which has been highly dependent on the existence of trash heaps from past cultures as a source of data.

Erosion and accretion traces may have certain systematic sources of error built into them. The amount of wear on the floor in front of an exhibit may be contaminated by the fact that the exhibit is in a particularly favorable or unfavorable place, or that it is to the right of the entrance door and, hence, in the direction in which visitors tend to turn. Despite the fact that these are conditions that depress the validity of measurement, such measures are not usually disturbed by the research worker's intrusion on the situation, although sometimes such intrusion may have an impact. For example, if it became known that the doodles of school board members were being studied, the subsequent doodles would show the effect of that knowledge.

There are also many other unobtrusive measures that are not influenced by the intrusion of the observer. School records of various kinds form a rich source of data in some school systems. Even as simple a record as the absentee rate for each pupil has proved to be a very interesting variable in some studies. Where teachers are encouraged to enter anecdotal material on the cumulative record, the notes thus entered may be a rich source of information both about the pupils and about the teachers who recorded them. Some archival records suffer from having been severely and deliberately distorted. The minutes of school board meetings commonly present only selected material of which the board wishes to have a record, and the more interesting aspects of the evening's deliberations are never entered.

The unobtrusive measures considered up to this point are all derived from the interaction of the individual with his environment, but there is also another category of observation or measurement where the research worker does not react with, and change, the object on which he focuses attention. This category includes the physical characteristics of the environment of pupils, teachers, and others engaged in education. However, we cannot go very far in educational research if we limit our observations to the educational environment. The latter is of interest only because it is believed to have some effect on learning and behavior; hence, the study of the educational environment always involves the study of those aspects of behavior that the environment is expected to influence.

Some Observable Characteristics of the Pupil's Environment

The material aspects of the environment having the greatest immediate impact on the learner are those closely associated with the curriculum, such as textbooks and other items of educational equipment. The analysis and assessment of the properties of these materials, a difficult and complex matter, will be treated in the next chapter. For the present, consideration will be given to those aspects of the educational environment that can be more easily appraised and studied.

Although materials related to the curriculum impinge most directly on the pupil, other aspects of his environment may also contribute to or interfere with learning even though their influence is less direct and probably less extensive. Administrators agree that the arrangement of a schoolbuilding may facilitate some activities but interfere with others. In recent times schools wanting to introduce team teaching have often been hampered by the fact that traditional schoolbuildings are not well suited to a team-teaching approach. Architects and administrators have worked together on the development of floor layouts that would permit team teaching and provide a situation in which groups of children can be readily divided up into smaller groups for some purposes and reassembled for others. Little is known about how space provisions in schools are related to function. Even some of the more easily appraised characteristics of the environment, such as the amount of playground space per pupil, have not been properly studied in relation to pupil utilization. State recommendations for minimum amounts of playground space per pupil are based on judgment rather than on knowledge. Such questions as the amount of playground space actually used can be investigated by fairly straightforward observational techniques with interesting results obtained. Other relationships of pupil behavior to directly measurable aspects of the environment need to be explored. For example, classroom space per pupil may be expected to have an effect on quality and frequency of pupil-pupil interactions.

Research is still lacking on the effect on learning exerted by some of the more easily identified characteristics of the pupil's social environment. Size of class has been extensively studied, but probably not in the size range that make a difference. A comparison of the learning of students in classes of thirty students with learning in classes of three hundred generally shows insignificant differences. It may not matter whether there are thirty or three hundred students in a class, but it may make a real difference whether there are ten or thirty. Yet the latter problem has hardly been touched on, perhaps because classes of ten pupils are almost nonexistent. The sex of the teacher is probably a very important factor in the lower elementary grades. An increasing body of evidence suggests that many of the problems encountered by little boys in school is a result of the fact that the environment there is designed and controlled largely by women and that it is probably more suitable for girls than for boys. A fruitful field of research involves the design of environments that will maximize particular aspects of learning. The modern elementary school classroom is a much better environment for learning than its counterpart of a century ago, but it probably needs extensive modification to bring it into line with what is known about child behavior.

Substantial evidence exists that the ease with which learning occurs in school is influenced by home conditions, yet not much is known about the effect of particular home conditions. Sociologists have developed measures of socioeconomic level, but these hardly seem suitable for identifying home-background conditions that are conducive to school learning. A beginning has been made in the study of the effect of such factors as whether the parent does or does not read to the child, and these studies seem promising. The other ways in which a parent can intellectually stimulate a child also need to be studied.

Rating as a Method of Reducing Data

Some of the events involved in educational research must be reduced to quantitative terms by means of a rating procedure. One may observe hundreds of interactions between the teacher and the pupils and reduce them to a single rating indicating the hostility or warmth of the teacher toward the class. Unless one is dealing with a case in which the rater judges the relative frequency with which an event occurs, the rating procedure involves the evaluation of numerous events, which individually have only small relevance and probably low reliability but that collectively may have value for prediction purposes. If it were possible to design a machine that would identify these events, score them for significance, and then add up the scores to give a total—and if it were possible for the machine to do this consistently—the results would probably be much superior to those produced by the human rater. The scores or ratings produced by human raters are based on a much less consistent performance than that of our imaginary machine. The rating is usually based not on a well-defined series of events but on a rather vague universe of events, often defined only in the most general terms. If the rater is viewed as a rather complicated machine for reducing data, it is evident that in order to have proper control over the measures derived by the procedure one must know what data is to go into the machine as well as the nature of the operation to be performed on it. The fact that there is very little control over the data that our rater is given to use accounts to a great extent for the unsatisfactory nature of ratings. An additional complexity in the use of ratings arises from the fact that two ratings (on two pupils, two teachers, or two whatever else) may not be based on the same data at all. This is not quite as damaging as it sounds, for we commonly compare the achievement of two pupils even if they did not take the same form of test and even though the items that they answered were different.

When two supposedly parallel forms of a test have been equated and it has been demonstrated that scores from the two can be used interchangeably, the researcher feels little hesitation in treating scores from one or the other as if they were alike. The equivalence of data derived from two sets of facts must usually be assumed in the treatment of ratings. A rater is employed to derive whatever significance may be possible from his observations, and this he does on the basis of judgment, which in turn is based on experience. An illustration may help to clarify this point. Suppose that one were to rate the children in a class with respect to their cooperativeness with the teacher. Cooperativeness might be manifested in a number of ways, such as doing assigned work quietly, attending to the teacher when she is speaking, volunteering to help with chores such as cleaning the blackboard, volunteering information in class discussions, helping other children with assignments, restraining aggressiveness when reprimanded, and through an immense range of additional and varied behaviors. The rater has at his disposal a sample of these behaviors, but no two children present the same sample, because each shows cooperation or the lack of it in a form that is compatible with his own personality structure. The rater must somehow evaluate the evidence provided by each pupil and make some judgment concerning what that evidence shows concerning general level of cooperativeness. The task is obviously an extremely difficult and complex one for the rater, particularly so because the ground rules for the whole operation have not been precisely defined. It is small wonder that the results of many studies that involve ratings produce only a mass of data to which there is little rhyme or reason and from which no useful scientific knowledge is derived.

If control is to be exercised over the rating process so that the product is meaningful, it is necessary to control both the type and quantity of information to be used by the rater and the processing that this information is to undergo. Let us consider the first of these problems.

It is extremely difficult to define for the rater just what are the events to be observed, and, in fact, this is not usually done except in the vaguest terms. For example, a teacher may be asked to rate pupils for their ability to work with other children in small groups. It is probable that the researcher engaged in this enterprise would supply the teacher with a rating scale in which various positions would be described in such terms as "Works well with group, seems to add to what the group accomplishes, contributes to the smoothness with which the group operates"; and perhaps at the other end of the scale the statement, "Generally seems to be a source of friction and irritation in a group." Now such a series of statements does very little to orient the rater in the matter of what to observe, but rather it assumes that the rater knows the kinds of observations that are necessary and relevant in order to arrive at the kind of judgment that the scale demands. There is no entirely satisfactory way of remedying this situation. An obvious partial solution is to provide a preface to be read as an orientation to the use of the scale. Although such a preface may help to orient the rater on the matter of what he is to observe, it can refer to only a limited sample of the universe of behaviors to be observed, because a long list becomes tedious to read and remember. It may also draw attention to certain specific behaviors, and the rater may easily forget that the behaviors listed are supposed to represent only a sample, not the total universe, of behaviors to be observed.

An alternative procedure, which has considerable merit, is to develop a rating scale consisting of many scales, each of which is directed to a fairly specific aspect of the total domain of behavior that is to be observed. If pupils are to be rated on their ability to work in small groups, each pupil might be rated with respect to each one of several aspects of the behavior and perhaps as many as twenty aspects might be listed. When such a procedure has been adopted, it is usually desirable to perform a factor analysis of the ratings to determine whether they can be considered to contribute to a single principal factor. One major advantage of the multiple-rating approach, in addition to the assistance that it gives in defining the domain of behavior to be observed, is that it usually helps to increase the reliability of ratings.

Efforts to Control the Rating Process

Efforts to exercise control over the rating process are familiar, for the common ones are cited in every textbook in educational measurement. The student is undoubtedly familiar with the following commonly stated rules:

1. Define several points on each scale with as great precision as possible.
2. Restrict each rating scale to a narrow range of behavior that can be well defined.
3. Change the ends of the scale so that the "good" end is not always at the top or always at the bottom of the scale.
4. Avoid words such as *average* in the middle range of the scale. The rater who does not wish to give too much effort to the rating procedure is likely to class too many as average.
5. In the directions, indicate the need for honest rating and, wherever possible, state that a low rating will not have any consequence for the person rated, either direct or indirect.
6. Assure the rater that his anonymity will be safeguarded.

But rules such as these, which are useful tips and provide some little help in rating, do not result in the exercise of adequate control over the rating process, at least not the type of control that an experimenter might wish to exercise over the way in which measures are produced. The usual suggestions are not to be disregarded, for they may perhaps convert wholly inadequate procedures into procedures that, although poor, have enough value to make them usable to a limited degree.

The various attempts to improve the traditional type of rating scale have not produced any instruments that represent a startling improvement over those of several decades ago. It is also doubtful whether any of the more novel approaches to rating have been more successful. One of these, which has been a source of considerable controversy, is the forced-choice approach. The reader is referred to J. P. Guilford's *Psychometric Methods* (1954) for a discussion of this technique.

Consistency of Ratings

In theory, if our directions concerning what is to be observed are sufficiently exact, if the observer has been precisely informed concerning the operations to be performed, and if the method of recording the final product of these processes has been well defined, it should be possible for two observers to arrive at closely similar if not identical ratings after observing groups of situations in which there are a range of differences. Interobserver reliability provides some evidence of the extent to which all of these factors have been specified in a satisfactory way. It is possible that good interrater agreement may be achieved even though adequate specifications for the entire procedure have not been provided. For example, teachers may agree on rating pupils for social adjustment even though they cannot provide an adequate definition of what is meant by this characteristic. On the other hand, if all specifications have been accurately made and are capably followed by two observers, it is inevitable that the resulting ratings will agree.

If ratings are to be meaningful, it must be possible to communicate the rating process so that different individuals can achieve the same results. If the procedure is not communicable, then it is evident that the particular research is not replicable (reproducible) because of the lack of communicability of the operations that it involves. For this reason, in all studies that involve ratings it is necessary to demonstrate that there is interrater reliability, for lack of such reliability probably indicates lack of communicability of the procedures that the research involves.

There is also considerable value to be achieved in determining the consistency of rating from occasion to occasion. If there is consistency among raters but not from occasion to occasion, it indicates that the phenomenon studied is not a stable one. If teachers were to be rated for some aspect of aggressive behavior shown toward children in the classroom, it is quite probable that raters would agree well among each other concerning the amount of aggression shown on a certain occasion, but the teacher might show little or no consistency in this trait from one occasion to another. Indeed, the amount shown might depend primarily on such factors as the time of day and the presence or absence of petty out-of-school frustrations.

In most rating studies an effort is made to work with characteristics that have stability over time, but it is quite conceivable that studies might be run in which changeability of the characteristic rated was sought—as, for example, if the researcher were investigating changes in the behavior of the new pupil as he adapts to the school situation. Under such a condition, the researcher would want consistency from rater to rater, but not from occasion to occasion if the occasions were so spaced as to cover a period of time over which changes were hypothesized to occur. Sometimes it may be desired to collect data in such a way that the effects of certain changes in the phenomena to be observed will be eliminated. Thus, in the hypothetical study of the aggressive behavior of teachers, it might be desired to eliminate variations that occur during the course of a day, and for this reason it might be planned to collect ratings only during the first hour of each day of teaching. By means of an analogous procedure, variations during the course of the week might also be eliminated.

The Interview As an Observational Technique

Up to this point, our discussion has mainly centered on the problem of observing classroom and group-activity situations. In such cases the observer is almost always external to the situation observed. In the interview, on the other hand, it is usual for the observer to be the interviewer and thus to form a part of the total situation within which observations are made. Attempts have been made to introduce observers who are outside of the interview situation, but this is not a usual technique. Sometimes interviews are recorded. When the latter technique is used, the interviewer can play a role in which he has been thoroughly drilled, and can do so unhampered by note-taking procedures.

Interviews may vary in the extent to which they are structured. The chief advocates of the unstructured interview have been clinical psychologists, who have used extensively the type of interview in which the conversation is left to wander where it will. The argument has been that, because the causes of particular characteristics of behavior vary from person to person, questions that are appropriate for probing in one case are inappropriate in another. The clinician feels a need to vary his tactics as the situation demands. One consequence of this flexibility is that he is not likely to discover laws that apply to a number of individuals, and indeed that is not what he is looking for.

The researcher, on the other hand, is looking for general laws and has little, if any, interest in the idiosyncrasies that make each patient a unique person. He cannot possibly consider the idea of collecting each item of data under different conditions from every other item. For this reason, when he conducts an interview the data from which are to be used for general scientific purposes he attempts to introduce as much uniformity as possible into the procedure. If the interview is to be highly structured, he asks the same series of questions of each person interviewed and does not vary either the order of the questions or the tone of voice in which they are asked. He establishes a uniform procedure that he applies whenever the respondent becomes discursive and wanders too much from the question asked. He uses the same introductory and concluding remarks.

If a structured interview is used, and if it proceeds with an organized list of standardized questions, the interviewer may ask questions that are open-ended or those that restrict the possible responses that the interviewee can make. In the former case, the interviewee is expected to *recall* or generate an answer. In the latter case, it is necessary only for the interviewee to recognize the response of his choice. There is some evidence that recognition, at least in a test situation, produces more information, and more accurate information, than recall. One presumes this is true also of an interview situation, but there is little empirical fact to support this view. When the interviewee is free to give any answer to the questions of the interviewer, there is danger that the interviewer may incorrectly record what is said or the gist of what is said. Although the amount of distraction undoubtedly varies from situation to situation, there is at least one study by S. L. Payne (1949) in which 25 per cent of statements recorded by the interviewer were found to be incorrect when they were compared with a recording of the entire interview. Such errors are much less likely to occur when the interviewee indicates to an interviewer which one of a number of statements printed on a card represents his particular choice of response. However, even in the latter case, the procedure for recording the response is not entirely devoid of error. There are also a few persons who refuse to choose any of the responses provided, preferring to modify one of them before they accept it.

An important aspect of the interview situation is the interviewer himself. For a long time it was not realized that it is necessary to know something about the characteristics of the interrogator if the products of the interview are to be evaluated. Those engaged in public-opinion polls have found that interviewers not only tend to select certain types of persons to interview, but the responses of the interviewee are related to the characteristics of the interviewer.

Webb, *et al.* have summarized the findings of research concerning the effect of interviewer characteristics on the responses of interviewees. They note, as one would expect, that the race of the interviewer has been shown to have an important effect, although one suspects that the topic discussed would largely determine the magnitude of this influence. An interaction related to the matter of civil rights would be much more likely to be influenced by the race of the interviewer than would the interaction required of a census taker. Younger interviewers seem to elicit rather different kinds of responses than older interviewers and they evaluate the responses rather differently. The social class and religion of the interviewer comes out as a factor in some studies; but the most overwhelming effect appears to be produced by sex. As a general rule one can say that women obtain more responses than do men. The fewest responses are produced when men interview men. However, there is one exception to all this, namely, that the most talkative of all interviewees is the young woman who is being interviewed by the young man.

The fact that there are so many characteristics of the interviewer that influence the data, suggests that the greatest caution should be exercised in the design of interview studies. The study involving the single interviewer should be avoided, for there is always the possibility that the particular characteristics of this individual may be producing whatever results are found. Even when studies involve many interviews, the bias produced by interviewer characteristics can hardly be avoided—a conclusion that should lead the research worker to search for other techniques.

Advantages and Limitations of the Interview
for Data Collection

The novice in research is likely to believe that interviews and methods by which the personal inner life of the individual can be studied offer special promise for yielding knowledge that can be used ultimately for the prediction of behavior. The behavioral sciences started out with this contention, which dominated nineteenth-century psychology. The notion has been perpetuated by psychiatrists, who have consistently advocated the use of individual interviews for selecting persons for special assignments. Yet the rather puzzling fact remains that researches involving inquiry into the inner life of the individual have been extremely unsuccessful. The reasons for this remain quite obscure, but it is perhaps of some value to the would-be researcher to consider certain sources of difficulty in the methodology of studying the individual, with the hope that this may help the student to avoid them.

1. In any interview in which one person conducts an inquiry into the inner life of another, the situation is much more complex than can be described in terms of an observer and the observed. The situation is more accurately described as involving an observer and a person responding to an observer. The responses are a result of the behavior of the observer and the characteristics of the observed. It is quite possible that relatively minor changes in the behavior of the observer could produce quite pronounced changes in that of the observed. The latter can be clearly seen in the administration of the Rorschach. Any behavior on the part of the Rorschach administrator that indicates that the situation involves threat to the ego of the examinee results in restrained responses. What the observer notes is as much a product of his own behavior as it is a product of the observed's characteristics.

2. It follows from what has been said that, unless the observer can manifest the same uniform patterns of behavior toward all those who are observed, he introduces a series of quite irrelevant variables into the situation. It is clear that observers are unable to reproduce uniform patterns of behavior when faced with varied situations. Even among actors who in the same play, night after night, face the same situation, there is considerable variation in performance. Many times greater is the variation in the performances of a person interviewing another. This variation is quite beyond the control that an individual can exercise over his behavior.

3. Interviewing procedures are usually based on the assumption that the person interviewed has insight into the causes of his behavior. Clinical psychologists, through experience now covering several decades, have come to the conclusion that insight into the causes of behavior is something rarely achieved, and that even with the extended help of the clinician, it is acquired by dint of long and hard effort. The assumption that it is possible to discover the causes of behavior by means of a short interview is a conception of psychological research that has long since been abandoned.

4. There are difficulties in quantifying the data provided by the interview. Often the data are such that they do not lend themselves to quantification. Rarely is it possible to quantify by enumeration, as when the scientist counts the number of words that refer to a given content category. The best that can be done is to rate certain characteristics of the interviewee's behavior.

5. In individual methods of appraisal, the psychologist is often looking for the laws of the behavior of the individual. Insofar as these can be discovered, they yield qualitative statements that summarize trends in past behavior, but these trends may not be related to the making of the desired type of prediction. In contrast, objective methods of appraisal are always designed to measure variables that are empirically or rationally related to the variables that psychologists have sought to predict. The material derived from an interview may have only the most remote relevance.

6. A person who is being studied by another may not be willing to reveal information. There is a real difference between the behavior of a person who visits a clinical psychologist in order to seek help and a person who is not motivated in this way to lay bare his innermost thoughts. In the latter case, there is a certain defensiveness about the individual's performance and an unwillingness to reveal what is in his mind. Indeed, there are some who refuse to answer the simple questions asked by public-opinion pollsters because they say that this would be an infringement of their privacy. The same difficulty arises in the administration of certain types of tests, particularly instruments of the projective type. The patient at the clinic may be expected to give a much richer range of responses on the Rorschach test than the one who is taking the test as a part of some research study.

Finally, what has been said here does not mean that it is not possible to study individual cases over a period of time, for this can be done by many methods that permit the use of objective measuring devices.

At this point, the reader may well ask, "Why not just pass out a questionnaire? Why go to all the trouble of conducting an interview when both the questions and the responses are standardized?" The answers are, to a considerable extent, matters of opinion, but there is substantial consensus among experts.

1. It appears to be well established that it is possible to obtain a much higher percentage of respondents with an interview than when questionnaires are handed out. Interviewers commonly report less than 5 per cent refusals to answer questions, whereas returns from mailed questionnaires rarely exceed 40 per cent. There is also a tendency for those who answer questionnaires to omit the answers to some questions, through either forgetfulness or a distaste for facing the particular issue. Incompleteness of returns is rarely found when data are collected by interview.

2. The interviewer is able to answer questions concerning the purpose of the interview, and the interviewee may be put at ease in a way that is not possible with questionnaire techniques. He is thus able to build up a feeling of confidence that makes for both cooperation and truthfulness.

3. Questionnaires present difficulties to persons of limited literacy, and the respondents to a mailed questionnaire study are likely to represent an undue proportion of the more literate public. In addition, persons who read with difficulty may not exercise the care that they should in finding and selecting the right answer, whereas the interviewer can take care of all such mechanical details.

4. An interviewer can conduct an interview at a proper speed, whereas questionnaires are often filled in hurriedly. The writer can recall having to fill in a questionnaire late at night in order that it be available for collection the following morning. True, the questionnaire had lain around the house for two weeks, but somehow time had not been found to answer the questions. This kind of problem can be avoided if an interview is used.

On the other side of the picture, it may be said that it is often much more feasible to present in questionnaire form long and extended lists of questions that it would be very tedious and expensive to present orally. Such questionnaires, administered to highly literate groups, may yield large quantities of information that could not easily be obtained by the oral interview.

Recording Interview Data

Many different methods are available for recording interview data and each has its own advantages and disadvantages. Circumstances must determine which one will be selected for a particular study.

A first point to note is that the interviewee provides a great wealth of information, only a part of which is likely to be noted and recorded. Although the verbal behavior of the interviewee is generally a matter of central interest, he also provides information through his facial expression, body movements and gestures, and even through his dress. The research design involving the interview must specify what aspects of the information provided by the interviewee should be recorded and which of the recorded aspects should be coded. The recording of the interview, as the term *record* is used here, involves the procedure of obtaining a reproduction of what happened without summarization or interpretation. A transcription of a shorthand report of an interview taken down word for word approximates such a record as does a tape recording or a sound movie. On the other hand, the notes taken by an interviewer summarizing what happened do not constitute a record in this sense. They represent the combined processes of selecting, summarizing, and interpreting information which is referred to as the *coding process.*

There are substantial advantages to be accrued from the procedure of recording an entire interview and then, later, coding the information that it is desired to code. Such a procedure presents ethical as well as technical problems. With the development of pocket-size tape recorders there is the possibility of making a complete record of the verbal communication. Many if not most psychologists consider it unethical to record interviews without obtaining permission from the interviewee. The federal government has taken the position that the recording of telephone conversations without the knowledge of the conversants is illegal and the same general principle would appear to apply to the recording of verbal communications under other conditions. But one has to recognize that, if the interviewee knows his words are to be recorded, this fact will exercise some influence on what is said. The same applies to the making of visual as well as auditory records.

If a record is kept of an interview, it can be analyzed at leisure and in a much more thorough fashion than when responses are coded at the time they are made. The reliability of the coding procedure can also be investigated when a record is available that can be played back to different coders. In this way a comparison can be made of the coding undertaken by one person and the coding undertaken by another.

A major difficulty involved in the use of complete records of an interview is the voluminousness of the material involved. If one hundred interviews are recorded on tape and each interview lasts thirty minutes, the total time recorded is fifty hours. If each tape has to be replayed four times for obtaining and coding the information an additional two hundred hours of listening time are involved. Because such listening is very tedious, the listening procedure may have to be extended over months, if a conscientious job is to be done. For this reason the records of interviews are not widely used in research, and most research workers have preferred to record certain limited observations during the interview, frequently coding them at the same time.

The Situation in Which Observations Are Made

There are certain aspects of all situations used as bases for observational data that have to be controlled if meaningful data are to be collected. First, there is the orientation that those observed are given to the situation. Usually this is a verbal orientation, and great care must be exercised in this process. It is not just when social behavior is being observed that this orientation procedure is of crucial importance. Even when a test is to be administered, the orientation procedure is a matter that may be of major importance in determining the score. It is now well known that, in the case of the Rorschach test, the responses depend to a very great extent on the circumstances surrounding the administration.

A dramatic example of the effect of a small change in a testing situation is brought out in a study by V. S. Gerlach, R. E. Schutz, R. L. Baker, and G. E. Mazer (1964). The background for this study is the large body of research in which individuals have been given what is claimed to be training in creativity. In these researches, the Guilford tests of creativity are commonly administered before and after training in order to determine the effectiveness of the program; a control group, which is not exposed to training, is also administered the tests. The finding in most of these studies is that the trained group shows a much larger gain on the creativity tests than does the control group. These results seemed to speak well for creativity training until Gerlach and his associates undertook their experiment. What they showed was that merely expanding the directions for the creativity tests so that the person taking them knew exactly how they were expected to respond produced a greater increment in score than training over a substantial period of time. The data suggest that perhaps what training does do is explain to the student what he must do to obtain a better score on the tests he has taken and will take again at the end of instruction. Little things such as slight changes in directions can make a difference. Another example of how a feature of a situation that might be overlooked can change the data produced comes from experience with Air Force research. Those who have worked with the Air Force typically report that, when enlisted men are used as subjects, much better data is produced when a noncommissioned officer is in charge than when a civilian attempts to run the experimental session. The noncommissioned officer seems to produce a set that leads to the careful following of directions.

Secondly, if stooges are used as a part of the situation to which persons are to be exposed, it is important that they be well trained so that they respond in the same way to all. Those who are to function as a part of an experimental situation must learn not to respond differently to different personalities. Learning in this respect is probably only partial, because most persons are not aware of the extent to which they are responding to others.

Thirdly, it is important to develop safeguards so that information about the situation is not transmitted from those who have been exposed to those who are still to be exposed. Sometimes the mere separation of subjects from others who have been exposed will suffice. Sometimes other precautions are necessary, such as the selection of persons from different classes or from different schools. It may help if subjects are asked not to divulge information, but even when this is done, there is likely to be some leakage of information.

Finally, it is hardly necessary to point out that some of the more obvious factors affecting behavior, such as time of day, should be carefully controlled, or that designs permitting the separation of the variance attributable to these factors should be used.

Role Playing as an Observational Technique

An interesting extension of the interview technique, in which there has been much interest in recent years, is found in role playing. An example is given in an unpublished study in which it was desired to explore the personalities of prospective teachers by means of this technique. For this purpose a number of situations were developed. In one of these, one of the participants was given a rather detailed account of the behavior of a pupil in a class that the student was theoretically teaching. The student was given fifteen minutes in which to study the material, and was told that at the end of that period she would have to interview the mother of the pupil in order to discuss with her the problems of the child. Another student playing the role of the mother was instructed to take a very defensive attitude toward the child and a hostile attitude toward the teacher, placing the blame for the child's behavior on the way in which the school was managed. The scene was then spontaneously enacted by the two participants.

The reader can see that there are extensive possibilities for personality measurement and assessment in such a situation. The behavior of the persons involved can be rated for various characteristics, and there are also possibilities for using checklists for enumerating the frequency of occurrence of specific aspects of behavior. Although the technique is still in the exploratory stages of development, promise is offered by the fact that persons placed in role-playing situations become deeply involved emotionally. Many play their parts as if they were completely identified with the character portrayed. The technique cannot yet be considered as a ready-made usable product, but it is an interesting invention.

Role playing also has potentialities as a training technique. It offers promise as a direct means of teaching persons to handle rather complex social situations.

Mechanical Instrumentation

Physical instrumentation in research can serve two primary purposes. Initially it can simply provide a record of events as they occur. Motion pictures and sound recordings of classroom happenings are of this character. These serve only the purpose of making it possible to reproduce the essential elements of a particular situation again and again, so that the material may be reevaluated or reassessed in some way by other raters or other observers. The bulk of the material that this involves is always substantial, and the process is costly. Instrumentation that permits reproducibility should be embarked upon only when there has been the most careful planning and where adequate funds are available for the purchase of materials and the employment of personnel.

The second purpose of physical instrumentation serves more than to record events as they occur, for the product is not just a record but a quantification and reduction of events to measures that can be used. For example, it may be possible to determine how much movement the teacher makes around the classroom in a given period of time by equipping him with a pedometer. The pedometer will provide a single over-all score, which indicates the number of steps taken during the period of observation. However, it is rare to have instruments permitting the recording of particularly relevant behavior attached to a teacher or to pupils in a classroom situation. Instrumentation is much more appropriate to a laboratory situation in which special provision is made both for the appearance of particular aspects of behavior and for their measurement. An interesting proposal has been made by Uldis Smidchens that observers in classrooms might record events by dialing numbers on a telephone dial wired through a plug in the wall directly to a computer. For example, the dialing of a 9 might mean that the teacher had just given directions to a pupil, and a 2 might mean that a pupil had asked the teacher a question. By feeding the numbers dialed on the telephone directly to a computer, the observations can be analyzed and compiled without the need of a great amount of tedious clerical work.

It needs to be pointed out at this time that the use of physical instrumentation necessarily places restrictions on what is to be observed. Most physical instrumentation results in the measurement and recording of only a limited aspect of phenomena. This is true regardless of whether the phenomena are derived from the physical or from the behavioral sciences. Usually, those selected are believed to be crucial elements of the phenomenon that is being studied; and because few can be measured, it is essential that these elements be crucial and that they be of theoretical significance.

The student of education may not be fully aware of the complicated measurement function of instruments in research. An example may illustrate this function. A relatively simple electronic device can be constructed to record the noise level in a classroom. This device registers the various physical disturbances of the atmosphere that fall within the range of audible frequencies, combines the energy values of these various disturbances, and indicates on a meter some linear or other function of these energy values. The device can be arranged so that it will give an average reading of the noise over, say, a ten-minute period. The instrument can be adapted to provide a numerical reading related to the particular function of noise that it is desired to record. It can thus automatically summate and eliminate the need for numerous readings, which otherwise would have to be summated by hand.

Finally, there is one important advantage to be achieved through the mechanization of data collection that often makes mechanical procedures an imperative. This advantage is the uniformity it provides in the collection of data. Consider, for example, a simple concept-learning task in which each subject views a number of cards and decides, in each case, whether the drawing of the creature on the card is or is not an example of a mollusk. This is a familiar concept-learning type of experiment in which the subject learns the characteristics of mollusks. After each trial the subject is told whether he is right or wrong. Now one way of carrying out this experiment is for the research worker to hold up each card, one at a time, to each subject, and to ask the subject to decide whether it is or is not a drawing of a mollusk; however, there are many features of this procedure that limit the value of the data derived from it. First, it is difficult for the experimenter to control the rate of presentation. Secondly, a very important factor is difficult to control—namely, the amount of time the subject is allowed to look at each display after he finds out whether his answer was correct or incorrect. There is ample evidence to show that the time of exposure of the stimulus display after the reinforcing event is important in human learning. Thirdly, the tone of the voice of the experimenter may vary from one occasion to the next, and hence some aspects of the reinforcements administered may vary. Fourthly, under these conditions, the subject is likely to be tempted to interact with the experimenter and disrupt the experimental procedure.

Data collection in the situation described should be entirely mechanized. Initial directions should be administered through a tape recorder that can also be used for triggering a slide projector used to display the material on the screen. The mechanism should control with some precision the time following a response during which the subject can continue to examine the display. The response should involve the pressing of one of two keys so that supplementary data on time of response can be recorded.

Without suitable instrumentation and mechanization the data collected are likely to be of only the most limited value. Such data are commonly referred to as "dirty" because any findings are likely to reflect the influence of a host of important uncontrolled variables. Data collected must always be as "clean" as possible.

Where devices are used for the collection of data, the research worker must remain aware of what these may do to the behavior of those observed. The placement of a television camera in a classroom will produce a reaction in both the teacher and the pupils. Most teachers will also demand that a signal be given when a recording is being made. Thus one cannot generally place a television camera in a classroom and record small samples of what is happening without the teacher knowing when a record is being made. Teachers and administrators take the position that a person whose performance is to be recorded has to give his consent. The issue involved is a matter of ethics and cannot be ignored.

Construction of Apparatus for Educational Research

Many theses and dissertations in the field of education have had to be abandoned because of apparatus problems, and some have been extended years beyond the expected date of completion for the same reason. It is therefore appropriate that a few comments be made here in order to steer the student away from some of the deeper pitfalls in in the use of apparatus.

It is perhaps worth pointing out that the author has known a number of graduate students who insisted on developing research projects involving apparatus that took years to build. Some of these students failed to reach the point of obtaining a doctoral degree simply because they never completed the apparatus. If the student doubts that he can build the required equipment within the space of a few months, he usually should abandon his dissertation problem and find another. Students differ greatly in their ability to build apparatus, and only the student himself can judge his capacity for building experimental equipment. One suspects that the person who has high competence in this respect is also the individual who can show the greatest ingenuity in developing simple designs. Many apparatus troubles result from a failure to simplify apparatus to the point where it will achieve the desired purpose with a minimum number of working parts.

In the planning of apparatus, it is most desirable to incorporate working units that are already available, such as slide-projectors, camera shutters, chronoscopes, and amplifiers. Much equipment that is available around a college can be adapted for experimental purposes.

It is also of the utmost importance that equipment be such that it will be relatively free of malfunctions. Apparatus that breaks down during the course of data collection wastes one of the assets that the experimenter has to conserve most carefully—namely, the time given him by his experimental subjects. Freedom from malfunction is partly a function of complexity and partly a function of good design and the use of appropriate materials. Do not, for example, build apparatus in which moving parts are made of wood. These are always unsatisfactory. If metal parts cannot be made, then try using plastics, which will not shrink and expand with changes in the humidity of the atmosphere, as will wooden parts. Plastics such as Lucite can be easily bent into desired shapes when warm and can be filed and machined when cold. Electrical contacts are always a serious source of malfunction, and for this reason all connections should be soldered. Where switches are required, it is important that good quality products be used, and the experimenter should never use the homemade variety. Particularly useful are modern microswitches and relays, which can be obtained in good quality at a cheap price.

The equipment available for research in most colleges of education is extremely limited. In many ways this is surprising in view of the fact that, in the early part of the century, these same colleges were centers for experimental psychology. Lack of leadership at the top levels of administration and the tendency to draw deans of education from the field of educational administration must be given substantial blame for this state of affairs in which the only device for collecting data is the paper and pencil. However, even though schools of education have slept, the rest of the academic world that has an interest in research on learning has forged ahead in the development of apparatus. Fine equipment can now be obtained for controlling almost every aspect of the learning process. A student who is interested in investigating a problem in learning should become familiar with that equipment, lest he find himself conducting research along lines that competent research workers discarded many years ago. Much of the modern equipment designed specifically for research on learning comes in *modules*, which can be assembled on racks to control the inputs to subjects and to record the responses they make. Such apparatus can also be used to control slide projectors and film-strip projectors.

Some sophisticated research on verbal learning requires the use of a computer to control the supply of information to the learner. In such research a computer is necessary to store the information that *may* be supplied to the subject and the conditions under which the information is supplied. For example, a subject may be given a problem to solve and, if he does not solve it in a given time, he may ask the computer for a particular piece of information. The computer, which has been programmed to answer questions related to the problem, is able to interpret the question and provide an appropriate answer.

The building of complicated electrical equipment should be limited. It is rarely desirable for the student to work out his own electronic circuits, because those already available are likely to represent the limit of what can be accomplished at the present time. The solution to the problems lies in obtaining ready made equipment, because the cost of having an instrument company build apparatus is usually prohibitive. This statement does not mean that instrument companies charge unreasonable prices, for the actual cost of producing such equipment is high. Not only does it require expensive and elaborate machine tools—hence, high overhead charges—it also requires relatively well-paid craftsmen and highly paid supervisors. In addition, even the smallest part that is to be custom made must be drawn by a skilled draftsman before the task of making it is assigned to the machinist.

Finally, whenever a piece of apparatus is made for conducting an experiment, it is desirable that the entire experimental procedure, once it is started with a particular subject, be completely automatic and not require the intervention of the experimenter. Although there are exceptions, it is by and large most undesirable for the experimenter to have to stop the apparatus from time to time in order to interject some addition to the directions. Thus, if the experiment is conducted by running a sound-recording tape, it is desirable that the full directions to the subject also be recorded on the same tape.

SUMMARY

1. The scientist uses the term *observation* in a different sense from that ordinarily used. The scientist refers to an item of data as an observation.

2. There are two distinct classes of observations that are made in the behavioral sciences. Observations may pertain to the characteristics of the environment or to the responses of living organisms to that environment.

3. The process of observation involves sorting out from a vast array of events presented to the senses those that are believed to have special significance. The plan or scheme that is used in selecting events for observation is referred to as the *frame of reference* of the observer. The observer should approach a situation with a clear idea about what is to be observed and with some rudimentary theory about the significance of his observations.

4. Information is available concerning the characteristic of persons who distort their observations. Even with the best selection of observers, training in the procedures to be used is generally necessary.

5. Many sources of error in observation can be reduced through proper training of observers who should participate as much as possible in the development of the techniques to be used or in trial runs of techniques already developed.

6. The research worker often influences the situation that he is attempting to observe. These "reactive effects" are quite varied in character. The more common ones are those produced by the fact that (a) the person observed realizes he is part of an experiment; (b) there is a tendency for persons to assume particular roles; (c) the

initiation of learning in the subject may be through the behavior of the research worker; and (d) tendencies for respondents to give particular classes of responses.

7. One approach to the elimination of reactive effects is to collect data in such a way that the method of collection has no impact on those whose behavior is to be studied. Erosion methods and accretion methods of collecting data about human behavior are suggested for this purpose. The erosions and traces of human behavior have long been used by archeologists and have had a reputable scientific history. These so-called unobtrusive measures may still be subject to certain systematic errors that must be recognized in their interpretation.

8. The observation of the environment of the pupil does not generally involve the same hazards as does the direct observation of behavior. Much needs to be learned concerning the relationship between the design of the pupil's environment and the learning of the pupil.

9. The classroom data collected by the teacher usually differ in many respects from those collected by the scientist. One marked difference is that the teacher uses his data directly, whereas the scientist uses them only after they have been processed in some way.

10. Rating is a way by which numerous events that are observed are somehow summarized and combined. Control over the rating process requires that control be exercised over both the nature of the information that is used and the way in which it is used. The unsatisfactory nature of most ratings is a reflection of the difficulties involved in introducing such controls over the selection and processing of information. When these controls are made explicit, then the rating process can be communicated.

11. The interview is a commonly used technique for obtaining observations concerning individual behavior. It presents a highly complex situation from which it is difficult to obtain data that can be reproduced in other studies.

12. Although interviewer characteristics are important variables in the situation, they are difficult to identify and control. It is even difficult to train interviewers to make accurate records of what happens.

13. The interview must be considered as a complex social situation in which the interviewer and the interviewee are making continuous adjustments to the responses of one another.

14. In planning interviews, caution should be observed in making assumptions about the extent to which the interviewee has insight into his behavior.

15. The interview has certain advantages over the questionnaire,

such as a higher percentage of respondents, superior cooperation, and a lack of dependence on the ability to read. It does present many problems of recording information.

16. Attempts have been made to place persons in situations that represent reproductions of real-life situations in order to observe their behavior.

17. Instruments can be introduced into the observation process for various purposes. They may improve the precision of the resulting observations. They may eliminate the need for human observers over long periods of time. They may summarize observations that would otherwise be bulky and cumbersome to handle.

18. As far as it is feasible, any instruments or devices used as a part of a research should consist of standard parts that are easily maintained and highly reliable in operation.

19. The underdeveloped state of the art of educational research is such that instruments have only the most limited value. Most of the data that such research involves must be collected by other procedures, and direct observation is probably the most widely used of these.

‖‖‖‖‖‖‖‖‖‖‖‖‖‖‖‖‖‖‖‖‖‖‖‖‖‖‖

CHAPTER 7

Using Multiple Observations in Measurement

COMBINING OBSERVATIONS TO PRODUCE MEASURES

The Single Observation

MOST inferences that can be made as a result of educational research are based on multiple observations. From observing a child's response to but a single problem assigned by the teacher, no responsible person is likely to make inferences concerning the child's educational achievement level or his scholastic aptitude. The single observation provides insufficient information for making either one of these inferences. Multiple observations can be used for making fairly accurate inferences about a child's achievement. Achievement tests are a means of providing multiple observations about a child's achievement, and the scores derived from these multiple observations have been demonstrated to measure certain achievements satisfactorily.

In other phases of educational research a similar state of affairs is found; the single observation has only the most limited value. If a socioeconomic index is desired for comparing the background of children, it is unlikely that reliance could be placed on a single observation, such as whether or not a child's home is equipped with a telephone. Although the presence or absence of a telephone is undoubtedly related to general socioeconomic conditions, it is only one of many possible criteria. A checklist of a number of items could be prepared, with each item hypothesized to be related to socioeconomic conditions. The list might include the presence or absence in the home of a telephone, a bathroom, an encyclopedia, a refrigerator, a separate bedroom for the child, and so forth. The scores on each of these items would be arrived at by counting the checks according to a key. The total information provided by all of the items might be of use, whereas the individual items considered separately might be almost useless. The small amount of information encapsulated in each single item makes the use of many items necessary.

The reader should not conclude that there are no areas of science in which single observations are of great importance. Medical science is replete with examples of instances in which a single test provides almost certain knowledge about the presence or absence of a particular disease. Chemical analysis depends on sequences of observations, each one of which is quite unambiguous in its interpretation. In physics, too, a single observation, such as is made in the determination of the density of a body, may provide highly valuable information to predict the behavior of the body in a multitude of situations. The contrast with educational research is marked.

Combination of Observations

Once it is recognized that observations must be combined in order to provide information that has any utility, two problems immediately arise. First, there is the problem of *what* observations are to be combined. Secondly, there is the matter of *how* they are to be combined. Most of the knowledge available about these two problems has been derived from studies of verbal responses to verbal problems such as appear in tests. Such knowledge, however, does have applicability to the wider range of materials used in educational research.

Consider the problem of estimating the size of a child's vocabulary or the relative size of the vocabularies of different children. One way of doing this might be to ask the child to define a series of words selected at random from a standard dictionary. If in this way we were to ask the child the meaning of ten words, and the child were to define five accurately, we might infer that the child could define 50 per cent of the words in the dictionary. However, a random sample of ten words would provide only the most limited amount of information about the child's total vocabulary. Chance may have resulted in the selection of common words, or perhaps very rare words, or words that the pupil happened to know. If any of these instances were to occur, our estimate of the pupil's vocabulary would be inaccurate. In order to avoid this eventuality, several courses of action could be taken. One of these would be to use a larger sample of words, the purpose of which would be to increase the precision with which it was possible to estimate the total vocabulary.

There is a second way in which multiple observations can be used, which can be described by returning to the problem of measuring vocabulary. If we were to draw a sample of one hundred words from the dictionary by taking the last word on each right-hand page, or every twentieth right-hand page, it is probable that our list would contain many common words with which almost everybody was familiar. The inclusion of these words in a test would provide little information since everybody taking the test would be familiar with them. Another procedure might be to select ten words that 90 per cent of the children to be tested would know, ten words that only 80 per cent of the children would know, ten words that 70 per cent would know, and so forth. This would form a rudimentary scale used to determine how difficult a level of vocabulary the individual can define. When such a scale is used, the purpose of measurement is no longer that of estimating the knowledge of the individual of all the words in the dictionary, although this can be estimated indirectly. The score of a child on such a scale would permit one to estimate how the child stood in relation to other children in vocabulary.

Dimensionality and Clustering Observations

There are unsatisfactory features in the procedures discussed for the measurement of vocabulary stemming from the fact that knowledge of vocabulary cannot be considered to be a unitary trait. Consider, for example, the case of the student confronted with a vocabulary test consisting of equal numbers of scientific and nonscientific words. Such a test might contain fifty test items in each of these two areas. Now it has been fairly clearly established that knowledge of scientific words is not very closely related to knowledge of general vocabulary, and thus the test measures two rather distinct abilities. If the student taking the test obtained a score of sixty items correct, it would be impossible to determine from the score alone whether the student had answered most of the scientific items correctly, or most of the nonscientific items correctly, or a considerable number of both types of items correctly. Two persons might obtain equally high scores, one by obtaining a high score on the scientific items, and one by knowing the nonscientific items. The score alone would not indicate whether the person was strong in the one area or in the other. This is because the test does not consist of a homogeneous group of items all measuring the same ability. If a measuring instrument is to have maximum utility, it should be designed to measure only one variable.

If a collection of items has such a mixed nature, then the score derived from it has only limited meaning. What is needed for meaningful measurement is a group of observations or items that belong together in some significant way and that can be used collectively as a measuring instrument. Such a group of items is sometimes referred to as a *homogeneous scale*, but one has to be careful about the use of the word *homogeneous*. Some writers who talk about a homogeneous group of items mean only that the items all *appear* to be measuring the same kind of variable, as would be the case with a test of scientific vocabulary or a checklist for measuring the socioeconomic status of the home. Others use the word to refer to a group of items that all belong together because it can be shown statistically that they all measure the same variable. What one really needs for meaningful measurement is a group of items or observations that not only belong together in some meaningful way but that also can be demonstrated by statistical means to measure a common property.

The research worker commonly is faced with the problem of having at his disposal numerous observations that must be grouped together into separate and distinct scales in order to provide meaningful measures. It is this problem of grouping that must now be considered.

Combining Observations in Meaningful Ways

The scientist who approaches educational problems is commonly faced with an abundance of observations and must find some way of grouping them so that they provide useful information. In the conduct of many types of school surveys, such as are undertaken by school- and college-accrediting associations, the accrediting agency may accumulate large numbers of items of information about educational institutions. Such information is not easily handled as a mass, and in some way the observations must be combined into groups if they are to be easily interpreted. If the home backgrounds of children are being studied, the social worker or research worker may collect hundreds of items of information about each child. Such data may include items indicative of socioeconomic level—home ownership, car ownership, size of home, value of home, and the number and type of appliances in the home. In addition, data might be obtained on a range of phenomena such as the number of brothers and sisters, the health of the parents, the sibling rivalries manifested by the children, the education of the parents, the number and type of books in the home, the preferences of the parents for the children, the father's occupation, the age of the parents, the number of neighborhood friends of the child, the religious affiliation, and the like. If, say, three hundred items of information were collected about each of two hundred children, the resulting collection of sixty thousand items is not usable for most scientific purposes until it is organized in some way. Some of the ways of doing this must now be given brief consideration.

The a priori method. It is probable that the research worker who planned to obtain a large quantity of information about the backgrounds of the pupils had some theory about the characteristics of the backgrounds that were relevant for his purpose. Suppose the goal was that of predicting the pupils' levels of academic achievement. He might have started out by postulating a number of different kinds of conditions in the backgrounds that might be related to achievement. One of these conditions might be the economic status of the home; another might be the degree to which tensions and frictions were absent from the home; another the cultural status of the home as indicated by the number of books or the presence or absence of a piano; and so forth. The list of items of information to be collected might well have been drawn up after a set of broad categories had first been established. After the data had been collected, the items would be grouped into these broad categories and a score derived for each. Thus, one score would indicate the relative socioeconomic status of the home; another the degree of psychological tension in the home; and another its cultural status. Thus, the three hundred items might be made to yield a dozen or fewer scores and the data would be reduced to manageable proportions. The advantage of the method is that it produces a set of measurements closely related to the theory on which the study was originally based.

Although this method is attractive, it has its limitations, particularly in studies in which not too much is known about how the items of information should be grouped together. The latter is true of such an area as school characteristics, in which a checklist might be used to describe a school by summarizing what are believed to be certain important facts about it. On the other hand, there are areas in which much is known about how items of information should be grouped. If the items referred to the biographical history of adults, it might be useful to group them in terms of the extent to which they reflected mechanical interests, scientific interests, clerical interests, and so forth.

The a priori method of grouping items of information rarely produces measuring devices that have particularly desirable properties. Too often the scales thus produced are too highly correlated with one another, which means that they measure characteristics that overlap. Considerable further work often has to be performed with these scales to refine them to the point where they are actually useful. A discussion of these additional steps is beyond the scope of this book.

Methods of grouping that depend on the interrelationships of the items. The student is familiar with the concept that two tests are said to measure the same variable when they are highly correlated, and that they measure different variables when they are uncorrelated. The same concept can be applied to items of information of all kinds. On the basis of this concept, it is possible to sort a pool of items into groups on the basis of whether the items are or are not correlated. Each group of items would then include all those items that were highly interrelated from a statistical point of view. Also, the items in one group would have little correlation with those in other groups—at least this would be so under ideal conditions. The actual procedure for doing this and the technical concepts involved are considerably more complex than is indicated here. Those who wish to explore the matter further are referred to an article on a special technique for doing this, called the *homogeneous keying technique*, which was developed by J. Loevinger, G. Gleser, and P. H. DuBois (1953).

Procedures for grouping items of information according to their interrelationships can be applied quite mechanically. Indeed, some of these can be undertaken almost completely by electronic computers. This is an advantage in terms of the speed with which the work can be performed, but the results are often difficult to interpret. Items that do not appear to belong together in any way are often grouped together. It is not that there are no good reasons why the items should be grouped in this way, but the reasons are not at all apparent. The reasons for the grouping often lie in the accidental way in which events happen together in our culture and in perhaps remote historical causes. For example, in one study of biographical material, it was found that three items grouped themselves together. These were (1) a knowledge of Latin, (2) a conservative political attitude, and (3) the ownership of a small business by the parent of the person being studied. It happened that in the city in which the study was undertaken, adherents to the Catholic faith were likely to share these three characteristics. This resulted in these three items being grouped together, but without a knowledge of the community from which the data were derived, the grouping would be meaningless.

A second approach to the sorting out of items of information in terms of their relationships depends on a whole series of techniques that have collectively become known as *factor analysis*. These techniques have evolved mainly for the purpose of attempting to identify the abilities that can be considered to underlie most of the aptitude tests that have been developed. Thus it can be shown that most of the numerous aptitude tests at present available can be considered to measure relatively few variables. One can classify tests in terms of the extent to which they measure each of a small number of reference variables, such as verbal ability, numerical ability, arithmetic reasoning, and so forth. By this means tests are grouped together in terms of the *factor* that they measure, but difficulties are introduced by the fact that the procedures usually permit more than one interpretation concerning the variables that are to be considered to underlie the battery of tests.

These same types of procedure can be applied to the grouping of test items as well as to the grouping of tests. One cannot point to examples where this procedure has used such items of information with striking success, but it is a procedure that is widely suggested in the literature. A major difficulty in its application stems from the fact that the arithmetic becomes extremely elaborate if the technique is applied to any large pool of items. Other difficulties arise in choosing, from the many possible sets of underlying variables that might be considered, the one that is most useful for the purpose at hand.

One of the problems encountered in the application of most factor-analysis techniques is a product of the approach not providing a unique solution to the problem of establishing variables. One does not necessarily end up with a set of independent measures, each one measuring a separate and distinct characteristic. Sometimes items of information are more conveniently organized in other ways. One alternative is called the *hierarchical model* of grouping tests or test items. The word hierachy was originally used to describe the organization of churches into clergy, bishops, archbishops, and so on, with many at the bottom of the hierachy and few at the top. L. G. Humphreys (1962) has an interesting example of how tests measuring knowledge about mechanical problems can be arranged within an hierachical system. Tests in this area can be built on at least four different levels: First, one could build a single broad test of general mechanical information covering many different mechanical areas such as plumbers' work, automotive work, machinists' work, sheet metal work and so forth. This would measure over-all mechanical knowledge. Secondly, one could build series of tests, each covering knowledge of one of these trades. Thirdly, one could build a much larger number of tests, each measuring knowledge of a particular group of tools within each trade (for example, a test on the various saws used by carpenters). Fourthly, one could build numerous short tests, each covering the use of a particular tool. The four levels of tests represent a hierachy of measuring devices from a test that measures broad general knowledge, at one extreme, to a large number of tests covering small areas of tool usage at the other extreme. The level at which one may want to build a measuring device would depend on the purpose involved. If one wanted to find out the specific areas in which craftsmen needed retraining, then the fourth level or perhaps the third level would be most appropriate. If one wanted to hire men with broad skills in particular trades then the second-level test would be what would be needed. On the other hand, the selection of men for training might involve the use of the first-level test.

One can also make a case for the position that the same kind of hierarchy occurs in the case of aptitude and intelligence tests. At the first level are tests of general intelligence, whereas at the fourth level are tests of very specialized skills, such as knowledge of particular types of technical terms.

The grouping of items of information in terms of the variables it is desired to predict. In a later chapter on problems of prediction, it will be pointed out that items of information are often assembled in order to make predictions. There are, for example, many studies in which information about the home and cultural background of children has been collected in order to predict and anticipate difficulties in school. Let us consider such an example in order to illustrate the method of grouping items of information.

Let us suppose that items of information about home and cultural background were collected for the purpose of predicting (1) reading disability, (2) social difficulties in school, (3) absenteeism, and (4) degree of success in an academic curriculum. The research worker collected 150 items of information about the background of each child entering a junior high school in a large city. The school served a residential area of varied economic circumstances. The data collection was continued until a record was obtained of the backgrounds of each of four hundred pupils. These pupils were followed through the school. A reading-disability group was slowly and carefully identified. Reports that enabled the research worker to identify a socially maladjusted group were obtained from teachers and added to by counselors. Records of absenteeism were available, and so were records of grades. Once the research worker had obtained all this information, he selected from the pool of background-information items a group that predicted reading disability. When a total score was derived from this group of information items, the score was found to predict reading disability with considerable success in subsequent samples. A similar procedure was adopted for predicting each one of the remaining three variables that the study had been designed to predict.

This method of using multiple items of information has been used successfully for combining items for all kinds of purposes. It has been used for predicting performance in various types of training programs; for predicting success in certain occupations, such as that of salesman; for predicting delinquency; and so forth. In most studies that have used items of background information, the resulting predictions have been extremely limited in accuracy. Of course, this does not mean that the method might not provide highly accurate predictions when used to combine other types of information.

The disadvantage of the method lies in the possibility that the measures it produces, as in the example discussed, often are closely related to one another. It is possible that three of the four scales produced were measures of the extent to which the atmosphere of the home was favorable to intellectual development. The fourth scale, related to social adjustment, may have measured a different characteristic.

Although this procedure does have a certain logic in it, there are procedures considerably more complicated that could be used to provide more accurate and efficient predictions. These other methods take into account not only the relationship of the items to the variable to be predicted, but also the extent to which the items provide overlapping information. This involves complicated statistical procedures requiring the use of computers to be efficiently undertaken.

Some Cautions Regarding the Fractionation of Pools of Items

The procedures discussed in this chapter are analogous to mechanical procedures for the fractionation of crude oil. The crude oil is fed in at one end of the fractionating plant, and a whole range of petroleum products, some useful and some not, comes out at the other. Procedures for grouping and selecting test items are of this character. They can be applied and used without much knowledge of the why and the wherefore, and their application can be considered in most cases as a step in the direction of developing tools for research; but it can hardly be considered research.

This point is made because the author has frequently been faced by a graduate student coming to him with a proposal for a doctoral dissertation to consist of the application of a certain technique to a pool of items the student proposes to build. This is not an activity that should be encouraged in the graduate student. It represents a laborious and time-consuming routine. It does not encourage the type of activity often considered to lie at the very core of a program of doctoral studies —namely, the thinking through of an important problem to the point where ways are found of arriving at a solution. Research of any consequence requires more than the mere application of a mechanical routine. If it could be undertaken by the latter means alone, it could be produced in a factory by a relatively uneducated labor force.

Much of what is undertaken in the name of research, and which is the wholesale application of a technique to some collection of items, fails to note that the mere identification of a variable is no guarantee that it is going to be of any use. As a matter of fact, new measuring instruments in the behavioral sciences can be developed very easily. The great difficulty is to discover and develop variables that have predictive value. This usually requires prolonged endeavor and what has been termed scientific insight. It does not result from any mechanical procedure, but rather from the development of a sound theory and the testing of deductions from this theory.

It thus behooves the scientist to begin all work on the development of measuring instruments with a theory concerning how the variables he is attempting to measure relate to the specific aspects of behavior that he is studying. If this is done, it will be necessary to test the instruments in order to determine whether the measures they provide permit the making of the predictions that were anticipated. If they do not, one should discard not only the instruments but also the theory on which they were based. Measures that have merit in terms of their internal properties do not help in building a sound theory and do not contribute to knowledge if they show no signs of operating in the way expected.

Finally, it must be reiterated that the information provided by a single observation related to education is extremely limited, and even a group of relatively homogeneous items cannot be expected to provide more than a hint about other types of events. This may be looked upon in another way in the case where the observations refer to behavior. If a group of test items occupies five minutes of time, this must be recognized as an extraordinarily small sample of a person's behavior.

What a person does in a five-minute period is only the most limited basis for generalizing about what the same person will do during other five-minute periods. At the same time it should be recognized, of course, that a test situation is not *any* sample of behavior, but should be a sample of behavior that has been demonstrated to have particular significance for predicting how the person will behave in certain other situations. Nevertheless, there is a definite limit to the amount of information that can be obtained about behavior in a given period of time.

RELIABILIITY AND VALIDITY

The purpose of grouping together observations is to provide measures of greater significance than can be provided by single observations. Up to this point, the reader has been left with only an intuitive understanding of what is meant by the *significance* of a measure. It is now necessary to define more precisely the meaning of the latter term and to consider the two aspects of significance—namely, reliability and validity.

Reliability of Measurement

A measuring instrument used for either research purposes or for some immediately practical purpose, such as the measurement of the length of a piece of fabric, must have useful properties if it is to perform satisfactorily the task at hand. One of these properties is *reliability*. Although this is an abstract and theoretical concept, let us develop it, first, within a practical context. Suppose that we were engaged in measuring the height of some small saplings and that the measuring instrument available was a tape measure such as housewives use when they sew. We might start by checking our measuring tape against a highly accurate measuring rod that was known to be almost exactly 60 inches. Let us suppose that this standard was guaranteed to be within 0.01 inch. In comparing the tape with the rod we would probably note that if we stretched the tape by just the right amount, the tape and the rod would be precisely the same length. We might then go out and measure each of the young trees, each time trying to stretch the tape by just the right amount so that it would provide us with an accurate measure. However, try as we might, sometimes the tape would be pulled too taut and sometimes it would not be pulled tight enough. The result would be that the height of some of the trees would be overestimated while the height of others would be underestimated. The instrument is obviously not perfectly reliable. We might find that if we remeasured the trees on a later occasion that the two measures might differ by perhaps as much as 2 inches. If the trees varied from 24 to 60 inches in height, we might regard an error of measurement of this size to be quite unimportant. However, if we had been conducting an experiment on the growth of trees and the trees varied only from 55 to 60 inches, then this error of measurement might be too large for our purposes. We would then have to find a more precise measuring instrument—that is to say, a more reliable instrument. From this example it is also evident that the significance of errors of measurement depends on how much variability they produce in comparison with the total amount of variability among the objects measured. A useful measuring instrument is one in which the variability produced by errors of measurement is small compared with the variability of the objects measured. Another point to note, in this case, is that some idea of the size of the errors involved can be obtained by repeating the measurement procedure.

Now the tape measure is obviously a poor measuring instrument and, in any experiment involving the measurement of length, we should use a more accurate and reliable device such as, perhaps, a steel tape. The example of the fabric tape is of value here because it has similarities with measuring instruments used in the behavioral sciences. A psychological test, for example, provides us with a score for each individual to whom it is administered. However, we know that even when the same test is given again to the same individuals, they do not obtain exactly the same score on each administration. Scores vary from one administration to the next just as the measured height of the saplings varied. There would be even more variability if another measuring instrument, made as similar as possible to the first, were used for the second measurement. The point to note is that repeating the measurement permits us to estimate the general order of magnitude of the error of measurement.

A measuring instrument provides a score that can be regarded as consisting of two components: one is the true score and the other is an error component. When the measuring instrument has been applied and a distribution of scores has been produced, we would want most of the variability of the scores to be attributable to variations in the true score. The measuring instrument would be most unsatisfactory if most of the variability were only a reflection of errors of measurement. The degree to which the variation reflects variation in true scores represents the degree to which the measuring instrument is reliable. On the other hand, in a highly unreliable test most of the variation in observed scores is attributable to errors of measurement.

Now one cannot disect each measurement into a true component and error component, for all one has is a single score for each individual that cannot be readily taken apart. For this reason, the reliability of a measuring instrument has to be estimated by indirect means. The key to the commonest methods of estimating reliability has already been indicated and involves the making of repeated measures. The repeated-measures approach involves the use of either (1) parallel forms of the measuring instrument; or (2) reapplication of the same form; or (3) various split-half methods, such as where performance on the even-numbered items is compared with performance on the odd-numbered items. Let us consider each of these in turn.

Parallel forms of a test are two forms designed to provide instruments that match one another as closely as possible without using the same items in each. In terms of measurement theory, parallel forms can be defined as those on which the true scores for an individual are the same and on which the errors of measurement are, on the average, equal. This does not mean that when the same individuals are measured on both instruments that they obtain equal scores. They do not, because the error component of the score for the particular individual may vary from the one test to the other. This makes his observed score vary, but, if the instruments are reliable, then only a small amount of variation is to be expected. If, on the other hand, the individual's score varies a very large amount from the one parallel form of the test to the other, then the error of measurement is high and the instrument can be considered relatively unreliable. The measure of reliability commonly derived through this procedure is the correlation between performance on the one form of the test and performance on the other form. Thus in a test manual one will find a statement such as, "The parallel-form reliability for the test was found to be 0.92 when the two forms of the test were administered one week apart to 350 fifth-grade children in a metropolitan area." In the interpretation of such a statement, the assumption is commonly made that the test measures a stable characteristic that does not change appreciably over a week. If the characteristic is not stable, then a low correlation may reflect merely that differences in the scores on the two forms of the test largely represent a change in the characteristic measured, rather than errors of measurement. There are methods available for discriminating between a variation in score, from form to form of a test, that is the result of a change in the characteristic measured, and a change that can be attributed to error of measurement. The reader who wishes to explore such methods is referred to P. Horst (1966).

Very often two or more parallel forms of a measuring device are not available and the procedure of administering the same instrument twice has to be adopted. This is not a very effective procedure for the estimation of reliability, partly because the individual tested often remembers how he marked the items on the first administration of the device and marks them in the same way on the second administration. The result is a spuriously high correlation between the performances on the first and second administrations. Thus a test-retest measure of reliability tends to provide an excessively high estimate.

When only one form of a test exists, another method of estimating the reliability of the instrument is still open to us. One can regard the items of the test as consisting of two separate tests, each of half length. One can, for example, consider all the even-numbered items as one form of the test and all the odd-numbered items as another. If the test is highly reliable, then the scores derived from the one half of the items should be highly correlated with the scores derived from the other half. The correlation will be lower than if two full-length tests were used because, within limits, the generalization is true that the longer the test the higher the reliability. However, a formula can be applied to the correlation between the two half-length tests that will estimate what the correlation would have been if two full-length tests had been used.

Many methods exist for dividing up a test into two shorter forms for the purpose of estimating reliability. The purpose of the division of the items is to provide two tests that have, as far as possible, the properties of parallel forms. The odd-even approach does this by taking two samples in a systematic way that, one hopes, distributes the items in different categories appropriately over the two forms. An important point to note is that any split-half method of estimating reliability should not be applied if the test is speeded and not all persons complete the test.

Although we can regard the methods of estimating reliability considered to this point as ways of estimating the extent to which scores are contaminated with errors of measurement, we can also view the parallel-form method in another light. The latter method can be viewed as an attempt to discover the extent to which a score derived from one sample of items can be used to predict a score derived from another sample of items, when each sample is derived from the same "universe" of items. There is also another way of viewing the problem of estimating reliability that brings us back to the problem of homogeneity.

The estimation of reliability by means of the Kuder-Richardson type of formula refers again to a different type of phenomenon. L. J. Cronbach (1951), who has made a careful study of this approach, refers to the coefficient derived from this procedure as *alpha*. He has also shown that alpha refers to an internal property of a test, which is a product of the statistical relationship among the items. This property is known as homogeneity, and refers to the extent to which all the items on a test can be considered to contribute to the measurement of a single common variable. The coefficient alpha is for this reason now most commonly referred to as a measure of homogeneity rather than as a measure of reliability.

There are also other approaches to the problem of estimating reliability and some of these approaches make it possible to investigate far more complex situations than have been discussed. Consider, for example, a problem investigated by J. C. Stanley (1962) of determining the reliability of an essay test. Let us suppose that two essay tests, A and B, were administered to two hundred students. Let us suppose that, on the first day, half of the students took Test A and half Test B, and that on the second day those who had previously taken Test A took Test B and those who had previously taken Test B now took Test A. Let us suppose also that the papers were retyped before the scoring was begun, and that the papers were assigned at random to the examiners except for the added restriction that no examiner ever scored both essays of the same student. In addition, let us have four examiners who read the tests; each examiner reads 25 of the A papers and 25 of the B papers from the first day and a similar number of each from the second day. After all the papers were scored, a study of the marks would probably show quite clearly that many factors entered into a student's mark. One might be the examiner. Some examiners are tougher than others. Another might be whether it was the first day of the examination or the second. An additional factor, and the one in which the examiners were interested, was the ability of the students to perform on such a test. The examiners would hope that the scores on the essays would indicate primarily the differences in ability of the students to perform, and not differences between examiners or other irrelevant features of the testing and scoring situation.

A technique known as *analysis of variance* (commonly called Anova) can be applied to these kinds of data for the purpose of sorting out the various factors influencing the final scores. Through the application of this technique, one could determine from the data the extent to which examiner peculiarities influenced scores, the extent to which the day of the examination had an effect, and the extent to which students showed consistency of performance from the first test to the second. If the procedure were further complicated by requiring that each paper be scored independently by two different examiners, then the analysis of variance could also be used to determine the extent to which two examiners agreed with one another, a further aspect of reliability that has not been considered up to this point. The advantage of the analysis of variance procedure is that it permits the sorting out of the various factors and an estimation of the relative effect of each on the scores given to papers.

Validity

Before any measuring instrument is applied, some data should be available to show that it is possible to make some true inferences from the resulting scores. The statement that the parallel-form reliability of a test is 0.95 ($N = 200$), enables one to infer from the person's score on one form of the test what his score would be on another form. This is far from being the most interesting or useful inference that can be made. The term *reliability* is used in discussing such inferences about how persons would perform if a parallel form of the instrument were administered; or if the same form were administered again; or if another sample of test items from the same universe of test items were administered. Although it is true that if one cannot make even such relatively trivial inferences the device is useless, a measuring instrument, useful in research or practical application, also has to be one from which much more significant inferences can be made. A personality test that is reliable, but does not predict anything about a person or about what the person does, is worthless. The user of an instrument must be able to make inferences that go beyond how a person would perform on other similar test items before he can be said to have in his hand a useful device. Such inferences pertain to what is called the validity of a measuring instrument.

Most measuring instruments are used on the assumption that a score derived from the instrument can be used to predict some aspect of behavior in situations different from that in which the measurement has been made. College admission tests are given on the assumption that they will predict success in college and that, on the basis of a student's score, one can make true statements about the probability that the student will complete a college degree. If one cannot make true statements of this kind it would be said that the test has no predictive validity. Such statements involving predictions from a test score do not imply a cause-effect relationship. Although one may be able to say that the score on an aptitude test predicts scholastic success in a particular educational institution, this statement must not be interpreted to mean that high aptitude *causes* high scholastic success.

Statements that pertain to predictive validity have to be based on sufficient quantities of carefully collected data, but these statements hold true only for those situations that are closely similar to the situations in which the data were collected. If, for example, a measure of motivation were shown to be related to scholastic achievement in the case of children in middle-class elementary schools, one could not assume that the same relationship would hold for children in underprivileged areas, or even for children in different geographical regions. Until one has a sound theory about why predictions can be made, great caution has to be exercised in making any generalizations from data showing that a particular prediction can be made in a particular situation.

A distinction must also be made between predictions of immediately occurring events and the prediction of events occurring at a later date from the time when a particular instrument was applied. The fact that a measuring device can be used to predict other immediately occurring events does not mean that it can be used for making predictions over greater time spans. For example, a simple test measuring interest in each school subject given in elementary school can predict the grades of pupils in related subjects, because the interest test scores reflect the immediate success that the pupils are enjoying. However, the same test scores may be useless for making predictions during subsequent school years. As a general rule, it can be said that the longer the period over which predictions are made, the less likely an instrument is to be an effective predictor.

Psychologists sometimes use the term *concurrent validity* when referring to statements about the prediction of events that occur at roughly the same time as when the instrument is applied. These statements are to be contrasted with statements involving the prediction of more remote events to which the term *predictive validity* is applied.

Although statements that a test or measuring instrument can be used to predict this or that have a certain practical utility if they are true, they still present only fragmented pieces of knowledge that do not constitute an organized body of scientific knowledge. A measuring instrument useful for research has to be one that has produced at least some findings that fit into a body of knowledge. Consider an example from another field of knowledge: The statement that the prolonged elevation of sugar in the blood after a test meal indicates diabetes represents much more than the discovery of the simple empirical relationship between the appearance of the symptoms of diabetes and the elevation of the blood-sugar level. The statement is one of a set of interrelated statements representing knowledge about the metabolism of sugar, the function of the pancreas in producing insulin, the storage of sugar in the liver, the glycogen cycle in the muscles, and so forth. It is not an isolated statement representing some odd but interesting experimental finding, but a part of an organized body of knowledge. This situation is to be contrasted with most of the statements that can be made about measures used in the behavioral sciences and in education. For example, although it can be said that a measure derived from a test of intelligence enables one to predict performance in school, only rather vague statements can be made about the conditions, genetic or environmental, that produce intelligence. In addition, one cannot make any statements about how intelligence test scores are related to the structure and functioning of the nervous system. The statements that can be made about intelligence-test scores are very limited in scope and fit into a poorly organized body of scientific knowledge at this time—in contrast with the statements about level of blood sugar, which are not only clear and precise but also fit into an organized body of knowledge about physiology.

When statements can be made about a measuring instrument that fits into an organized body of knowledge, the instrument is said to have *construct validity*. When this term is applied to an instrument, it implies that the measure represents a variable that has a role in a scientific theory. Very few of the measures used in educational research can be said to have construct validity in this sense, although construct validity is always a matter of degree. In the case of some measures of anxiety, such as the Taylor Manifest Anxiety scale, a considerable body of information has emerged suggesting that the variable measured has many properties similar to a drive and that predictions can be made of limited validity based on the assumption that one is dealing with a variable that is, essentially, a measure of the extent to which behavior is energized. This is the beginning of construct validity. The measure is on the threshold of fitting into a theoretical framework, but it is still far from fitting into a tight system of ideas, as measures in the better-established sciences do.

Summary

1. In educational research it is usually true that a single observation provides only a very limited amount of information. In order to overcome this limitation, it is usually necessary to combine together several observations.

2. Items of information must be grouped together in some way so that they form a meaningful measuring instrument. Under ideal conditions the items should all belong together in terms of some theory; but they should also all belong together in a statistical sense, and in this sense should all measure a common variable.

3. Items of information can be combined together on the basis of judgment either because they appear to belong together or because there is some theoretical basis for grouping them together. This method of grouping together items of information is referred to as the a priori method.

4. A series of methods of using multiple observations have been developed in which the grouping depends on the statistical relationships among the items. Two general classes of techniques for this purpose have been developed:

    a. The homogeneous keying technique represents a method that has been evolved specifically for the purpose of sorting a large number of items of information into groups, each of which forms a measuring instrument.

    b. A second approach is that of factor analysis, which evolved more as a procedure for the grouping of tests than a procedure for the grouping of items.

5. Observations can be grouped also in terms of the extent to which they predict some other variable.

6. A measuring instrument has no value unless some inferences can be made from the scores derived from it. If one can accurately infer from the scores derived from an instrument what scores would have been obtained from a parallel form of the instrument, or if one can make a similar inference then the instrument is said to be reliable. Although reliability is an essential feature of a satisfactory measuring instrument, other features must also be present if the device is to have utility.

7. A measuring instrument that has utility must also provide scores from which valid inferences can be made concerning the scores that would be obtained on other variables. Statements of validity often

make references to the predictive power of an instrument. The distinction is also commonly made between concurrent validity and predictive validity, depending on whether the instrument is used for predicting other events occurring about the time when the instrument is used, or whether some event more remote in time is predicted.

8. In the case of an ideal scientific measuring instrument, one is able to make statements about the relationship of the variable measured to other variables; these statements fit into a system of knowledge. The validity statements are then no longer just odd items of information that do not fit in with other knowledge; they constitute a part of systematic knowledge. When that is the case, the instrument is said to have construct validity.

‖▮‖▮‖▮‖▮‖▮‖▮‖▮‖▮‖▮‖▮‖▮‖▮‖

CHAPTER 8

Instrumentation of Classroom Observation

THE types of instruments to be considered in this chapter have been developed for the purpose of helping the observer to organize his work when he is faced with the task of identifying and recording some of the happenings in the classroom. These instruments are means of controlling the observer's attention so that he focuses on the particular kinds of events that are under investigation. Without the use of such devices, the events selected for observation and record are likely to reflect the personal whims of the observer. In addition, these devices also provide a systematic means of recording observations in a form permitting the subsequent systematic analysis of the data.

Classroom Observation Schedules—Problems in Their Development

The reader can turn to a textbook on educational measurement to acquire information about the development of rating scales, but he will not find information about the development of observation schedules so readily available.

The development of observation schedules to be used in the recording of events in the classroom is a matter that requires considerable technical knowledge. In order to familiarize the reader with some of the problems that this involves, the development of an observation schedule as it occurred in one study is presented here. The study selected is that by J. E. Morsh (1955), which is also discussed in other parts of this book. Examples of other observation schedules are then presented.

In his study, Morsh was concerned with determining the relationship between instructor's and student's behavior and the amount students learn. The study was conducted in technical courses given in Air Force schools. In this research, it was decided to study behavior at a level that involved fairly small segments, or what would commonly be called specific behavior. Observers were sent to classrooms to obtain lists of what seemed to be relevant teacher behaviors that could be postulated to effect the course of student learning. Lists of relevant student behaviors that could be hypothesized to be symptomatic of efficient and inefficient learning were also prepared. On the basis of these preliminary observations, a list of 160 behaviors was prepared. But it was soon found that observers who used it as a checklist could neither keep all the items in mind nor observe on such an extended front. This difficulty resulted in the reduction of the checklist to eighty items.

At this stage of the inquiry, certain observational difficulties soon became apparent. The first of these was mechanical. It simply did not seem feasible to provide observers with an instrument lengthier than a single page. Searching through more than one page to record an entry was not a feasible task, particularly when, as in any classroom, much was happening and several different but relevant behaviors occurred concurrently. Secondly, there was little point in the inclusion in a checklist of those items that happened so rarely that they were not likely to be noted by the typical observer in the study. Thirdly, the observer had only limited time in which to record his information, and thus items that required some reflection before the decision to record was made should not have been included unless they provided information essential to the study. There is, of course, no clear-cut line to be drawn between items that involve judgment and items that do not. Rather it is a matter of degree. In many areas of observation, if judgment items are discarded little of value remains. A simple and familiar example of this is the typical English theme or composition. Systems of judging such compositions that are limited to objectively observable items, such as spelling, capitalization, agreement of subject and verb, and so on, have been found to measure only the most trivial aspects of teaching in English. Fourthly, it was considered desirable that the lists be usable by an observer who had had only very limited amounts of training. Fifthly, it appeared to be important to make the lists short enough to be memorized by the observer. Sixthly, only those items were to be retained that had some logical relevance to the learning process as it occurred in the classroom. (This is a point stressed all the way through this book, and is merely the application of one aspect of acceptable scientific methodology.)

As a result of these practical considerations, still further reductions were made in the checklists. That for recording observations pertaining to the teacher's nonverbal behavior consisted of a list of thirty-five items. Another list of thirty-three items pertained to the instructor's verbal behavior. A third list of twenty-five items was used for recording observations of student behavior.

Three observers were given preliminary training and were then assigned the task of collecting data in fifteen-minute observation periods in thirty classes. On the basis of these data, the reliability (consistency) of rating was determined for each item in the checklist. Through this computation most of the items were found to have adequate interobserver reliability. Those that did not were almost without exception items that occurred very infrequently. Examples of such items (sad to say) from the instructor's verbal behavior were "praises student, praises class, admits mistake." From the list of nonverbal behavior, infrequent items included such matters as "uses blackboard for key term, checks time, ignores student answer." All of the items except one in the student-behavior checklist showed satisfactory interobserver reliability.

Now Morsh was aware of the fact that raters might well agree among one another and in this sense the measure might have reliability, but this would not necessarily mean that the measure would have consistency from occasion to occasion. Indeed, from the evidence presented up to this point, it is quite possible that the incidents that occurred during the particular fifteen-minute periods were not typical.

In order to determine whether the observations during the particular fifteen-minute periods of observation could be used to generalize about behavior in other periods, a further study was made. In this subsequent study, each observer visited a large number of instructors for six fifteen-minute periods. These were combined into three half-hour periods for the purpose of determining reliability of observation from occasion to occasion. As a result of this procedure, it became necessary to eliminate certain additional items from the checklist because they did not show sufficient consistency from occasion to occasion. As a result of this elimination procedure, there remained thirteen items on the instructor verbal-behavior form, twelve items on the nonverbal-behavior form, and ten items on the student-behavior checklist. The lists were then set up for six five-minute periods of observation to provide a total period of thirty minutes of observation on each form. What were some of the items that were retained as reliable after such an elaborate process of elimination? In the case of the student behavior checklist, the following items were retained:

Talks	Ignores instructor
Answers question	Slumps
Asks question	Yawns, stretches
Looks around	Sleeps or dozes
Doodles	

Although the extent to which the student manifests such behavior can be considered as evidence of conditions unfavorable to learning, the same cannot be said of the teacher-behavior items. The final teacher-behavior checklist included an excess of items such as "stands behind desk, stands at board, stands at side, moves, leans on desk, sits on desk." Undoubtedly such items tended to be retained by the procedure because they could be observed reliably. On the other hand, some items were also retained that it seemed reasonable to suppose were highly related to the teaching process. Examples of these were "ignores student with hand up, smiles, demonstrates at board." The data demonstrate the tendency for highly reliable items of behavior that refer to gross bodily positions to be retained in checklists, whereas the more difficult to observe and more subtle aspects of teacher behavior tend to be omitted.

There is much to be learned from this. The principal lesson is that aspects of teacher behavior likely to be related to learning effectiveness may be difficult to identify and will probably have to be rated or assessed through instruments that the investigator has prepared after long and painful effort. This may mean that the researcher will have to experiment with recording numerous different aspects of behavior until those that can be reliably observed are identified. A satisfactory instrument for use in observing teacher behavior can be prepared only after prolonged effort.

Although the previous discussion was presented in order to illustrate the problems of preparing schedules and checklists for recording observations, it would be unfair to the reader not to present some of the consequences of the Morsh study. As might be expected, the items in the teacher-behavior checklist showed little relationship with the extent to which the students showed gains in achievement (corrected in terms of both their initial knowledge and relative level of ability). The difficulty of recording relevant aspects of teacher behavior are indicated by these results. The only alternative explanation would be that teacher behavior does not provide important variables in the teaching process. The latter just does not seem to be an acceptable hypothesis in terms of what is known about conditions affecting human learning.

In contrast, the behavior of the students as recorded on the checklist was indicative of the extent to which learning was taking place. This is, of course, entirely reasonable. Students who are yawning, dozing, or sleeping cannot be expected to be learning with any degree of effectiveness. Morsh draws the interesting conclusion that if the supervisor visiting the classroom wishes to make an assessment of the amount of subject-matter information that is being acquired by the student, he might do well to observe what the students are doing. Observable student behavior may provide more valid evidence of teacher effectiveness with respect to certain goals than can the information derived from the observation of teacher behavior. When we learn what aspects of teacher behavior to observe in this connection, this statement perhaps may need modification.

The Morsh study has been presented here because it illustrates some of the precautions that must be taken and the care that must be exercised in developing observation schedules. It also reflects the fact that the screening process may eliminate from consideration all but the most trivial of observations. When this happens, the researcher should not be content to pursue his inquiry with the reliable but trivial. He has a choice of making another attempt to observe relevant events or of dropping the investigation.

Some Characteristics of Observational Procedures

Many different procedures for collecting and handling data that involve the observation of behavior are available. Some procedures involve the collection of raw data that is later classified and analyzed. If behavior has to be classified into many categories, there are substantial advantages in obtaining a record of the behavior to be observed. Later, the record is studied and the events it presents can be placed in categories or scored in some way. Sound recordings, videotape recordings and motion pictures all have been used for recording information about the classroom. Sometimes the services of a stenographer have been used. None of these procedures is entirely satisfactory. Sound recordings are often difficult to decipher because the noise level is typically high in relation to the loudness of the spoken word that one may desire to receive. Also, if the research worker wishes at some later date to determine which words were spoken by which person, not even the teacher may be able to recognize the voices of pupils sufficiently well to identify the sources of particular communications. The employment of a stenographer does not entirely overcome this difficulty, partly because he will experience difficulty in keeping track of thirty or more names and partly because several communications may occur at the same time. The problems of recording classroom events are far from solved. The alternative procedure is to observe classroom events on a limited scale and classify them as they occur. What a teacher says to particular pupils may thus be classified into a set of categories, provided the number of categories is limited. The problem to be solved is that of setting up a data-collection system that does not overwhelm the observer. Thus it may be necessary to limit observation to the interaction between the teacher and the particular pupil with whom he interacts. Time sampling is often particularly helpful. The observer may be instructed to observe and classify only the first activity the teacher undertakes after the beginning of each minute. If the activities of pupils are to be observed, then the activities of only certain pupils may be selected for observation.

The first decision in designing an observation device is to establish whether the observer is only to record observations or whether he is to observe and classify the events observed. The decision depends on such factors as the number of categories into which the observations are to be classified and whether the observer will have enough time to classify the events while in the observation situation. A second related decision that the person preparing an observation schedule must also face is whether the events to be observed are to cover a wide range of classroom activities or whether they are to be derived from only a limited range of situations. For example, one observation schedule known as the OScAR covers all the major broad categories of events that are believed to be related to pupil learning in the elementary school. In contrast, a device developed by B. O. Smith and M. O. Meux (1965) is concerned only with teaching events that can be assumed to be related to the development of concepts during teaching. Devices that are limited in scope are often applicable only when the teacher is willing to teach a particular lesson. Instruments broad in scope have commonly been developed in the past, perhaps because of the interest in obtaining a measure that might reflect general teaching ability. The fact that such enterprises have not been particularly successful has led recent workers to develop more limited devices that probe very restricted aspects of the teacher's performance.

For a review of devices that have been developed for the study of classroom situations, the reader is referred to I. J. Gordon's volume (1966) entitled *Studying the Child in School.*

Devices for Classifying and Recording Classroom Observations

A widely used instrument that has been carefully developed and that has considerable breadth and scope is a device developed by D. M. Medley and H. E. Mitzel (1958) known as the OScAR 2a.* The peculiar name is an abbreviation for *Observation Schedule and Record.* The authors of this device claim that it can be used by a relatively untrained observer, which gives it a considerable advantage over other devices. Let us consider an early version of this device, the 2a version, before discussing later revisions and elaborations. The reason for presenting the early version first is that it is still the version most widely used by research workers.

The essential core of the OScAR 2a is a fairly elaborate schedule on which observations are recorded. The observer begins by starting his stopwatch and entering in the Activity Section as many of the activities listed as he observes. This section includes such items as "pupil laughs" and "teacher works with individual pupil." The observer then turns to the Grouping Section in which he records the nature and size of the groups observed. In the Materials Section he records the equipment and learning aids available. In the Signs Section he records evidences indicative of the social climate of the classroom. He then records the elapsed time and resets the stopwatch to zero. The observer then records the subject matter area that received the most attention during the period of observation. Finally, the observer starts again and tallies statements the teacher makes in five categories: Pupil-supportive, Problem-structuring, Miscellaneous, Directive, Reproving. In addition, he records gestures of the teacher that might indicate affection, approval, hostility, or reproof. The total procedure also involves certain additional operations. Most studies involving the OScAR call for at least two separate visits to each classroom. The data thus collected are finally scored on fourteen scales:

1. Time spent on reading
2. Problem-structuring teacher statements

---

* The most recent version of this device, the OScAR 4V, is less well accepted by research workers and is less widely used.

3. Autonomous administrative groupings
4. Pupil-leadership activities
5. Freedom of movement
6. Manifest teacher hostility
7. Supportive teacher behavior
8. Time spent on social studies
9. Disorderly pupil behavior
10. Verbal activities
11. Traditional pupil activities
12. Teacher's verbal output
13. Audiovisual materials
14. Autonomous social groupings

A factor analysis has demonstrated that the fourteen keys serve mainly to measure three variables, which are described as emotional climate, verbal emphasis, and social structure.

The more recent version of the instrument, the OScAR 4V, shows both the fruits of years of careful thinking and added complexity. The categories of behavior in this latter version have been increased to fifty, all of them fitting into a system, but this increase calls on the observer to make a detailed analysis of teacher behavior and its consequences while sitting in the classroom. This version of the instrument would seem to provide a device that could be used only by those who had been given extensive training in its application. Although this is a serious disadvantage, one also has to bear in mind that the more complex observation schedules are generally those based on a more rigorous analysis of the problem and that, hence, they are also more likely to yield data of significance.

Many devices for use in classroom research lack, as a foundation, any careful analysis of the teaching task. One device, against which this criticism *cannot* be leveled, is that by M. M. Hughes (1959) which is, beyond any question, based on the most careful and systematic thought concerning the nature of teaching. Hughes regards the dynamics of effective teaching as being extremely complex and, hence, classroom data must be collected and analyzed in terms of a complex framework. She sees the classification of classroom events as involving an extremely difficult task—much too difficult to be undertaken on the spur of the moment while the observer sits in the classroom. In order to use her system, data are first collected by an observer or tape recorder and these data are restricted to verbal interactions between teacher and pupil. The original data, on which the device was extensively used, were collected under standardized conditions, in that the teacher taught a particular lesson. The data collected by observers is then divided into units referred to as teaching acts that are then classified into categories. Although Hughes has developed quite detailed descriptions of what does and does not belong in each category, we can present here only the briefest description of the categories as follows:

1. Structures
2. Regulates
3. Sets standards
4. Judges
5. Admonishes
6. Reprimands
7. Accuses
8. Refuses request
9. Checks
10. Demonstrates
11. Clarifies procedure
12. Informs (not requested by pupil)
13. Acts as resource person on request of pupil
14. Stimulates by offering alternatives to pupil
15. Clarifies idea
16. Interprets (a more detailed process than clarification)
    a. Interprets feelings (emphasizes)
17. Evaluates
18. Supports (praises, reinforces positively)
    a. Support (stereotyped as in saying "Thank you")
19. Solicitous (shows concern for welfare of pupil)
20. Encourages
21. Does something for (highly personal rather than connected with class work)
22. Moralizes
23. Verbal (brush off)

The classification system is extraordinarily comprehensive, but requires the most painstaking effort for its proper application. The fact that it is based on a theory of teaching gives encouragement for its future utility.

Many variations can be introduced into the procedures used for collecting classroom observational data and the categories involved. H. V. Perkins (1964, 1965) has developed a procedure for assessing the classroom behavior of students and teachers that overlaps considerably the Hughes device in the categories used but involves a fundamentally different method of collecting the data on which the assessment is made. Perkins' device does not appear to have been based on any careful analysis of the characteristics of the teaching act that facilitate or inhibit learning but rather on a compilation of the ideas of others. It does, however, reintroduce into education a recording device, known as the Bales-Gerbrands recorder (1948). In the application of this device, one source of behavior is observed and studied at a time.

The Bales-Gerbrands device consists of a box with a narrow vertical slit across the lid with paper moving at a constant speed behind the slit. The categories of behavior that are to be recorded are listed in a column beside the slit. Suppose that during a particular two-minute interval the schedule of observation calls for the observing of the behavior of a particular pupil whom we designate as John. Let us suppose also that, at the beginning of the observation period, John is seen daydreaming. In order to record this fact, the point of the pencil is pressed against the moving paper in the slit opposite the category "Withdrawal." As the paper moves, the pencil leaves a line on the paper. If John continues to daydream for one minute, then the length of the line drawn represents one minute. If at the end of the minute John stops daydreaming and begins to chat with his neighbor about what he did last weekend, then the pencil point is moved opposite the category "Social, friendly." The point then begins to draw a line representing the length of time that the pupil continues to engage in this category of behavior. This recording system can be used only when there are a limited number of categories and when the classification of behaviors can be made almost instantaneously by the observer.

The only system for collecting and categorizing classroom events that has had any extensive tryout is that by N. Flanders (1962). The system has been used by him and others in a virtually unchanged form for over a decade.

Flanders collects data on classroom interactions by using trained observers who classify verbal behavior occurring during each three-second period. The statements are classified into the following categories:

1. Clarify feeling constructively
2. Praise or encourage
3. Clarify, develop, or make use of
   ideas suggested by students

Teacher talk 4. Ask questions

        5. Lecture
        6. Give directions
        7. Criticize

Student talk   8. Student talk in response to the teacher
        9. Student talk initiated by the student

      10. Silence or confusion

From the record, which consists of a set of numbers entered by the observer at the rate of one every three seconds, one can tabulate the frequency with which each one of the events occurs. The data-collection procedure obviously requires the use of trained observers because of the speed with which it occurs. It also involves a very crude system of broad categories and little of the pedagogical sophistication that characterizes the Hughes system.

The data permit an analysis of the ongoing classroom teacher-pupil processes. This is done by preparing what is referred to as the *matrix*, which consists of a table with ten vertical columns and ten horizontal rows, as shown in Figure 3.

Category	1	2	3	4	5	6	7	8	9	10
1. Clarify Feeling Constructively	—	—	—	—	0.4	—	0.1	0.1	—	0.1
2. Praise or Encourage	—	0.9	1.8	0.9	2.5	—	0.1	0.2	0.9	1.0
3. Clarify, Develop or Make Use of Ideas Suggested by Students	—	0.9	27.8	11.0	20.3	1.7	0.5	4.3	9.9	8.5
4. Ask Questions	0.1	0.1	0.2	13.5	4.4	1.0	0.4	36.5	11.5	3.0
5. Lecture	0.6	1.1	1.6	25.5	440.3	5.1	3.2	0.3	14.7	9.7
6. Give Directions	—	0.1	0.1	1.7	5.5	10.4	1.1	1.7	1.6	6.4
7. Criticize	—	0.1	0.1	1.4	3.6	1.0	9.6	0.4	0.4	2.9
8. Student Talk in Response to the Teacher	—	2.3	16.9	9.1	8.7	1.7	0.7	63.0	3.0	2.8
9. Student Talk Initiated by the Student	—	2.6	35.5	3.8	6.9	0.9	0.9	0.4	45.9	4.1
10. Silence or Confusion	0.1	0.3	0.9	3.7	9.6	6.7	2.7	1.3	13.1	37.4
Total	0.7	8.4	84.8	70.7	502.2	28.6	19.5	108.1	101.2	75.8

per 1000 tallies

N= 13,593

FIGURE 3. *Interaction matrix for content centered social studies teachers, N = 3 adjusted for 1,000 tallies.* (Data from Flanders, 1962, p. 116.)

In this matrix the ten columns and the ten rows correspond to the ten categories of observed behavior. The purpose of the matrix is to permit the tallying of the recorded events in pairs. This is done by taking the first pair of events, which might have been recorded in categories 6 and 9. Such a pair of events would be tallied in the cell where row 6 intersects with column 9. Then the next pair of events is tallied. This pair would be the event classified as 9 and the event that followed it. These are tallied in the same way—and so the analysis is continued. Because this may become a very tedious process when thousands of events have to be tallied, the material is best handled by a computer.

An examination of the matrix indicates some of the characteristics of the teaching process as observed. For example, in the case of the matrix given as an illustration, any period of lecturing by the teacher is most likely to be followed by more lecturing. In only 8.25 per cent of the cases does a comment by the teacher stimulate the student to make a verbal contribution to the class. In the case of this particular classroom for which the data are provided, a little more than 70 per cent of the time is occupied by teacher verbal activities and only about 21 per cent by pupil verbal activities. Very little verbal activity is initiated by the pupils, and more than half of the pupils' verbal activity is in direct response to the verbal activity of the teacher. The classroom is conducted along traditional lines, the teacher holding forth and the pupils supposedly absorbing knowledge.

A very comprehensive study has been made by W. D. Coats (1966a, 1966b) of the relationship between the measures derived from the Flanders type of interaction analysis and measures of attitude and achievement. The study generally confirms the opinion that the inter-action-analysis procedure does *not* produce measures of variables that are causally related to achievement. In the Coats study, some small relationships were found between achievement measures and measures derived from the interaction-analysis procedure, but these relationships appear to be artifacts. A worthwhile lesson in the interpretation of research data can be had by considering how such artifacts could occur. In examining this problem let us begin with the well-known fact that a measure of IQ is both a predictor of achievement and also a predictor of the ability of the pupil to engage in an academic dialogue. Now let us suppose that research demonstrates that a measure of pupil-teacher interaction, represented by the amount of expansive dialogue taking place between a pupil and a teacher, is also related to the achievement of the pupil (a large amount of dialogue being related to high achievement). One is immediately tempted to interpret the latter finding by saying that, obviously, constructive dialogue between the teacher and the pupil is an important factor contributing to pupil achievement; but this interpretation is almost certainly incorrect. A more reasonable interpretation is that the high-achieving pupils are those with whom the teacher can most readily engage in dialogue. In the Coats study, the only variables derived from interaction analysis that show even a small relationship to achievement are those that are related to measures of IQ. Whatever is measured by the Flanders interaction-analysis procedure has little to do with pupil achievement.

The instruments considered up to this point were designed for the purpose of providing a blanket coverage of events of the classroom that the author of each instrument considered to be of critical importance for facilitating or inhibiting the learning of pupils. Other instruments have been developed that concentrate either on certain limited aspects of classroom phenomena or on events believed to be related to particular outcomes.

An early device that limited the scope of observations to the verbal behavior of the teacher was developed by J. Withall (1949) who made the assumption that the verbal behavior of the teacher represented the most important single class of events in the classroom related to pupil learning. The application of Withall's technique requires that the statements made by the teacher be sampled in some way to ensure that those recorded are representative of the utterances of the teacher. Once they have been recorded—and this is done at the time of observation in the classroom—they are available for later classification, which can be undertaken by persons who were not involved in the original recording process. The reliability of the classification procedure can then be determined. The system of classification of verbal behavior proposed by Withall uses the following categories:

1. Learner-supportive statements given with the intent of reassuring or commending the pupil.
2. Acceptant and clarifying statements conveying to the pupil that he was understood or to help him gain insight.
3. Problem-structuring statements or questions.
4. Neutral statements comprising polite formalities, administrative comments, verbatim repetition of what has already been said.
5. Direct or exhortative statements requiring the pupil to follow a recommended course of action.
6. Reproving or deprecating comments.

7. Teacher self-supporting remarks justifying the teacher's position or course of action.

Some of the advantages of the Withall technique over the more familiar observational and rating techniques should be pointed out here: It permits the summation of scores derived from a great number of behaviors. In this way, it is possible to build up reliable scores from a great variety of classroom events. The work and thought of categorizing behavior, which may occupy so much of the time of an observer in the classroom as to detract from his observations, is undertaken at leisure after the observations are made. The technique also recognizes the overwhelmingly important role played by verbal behavior in structuring events in the classroom, a fact that has been commonly overlooked in most observational techniques.

The Withall categories do not focus on cognitive learning but are centered on problems of motivation and reinforcement. More recent classifications of verbal behavior in the classroom have tended to use categories that are related to the teacher's role in the intellectual development of the pupil. Those of A. A. Bellack (1965) and Smith and Meux (1965) concentrate on this aspect of education.

Bellack approaches the study of verbal behavior in the classroom by viewing the interactions involved as a performance similiar to that involved in a game—a notion he states is derived from the philosopher Wittgenstein. The verbal interplay is a game insofar as one can consider a statement made by a pupil or teacher to represent a move that is made with the expectation that the person toward whom it is directed will make another particular kind of statement or move. The game is played according to certain rules. An example of an implicit rule is that when the teacher asks the pupil a question, the pupil's correct move is to answer the question. Bellack classifies pedagogical moves into four categories:

1. *Structuring.* Moves that set the context for what happens next; as when a teacher draws attention to a topic or problem to be discussed.
2. *Soliciting.* Moves that elicit directly a verbal response from those toward whom they are directed; these include questions and commands.
3. *Responding.* This is the response to a soliciting move; a student's answer to a question falls into this category.
4. *Reacting.* These moves are occasioned by the other moves but are

not directly related to them; a teacher's evaluation of a pupil's response is an example of a move in this category.

Bellack points out that the moves tend to occur in cycles beginning with a structuring move and ending with a reacting move. In addition, he classifies each statement in terms of the nature of the meaning it conveys.

The classification of teaching episodes developed originally by B. O. Smith and elaborated on by Smith and Meux (1965) is of particular interest because it departs from a fundamentally different viewpoint from any previous classification system. The classification is based on the nature of knowledge and the development of knowledge in a learning situation rather than on the nature of the learner. In a sense, the classification system represents the approach of the epistemologist and philosopher rather than that of the psychologist or behavioral scientist. The system is used for classifying what are termed *episodes* in teaching. These generally involve an interaction between pupil and teacher and typically begin with a question. An inspection of the following categories used by Smith and Meux brings out this point:

1. *Defining.* This category refers to episodes in which words and other symbols are related to objects and events.
2. *Describing.* This category refers to the naming of attributes of particular objects or events or giving an account of what happened.
3. *Designating.* These are episodes in which an object or event is named, as when the teacher asks, "Tell me which figure is an isosceles triangle" and the pupil points to the appropriate figure.
4. *Stating.* These episodes involve questions that call for an answer to be given in the form of a statement.
5. *Reporting.* These episodes call for a report on some happening or document.
6. *Substituting.* In these episodes the student is asked to perform an operation with symbols in which one symbol is substituted for another.
7. *Evaluating.* This category is self-explanatory.
8. *Opining.* In this category a conclusion is drawn but the conclusion is not fully warranted in terms of the available facts. An episode involving the question "How effective is the United Nations Organization?" would fall into this category.

9. *Classifying.* The general intent of this category is fairly clear.
10. *Comparing and Contrasting.* In this category two or more events or things are compared.
11. *Conditional Inferring.* These episodes involve the student being presented with an "If this . . ." kind of statement from which he must give a "then that . . ." kind of statement. In some of the episodes included in this category, the student is given a conclusion and he is asked to judge whether the conclusion is, or is not, true.
12. *Explaining.* This is quite a complicated category because Smith and Meux make a distinction between mechanical explaining, causal explaining, sequent explaining, procedural explaining, teleological explaining, and normative explaining.
13. *Directing and Managing Classroom.* These episodes include those that have little or no logical significance but are designed to keep the classroom activities moving along in an orderly manner.

Smith and Meux found that substantial differences existed in the frequency of each category of episodes in different subject-matter fields. They also found that there were differences between teachers in this respect. Much still has to be learned from this promising technique, which may well indicate the kinds of logical developments that are most effective in promoting organized learning.

Pupils as Classroom Observers

Attempts have been made to enlist pupils in the task of determining the nature of classroom events generally through the use of a questionnaire. The advantage of this technique is that it may throw light on the pupil's perception of the characteristics of classroom activities and such perceptions could, conceivably, be much more important than the perceptions of an adult observer.

The earliest devices used for this purpose were developed by W. A. McCall (1937, 1941) at Columbia University, Teachers College, in cooperation with the professional staff of the Board of Education of the City of New York. These devices were developed for the purpose of determining the extent to which the introduction of a new curriculum had actually changed classroom practices. For this purpose a "School Practices Questionnaire" was developed for use in grades 1–9. Later, as a result of experience with this questionnaire, a similar device was developed for use at the junior and senior high school levels, titled

"Comprehensive Curriculum Tests." The *School Practices Question-naire* included such items as

1. "In the last four weeks did the teacher usually give you work to do that was the same for all the class?"
2. "In the last four weeks did you help decide important things on most school days?"
3. "In the last four weeks did the school help you do anything you wanted to do?"

A more recent device, which attempts to use pupils as observers, has been developed by M. L. Cogan and was used as a part of a series of researches (Cogan 1953, 1958). The Cogan device carries the inno cent title of *Pupil Survey* and covers a great many areas in which the teacher relates to the pupil. The first section of the survey relates to the kind of homework assignments given the pupil by a particular teacher. The second section covers "extra things you may do, not counting assigned homework." The third section contains eighty ques-tions covering a wide range of matters including how often the teacher loses her temper, the orderliness of the class, the extent to which the teacher allows the pupil to exercise choice, and the punctuality of the teacher.

The main scales derived from the items pertaining to teacher be-havior are described by Cogan (1958) as follows:

I. Inclusive
    A. Integrative
    B. Affiliative
    C. Nurturant
II. Preclusive
    A. Dominative
    B. Aggressive
    C. Rejectant
III. Conjunctive
    A. Level of demand made on the pupils
    B. Ability to communicate
    C. Competence in classroom management

The three terms, *inclusive, preclusive,* and *conjunctive,* are each described by the categories that fall under them.

The devices of this kind have not reached the point where the developers agree that there are certain variables that can be profitably measured by them. Indeed, each new one developed seems to present a new set of categories reflecting the fact that there is little knowledge available concerning what can be profitably measured. Contrast, for example, the scales used by Cogan in developing his device with those used by D. M. Medley and A. A. Klein (1957). The pupil inventory developed by the latter researchers provides four scales of measurement. First, there is the *halo scale* designed to reflect the feelings that the pupils have for the teacher. The scale reflects the extent to which the pupil enjoys the class and feels that it provides opportunities for him to develop. The second scale, the *disorder scale*, reflects the extent to which there is orderliness or chaos in the classroom. The scale places emphasis on the extent to which there is disruptive activity such as teasing, showing off, or wasting time because no work had been assigned. A permissive classroom in which pupils go about their work in a free atmosphere would score as an orderly class. The third scale, the *supportive scale*, can well be described as reflecting the extent to which the teacher avoids negative reinforcement, utilizes positive reinforcement, and provides feedback. The fourth scale, the *traditionalism scale*, indicates the degree to which the class is run along traditional lines, in contrast to modern lines with a considerable emphasis on individualized instruction. In the case of this instrument, as with others, there is not too much evidence that the responses of the pupils are related to objectively identifiable categories of events in the classroom. Medley and Klein provide a little evidence by showing that the scores on the disorder scale are related to the observations made by adult visitors to the classroom. A point to note in this connection is that L. M. Heil and C. W. Washburne (1962) found that orderliness and good organization on the part of the teacher were related to the academic achievement of the pupils.

SUMMARY

1. The observation of behavior in the classroom and in other complex situations usually requires the use of observation schedules.

2. Observation schedules should include no more items than the observer can remember and easily locate on the list. The schedule should usually refer to items of behavior that occur with fair frequency. It should also be easy to recognize when an item of behavior has, or has not, occurred.

3. Observation schedules should be based on a theory concerning

the relevance of the items of behavior observed to the purposes of the study.

4. The student should be on guard against a procedure for selecting items that results in the retaining of those that are highly reliable but rather inconsequential. A checklist type of schedule may be quite unsuitable for the purpose of assessing the more subtle aspects of classroom phenomena, and the latter may have to be appraised in terms of the general impressions of the observer. The latter is a practice that research workers have strenuously attempted to avoid.

5. Procedures for handling classroom data can be designed so that both the collection of observations and their classification takes place at the same time or so that the collection of observations takes place first and their classification second.

6. Many instruments have been developed for the classification of classroom observations. The most systematically developed of these in terms of a theory of instruction is that of Hughes. Another approach is represented by the device of Smith and Meux, which has been developed in terms of a theory of the structure of knowledge. A theory of the structure of knowledge is closely related to a theory of teaching. The nature of knowledge must determine, to some extent, the nature of teaching. A third type of model for the analysis of classroom data is found in the work of Bellack, who views the verbal interactions of the classroom as representing a game.

7. One of the most widely used devices is the OScAR 2a. Although the authors of this device have produced a number of later revisions, the simplicity of the 2a version has continued to make it attractive to research workers.

8. The Hughes system of classifying classroom observations differs from the OScAR in many respects, one of the most important of which is that the classifying of the observations is *not* made at the time when the observations are recorded. The Hughes system also has the virtue of having been built on the basis of a thorough psychological analysis of teaching. Although it is much more tedious to apply than other systems it may have important advantages.

9. Some effort has been made to introduce mechanical instruments that will facilitate the recording of classroom observations. Perkins use of the Bales-Gerbrands recorder is an example of an attempt to do this.

10. Flanders' system of interaction analysis still continues to be widely used despite the fact that it has not been very successful in yielding knowledge about classroom phenomena. The data derived

from this system are easily misinterpreted and often have been in the past.

11. Other devices have been developed to explore more specific aspects of classroom phenomena. Withall's technique provides an analysis of the verbal behavior of the teacher. Smith and Meux have developed a system for recording and analyzing the logical development of ideas and concepts in the classroom.

12. Pupils have sometimes been enlisted as classroom observers, and schedules have been developed on which they can record their observations. Such schedules have the advantage of providing information concerning the way in which the pupil views the learning situation. The pupil's perception may well be different from that of an adult observer.

‖‖‖‖‖‖‖‖‖‖‖‖‖‖‖‖‖‖‖‖‖‖‖‖‖

CHAPTER 9

Survey Methods

RESEARCH THROUGH SURVEYS

Common Survey Problems

SURVEYS are conducted to establish the nature of existing conditions. A school survey is commonly conducted in order to determine which services the school can render its community or perhaps to compare these services with those that are provided by other schools.

A distinction must be made between a survey and sample survey. In a sample survey, data are collected about only a portion of the events with which the surveyor is concerned. The design of the sample survey is such that the events examined provide data from which inferences can be made about all of the events. Thus an examination of one hundred rural high schools within a particular state may permit the making of inferences about conditions in the other five hundred.

The survey is an attempt to build a body of knowledge through the use of direct observation, but direct observation is probably limited in the knowledge it can produce. Chemistry and physics could not have been produced by merely observing naturally occurring chemical reactions, and even wise men were unsuccessful at achieving understanding of human nature by observing the behavior of their fellow humans. Not only chemistry and physics, but also psychology, required for their advancement the development of experimental procedures to supplement observation before even limited understanding could be achieved. Direct observation, even in its more sophisticated form, represented by the survey method, is limited in the knowledge it can achieve. Nevertheless, there are many situations in which experimentation is impossible or impractical, and the survey method can help us to achieve understanding under such circumstances.

The events or conditions that may be enumerated or measured during surveys include a great range of phenomena. The popularity of the public opinion survey as a newspaper feature makes one think of attitudes and opinions as the main source of data in surveys, but this is not necessarily so. Various classes of events that may form the central core of an educational survey must be given brief mention here.

Physical conditions related to learning. Many characteristics of the physical environment can be measured, such as the floor space per pupil in different schools, the number of books per pupil in the library, the intensity of the natural illumination on the pupil's desk, the mean temperature or humidity, and the like. Many school surveys devote considerable effort to the measurement and evaluation of such characteristics of a school program, and on the surface they would appear to be on a solid foundation; for it is clear that the *measurement* of these variables is objective and does not involve the judgment of the investigator. These measures have satisfactory reliability, and thus their weakness is not at first apparent. The inadequacies of the procedure are a result of the fact that its usefulness depends on the choice of suitable environmental variables—that is to say, variables that are genuinely related to the effectiveness of learning of the pupil. But very little is known concerning the relationship of such variables to learning processes in pupils. If the student looks back over research in the area, he is likely to find, not only little positive evidence to help in the selection of variables, but much negative evidence indicating the apparent lack of relevance of many variables he might choose. Such studies may have failed to demonstrate the relevance of some of these physical variables because any effect they may have is perhaps long-term and not sufficient in magnitude to manifest consequences over a period of a few weeks or even a semester. Long-term studies of the effect of these physical conditions are rarely feasible.

Behavior of teachers and other behavioral conditions related to learning. Numerous studies have been conducted that attempt to determine what teachers do in the classroom or how they spend their time. Some of these studies serve the purpose of providing data necessary for rethinking and redesigning classroom procedures to make more effective use of the time available. For example, if it is found that, say, 50 per cent of the teacher's time is devoted to minor administrative routines, then some steps can be taken to eliminate these routines.

Much of the data derived from surveys of teacher behavior in classrooms has been used for scientific purposes such as that of attempting to identify major variables in terms of which the complexities of teacher behavior can be conveniently and compactly described. For example, D. G. Ryans (1960) undertook extensive observations of the behavior of teachers for the purpose of identifying some dimensions of teacher behavior. From a statistical analysis of such data he was able to tease out three major characteristics as follows:

Pattern X_0—Warm, understanding, friendly vs. aloof, egocentric restricted teacher behavior

Pattern Y_0—Responsible, businesslike, systematic vs. evading, unplanned, slipshod teacher behavior

Pattern Z_0—Stimulating, imaginative, surgent vs. dull, routine, teacher behavior

Pupil achievement. Surveys that are most likely to reveal facts of importance for educational administration are those provided by the pupils themselves. Such information has direct relevance to the control and study of the learning process that the other classes of facts revealed by surveys do not. Another chapter in this volume is devoted entirely to observation procedures that may be used to conduct surveys of pupil-teacher interactions in classrooms. In addition, surveys may be made regarding the reading achievement of pupils or their achievement in other so-called basic skills. Sometimes surveys of the information of the pupils may be made, as when a school determines what the pupils know or do not know about their local community, about health practices, about contemporary affairs, or about some other matter judged to be of significance in the educational program. Such surveys need not be confined to matters of student knowledge but may also include events in the attitudinal field.

A new venture in surveys emerging on the scene is the National Assessment Program. At the time of writing this it is perhaps the most controversial educational innovation of recent years. Because this program poses certain technical problems that will have to be overcome if it is to bring success with it, a brief discussion of these problems is in order here despite the fact that the program has not, as yet, gone very far.

Like many other innovations of recent years, this program appears to have been developed through the initiative of a large philanthropic foundation, in this case the Carnegie Foundation. Although during the fifties, the Ford Foundation was on the forefront of educational innovation, this same role was taken over by the Carnegie Foundation during the sixties. There is no question that both of these large and financially well-supported organizations were instrumental in producing extensive innovation during their decades of power, but there remains substantial controversy over whether they were effective in producing educational progress. Innovation and progress often belong to different worlds. The concern of the Carnegie Foundation for educational change seems to have been generated by the president of the foundation, John Gardner, who became Secretary of the Department of Health, Education, and Welfare. Gardner's book on the topic of excellence in education (1961) reflects his interest in the problem of educational assessment. Through money provided by the Foundation, a group was formed to consider the problem of developing a procedure for obtaining information concerning the current state of academic achievement of students in the schools of the United States. The central idea was that such an assessment, undertaken periodically, would perform a function analogous to that of the Public Health Service, which collects information periodically on the health of the population. The analogy is probably not a good one, but it has been widely cited by those sponsoring the program.

The analogy with the Public Health Service is far flung and misleading. When the Public Health Service finds that there has been an increase in, say, malaria in a particular district, remedial measures can be introduced to prevent the spread of the causative agent. Because the causes of malaria are well established, knowledge is available that can be applied to the solution of the problem turned up by a health survey. On the other hand, if a National Assessment survey showed that children in a particular locality were deficient, as compared with children elsewhere, in some of the critical skills involved in reading, one could probably find as many remedies as there are experts and none of the proposed remedies would be backed up by any substantial body of established knowledge. The discovery of deficiencies in education is very readily undertaken either by National Assessment programs or by the less formal means of the "arm chair reformer." But what is the use of turning up deficiencies if remedies are not available. Energy diverted into the discovery of remedies for the more obvious deficiencies in student achievement is much more likely to have payoff over the years than energy devoted to assessment. The analogy with the Public Health Service is dangerously misleading, partly because it is so attractive.

The concept of national educational assessment has still another, and far more serious flaw, connected with its development. Claims have been made that the data provided by such an assessment will permit the making of such a statement as, "Eighty per cent of 15-year olds in high schools were able to read and understand an editorial from a newspaper." Although this reads like a nice clear statement concerning the educational achievement of the country as a whole, what does it really mean? Let us suppose it refers to a particular editorial that was presented to a representative sample of 15-year olds in high school and that the editorial was followed by a number of multiple-choice test questions. Let us suppose also that 80 per cent answered all the questions correctly. In a sense it can be said that this 80 per cent understood the editorial, until somebody points out that the questions did not cover the subtle points of the editorial and, hence, gave a false picture of level of comprehension. On the other hand, it might happen that the questions did cover the extremely subtle points, in which case some would say that the test was really too difficult and that a greater number understood the editorial than the statistics seemed to show. The statement made about the level of comprehension of the 15-year olds is not a meaningful statement. In fact, it is quite meaningless.

Then there is another problem. From a knowledge of how much understanding the pupils displayed of the particular editorial, can any inferences be made about how the pupils would respond to other editorials? Probably not, for editorials differ enormously in content, in complexity of language structure, in length, in vocabulary, and in other features. The selection of an editorial that is representative of all editorials is probably an impossible task. All one could find out by the administration of a single editorial to a group of 15-year olds would be something about how they responded to that particular editorial, and not much at that. The administration of a more extensive series of editorials does not overcome all the difficulties involved.

Then again, even if a representative group of editorials were administered, and if the difficulties related to the adjustment of the difficulty of the test items were somehow met, nothing much of use would have been learned. Because little is known about the conditions that produce deficiencies in the reading skills involved, little could be recommended to remedy any deficiencies found.

There are many areas in which survey techniques can be appropriately and productively applied, but surveys of pupil achievement very rarely produce knowledge of any value to education.

Surveys of Aptitude. Considerable interest has been stirred in recent years by a large-scale survey of aptitudes conducted through an enterprise known as *Project Talent.* As a part of this survey, a very large and comprehensive battery of aptitude tests was administered to a cross section of high school students in the United States. A careful follow-up of a sample of these students permitted a great amount of useful information to be collected. For example, such a study permits one to find out the extent to which students with high-level talent fail to find jobs commensurate with their level of ability and, hence, a determination can be made of the degree to which talent is wasted in particular groups.

The data from Project Talent are so extensive that research workers outside the staff of the study have been encouraged to make use of the material. The library of information that has thus been made available will become the basis for many doctoral dissertations for years to come. Much of the data will also increase in scientific value as time goes by for it will provide a bench mark on the national utilization of talent against which the data from future surveys can be compared.

Pupil Attitude Surveys. An ambitious attempt to study pupil attitudes by survey methods is the Purdue Public Opinion Panel, which conducts an opinion poll in cooperating high schools, mainly at the junior and senior levels. Schools that participate pay a very small fee to help cover expenses and in return obtain a report on the responses of their own students as well as on the responses of a wider sample of pupils. Surveys conducted in this manner are usually related to matters of rather widespread interest, such as the attitude of pupils toward various aspects of the curriculum or toward their parents. The results serve the purpose of stimulating thought rather than that of solving specific problems.

Much of the material collected about pupils by means of surveys is collected through the medium of paper-and-pencil devices, but information about pupil behavior can sometimes be collected by other means. It is possible, for example, to obtain records of the number of books borrowed by each pupil from the library if a survey of reading is being made. The consumption of foods in the cafeteria can provide some evidence of eating habits in relation to health. Absentee rates are of considerable interest. Artistic products and other products of the pupils' hobbies can provide evidence of how leisure hours are spent. There is a wealth of objective pupil data that can be incorporated in a survey, data that do not derive from verbal responses of the pupils.

Survey Data and Subsequent Complex Analyses

Sometimes the results of surveys are presented in fairly simple tables that provide the needed information, but also they can lead to very complex analyses. For example, numerous surveys have been conducted related to the problem of determining the best routes for school buses to take. These data have generally been used in straightforward and commonsense ways by administrators to establish the routes that are optimum for the particular school districts involved. There are other uses for such data and an important one is to develop some general solution to the problem of locating bus routes in such a way that they minimize the loss of pupil time in transportation. N. A. Fattu (personal communication) has developed a generalized solution to this problem and, although the solution requires the use of a small amount of computer time, the advantages to be achieved by applying his solution might well outbalance the cost. The kind of utilization of survey data that Fattu has undertaken is an excellent example of how much can be achieved when survey data are placed in the hands of a person highly sophisticated in the use of modern scientific procedures.

The value of a survey depends greatly on the extent to which data are fully and properly analyzed. Many reports on surveys provide little useful information because the data were not sufficiently analyzed. For example, a survey was made of the use of various forms of punishment in schools. The report of the results included tables showing the distribution of the age of the teachers, the number of teachers at each grade level, and the frequency with which each form of punishment was used. The research worker should have further analyzed his data to show the relationship between the age of the teacher and the form of the punishment used and the relation of grade level to form of punishment. The data were underanalyzed.

TECHNICAL ISSUES IN THE CONDUCT OF SURVEYS

Surveys are mainly of the "what exists" type; that is to say they are designed to determine the nature of an existing state of affairs. They result in the accumulation of knowledge, but the survey technique runs into difficulties if one wishes to discover the kinds of conditions producing particular effects. For example, if in the survey of punishments used by teachers the data showed that the older teachers used fewer and different forms of punishment from the younger teachers, one would have difficulty in knowing what to make of this finding. Perhaps as the teacher ages, his views on education change and he alters his practices. This is one explanation. Another possibility is that the older teachers were trained differently from the modern teacher. Survey data generally does not permit us to choose between many different explanations of findings. Sometimes very extended research involving surveys can help us to choose one explanation rather than another, but the survey technique is not well designed for this kind of purpose. The simplest surveys attempt to discover only the frequency with which certain events occur, but to achieve much understanding one has to study the interrelationship among events. Thus we may identify at this point two general classes of survey that differ mainly in the complexity of design they involve and the depth of understanding they achieve.

The frequency-count survey. The best-known surveys of this sort are those designed to determine the number of persons in a group who expect to vote in a particular way at a forthcoming election. Schools may conduct surveys to determine how many children have received immunization shots of various kinds or how many teachers have M. A. degrees. Such surveys necessarily provide limited but often highly useful knowledge. However, they cannot be said to contribute in any way to an organized body of scientific knowledge about education.

The interrelationship-of-events type of survey. In many surveys, much more than a mere frequency count is sought; in addition, an attempt is made to find the interrelationship among events. Familiar studies of this type are those published by Dr. Gallup in which tabulations are shown of the voting preferences of adults split according to their socioeconomic level. Such surveys are usually based on some kind of theory concerning the interrelationship of events, and indeed should not be undertaken unless they are based on some fairly definite theory. It would be quite ridiculous to conduct a survey to discover the interrelationship of the physical characteristic of redheadedness and voting behavior. On the other hand, it would be quite reasonable to study the relationship between religious preference and party preference, for it is easy to see numerous reasons why there should be such a relationship. The study of such relationships is unlikely to provide direct evidence concerning causal relationships, and indeed they are extremely difficult to interpret. Although a particular religious affiliation, for example, may be related to preference for one of the major political parties, it is clearly unreasonable to conclude that the affiliation *causes* the individual to vote for, say Republican candidates. Yet it is clear that such a relationship, if well established, must be a result of complex causal relationships that may produce both phenomena. The survey itself is unlikely to establish the nature of these complexities.

The Role of Theory in Conducting Behavioral Surveys

Surveys of behavioral phenomena need to be most carefully planned if they are to yield useful data. The information-gathering process should be based on some theory of the nature of the phenomenon that is being investigated. In most cases this is likely to be a fairly complicated matter, and it may require very extensive information if answers are to be found to important questions. A classic case of a behavioral survey based on well-developed concepts and calling for a large number of items of information is the Kinsey study of sexual behavior in the human male. In this study, several hundred items of information were collected about each male included in the sample. The purpose of obtaining such extensive data was to be able to check and crosscheck a number of hypotheses concerning sexual behavior. The type of survey conducted by Kinsey contrasts with that conducted by Gallup and others whose data are published on a nation-wide basis through the newspapers. The latter type of survey collects a very limited amount of data about a matter of vital concern to the public. It is not designed for the purpose of developing understanding concerning the nature of voting behavior. Its usual purpose is to predict a particular event, such as the outcome of an election, and although the pollsters have come to realize that some understanding of voting behavior may contribute to the accuracy of prediction, this is a secondary and minor goal. In contrast, Kinsey was not concerned with keeping a newspaper column going. His interest was a scientific one, and its goal was that of providing an organized account of certain aspects of human behavior, with some attempt to discover interrelationships.

The theoretical framework used as a basis for a survey should, as far as possible, be stated as a theory, in the way outlined in earlier chapters. The limitation on this arises from the fact that surveys are commonly conducted in situations in which not much is known about the phenomena concerning which inquiry is made, and some of the data-collecting may be analogous to the grasping of a blind man in a new environment. The result of such grasping is the acquisition of information that will help him in developing a concept of the way in which his environment is arranged. The analogy does, of course, represent an extreme case, and the fact is that researchers, at least in their early years of development, would be most unwise to explore entirely unknown territory. They would be more likely to achieve positive results and to have a profitable learning experience if they were to conduct an inquiry into an area already partially explored and in which earlier workers had already developed concepts for use in understanding.

Where limited surveys are conducted, the theory involved should be stated in the simplest terms and should consist of no more than a single sentence. Perhaps a good beginning for the development of a conceptual framework is to recognize that a survey that accumulates data by asking questions and recording the answers is not just an easy process of obtaining information.

The matter of stating questions and obtaining answers is far from being the simple one that it is commonly believed to be. Perhaps all who have used this technique for collecting data during the past twenty years have shown a surprising naïveté in this respect. We owe a debt to J. W. Getzels (1954) for calling attention to our lack of sophistication.

Getzels has pointed out that, although numerous studies have been conducted to show that all kinds of conditions affect responses to visual patterns, no parallel research exists to describe conditions that affect responses in question-and-answer situations. He has borrowed a number of concepts from the field of perception to build a model that attempts to account for variations in the answers given to the same questions as the situation in which the question asked is changed. According to the model provided by Getzels, the asking of a question first produces an internal response, which is not verbalized. This immediate response is, in a sense, an answer to the question, and it is described as the *personal hypothesis* in this theory. Secondly, responses are made to various aspects of the situation in which the responses occurs. This is referred to as the stage in which the demands of the situation are sized up in terms of the individual's personal adjustment to that situation. Thirdly the individual formulates a response that will facilitate his adjustment to the total situation.

According to this theory, there would be a tendency for the respondent to reply to a question in such a way that his answer reflects what he perceives to be an appropriate response to that situation—

that is to say, he answers in the way that he believes is expected of him.

The point here is that a theory to be used as a basis for a survey involving verbal responses must take into account the adjustments that are made between interviewer and interviewee. This complicates considerably the theory requirements for this type of work and recognizes at the outset that data thus collected cannot be taken at face value.

At a minimum level of development, a theory must postulate the ways in which the phenomena can be measured. If various methods of measurements are possible, then there should be some statement of how these measures are related to one another. For example, if a survey is being made of parental disciplinary actions in the home, one might postulate that the parents' account of frequency of disciplinary action should be related to the child's account. If the two accounts are unrelated, then the data are quite probably worthless. One might also postulate that a more truthful answer would be given if a parent were asked to indicate what he thought would be the best way to handle a common behavior problem than if he were asked how he would handle his own child.

A theory on which a survey is based must usually postulate the relationships of the phenomena investigated to possible causes. In the case of the disciplinary behavior of parents, a survey would be a barren and dull affair if it stopped at the point of finding out how frequently parents inflicted different types of punishment on their children. The investigator would almost certainly want to know something about the characteristics that differentiated parents who punished frequently from those who punished rarely. To do this, it would be necessary to construct a theory of the determinants of punishing behavior. This theory would then form the basis of the inquiry.

A theory on which a survey is based must have something to say about the specificity or generality of the phenomenon that is to be surveyed. If the behavior of parents is being surveyed concerning the extent to which they attempt to exercise control over the behavior of their children, it is important to know whether the phenomenon is a general one; that is to say, it is important to know whether a parent who exercises extensive control in one area of child activity also tends to exercise control in other areas. If no information is available concerning this matter, then the survey must be conducted so that it samples the various areas of parental control and provides information concerning them. Unless such information is given, the results of the survey will have little meaning.

Types of Data Collected in Behavioral Surveys

The data collected in surveys may vary in the degree to which they represent directly the phenomena in which the surveyors are interested. The collection of data directly about behavior relevant for an educational survey is difficult to achieve. Examples of such data are found in many studies—as, for example, those in which pupils' food choices in the school cafeteria have been studied. This can be done by direct observation, and such a procedure is obviously much superior to that of asking the pupils what they will eat or have eaten. Spelling behavior may be surveyed by the inspection of samples of pupils' work. There is some evidence, incidentally, that the latter procedure provides information superior to that which can be derived from spelling achievement tests. Such data, however, represent only the most fragmentary records of a person's behavior in a particular area. It is possible, if not probable, that deplorable deficiencies manifested by pupils in their choice of food in the school cafeteria can be justified in terms of their diet over an entire day. This sample of behavior, like most samples of directly recorded behavior, is too restricted and narrow to provide much useful information concerning the total eating habits of the pupils. Most surveys that attempt to obtain data directly without resorting to the collection of verbal reports suffer from this defect. This does not mean that observational techniques of the types previously discussed cannot yield valuable data and form the basis of worthwhile research, for they can.

A second source of data for surveys about behavior is found in existing records. Previous school grades and test records are examples of such data. Comparisons of the performance on tests administered at the same level but ten or twenty years apart represent a particularly interesting use of this technique. There is a very substantial body of data in most school systems about pupil personnel and teacher personnel to form the data of useful surveys. A word of caution should be injected here. Such data often include gross inaccuracies as a result of clerical errors made at the time they were recorded. Further discussion of this matter will be presented later.

Because the collection of data about behavioral phenomena for the purpose of conducting surveys must involve mainly a question-and-answer procedure, it is necessary at this time to discuss the matter of formulating questions. The design of the questions to be used has come to be recognized as a matter of crucial importance in the planning of surveys. Suggestions for the design of questions can now be found in many sources. The reader is referred to sources such as H. Cantril

(1947), M. B. Parten (1950), and C. H. Backstrom and G. D. Hursh (1963).

It would be inappropriate to attempt to discuss here at length the design of questions to be used in surveys, because this is a subject about which there is an extensive technical literature. Nevertheless, it is necessary to provide a brief orientation.

First, note that the design of effective questions is much more than a matter of writing out clearly what one wants to ask. It is much more than a matter of the effective use of English. The question should be regarded as a stimulus to which there is a relatively stable response. If there is not a stable response or set of responses, then there is little point in asking the question, for responses to it will lack what is ordinarily termed reliability.

Secondly, the questions should be such that the responses are made to the questions themselves rather than to other aspects of the situation. For example, questions asked in a survey about the pay of teachers are likely to elicit a very high frequency of response to the effect that they are underpaid. Yet the same individuals who state that teachers are underpaid are likely to vote against increased state and city budgets that would make increases in their salaries possible. In answering the survey questions, these individuals are responding to the social pressures of the situation as much as to the question itself. Such responses are commonly referred to as stereotyped responses.

Thirdly, the questions should draw responses that can be elicited with some uniformity. This is really saying that the procedure should have reliability and be reproducible. This is clearly not a sufficient condition to make a question useful, because questions to which there are stereotyped responses provide high consistency but little else.

Fourthly, the questions must be such that inferences can be made from the responses to responses in other situations. This may not seem obvious when it is first considered, but it is precisely what is wrong with the question that elicits a stereotyped response—one given in the particular situation but presumably not given in other situations. If a survey is made to determine how the electorate will vote in a certain election, it is important to be able to assume that behavior in answering the survey questions will be related to behavior in the voting booth. If these two aspects of behavior are unrelated, the survey ceases to have any purpose. All questions asked in the survey method must be such that it is reasonable to assume some generality of the response. The reader is reminded that the relationship between verbal behavior and other aspects of motor performance is complex, and that a simple one-to-one relationship can rarely be expected.

The trend in collecting behavioral information about populations of individuals has been to standardize the questions asked by the interviewer. The opinion poll as it is commonly conducted represents a series of brief but standardized personal interviews, in which interviewers always ask the same questions and in which the responses of those interviewed are generally restricted to a few categories. It is possible to remove restrictions on the behavior of both the interviewer and the interviewee until the point is reached where a relatively free interview takes place, perhaps restricted only to the topic to be discussed. However, in surveys the difficulty of quantifying the data based on free interviews is such that they are not practical. The most that is likely to be done in departing from the situation in which both the question and the responses are restricted is the elimination of restrictions on the response. Such open-ended questions provide a range of responses that must ultimately be tabulated and codified.

While a number of general considerations are being taken into account in planning questions, the actual questions must be carefully examined to make sure they do not reflect certain technical deficiencies. The common deficiencies have been well reviewed by Backstrom and Hursh (1963), who also provide an excellent review of the other practical problems involved in conducting survey-research interviews. Backstrom and Hursh list the following points as of prime importance in preparing questions:

1. Avoid ambiguity, but ambiguity can generally only be identified by running trial interviews.
2. Be precise.
3. Be on your guard lest the person answering the question misperceive it because of his particular background. Backstrom and Hursh tell a delightful story about a question involving the government control of profits. The uneducated population asked this question was almost unanimous in stating that they thought "prophets" should be controlled only by God.
4. Avoid loaded questions. An example of such a loaded question is "Some people criticize the teaching of reading in our schools. Do you agree?"
5. Avoid emotionally loaded words such as unpatriotic, Communist, extreme right, progressive educator, permissive classroom, and so forth. In a question such as "Superintendent Smith says that the schools are better today than they were ten years ago. Do you believe he is telling the truth?" The respondent not only has to decide whether the schools are or are not better than they were, but also

has to decide whether or not to call the superintendent a liar. The question is emotionally loaded in a way that will bias the responses to it. Do not drag prestige names into questions. Do not ask a question stated in the form, "President Kennedy believed that the Federal government should provide financial support for education. What do you think?"

6. Do not use questions that may place the respondent in an embarrassing position. For example, do not ask the question, "Did you vote on the recent school bond issue?" A person may be embarrassed to admit he did not.
7. Avoid lengthy or complicated questions.
8. Make sure that the questions involve issues with which the respondents have some familiarity.

Interviewer Characteristics

The interviewers who collect survey data are not all equally successful. M. Hauck and S. Steinkamp (1964) sent out interviewers to collect economic data from a rural population and found sizeable differences in the capability of different interviewers to obtain the data and to obtain it with accuracy. Some of the data involved the amount in savings accounts and could be verified. Interviewers differed both in the accuracy of the data they were able to elicit from those questioned and also in the completeness of the data provided. An attempt to identify the characteristics of the successful interviewers suggested that they showed greater self-confidence, dominance, and likeableness than the less successful interviewers.

Direct-Mail Questionnaire Methods

The last fifty years have shown a transition in survey techniques from the use of questionnaires sent through the mail to quite elaborate interview techniques. It is unfortunate that the same trend has not been apparent in educational research, where direct-mail techniques are still commonly used.

The central difficulty in all direct-mail techniques is that the percentage of returns is small. A questionnaire of some interest to the recipient may be expected to show only a 20 per cent return, even when conditions are favorable. If nonrespondents are contacted a second and a third time, the return may be increased to 30 per cent. Only rarely does it reach the 40 per cent level. Attempts may then be made to contact personally the final group of nonrespondents, but if this is done, it might be as well to perform the entire operation by interview.

A considerable amount is now known about who does and who does not respond to mailed questionnaires. At one time it was believed by many that it was largely a matter of chance whether a person did or did not respond to a questionnaire sent to him through the mail. If it arrived at a convenient time, he would respond to it; if it did not, he would not respond. Research has shown that this is not the case at all. A study by D. Wallace (1954) is particularly revealing in this respect.

Wallace sent four questionnaires at intervals to the same group. Some failed to return any, whereas others returned all four. The tendency was for a person who returned one questionnaire to return all four. In other words, there are those who, by and large, tend to return questionnaires, and there are those who do not. Insofar as these groups differ in relevant respects, the results achieved with direct-mail questionnaires are likely to be biased.

Wallace's study also throws some light on the characteristics of those who return direct-mail questionnaires and those who do not. Of particular importance is the fact that those who return them show a marked tendency to have a college education, whereas those who do not have relatively less education. Because differences in education are related to a host of other variables, it is hard to find an area in which questions are not likely to elicit a different response from a well-educated group than from a less well-educated group. Thus the returns may be considered to be biased by an unknown quantity. It is of some interest to note that, although the returnees and nonreturnees did differ in education, they differed little in the Wallace study in socioeconomic status. Wallace states that the safest rule in deciding whether or not to use direct-mail questionnaires is: Don't.

Surveys of Behavior in Simulated Situations

A new approach to the problem of conducting surveys of behavior is found in a very large-scale research by Hemphill, et al. (1962). The basic purpose of the study was to discover some of the dimensions of administrative behavior in elementary schools and also to obtain assessments of how teachers and superintendents regarded and evaluated each aspect of administrative behavior. It is not a study of administrative effectiveness as such but rather is it a study of what administrative behaviors occur and who considers them desirable or undesirable.

Although there would be merit in studying principals in the actual job situation and in finding out how they handled the many situations that arise during the course of a typical school day, such an approach is not feasible. An observer would hardly be permitted to sit with the principal, listen to conversations often of a confidential nature, record the statements made by visitors, review the daily correspondence and the replies to it, and so forth. In the Hemphill study this problem was avoided by bringing principals from the schools into artificially constructed administrative situations. The principals were invited in groups of twenty, to the centers conducting the research. There, they were told that their name was "Marion Smith" and that each was the principal of the Whitman Elementary School in the town of Jefferson. They were then given an orientation to the community and school by means of a sound movie, filmstrip, personnel files, handbook, a school survey, a school census, test scores of pupils, and other information. After the fairly lengthy orientation session, each principal was then taken to what was to be considered the school office. There they were told to imagine that this was the office on Labor Day and that they were to prepare for the first day of school. The in-basket on the desk was filled with items that needed immediate attention. One of the tasks was to go through the in-basket and take appropriate action on each of the documents it contained. Another task involved the observation of three teachers still on a probationary status. The latter observation was undertaken by viewing kinescopes of teachers in classrooms. In addition, an attempt was made to assess the speaking abilities of the principals who were required to prepare and deliver a speech to the Whitman Parent-Teachers Association. In a second social situation a group of the principals were brought together by a mythical "Mr. Davies," the business manager for the district, with the object of selecting a new principal. The situation permitted observers to record relevant aspects of the participants behavior.

A major outcome of a study of this kind is a set of variables that can be used in subsequent research. Before studies can be undertaken that attempt to find means of predicting administrative behavior, a set of measurable characteristics of administrative behavior must be established. The study of the principals served this purpose and fifteen major characteristics of administrative behavior were identified. These are described in general terms as follows:

1. General ability to reason and understand
2. Superiors' over-all impression
3. Concern for human problems versus conventionality

 4. Gregarious friendliness versus independent initiative
 5. Involvement with others in in-basket work
 6. Effective participation in group interaction
 7. Anxiety versus emotional maturity
 8. Analyzing the situation
 9. Directing the work of others
10. Job-performance values
11. Complying with suggestions
12. Teachers' impressions
13. Age and experience
14. Preparing for decision versus taking final action
15. Instructional awareness

This list of variables does not include many characteristics that one would expect to appear. For example, there is nothing included in it which covers such behavior as "improves working conditions" or "backs up staff." Another category that is notably absent is "delegates authority." These absences do not represent deficiencies in the appraisal procedure but simply reflect the fact that the principals studied showed an almost complete absence of these behaviors. The same is true of other categories that authorities on educational administration agree to be important but which do not emerge from the study.

The point just made here brings out one of the major values of the survey. It can serve to identify characteristics that show a sufficiently wide range of values so that individual differences can be reliably assessed; but it also serves to identify those characteristics that have not been developed and to which training programs should give special attention.

The identification of variables that can be measured provides a basis for future research. In a sense, the kind of survey under consideration provides a foundation on which future research on the prediction of administrative performance and on the training of administrators can be built. Too many studies are undertaken without the ground having been thoroughly explored and cleared by a study such as this one. A too hasty attack on problems of training and prediction of success leads only to failure.

Checks on the Data-Collection Process

It is apparant from what has been said that the collection of verbal survey data is likely to leave the investigator with feelings of insecurity

concerning the meaning of the information collected. It is usually recognized that empirical errors have been introduced into the data, and
the size of these errors needs to be estimated if the results of the survey
are to be interpretable. The experienced survey researcher will build
into his study empirical checks that will provide him with information
concerning the meaningfulness of his results.

Of primary importance are checks on the adequacy of the data-
collection process itself. The early organizers of surveys of consumer
preferences discovered that paid interviewers sometimes omitted the
important detail of actually conducting interviews and adopted the
short cut process of filling out the interview schedules at home. Many
ways have since been devised for checking on the honesty and accuracy of interviewers. One of these is to include on the interview
schedule questions such that the distribution of responses in the population to be interviewed is known. Another common procedure is for
interviewers to obtain the name and address of each interviewee and
for a sample of these interviewees to be followed up independently.

Certain types of errors, known as *response errors*, are particularly
difficult to estimate and control. Those who respond to interviewers
are likely to show a tendency to overestimate those characteristics
that are highly esteemed. Estimates of education and income are likely
to be inflated unless they are preceded by questions that ask for such
details as make subsequent falsification of answers hazardous. For example, if it is desired to determine a man's income, it may be well to
start by establishing his place of employment, his grade within the
organization, and the base rate of pay for that grade, before direct
questions pertaining to income are asked. The early questions in such
a series provide data against which subsequent responses can be
checked.

The internal checking of responses is probably the simplest and
commonest way of testing the consistency of data. A person's given age
can be verified against data such as the age of his oldest child and his
age when the child was born. The latter two questions can be separated from one another by other material and separated from the original question on the topic. Sometimes a question on birth date can also
be included as an additional check. It is possible for a respondent
to be consistent in answering all these items yet provide a completely
false record, but the likelihood of this is small.

A type of check that has been used extensively for determining the
trustworthiness of responses to personality test inventories has also
been used in the conduct of opinion polls. The technique is simply that
of asking a question to which the reply itself provides some estimate

of the extent to which the respondent is providing trustworthy answers. If a person is asked, "Do you ever tell lies?" one may suspect that he is not telling the truth if he answers "No!" There are few, if any, who never tell lies. It is possible to introduce a series of such questions, which may be used to provide a so-called validating score. Nevertheless, the technique is not without its pitfalls. The reader should take note of the fact that such questions, if they are answered honestly, usually place the respondent in a rather bad light; for this reason the tendency to falsification may be much greater than would be the case with more innocuous items. The answers to such so-called validating items, or scores derived from them, cannot be unequivocally interpreted at this time.

If checks based on internal consistency are used, it is sometimes possible to determine the adequacy of these checks by separating from the population a group that may be expected to have an unusually high consistency of response. For example, if questions are asked school personnel about the behavior of individual pupils, one may expect principals to be less consistent than teachers, simply because principals have fewer opportunities to observe pupils. If a check showed that the principals were more familiar with the pupils than were teachers, the data would be open to suspicion.

The information given by internal checks provides evidence mainly of the internal consistency of the data. This is information related to reliability rather than to the trustworthiness of the data as a basis for inference. For this reason most opinion polls include checks whereby a part of the data collected are compared with equivalent data from some other source. A rich source of data in the educational field, which may be used for making many such comparisons, is that collected by the Purdue High School Opinion Poll. Other sources in the educational field are limited, and for this reason difficulties are encountered in the application of this method of checking the data. Hence a second and much less satisfactory method is commonly used; it involves the collection of observations additional to those ordinarily gathered in survey interviews. We are referring here to observations made by interviewers concerning the forthrightness or evasiveness of those interviewed and such behavior as may indicate whether or not trustworthy responses are being given.

Identification of the Sample to Be Surveyed

In solving strictly local educational problems, surveys are commonly conducted to cover every member of the designated population.

In such cases we have no sampling problems, but there is also no population to which the results can be generalized. Sampling becomes a problem when it is desired to make a generalization from a sample of a specified population, either to other samples not yet drawn or to the population itself. The problem of sampling arises simply because it is desired to make a generalization.

There is an important distinction between a random sample and a representative sample. A *random sample* is one drawn in such a way that each member of the population has an equal chance of being included. Of course one random sample will be expected to differ from another random sample; and, other things being equal, the larger the two random samples, the less will be the expected differences between their means on the characteristic sampled. On the other hand, in a *representative* or *stratified sample* cases are selected in such a way that the characteristics of the sample are similar in important respects to the characteristics of the population sampled. Thus, in polling the public on their choices in forthcoming elections, it is common practice to select a sample so that it is representative of the entire voting public with respect to certain characteristics that are related to voting behavior. For example, because voting behavior is related to income, it is important that the distribution of income in the sample be similar to the distribution of income in the universe. A similar control can be exercised over numerous related variables if the characteristics of the universe are known. This process of matching the sample to the universe permits greater validity of inference from the sample to the universe and from the sample to other variables than when the sample has been selected at random.

Present plans for the National Assessment Program call for the administration of tests to a very small sample of people, carefully chosen, so that inferences can be made from the sample to larger populations. In addition, present plans also propose that no pupil be required to take a complete test in any particular area, but only part of a test. In this way an effort will be made to avoid imposing on the time of any one student, for the tasks involved in the survey will be distributed over many pupils. The researcher should avoid preparing an alphabetical list of names and then proceeding down the list until he has included a sufficient number in his sample. It is well known that some letters of the alphabet include more names from certain European groups than others, and this may produce bias in a sample selected on the basis of name alone.

In order to avoid the difficulties that are likely to arise from sampling an alphabetical list, a good plan is to select every fifth or sixth or tenth name, or whatever interval will yield the needed number while still distributing them over the entire list. Those who are absent on the day when the data are collected should be included as soon as possible thereafter. Substitutes should not be sought for these subjects, because it is possible that absentees have relevant characteristics that the substitutes do not have. Also, there should be as little delay as possible in the testing of the absentees, for in any interviewing period the characteristic that is being measured may change. The researcher should also avoid the practice of depending on volunteers as a basis for selecting a sample, because volunteers are likely to be differently motivated from nonvolunteers. In the latter connection, the author can recall an instance where volunteers were compared with nonvolunteers on the Rorschach. The main difference between these two groups was that the volunteers came to the testing situations determined to reveal as much as possible of their inner lives, whereas the nonvolunteers wanted to reveal as little as possible. Related influences may well affect scores from achievement tests.

Problems of sampling in educational surveys at the local level can often be completely avoided by including the entire universe of possible cases in the "sample." If a high school principal wishes to conduct a survey of the reading skills of the twelfth-grade pupils in his high school, it may be possible for him to include every one of them in the survey. In most high schools this would be a practical matter, but in large city high schools where enrollments can be as great as ten thousand, it becomes quite unnecessary to test every pupil in the senior class in order to obtain the desired data. The decision concerning which of the pupils to include in the survey is greatly facilitated by the fact that there is available a complete list of the names of all cases in the universe from which the sample is to be drawn. When such a list is available, major difficulties associated with the problem of sampling are eliminated

A common error in sampling school populations is to sample by seating position in an assembly hall. This would happen if the first four rows in an assembly were retained for a brief period to fill in a questionnaire whereas the others were dismissed at the end of the meeting. If the pupils were free to seat themselves in any way they wanted in an assembly, it is likely that those who chose the rear of the room would be different in many respects from those who chose the front of the room.

Difficult problems of sampling arise when it is not possible completely to identify the universe to be sampled. The typical public opinion poll faces this difficulty. If a representative sample of the adult population has to be identified to determine public attitude with respect to some issue, there is no way of locating and identifying in advance of the poll the names of those to be questioned. This fact makes it difficult to insure that the sample is representative of the universe, or that it has not been selected in some way so that a systematic bias has been introduced. Fortunately, most populations that the educator may wish to sample have been inventoried for him, as is the case with populations of pupils and parents. However, when he wishes to extend his inquiry outside of these groups, he runs into the difficulty of identifying the population that is to be sampled and therefore has difficulty in identifying an appropriate sample.

The problem that this situation presents is a difficult one, and we must pause here to consider some of the historical solutions and their weaknesses. The oldest method of all is to avoid the problem and include in the sample just those cases that can be easily located or that volunteered. The disastrous *Literary Digest* straw ballot on the outcome of the 1936 Presidential election was run on this kind of a basis. Millions were included in the sample—indeed, it was one of the largest ever included in a ballot—but circumstances beyond the control of the investigator caused the sample to be biased. Roosevelt was predicted to be the loser, but he won with a large majority.

The trend in the late 1930s was to select better-chosen samples distributed geographically and to instruct interviewers, who were also distributed geographically, to obtain interviews with certain specific percentages of individuals in each economic structure, each race, each sex, and so on. For a long time this appeared to be a satisfactory procedure. However, it eventually became clear that the procedure of allowing interviewers to select those to be interviewed resulted in a bias in the sample thus selected. Interviewers tend to select interviewees who are rather like themselves. Thus, if the interviewers belong to an upper socioeconomic group, they are likely to include too few individuals in the lower-income brackets. Interviewer bias is now a well-known and well-established phenomenon. Thus the interviewer should not select those to be interviewed.

One improved approach to the problem of selecting a sample is referred to as *area sampling*. In this technique, highly detailed maps of the regions to be sampled are used and the area is systematically sampled. If, for example, a particular small area is to be included in the sample, then all persons living within that identified small area are included in the sampling. The sample thus selected is largely independent of the whims, likes, and dislikes of the persons collecting the data. Nevertheless, the method is not as simple as it seems, and difficulties are encountered in tracking down the persons identified. There are also definitional problems. If a person has residence in a particular locality, it does not necessarily mean that he lives there, and decisions have to be made about such matters.

In some localities, samples can be identified in advance of the process of collecting data by obtaining complete lists of residents. Here again, the procedure appears to be highly satisfactory on the surface, but difficulties arise in its application. Lists of residents are often inaccurate because of faulty methods of collecting the data on which they are based. An even greater source of difficulty arises from the time lag between the collection of data for making lists of residents and their subsequent use for survey purposes. In many areas, a lag of only a year may render such lists quite unsuitable for identifying any kind of sample. On the other hand, other areas may show a high population stability.

Special problems arise when follow-up surveys of school graduates are made. Studies of these groups are commonly undertaken in order to determine the successes and failures of the graduates so that the program of the school can be improved. In these follow-up studies, it is easy to obtain a complete list of the names of the population to be studied—the difficulty arises in locating these individuals. Young groups are particularly mobile, but fortunately their parents represent a population much more stable in terms of home address. Many graduates can be contacted through their parents' homes; however in some localities it may not be possible to do this, because entire families may move to different parts of the country. If the survey is a follow-up of college graduates, then the alumni organization may be of great value in locating individuals. Classmates can also be consulted to determine addresses of cases that cannot otherwise be located. The investigator must be resigned to the fact that, in the educational follow-up survey, it is likely that a substantial fraction of the cases to be included in the sample will not be located despite intensive efforts on the part of the investigator.

Sometimes in conducting follow-up studies, one can check on the extent to which the sample collected is representative of the total population included in the study. For example, if the school files still retain the scholastic records of the population, it is possible to determine the extent to which the sample is representative of the school class that is sampled with respect to scholastic achievement. This would be an important fact if scholastic aptitude could be considered to be related to the phenomenon under study. If, in this case, a serious discrepancy existed between the sample and the school class, questions might be raised concerning the validity of inferences that could be made from the sample.

Some Misuses of Survey Methods

The survey as it exists today within the framework of educational research finds its greatest misapplication in the local study of the type that educational institutions usually undertake for the purpose of justifying their existence. For example, the author has watched the development of a study designed to provide an evaluation of selected aspects of teacher education. Some of the questions that those conducting the study proposed to answer were truly answerable, such as, "What has been the effect of state aid on the program?" Such a question can be answered mainly by consulting the budget office and by determining just how the money has been spent. However, an answer is likely to add but little to what is already known through the channels of common gossip. Most of the answerable questions posed by the committee running the survey were of this character. However, it was the questions that were much more difficult to answer, if they could be answered at all, that dealt with the problems of central importance to this survey; for example, "Does the institution graduate students who can teach successfully?" and "What are the weaknesses and strengths of the teacher education program?" Such questions and related questions, unfortunately, cannot be definitely answered by any means at present available.

Now in the case of the particular survey, those who asked the questions soon realized that there was no satisfactory way of answering them. They saw that there was no way of determining whether the teachers produced by the program could teach successfully. Thus an alternative question was formulated, "Are the principals who employ the graduates of the college satisfied with these graduates as teachers?" In order to answer this question, a questionnaire was sent to the principal of each school employing one graduate or more. This questionnaire asked for information concerning the extent to which the graduates were satisfactory as teachers. As one might well expect, those principals who did reply rated almost all the teachers trained in the particular institution as satisfactory or very satisfactory. This, of course, meant absolutely nothing. A person inclined to make a derogatory report would probably make no report at all. Thus such "data," if one will excuse this misuse of the term, were quite valueless for answering any significant questions that might be asked about the teacher-education program.

SCHOOL SURVEYS

The development of methods for undertaking school surveys has been intimately related to the development of accreditation procedures. This is hardly surprising, because the accrediting associations represent the major enterprises that engage in school-survey work, although professors of education, educational consultants, state and local superintendents, and others also engage in surveys of schools to varying degrees. Accrediting associations, however, have had to enter into the business of conducting school surveys with a certain amount of system to their methods because they are open to public criticism.

Procedures for the evaluation and accreditation of schools and their programs should not be confused with educational research. They are procedures for setting standards and for helping schools improve their programs. However, programs for the accreditation of schools have had an intimate relationship to research in that many of the procedures involved have been the products of major research programs. In addition, accreditation procedures provide data-collection facilities that have been used in the past by research workers and may be used more extensively in the future. This section is designed to give the reader some understanding of the data available in this connection and the instruments that have been and are being used for their collection.

The development of methods for evaluating schools by inspection has been closely linked with school and college relationships. In this process, the early stage was marked by the admission of students to college by examination, a procedure that tended to standardize the high school curriculum in terms of college admission requirements. The recognition of the fact that cooperation between secondary schools and colleges was a necessary prerequisite to the development of secondary and higher education led to the founding of the New England Association of Colleges and Secondary Schools in 1884; the Association of Colleges and Secondary Schools of the Middle States and Maryland in 1887; and the North Central Association of Schools and Colleges in 1895. The latter grew out of the Michigan School Master's Club, which held an annual meeting at which secondary school and college teachers discussed problems of mutual interest. The members of this organization believed that it might be profitable to bring together teachers from a wider area, and thus the North Central Association of Schools and Colleges was formed. However, the early college and school associations were primarily devices for bringing together individuals to discuss and solve common educational problems. It was not until 1901 that any activities were undertaken to develop a system of accreditation. In the latter year the Commission on Accredited Schools was established to investigate this matter. The commission was given broad authority to set up standards for high school courses that would be accepted for credit by colleges, and to set up standards for accreditation in general.

Parallel with the work of the North Central Association was that of various state departments of education, which were concerned with the problem of accreditation from the standpoint of setting up minimum standards at which all schools should aim. Since that time, the function of accrediting secondary schools has been shared by state universities and state departments of education, which in many states have performed this function cooperatively and at times interchangeably.

Although the initial interest in this area was in the accreditation of specific courses, the procedure soon broadened out to include a multitude of matters, such as the length of the school year, the number and length of the periods given each week in each subject, the training and experience of the faculty, the size and scope of the library and other physical facilities, and other matters too numerous to list here.

A study by W. E. McVey (1942) pointed out that the North Central Association of Schools and Colleges has been a powerful influence in the establishment of standards for secondary schools by the various states. He goes on to point out that this is partly a result of the fact that influential members of state departments of education have often been members of this association and have attended meetings where standards have been established.

The basic problem in the development of procedures for accrediting schools is to establish a basis on which schools are to be judged. Clearly it is insufficient to turn loose an observer in a school. Observation must be restricted to certain aspects of the school and its program that are considered of central importance to the effectiveness of the program. The essential characteristics observed during the accreditation procedure are referred to as *evaluative criteria*. The remainder of this section attempts to describe the general nature of the evaluative criteria that have been used in the accreditation of schools and colleges; that is to say, it describes the types of schedules that have been developed for guiding observers who are sent out to obtain information about schools by inspectional procedures.

Accreditation of Schools

The most comprehensive attempt to draw up a guide for the evaluation of schools was an outcome of the Cooperative Study of Secondary Schools Standards, first organized in 1933 by the representatives of six major regional accrediting associations. The results of this study appear in numerous publications. The purposes were the following:

1. To determine the characteristics of a good secondary school.
2. To find practical means and methods with which to evaluate the effectiveness of a school in terms of its objectives.
3. To determine the means and processes by which a good school develops into a better one.
4. To derive ways by which regional associations could stimulate and assist secondary schools to continue growth.

The same study led to the development of a series of schedules for evaluating secondary schools. These schedules were first published in 1950. In 1960 an expanded and revised series was published covering the following areas:

Agriculture	Industrial Arts
Art	Mathematics
Business Education	Music
Core Program	Physical Education for Boys
Distributive Education	Physical Education for Girls
Driver Education	Religion
English	Science
Foreign Languages	Social Studies
Health Education	Vocational Trade and Industrial
Home Economics	Education

In addition, schedules are included for use in evaluating the subsequent areas:

Student activity program
Instructional materials services

Guidance services
School plant
School staff and administration
Individual staff member

A very similar list of schedules has also been published for use in junior high schools. The latter appears in a volume entitled *Evaluative Criteria for Junior High Schools* published in 1963.

Each one of the schedules for the evaluation of work in specific subject-matter fields organizes the evaluation into the following areas:

1. Organization. This covers such matters as how the curriculum is developed, whether there is continuity in the organization of studies in the area, and the like.
2. Nature of offerings. This category explains itself fairly adequately, but it does include such matters as whether the courses provide opportunity for student responsibility and leadership.
3. Physical facilities. This includes such considerations as furniture, visual aids, and general classroom conditions.
4. Direction of learning, divided into these four areas:
   a. Instructional staff. This covers preparation, background, organization, and the like.
   b. Instructional activities
   c. Instructional materials
   d. Methods of evaluation
5. Outcomes. This covers assessments of what students have learned in the program, although few hints are offered as to how the assessments are to be made.
6. Special characteristics of the program in the area.

Under each of these areas a checklist is provided against which a mark or other symbol is entered according to the following system:

E   Provision of the condition is made exclusively.
S   Provision of the condition is made to a moderate extent.
L   Provision of the condition is very limited or missing but needed.
M   Provision of the condition is missing but its need is questioned.
N   Provision of the condition is not desirable or does not apply.

On the basis of all the evidence in any one area studied, an over-all evaluation is made of the effectiveness or worth of that aspect of the operation. These evaluations are summarized on a five-point scale, on which the points are as follows:

Scale Value   *Interpretation*

5	Excellent: The provisions or conditions are extensive and are functioning excellently.
4	Very good: (a) The provisions or conditions are extensive and are functioning well; or (b) the provisions or conditions are moderately extensive but are functioning excellently.
3	Good: The conditions or provisions are moderately extensive but are functioning well.
2	Fair: (a) The provisions or conditions are moderately extensive but are functioning poorly; or (b) the provisions or conditions are limited in extent but are functioning well.
1	Poor: The provisions or conditions are limited in extent and are functioning poorly.
M	Missing: The provisions or conditions are missing and needed; if present they would make a contribution to the educational needs of the youth in this community.
N	Does not apply: The provisions or conditions are missing but do not apply or are not desirable for the youth of this school or this community.

The items listed under each heading of each evaluation sheet vary in specificity. Some are highly specific, and many ask whether staff members have had specific types of experience—one item, for example, asks whether home economics teachers have had actual work experience in this field. Others are so general that it seems almost impossible to determine whether or not the condition exists. For example, it may be almost impossible to answer, in terms of the categories provided, whether the program of a school is based on an analysis of the educational needs of youth, for it is not clear whether the answer is to be based on systematic investigation. Also, it is not clear what is meant by "the educational needs of youth"—are these to be needs they have already experienced, or needs in terms of the problems they will face later in life? The term *need* is one with a multitude of meanings. As another illustration of the same difficulty, one may wonder how it is possible to determine whether a program "encourages enlargement and enrichment of the pupil's scope of interests."

The lists of evaluative criteria display no pretensions of being comprehensive, and indeed spaces are provided on the schedule for the addition of items that are relevant to the specific situation in which the evaluations are made but may not apply outside of those situations.

Any criticism of the schedules prepared in the cooperative study of school standards must take into account the purposes for which they were prepared and the background of thinking on which they were based. A superficial examination of the schedules reveals that although they bear some resemblance to orthodox psychological and educational measuring instruments they do not meet customary standards of acceptability. This criticism is not entirely fair, even though it may be pointed out that the end result of the use of the schedules is a single numerical rating based on a series of evaluations of a number of important elements in the situation. In addition, it may be pointed out that the ratings thus arrived at are produced by a highly subjective process and cannot be appraised in terms of norms because no norms are available. Finally, the measurement expert might point out that no evidence is given concerning the reliability of the assessments provided by the schedules, nor is there any evidence concerning the validity of these assessments. These criticisms are not entirely logical, for the following reasons: First, the history of school inspection and accreditation during the last fifty years has illustrated a trend away from the use of quantitative data and a return to qualitative standards. Therefore the schedules that represent a recent stage of thinking in this area do not represent a series of measuring devices to be used in a standard way; rather are they guides to the thinking of the person who is undertaking the evaluation. They present a series of topics that *may* be given consideration in the total assessment procedure, and it is recognized that some topics may be irrelevant in some situations and that some relevant ones may have been omitted from the list. Some guide to thought is better than none.

Secondly, numerical norms of the type provided by most publishers of achievement tests would be largely meaningless in the assessment of secondary schools, since different schools must be assessed by different standards. The curriculum provided by a large secondary school serving an industrial population must differ in some ways from that of a small school serving an agricultural community. The failure of schools of the latter type to meet the needs of an agricultural population is the most common criticism professional visitors level at them, an entirely different criticism from that directed against schools in industrial communities.

On the other hand, the criticism concerning the lack of evidence of the reliability or validity of the recorded assessments cannot be passed off lightly. If individuals cannot show substantial agreement with themselves or with others in the entries made on the schedule with respect to a specific school, then the schedules and the records made on them have no value. Evidence of reliability would be fairly easy to obtain, and the only real excuse for its lack is the large amount of money that such an undertaking would probably involve. Evidence of the validity of the end products of the schedules must also be produced.

Accreditation of Colleges

The need for developing a system for accrediting colleges arose from a different source than that which stimulated the development of machinery for accrediting secondary schools. G. F. Zook and M. E. Haggerty (1935, 1936) reviewed this matter and concluded that the movement for the establishment of standards for the accrediting of colleges arose from a need for exercising some social control over higher education, which expanded so vastly during the first half of the present century. These authorities point out that although there are many ways in which public control can be exercised over higher education, control by accrediting associations offers the advantage of freedom from political pressure and controversy. Accrediting associations can honestly raise standards of education without political intrigue or influence.

The problems of establishing criteria and of establishing standards are quite distinct. Two different accrediting agencies may use similar criteria, and yet, because their standards differ, they may vary in the percentage of institutions inspected that they accredit. Strictly speaking, the establishment of criteria should precede the establishment of standards.

The development of procedures for accrediting institutions of higher education has had a history covering over fifty years, and contributions to these procedures have been made by numerous individuals, many accrediting associations, divisions of the federal government, state departments of education, the American Council on Education, and other organizations and individuals. However, an overview of the situation would indicate that many of the major developments in the procedures have come from the North Central Association of Schools and Colleges, which has sponsored some of the few systematic studies in this general area.

In 1934, after many years of deliberation, the Association published a manual to be used in the accreditation of colleges and a series of schedules on which the data relevant to the accrediting procedure were to be recorded. In addition, a series of monographs published in 1935–1936 provided extensive data on the use of the criteria described in the manual, and even went so far as to provide some normative data for some of the measures used in the accrediting procedure.

The manual provides criteria for evaluating each one of the following aspects of a college:

Faculty	Student personnel services
Curriculum	Administration
Instruction	Finance
Library	Plant
Induction of students	Institution's study of its problems
Intercollegiate athletics	

Each one of the areas to be evaluated is broken down into elements. Consider the matter of evaluating the faculty. This is first broken down into the areas of (1) faculty competence, (2) faculty organization, and (3) conditions of faculty service. For the first of these three, criteria for determining the degree of competence are listed. Some of these criteria are

Percentage of total staff holding an earned doctor's degree
Average number of years of graduate study of the staff
Average number of years of experience in teaching and administration in institutions of higher education
Number of scholarly books and monographs produced per staff member
Number of memberships in national learned societies per staff member
Number of places on national programs per staff member

The criteria listed in the 1934 edition of the manual were tried out over a period of several years, and in 1941 a revision of the criteria was published. In the revised manual a substantial amount of normative data is provided to assist in the interpretation of data collected during the accreditation process. The normative data are based on the institutions of higher learning accredited by the Association. As an illustration of these data, with reference to the percentage of the staff holding an earned doctoral degree, average values are given respectively for junior colleges, teachers' colleges, liberal arts colleges, and universities, and in each case separate data are given for publicly and privately controlled institutions. In another table, data are presented showing the average number of books, monographs, and articles published per faculty member in each of these types of institutions. In recent years, more normative data have been provided by the American Association of University Professors.

The inadequacy of the evaluative criteria both at the secondary school and at the college level is well recognized by the North Central Association in its reports, which frequently emphasize the fact that the program of a school must be evaluated as a whole. It is also recognized that there seems little possibility at the present time that qualitative criteria can be replaced by quantitative criteria, and that fundamentally the process of accreditation must depend on subjective judgments. Frequent cautions are given that the criteria outlined should be considered more as a guide to thinking than as a series of basic dimensions along which assessment must be made. The emphasis on caution gives recognition to the fact that the process of assessment in this area is still in the earliest stages of development.

One of the more interesting developments of research in this general area in recent times is the exploration of the cultural climate of colleges and the effect this has on the development of the student. Colleges vary from the liberal to the conservative, and from the playboy to the academically oriented, as well as along other dimensions. Variations of this kind may well have much greater impact than those considered by people concerned with accreditation.

Criticisms of Evaluative Criteria Used in Accreditation

A number of important criticisms of the evaluative criteria discussed in this chapter must be considered, but these criticisms must be reviewed in the light of the fact that this type of measurement is relatively new, about as recent as the development of tests of intelligence. Nevertheless, these forms of measurements have not had as much concentrated thought bestowed on them by so many people as have intelligence tests. Work on accreditation procedures has been largely the spare-time activity of relatively few individuals.

1. It should be noted that there is no experimental basis for the evaluative criteria commonly used in the inspection of schools and colleges. There is general agreement that the main ultimate criterion of the effectiveness of an educational program is the extent to which

it produces desirable changes in the pupils. Evaluative criteria for use in accreditation are based on the judgments of educators that certain characteristics of a school do have an effect on the extent to which the objectives of learning are achieved. It is assumed, for example, that it makes a difference in the amount of learning accomplished whether a faculty of a secondary school does or does not have professional education training in the courses provided by departments in education. As far as the author knows, there is no evidence that teachers with professional training of this type are more effective than those who do not. One would assume that it would make a difference (all teacher training is based on this assumption), but many assumptions made by educators in the past have been shown to be unjustifiable on the basis of scientific experimentation.

2. The attempt to achieve rigorous standards of measurement may prevent the assessment of the outstanding characteristics of an institution. This is a problem well recognized even by those who have developed the evaluative criteria for the North Central Association. A secondary school may be performing a first-rate job even though its faculty has had limited training and the plant is poor. Desire to do a professional job may overcome deficiencies of formal training, and ingenuity may make up for deficencies in the plant.

3. Normative data may have relatively little value because they do not set minimum standards but only show how one institution compares with others. On the norms provided, one institution appears to be low and apparently inadequate because others are higher on the scale, although the fact may be that all the institutions are inadequate.

4. The normative material provided was developed during a period of great educational change, which included times of oversupply and undersupply of teachers. These changes would make it unreasonable to use norms of the types provided in other places and at other times.

5. The system of evaluative criteria does not take into account the fact that single items may be crucial. A school that has a program quite unrelated to the needs of its students should not be accredited even if it is adequate on all of the other dimensions listed. A rural school that fails to take into account the fact that most of the pupils will eventually enter agricultural pursuits is inadequate, even if it achieves high scores on other variables.

One may assume that eventually all of these criticisms will be met after careful studies have been made of the extent to which the various factors are related to the degree to which the objectives of learning are achieved. Before this can be done, it will be necessary to develop valid measures of a great number of outcomes and to measure the outcomes of teaching under a variety of conditions. The problem is complicated by the fact that, different institutions have different objectives, and consequently the achievements of the pupils in one place may not be comparable with those in another.

Overview of Accreditation Procedures

Survey procedures for assessing the effectiveness of schools and colleges in achieving particular objectives must be considered relatively crude methods of appraisal. They are all based on numerous assumptions, some of which are open to question. Although the validity of these procedures may be questioned, the process of inspection has certain intrinsic values that may justify it regardless of validity. First, accreditation and inspection procedures are becoming more and more a service; that is to say, they are designed to help schools and colleges improve themselves rather than to act as a threat. Accrediting agencies now often make available the services of special consultants to help schools with special problems. For example, the University of Michigan functions as the accrediting agency for the secondary schools of Michigan, and as a part of its function it provides consultants in a great many different areas.

Secondly, accreditation procedures encourage schools to examine themselves. This is always a healthy process, and a well-organized accreditation agency can perform a valuable function by encouraging schools to do this.

Although accrediting agencies may use the most primitive methods of assessment and measurement, that they are useful when their power is exercised with wisdom cannot be questioned.

SUMMARY

1. Survey research methods as they are currently employed by educational organizations represent research on educational problems at a rather simple level, undertaken mainly to solve problems of local significance only.

2. Surveys conducted in educational research are commonly undertaken as efforts to determine the nature of the physical conditions related to education. Sometimes surveys are made of the behavior of teachers or pupils. A further type of survey attempts to establish the achievements of pupils.

3. Surveys may merely enumerate the frequency of occurrence of some type of event, or they may study the interrelationship among events.

4. Surveys may attempt to undertake studies that could be undertaken by experimental methods, but they do not provide the same certainty of knowledge that experimental procedures might provide.

5. Surveys of behavioral phenomena should not represent a mere effort to collect a set of unrelated facts. The information gathered should be interrelated within a plan or framework.

6. Some of the more interesting kinds of survey study the interrelationship among events.

7. A survey should be based on a theory of the nature of the phenomena that are to be surveyed. Because surveys are often conducted in areas where relatively little is known, it is often difficult to develop an adequate theoretical basis. All surveys that involve a question-and-answer approach should be considered as studies involving a complex social interaction between a questioner and a respondent. The theory should specify the general nature of the phenomena to be investigated, the methods through which aspects of them can be measured, the conditions that produce them, and the population in whom the phenomena are to be found.

8. The direct observation of behavior in naturally occurring situations has limitations as a survey technique. It usually represents a highly selected sample of the total daily behavior of the individual. Surveys conducted through the administration of tests or through an examination of pupil products have had a long history of utility.

9. Problems and difficulties involved in the design of questions for surveys have been extensively explored by research workers, and the person who undertakes a survey involving the asking of questions should be familiar with what is known about the preparation of such materials.

10. Direct-mail questionnaires should be avoided unless no other method is available for obtaining the desired information. Those who return questionnaires delivered through the mail tend to be a more educated group than those who do not.

11. Surveys of behavior are sometimes conducted in artificial situations which simulate a realistic set of conditions.

12. In any survey, checks should be built into the data-collection process itself. The main type of check used is an examination of the data for internal consistency.

13. Because sample surveys are designed to obtain information from a sample that can be applied to a universe, it is most important that the universe to which the results are to apply should be specified

and that the method of obtaining the sample should be an appropriate one.

14. The research worker who conducts a survey should be sure that the resulting data will be meaningful. Too often the results of surveys provide biased information to support some person's prejudices.

15. The development of school-survey techniques has been intimately connected with the development of accreditation procedures. In this connection, the North Central Association of Schools and Colleges has played a leading role.

16. The Cooperative Study of Secondary School Standards was a comprehensive attempt to provide a guide for the evaluation of schools. This guide provided a system of rating scales through which the observations made concerning a school could be quantified.

17. The trend over the last half-century has been away from the use of quantitative standards, which have come in for serious criticism. The main difficulty in using such standards is that different schools have to be assessed along different dimensions.

18. Similar attempts have been made to provide quantitative criteria for the evaluation of colleges.

19. The numerous criticisms that have been leveled against present systems of evaluative criteria indicate that there exists here a fruitful field for research. There is a real social need for a continuing program of research in the area. The assumptions underlying the use of current accreditation procedures need to be investigated.

||||||||||||||||||||||||||||||||||||||

CHAPTER 10

Analysis of the Content of Verbal Materials

EDUCATIONAL research often involves the analysis of the content of verbal materials, which can be either spoken or printed. The analysis of content is a central activity whenever one is concerned with the study of particular curricula, or the comparison of curricula, or when one is concerned with the study of the nature of the verbal materials to which children are incidentally exposed. A review of research in any area involves the analysis of the content of the research articles that have been published. The analysis may be at a relatively simple level, as when one peruses a biology textbook and notes the major scientific concepts that are covered; but other analyses may be subtle, as when a research worker makes a study of the attitude of the press toward education by feature writers. In addition, computer methods for searching large bodies of technical literature for particular information require that a very systematic analysis be made of the content of that literature. In this way, special kinds of abstracts of each of thousands of articles can be rapidly scanned by computers in order to identify the few articles that throw light on some specific problem. The educational research worker should be familiar with these new methods of searching through library materials, because these methods will become widely used within a few years. Simple methods of content analysis appear to have outlived their usefulness and the little knowledge they have yielded is probably all the knowledge they are likely to yield. The trend is in the direction of the development of more sophisticated and elaborate techniques, which should form part of the repertoire of the modern educational research worker.

Curriculum Analysis: The Problem of Identifying Content

Content analysis refers to a group of techniques that have been designed for the analysis of verbal communications. The techniques are appropriate for the analysis of a great range of communications, including those to be found in textbooks, lectures, informal teacher-pupil interactions, written compositions of pupils, and other sources. Although the problems involved in the analysis of the content of a curriculum are of central concern to education, they represent an area of content analysis that has hardly been explored. Nevertheless, the significance of the analysis of the content of curricula is such that it will be given first place in the discussion of the area.

In recent years, emphasis has been placed in curriculum planning on the "content" aspects of the curriculum. Some courses are believed to contain more content, or more worthwhile content, than others and, hence, have been given a place of greater importance in the school program. Other courses, which are alleged to lack content have been squeezed into a smaller amount of school time, or have been excluded from the program. Just what constitutes content is rarely defined, and the term remains an obscure one with respect to curriculum planning. The definition given here is one the author finds convenient, even though it may not be universally accepted.

His position is that a teaching area has content insofar as it can be represented by an organized set of statements or propositions. These statements or propositions would include definitions, statements of fact, and generalizations and principles. The propositions representing the content of an area always have organization, but the organization may differ from field to field. In the case of geometry, for example, the propositions are organized within a logical structure, beginning with certain propositions referred to as axioms—which are essentially definitions. The content of physics has a somewhat similar structure. The structure of the content of history is different from either of these two in that the statements and propositions representing the knowledge in this area are organized in time as well as with respect to other characteristics. Some historical events occurred before other historical events and their sequence in time must be understood in order to understand history. The content of history is also organized in other ways. Some events in history belong together because they all reflect interrelated economic events. Some events in history can be grouped together because they all occurred in a particular geographical region. Thus Roman history is taught as a subject because the facts related to it are commonly grouped together. The same fact can be included in many different groupings. Thus the Russian revolution can be placed in the category Russian history, or in the category of economic history, or in the category of ideological movements as well as in other categories. The events of history cannot be placed in any simple order in designing a teaching program of the Skinner type. Their interrelationships can be represented much better by a web or lattice. The content of most other subject-matter fields is equally complex. Consider, as another example, English, the content of which is organized into a number of different structures. On the one hand there is the structure represented by grammar, which is a system of rules describing the customs that have evolved with respect to the use of words. But the teaching of English also involves the use of other structures within which the propositions representing the fields are organized. Because some of the content of English courses is historical, it involves the use of time sequences and a time structure similar to that involved in history. The reader should pause at this point to think of other systems in terms of which knowledge in the area of English is structured.

Those engaged in the development of Skinner-type teaching programs have commonly assumed that there is a best order into which the facts and skills to be learned in any particular course can be arranged. Although something approaching this situation exists in arithmetic and in other aspects of elementary mathematics, most areas of knowledge do not present a single simple way in which the content can be organized. Because the development of a teaching program is generally based on the assumption of the existence of such an order, the program writer is likely to "force" the subject matter into some kind of sequence that will give it the appearance of organization. However, the organization is likely to be quite artificial and probably no more useful than the many other ways in which the same subject matter might be organized.

There is also much learned in most subject-matter areas that is outside of content, as it has been defined here. Many motor and perceptual skills are not reducible to organized sets of propositions. In learning a foreign language, for example, the skill acquired in pronunciation is not reducible to a set of propositions that encompass all aspects of the pronunciation. Pronunciation must be learned largely by imitation. Although physical education has content in the sense defined here, a physical education major also acquires skills related to activities that cannot be represented as a set of organized propositions. A course in literature may have as one of its major purposes providing the student with the aesthetic and emotional experiences that accompany the reading of a great work. That such a course provides knowledge of a kind cannot be denied, but it is not knowledge reducible to a set of precisely stated propositions. These aesthetic and emotional experiences cannot be communicated to others by the same means as would be used for communicating physics or philology. That such experiences play an important part in the educational process cannot be denied, but they do not represent content as the term is used here. Literature is not the only area of study in which experiences other than that of the assimilation of content, as such, play an important role. Most areas of study call for the exercise of thinking skills; and they can serve many different objectives, including that of assimilating the content. The historian may ask his students what the historical consequences might have been if a certain decision of the Supreme Court had been the opposite of what it actually was. Such a question and the thought it inspires on the part of the student may help him to assimilate the content under discussion and to develop skills in the utilization of the content. Indeed, the assimilation of content without the operation of such processes seems unlikely.

A final point to be made is that any work on the analysis of the content of a curriculum or a subject-matter field requires an understanding of the organization of the content as well as of the content itself. A precise definition of the content would require the listing of the propositions that represent the content, although this might require much more labor than is feasible. For most practical purposes, curriculum research must settle for something far short of such a complete list—but it does not have to settle for so little as the broad general descriptions typically used in the past.

Content Analysis in Communication Research

The history of content analysis, particularly in communications research, has been summarized by Bernard Berelson (1952). Some of the earliest studies pertained to the development of scholarship. Analysis of scientific writings produced at different times in the past has shown the changing interests of scholars in particular fields and the growth and decline of particular emphases. Other early studies in this field attempted to show the extent to which particular newspapers gave coverage of the news. This was accomplished by defining what was meant by "full coverage" on particular days by listing the events to be covered. The newspapers were then analyzed to determine what percentage of these topics were covered. Similar studies were also undertaken to compare the reporting of news in different countries, and the analysis of radio broadcasts became an area of military intelligence research. From this there developed a whole area of systematic intelligence research based on analyses of enemy publications, statements by prisoners, and the like.

Although the trend in content analysis has been to develop quantitative methods, the possibility is still open that qualitative methods may have some merit. The clinical psychologist considers that a broad overview of the case he is working on may give him hunches that cannot be derived from the measures of personality he has at hand. The person making an analysis of intelligence data may believe that he can obtain hunches from looking at the data as a whole. The curriculum analyst may, for the same reason, hold the opinion that a broad overview of the content is important. These are matters that still have to be demonstrated—they are mentioned in order to indicate that although little attention can be given here to qualitative methods, they cannot be disregarded. Quantitative methods, on the other hand, are well developed and have had a history of success. They have had a long history in the hands of scientists working in many different disciplines, including linguistics, sociology, and psychology.

A volume edited by Pool (1959) brings together much of the knowledge concerning techniques in this area that have been evolved by workers in the several disciplines. He discusses the procedures under the paragraph titles that follow.

Intensity. Measures of intensity are attempts to indicate the emotional emphasis given a particular aspect of a communication. In the analysis of the content of a newspaper, emphasis can be measured in terms of the size of the headlines devoted to a particular topic, the number of words devoted to it, the number of pictures that accompany it, or the number of emotionally loaded words, and so forth. In the case of journalism such measures have often been used to reflect the bias in reporting. The emphasis given to one political party can be compared with the emphasis given to the other. Considerable skepticism has been expressed concerning the value of such measures despite their widespread use in studies of propaganda.

Frequency. The traditional method of undertaking content analysis is that of counting the number of times that particular ideas or words are presented; for example, one might attempt to determine the emphasis a textbook gives to the understanding of democracy by counting the number of times that the words *democracy* and *democratic* are used. Such a measure is not likely to fare very well. One can see this clearly when he realizes that such words might have a high frequency of occurrence in a speech by, say, Hitler, but with a derogatory connotation. The main fact recommending frequency measures is that they are simple to obtain and comparisons of the frequencies derived from different sources can be compared. For these reasons frequency counts continue to be used.

Contingencies. This form of analysis rarely appeared before 1950, but since then it has come into considerable prominence. This approach can be illustrated by referring back to the example given of the occurrence of the word *democracy* and related words in printed materials. The frequency count could be made in the way described or it could be made by tabulating separately the cases in which it was coupled with the implication that democracy was being rejected. On this basis the counts would clearly differentiate between the usage in an American high school text and that in a speech by Hitler. Contingency analysis takes into account the *context* in which particular words or ideas are expressed. In this way the content analysis is more likely to represent the materials from which it is derived than is a simple frequency count.

Many aspects of content analysis have not yet been well standardized, and each research worker must to some extent establish his own. One problem, for example, is the size of the units to be used as the basis for the analysis. A *unit of meaning* is sometimes considered the most appropriate unit for analysis, but there is some difficulty in deciding what is meant by the phrase. Despite the fact that on the surface the selection of a unit of suitable size appears to be an important problem, there is some research to indicate that the unit may be varied within wide limits without making too much difference in the result.

The categories to be used in content analysis must be appropriate to the particular problem under consideration. In many areas, sets of categories have been prepared that can be used by subsequent workers. This proliferation of systems of categories is unfortunate for, as Pool (1959) points out, what is needed are standardized sets of categories to be used for research in much the same way as standardized intelligence scales have been used in research on achievement. In certain areas, such as those involving the use of projective tests of personality, the value of standardized categories has been demonstrated.

Content Analysis in Educational and Psychological Research

In certain areas of educational and psychological research, the procedures of content analysis have had considerable impact. Some of the more important of these must now be given brief consideration.

A special case of content analysis that needs studying is that involved in the analysis of tests, particularly objective tests. The problem is a common one. Suppose a teacher or research worker wishes to use a published test for some specific purpose. He may be interested in making an analysis of the test to determine its relevance. In this connection, one group of educators (B. S. Bloom, 1956) has suggested that all test items of intellectual achievement be classified into a list of standard categories, which might then become generally used. Examples of the categories they employ are the following:

1.11   Knowledge of terminology
1.12   Knowledge of specific facts
1.21   Knowledge of conventions
1.22   Knowledge of trends and sequences
1.25   Knowledge of methodology
2.10   Translation from one level of abstraction to another
4.10   Analysis of elements
4.20   Analysis of relationships

This list gives just scattered examples from this attempt to categorize test items in terms of the achievement they are designed to measure. In the source from which these were abstracted, every effort has been made to define each category both in terms of general description and in terms of actual test items. However, despite the care with which this has been done, it is doubtful whether any two educators would show substantial agreement on the classification of items. The reliability of the process of classification needs to be determined experimentally.

This matter is closely tied up with the whole problem of determining the content validity of an achievement test. The term *content validity* is here borrowed from current usage. It is really inappropriate, because it refers, or should refer, to the objective properties of a test item. The so-called content validity problem is generally stated as that of determining the extent to which a group of test items can be considered to be a representative sample or a random sample of test items covering a particular area of knowledge. This problem of sampling is important in all fields of content analysis.

Attempts have been made to classify other aspects of behavior for the purposes of educational analysis. D. R. Krathwohl and his associates (1964) have proposed a classification of what they call the affective domain. This effort appears to be an attempt to classify behavior related to attitudes, value judgments, and perhaps even motivations.

An aspect of content analysis that has had great significance for educational research is that related to the appraisal of the comprehension level of printed material. A whole series of readability formulae have been developed, but there is still much controversy concerning their appropriate uses and limitations. The earliest attempts to measure this characteristic of printed material used the simple expedient of determining the percentage of difficult or easy words in terms of a list giving the frequency with which words appear in certain types of published materials. Those who undertook these early measurements were aware that this simple procedure was inadequate for handling the complexities that even the most straightforward prose presents. It soon became evident that these simple methods had very little use, but not until the mid-1930s had sufficient research been undertaken to permit the construction of more useful methods. W. S. Gray and B. E. Leary (1935), who pioneered in this field, published a complex formula for measuring readability, based on five characteristics selected from a list of eighty-two assumed elements. Nearly a decade later, I. Lorge (1944) developed a similar formula based on only three characteristics: the number of "difficult" words (as determined by a standard word list); the number of prepositional phrases; and sentence length. Other formulae appeared at about the same time as the Lorge formula; they included the Flesch formula (1951) and the Dale and Chall formula (1948). A review of the problem of measuring readability is available in a volume by G. R. Klare (1963).

An entirely different procedure for measuring difficulty, which has had a long history, has recently come into prominence under the name of the *cloze* procedure. If the readability of several passages is to be compared, an equal percentage of words are deleted from each passage. The words chosen for deletion should be selected at random. The passages are reproduced with the omitted words replaced by blanks of a uniform size. Subjects are then asked to attempt to fill in the blank spaces with the words they think should be there. The filled-in words are then scored as identical with those that were deleted or as different. The easier the passage, the greater is the probability that the words filled in will be similar to those that were in the original passage. This procedure for the measurement of relative reading difficulty is very easily undertaken when persons are willing to attempt to fill in the blanks. The resulting measures of readability or reading difficulty have been found to be highly correlated with those derived from the more conventional reading difficulty formulae.

Readability is closely related to the difficulty of the words used in the material. Two systems have been evolved for doing this. In the system used by Lorge and Thorndike the difficulty of a word is established by finding out how often it occurs in commonly read materials. The more frequently a word is encountered the easier it is considered to be. The difficulty levels of words given in the *Teacher's Work Book of 30,000 Words* (1944) are based on elaborate counts of how frequently each word appears in print. Although the latter procedure does give a rough indication of the difficulty of a word, a better procedure has been developed by E. Dale and G. Eichholz (1960). The alternative procedure is to administer vocabulary tests to children and to find out the percentage of children who know the meaning of each word. Dale and Eichholz claim that this new procedure provides far more useful measures of word difficulty than that provided by finding out the frequency of occurrence of each word. There seems to be considerable agreement that the characteristics measured by readability formulae are not entirely satisfactory and that the formulae cannot be applied to all kinds of materials. A formula that is quite satisfactory for measuring the readability of grade-school material may provide ridiculous results when it is used for assessing the readability of technical writing. A central difficulty is that the formulae do not take into account some of the more subtle aspects of style, which may have enormous influence on the difficulty level of reading material. An author may write in simple words, but his material may be difficult to read because he makes use of unusual analogy and innuendo in a way that conveys a richness of meaning through its overtones. No formula at present available takes into account this aspect of reading difficulty.

Reading difficulty is also a complex function of a person's previous experience. An elementary textbook in physics may be very difficult for a student before he has taken a course in physics, but easy once he has mastered the vocabulary and concepts of the field. Relatively slight differences in life histories can produce marked changes in readability of material. This fact illustrates the weakness of readability as a concept.

Measures of readability have many applications in the broader field of public education. They provide an objective means of determining the suitability of materials for various age groups and for various levels of pupil ability within these groups. They provide a means of adjusting existing materials to a more suitable level of readability. Many works of classical literature that are quite inappropriate to the current reading level of pupils have been adapted to make them suitable through the medium of readability formulae. In addition, such formulae have been used to measure the readability of announcements and other materials designed for public education programs such as are sponsored by various health and safety organizations.

Content Analysis and Problems of Sampling

Content analysis of the type thus far considered presents special problems of sampling, because it is not usually feasible to make an analysis of all of the material available. In the preparation of word lists indicating the frequency with which various words appear, the problem is acute. The purpose of such counts is to measure the "difficulty" of words, but the term *difficulty* has meaning only when it refers to a particular individual or group. A word is difficult if it is difficult to understand or if its meaning is understood by only a fraction of the members of a group. Thus if the difficulty of words for a particular group is to be estimated from their frequency in reading material to which the group is exposed, it is necessary to know what this group reads and to sample it. It may happen that the members of the group differ greatly in what they read, in which case it is necessary to assume that at least some of these various materials are equivalent. Of course care will be taken to insure that all the materials on which word counts are made are not by the same author, because individual authors often have their own favorite vocabularies. The difficulty of words assessed from a representative sample of specified materials may not provide a useful estimate of difficulty of words for other groups that have different reading habits. The common practice in this area is to sample so-called popular reading materials, such as the *Saturday Evening Post,* in the hope that the results can be applied to a wide range of groups; but this method of identifying the sample to be analyzed has always been criticized.

Content analysis at more complex levels than that of word difficulty ceases to be an entirely objective matter. The interpretation process involves the same subjectivity as does the interpretation of pupil behavior in the classroom. There should be agreement among judges concerning the interpretation of materials before anything more than the simplest content analysis can be made. This is fairly easy when the analysis is at the level of counting words in different categories, because there is good agreement as to which words are to be classified as nouns, as adjectives, as verbs, and so on. Greater difficulty is experienced in separating fact from inference. Perhaps little reliability might be found if an attempt were made to single out from a total speech those remarks that reflected hostile gestures. We can think of a continuum that varies from one end of the scale, where there would be no agreement among analysts, to the other end of the scale, where there would be complete agreement. Under the latter conditions there is objectivity of measurement, a term meaning that there is social agreement. It is not unusual to find that those aspects of content analysis on which there is complete social agreement are the most trivial of those it is desired to measure. It is thus necessary to move further down the scale and to sacrifice some objectivity in favor of relevance.

Content Analysis for the Measurement of Motivation and Other Attributes

The analysis of written and spoken responses for the purpose of identifying motives, attitudes, and values has had a long history in psychology. The scoring of the Rorschach test was one of the first devices using this kind of content analysis. In the early days of research with responses to inkblot materials, the tendency was to classify that person's responses into content categories such as plants, tools, animals, and maps. Such categories did not appear to be particularly useful and alternative categories were tried out. An alternative method of analysis, suggested by Hermann Rorschach himself, was that other aspects of the response be considered, such as whether it was a response to color, whether it involved the perception of a moving object such as a sheep *running*, or whether it involved a response to a small detail or to a large section of the inkblot. Such categories have generally been preferred to those classifing the objects perceived, but the usefulness of the measures derived still remains a source of controversy. At least a part of the problem is that the measures are highly influenced by the particular circumstances under which the instrument is administered. The response given to a Rorschach card is a response to a total situation rather than just a response to the inkblot.

A related kind of analysis became applied later to the responses to many other kinds of testing situation. The best-known and most extensive work involving this kind of content analysis was sparked by the work of H. A. Murray and the development of the Thematic Apperception test. The latter device became a prototype for a whole series of instruments designed to measure motivation. All of them present pictures of persons involved in life situations, but the details of the picture are sufficiently vague that the action involved can be interpreted in many different ways. Many of the pictures are highly suggestive of stress and tension. The task of the person presented with the picture is to provide an interpretation of what is happening. Generally he is given some guidance in this task by being asked such questions as, What is happening? What has led up to the situation? What is being thought? What is wanted? What will be done? For a common method of the analysis of the content of such materials, the reader is referred to D. C. McClelland *et al.* (1953). A much more complex method of scoring is found in S. S. Tomkins (1947). The general purpose of these scoring systems is to produce measures of motivation and, of particular interest to educators, to derive measures of achievement motivation. Similar scoring systems have been applied to strictly verbal tests such as those of E. French (April, 1956), which also provide measures of achievement motivation. The latter measures have shown some small relationship with achievement in school learning situations. A book by H. Heckhausen (1967) reviews the very extensive and intensive research that has been undertaken on achievement motivation, both with respect to how it develops and what its effect on behavior are.

Numerous other kinds of materials derived from standardized situations can provide interesting information if subjected to suitable content analysis techniques. For example, W. Rabinowitz and Travers (1955) asked students of education to make quick drawings of "a teacher with a class." An analysis of these drawings was used to study the student's concept of what teaching involved. Such concepts were found to differ as a result of the particular teacher-education program to which the student had been exposed. Examples of the kinds of drawings involved in this study, but collected by Rabinowitz in a later study, are shown in Figure 4. A comparison of these two drawings makes it very clear that students of education can present fundamentally different concepts of teaching through this medium. G. F. Gregersen and Travers (1968) asked children in the lower elementary grades to draw similar pictures and analyzed in terms of the extent to which

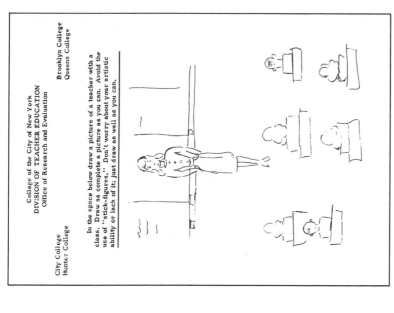

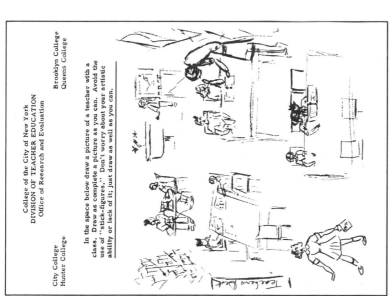

FIGURE 4. *A projective technique for studying concepts of teaching. Students of education and teachers were asked to draw a picture of a teacher with a class. This illustration presents two strikingly different concepts of how a teacher should behave in a classroom, and also how a classroom should be organized. (Illustration by courtesy of Dr. William Rabinowitz, and collected as part of a research study at the Office of Research and Evaluation of the Division of Teacher Education, Municipal College of New York City.)*

235

they reflected a positive or negative teacher-pupil interaction. The drawings, in the latter study, could be assigned to the positive and negative categories on the basis of quite objective features of the picture, such as the relative size of the pupil and teacher, the absence of any pupils, lack of facial features of pupils, and so forth. The study showed that the boys produced more negative drawings than the girls, but that the girls showed an increasing frequency of negative responses as they advanced through the grades. In addition, the proportion of pictures showing a negative interaction depended on the particular teacher involved. The classification of the drawings in this study could be made with a high degree of reliability.

Information Storage and Retrieval: A Special Problem in Content Analysis

The techniques of content analysis that have been developed by those engaged in curriculum research have been relatively crude. Much more refined systems for the analysis of verbal discourse have been developed by those engaged in the problem of storing the fund of human knowledge in such a way that information relevant to the solution of particular problems can be readily retrieved. The development of techniques for the storage and retrieval of information has become one of considerable importance with the extensive sponsorship of research by the Federal government and the resulting vast volume of findings that become hidden away in obscure research archives.

Merely adding books and pamphlets to the shelves of libraries does little to help the user of knowledge to locate the information he needs. This problem has become particularly acute in many areas including that of educational research where an extraordinary proliferation of studies has taken place. In order to handle this problem, considerable money has been spent on the development of methods of analyzing and coding the content of research documents that have implications for teaching and supervision. Some of these methods have implications for curriculum research that may also involve the analysis of documents.

Although library catalogs permit a search of those documents that are entered in the card catalog, the classification involved is a crude one. Furthermore, the card catalog does not attempt to present information on the content of journals and other sources in which research is published. One cannot go to a typical library card catalog and locate articles on, say, the effect of economic deprivation on school achievement, although the Ohio State University attempted, at one time, to prepare such a file for educational researchers. Before material can be cataloged, an analysis must be made of its content. The central problem of developing a storage and retrieval system is that of developing a method of identifying and coding the essential content of documents. The analysis of research literature for this purpose is not too different from that of studying a curriculum and preparing a summary of what it contains.

Those who have engaged in the problem of the analysis of the content of research reports for the purpose of storage and retrieval generally agree that the conventional abstract or brief summary is not particularly useful for this purpose. A storage and retrieval system requires that all information be handled through a number of steps.

1. An analysis must be made of each research report in such a way that the essential content can be reduced to an abstract written in a uniform language and in a standardized format. Ordinary abstracts and summarizing statements do not do this because each person writing a summary of a research report tends to use his own terms and his own preferred format.

2. In order that the information derived from the abstracts be readily available to users, it must be stored in a form that permits the user ready access. Card catalogs, with summaries printed on them, are not particularly useful, particularly when a very large number of studies is involved. The task of going through 1000 or more cards, in the hope of picking up a study that may be of use, is a tedious and time-consuming task. Systems for scanning the information in libraries exist, as L. H. Heilprin and F. L. Goodman (1965) point out, because the human is capable of scanning information at only a slow rate. Electronic and mechanical devices can scan suitably coded information at a much higher rate and, hence, provide the human with a capability of scanning vastly more information than he would have access to through his senses alone.

3. A good storage system permits rapid searching of sources of information and the retrieval of knowledge in a useful form. A retrieval system that has not been designed to meet these conditions is not acceptable.

Let us consider the first of these steps in the handling of information. It involves the summarization of knowledge in a very compact form in a special language developed for this purpose. Such a language has been developed for handling educational research. The language is one of the products of a series of projects on the storage and retrieval of information undertaken by the Center for Documentation and Communication Research at Western Reserve University. The summary that results from the coding of knowledge into a special language is referred to as a *telegraphic abstract* to distinguish it from a *conventional abstract*. The telegraphic language consists of a list of key words derived from the study, each one of which is paired with a special code word indicating the role played by the word in the description of the study. For example, KIS-Harvard means that the study was undertaken at Harvard, but KEJ-Harvard means that the study was a study *of* Harvard.

An example given by P. W. Reeves, *et al.* (1962) shown in Table 2, illustrates how a telegraphic abstract is used to provide a digest of the essential information in a study. In this telegraphic abstract, the words in parenthesis were added to help the reader understand what the coded terms mean. This abstract of the study is to be contrasted with that provided by a conventional abstract that this author prepared as follows:

A comparison was made of the teaching effectiveness of the captioned filmstrip, the captioned filmstrip with narration, the sound filmstrip, and the filmograph for teaching a sixth-grade social studies unit on the origin and way of life of the Maoris in New Zealand. Four groups of sixth-graders in Los Angeles, matched with respect to IQ, sex, age, and socioeconomic status, were derived from a population of 558 sixth-graders in the Los Angeles schools. Each group was exposed to one of the four teaching procedures. A pre- and post-test of achievement in the unit was administered and also a delayed retention test was administered after three weeks. Analysis of the variance of the gain scores for the pre- and post-tests showed that the means were significantly different, but a Tukey test indicated that no one method could be considered significantly superior to any other. Boys performed significantly better than girls. When a comparison was made of the pre- and delayed-retention test, no significant differences were found between the methods.

The telegraphic abstract is also carried one step further in that the ordinary English words in the right-hand column are then converted into a uniform coded language referred to as the semantic code. The coded telegraphic abstracts are then all placed on the kind of tape used to provide inputs to computers.

What has been done up to this point is to summarize a study through the use of a uniform set of symbols of the type that a computer can handle. If the procedure has been effective, it will mean that the essential nature of each of a very large number of studies can be fed

Col. 6-8	Role Indicator (Col. 28-80)	Col. 6-8	Description (Col. 9-27)
			Do not write in this space
1	. . KAB, (type of literature)	2	RESEARCH
3	. KIS, (location)	4	U OF SOUTHERN CALIF
5	. KQJ, (sponsor)	6	NDEA TITLE 7
7	. . KIT, (year)	8	1960
9	. . KEJ, (subject of study)	10	STUDENT (558)
11	. KIS,	12	ELEMENTARY SCHOOL
13		14	INTERMEDIATE
15	. KWV, (attribute)	16	IQ
17		18	AGE
19		20	SEX
21		22	SOCIOECONOMIC
23		24	MATCHED
25	KIS,	26	LOS ANGELES CO CALIF
27	. . KAM, (process)	28	TESTING
29	. KQJ KWJ, (means developed)	30	FACT
31		32	CONCEPT
33		34	TEST
35	. . KEC, (subject-matter taught)	36	SOCIAL STUDIES
37	. KQJ, (means)	38	FILMSTRIP
39	. KQJ,	40	FILMOGRAPH
41	. KWV,	42	CAPTION
43	. KWV,	44	NARRATION
45	. KWV,	46	SOUND
47	. . KAM,	48	DATA
49		50	ANALYSIS

Abstracter ————————————

TABLE 2. *A telegraphic abstract.* From Reeves, *et al.* (1962, pp. 181–182).

Col. 6-8	Role Indicator (Col. 28-80)	Col. 6-8	Description (Col. 9-27)
51	. KQJ,	52	VARIANCE
53	. KQJ,	54	TUKEY TEST
55	. . KUP KAP, (finding influenced)	56	IMMEDIATE
57		58	RETAINED
59		60	LEARNING
61	. KAL, (influencing factor)	62	IQ
63	. KAL,	64	SEX
65	. KAL KXL, (Sometimes not an influence)	66	CAPTION
67	. KAL KXL,	68	NARRATION
69	. KAL KXL,	70	SOUND
71	. KAL KXL,	72	FILMOGRAPH
73		74	
75		76	
77		78	
79		80	
81		82	
83		84	
85		86	
87		88	
89		90	
91		92	
93		94	
95		96	
97		98	
99		100	

into a computer that will then examine them. A person using the equipment can then ask the machine to sort out all the studies concerned with particular topics or problems.

In retrieving information, the person who wants information has to ask the data bank and the related computer a question. For example, a person may ask the computer the question, "What research has been done on social studies achievement in children?" The computer will then scan the tapes on which the telegraphic abstracts have been recorded and print out the numbers of those studies that pertain to the question asked. Once the list of numbers has been prepared, the person who asked the question can then go to the files and pull out the conventional abstracts for these studies. These abstracts can then be perused as they would be in a library; however, the machine has undertaken the task of identifying them, and has performed, in less than an hour, a library search that might have taken many weeks to undertake in a conventional manner.

The question about social studies achievement might have been asked in a number of different forms, which might have placed restrictions on the answer and, hence, reduced the number of studies located. For example the question might have asked, "What research has been done on social studies achievement in sixth-grade children?" This form of the question would result in the machine rejecting all social studies research that did *not* involve the sixth grade and the resulting list of studies produced would be much shorter than the previous list. The more specific the question, the shorter is the list of studies produced.

Although the system that has been developed for the storage and retrieval of educational research covers, at this time, some 4000 documents, funds have not been available to make the system available to most users. However, one can confidently predict that the kind of system envisaged will become an integral part of the library of the future. Users of educational research should be aware of the existence of such a system and not be taken by surprise when it becomes available. A similar system is already available to users in the field of chemistry.

The kind of analysis of documents that is required for a storage and retrieval system is not too different from the analysis required for much curriculum research. The analysis of textbooks commonly undertaken in curriculum research requires that the knowledge represented by the books be coded in some form that will permit the content of one book to be compared with the content of another book. Crude forms of coding the content of documents have long been used in curriculum research, but the kind of coding developed by the Center for Documentation and Communication Research represents a much more sophisticated system than any that curriculum researchers have developed in the past.

The procedure for the classification and retrieval of educational research that has been discussed here represents only one of many projects that have been developed for similar purposes in the behavioral sciences. For example, the National Library of Medicine has long been concerned with the development of a language for the analysis of medical literature and is now expanding this language to include a vocabulary for the behavioral sciences. In order to promote this effort, the Library is being aided by other bodies interested in the analysis and retrieval of information in the behavioral sciences including the American Psychological Association, which publishes *Psychological Abstracts*. If the language thus developed were suitable for the analysis of information in *Psychological Abstracts*, then a simple system could be developed for retrieving information from the abstracts. Although much of the activity in this area is directly concerned with the development of useful library systems, some of the activity is more concerned with the more general problem of the analysis of the content of verbal communication and the use of computers in the analysis of content. For example, Harvard has had a major project involving a computer approach to content analysis and has developed a system known as the *General Inquirer*. The problems involved are also closely related to those of developing computer languages.

At a practical level, numerous library information-retrieval projects, in addition to those already named, could be cited to show the extent to which the area is a vigorously developing one. Of particular interest to the reader is the Educational Research Information Center (ERIC), which is a central unit coordinating the work of a nationwide series of ERIC clearinghouses. This entire operation has been developed and financed by the United States Office of Education. Each one of the ERIC clearinghouses is a depository of research and related information in some fairly specialized area such as reading, science education, the disadvantaged, exceptional children, junior colleges, and so forth. A periodical is produced listing the various documents available and copies of these documents are obtainable at a nominal cost. Whether there is enough buried information that it is worth making available through such a costly system still remains to be seen. Opinions vary on this matter. Some believe they see an explosion in knowledge on the educational frontier, but others take the stand that the explosion has only the force of a popgun.

Another extensive project for the analysis of information is the

Science Information Centers Branch of the National Institute for Child Health and Human Development. Three units are being established by this organization that will survey, collect, analyze, and make available information pertaining to three periods of the human life span. The plan is to provide computer systems through which the information in the system can be scanned and selectively retrieved. In addition, some more conventional publications may be forthcoming.

A final example is the IMPRINT program developed by the Galton Institute. This program is designed to focus on information in the areas of perception, learning, and cognition. This center expects to explore new methods of scientific reporting that will both eliminate the long publication lag that is now typical and the unsatisfactory distribution of scientific documents. The hope is that new methods will be developed so that scientists will be quickly and efficiently informed of developments related to their own work, and so that they will no longer have to scan masses of material to find the few studies in which they are interested.

Even some simple devices may provide much more effective scanning and localization of information than is ordinarily provided, and they do not necessarily have to involve computers. F. L. Goodman (1963) has developed a simple device involving the use of thirty-six IBM cards that can be used for locating information within a bibliography of several hundred items. The cards are used without the help of any mechanical devices. Other simple devices have, of course, long been used for the retrieval of information from books. For example, the table of contents of a book is a device permitting the scanning of the content of the book at a highly abstract and general level. The index at the end of the book provides a more extensive means of scanning content and the location of particular aspects of the information presented. The index could, almost certainly, be greatly improved from what it is today.

Summary

1. The analysis of the content of verbal materials represents an important approach to the study of curriculum problems. Although simple techniques have been used in the past, newer approaches represent a high degree of sophistication.

2. The content of a curriculum is that aspect of it that can be reduced to a set of statements or propositions. Many aspects of the

curriculum cannot be thus reduced and, hence, are not included in content.

3. The content of a subject-matter field has some degree of organization. In fields that have logical organization, such as mathematics, the structure is readily identifiable. On the other hand, a subject such as history reflects many interwoven structures running through it. Areas of knowledge that have complex structures do not lend themselves easily to the development of teaching programs such as are involved in teaching machines.

4. Major developments of techniques used in content analysis have evolved in communications research. In the latter area, attempts have been undertaken to make an analysis of the "emotional" content of verbal communications.

5. The major development of content analysis in the area of education has been in the production of taxonomies of objectives of education. These permit the analysis of the content of objective tests, but have not as yet provided a means of analyzing the content of written materials or the content of the verbal communications of teachers.

6. Reading-difficulty formulae have been evolved for measuring the readability of verbal communications. Numerous formulae exist, each of which has its own merits and limitations.

7. An important characteristic of printed materials is the difficulty level of the vocabulary, which can be measured by two quite distinct techniques that give rather different results.

8. A special use of content-analysis procedures has been in the area of the measurement of motivation. These procedures are based on the assumption that a person's verbal responses to many situations provide information concerning his motives. The test situations that have been used include inkblots, pictures of life situations that can be given many interpretations, and brief, vague statements into which a person can read many meanings.

9. Most studies involving content analysis require the research worker to draw a sample of the materials to be analyzed. The identification of an appropriate sample is often a very difficult problem.

10. A special problem in content analysis is presented in the task of storing and retrieving research information. In order for knowledge derived from research to be available, it must be stored in a precise and compact form and also in a form permitting a mechanical search of the storage system so that needed information can be rapidly retrieved. Storage and retrieval systems generally involve the development and use of a special language that computers can use.

‖ ‖

CHAPTER 11

Prediction Studies

Research on Problems of Prediction

"WHAT is the state of affairs that exists?" is the type of question that surveys most commonly attempt to answer. The major purpose of surveys as they are conducted in educational research is not the prediction of events in the future. However, a great many educational research studies are carried out with the primary object of developing methods of making predictions. This type of study and problems attending its execution are considered in this chapter.

Prediction studies within the domain of educational research may be sociological, economic, or psychological. Attempts may be made to predict enrollments at some future date. Predictions may also be made of the future teacher supply and demand, and of funds to be available for teachers' salaries from direct taxation. Forecasts may also be made of the success or failure of pupils in different curricula. Sometimes attempts are made to provide predictions over a relatively long period of time—for example, studies that attempt to develop methods of predicting college success from tests given in junior high school. These studies are concerned with problems of the greatest importance, for the assignment of pupils to a proper curriculum in high school must depend on the ability of school personnel to predict how the pupil's talents can best be used at a later time in his career.

The Pseudo Science of Predicting Something from Anything

A word must be said about the type of educational study that involves predicting *something* from *anything*. Usually both the *some-*

thing and the *anything* are rather vague. Many such studies begin with the graduate student's dissatisfaction with current procedures for predicting scholastic success in some field of study in which he is interested. Such a student may have been a high school teacher of accounting. Greatly concerned with the fact that a large fraction of students who enter accounting courses fail to achieve satisfactory grades, he may feel there is a need for building a test that will eliminate those applicants who are almost certain to fail. Because various tests have been tried, but none has proved to be useful, he decides to collect a number of new tests and administer them to students of accounting in the hope that one will turn out to be a good predictor of grades. This might be called a shotgun approach, and it has disadvantages with which the graduate student should be familiar.

First, it is a departure from the type of scientific procedure that has yielded so much in the past and represents a return to a much more primitive method of achieving knowledge. It is a return to the kind of prescientific technique practiced by the medieval physician, who tried whatever herbs and techniques he had at his disposal in the hope that something would be found to help the patient. Occasionally this approach worked and the patient was cured, and in this way there accumulated a considerable amount of unconnected items of information that had their uses in the primitive practice of medicine. Such scraps of lore did not make medicine a science. Neither will large numbers of correlations between test scores and measures of performance in handling life's daily problems of work and play constitute a science of behavior. Only when these apparently disconnected facts are integrated into a system is there any hope that they may form the rudiments of a science.

Secondly, even if a correlation exists between a test and the *something* it is desired to predict, there is always a real possibility that the correlation may be the result of some irrelevant aspect of the *something*. For example, one might find that ratings of personal attractiveness of female college students correlated with grades in college. One might certainly suspect that this correlation was generated by the fact that male college professors might have a tendency to overestimate the academic achievement of outstandingly attractive college women. Such a hypothesis would be much more reasonable than to suppose that personal attractiveness has a genuine relationship to academic achievement.

Thirdly, because the shotgun approach is a hit-or-miss procedure, it is necessary to include a great many potential predictors—unless, of course, a theory is available that permits predictors to be selected in advance. Many studies of the predictive value of brief biographical items of information have been carried out by administering several hundred such items to groups whose behavior it was desired to predict and then selecting the items that had the greatest predictive value. Such procedures are laborious, require extensive statistical treatment of the data, and are costly. They are most appropriate where useful results must be achieved rapidly regardless of cost, and where new areas are being explored.

John Dewey (1910) elegantly compared the relative merits of the shotgun and the scientific methods of prediction in the following statement:

> While many empirical conclusions are, roughly speaking, correct; while they are exact enough to be of great help in practical life; while the presages of a weather-wise sailor or hunter may be more accurate, within a restricted range, than those of the scientist who relies solely on scientific observations; while, indeed, empirical observations and records furnish the raw or crude material of scientific knowledge, yet the empirical method affords no way of discriminating between right and wrong conclusions.

There are a few who might take the position that the endproduct of all prediction studies should be a kind of cookbook giving recipes for making particular predictions. One can imagine such a cookbook at this time although the knowledge available would not make a very impressive set of recipes if it were all assembled. Such an imaginary cookbook might tell one how to predict who is most likely to pass or fail each of a dozen different courses in algebra, or it might provide a recipe for selecting students most likely to profit from four hundred hours of instruction in Cantonese. Such a cookbook has some appeal in our present stage of ignorance, but it does not represent a worthwhile research goal. One can understand this point best by considering the limitations of such a cookbook in another field where prediction is a central problem.

Consider, for example, the problem of weather forecasting. At one time, weather forecasts for a particular locality were made by keeping records of *what followed what* in the sequence of weather conditions. Thus a high southeast wind in a particular locality might be taken to indicate rain, because rain followed more frequently than anything else on the tail of such a wind. Nobody knew why this was so. The probability of the occurrence was well established, but so long as nobody knew, there was no way of improving the accuracy of predictions. However, such a system of forecasting has been abandoned, because its accuracy could never be improved beyond that permitted by the data previously collected. The present system, which has replaced the old statistical system, is based on a knowledge of how weather conditions are produced. It is based largely on air-mass analysis and thermodynamics, and permits much more accurate predictions than the older statistical method. This does not mean, of course, that mathematical methods are not used for making predictions today, for they are. However, their function is to use data in accordance with some complex theory of weather prediction. Modern weather forecasting has in fact become highly mathematical and introduces the help of electronic computers in order that complex mathematical functions may be computed at a relatively rapid speed.

The example from meteorology illustrates the difference between predictions based on the accumulation of odd bits of information and predictions based on a well-organized body of knowledge. Predictions made within the context of educational research should stem from the knowledge available about the phenomena as well as from knowledge in organized disciplines such as psychology and sociology. However, sometimes the knowledge available is so meager that the research worker has no alternative except to try anything that, on a common sense basis, offers some hope of providing predictions. The latter represents a kind of prescientific activity that sometimes has to be undertaken as a prerequisite of later scientific research.

Reliability: An Essential Condition for Prediction

A necessary, but not a sufficient condition, for prediction is reliability. If the predictors have zero reliability, there can be no prediction. If the measure to be predicted has no reliability, there can also be no prediction. Consider, for example, a highly unreliable predictor such as my judgment of how a new employee is going to work out. In my particular case, such judgments depend on the whim of the hour. One minute the new employee does something well and I have high expectations, but a minute later he flounders and I reverse my judgment. If forced to make a prediction immediately after the employee reported to work, such a forecast would show no relationship to the performance of the employee over a year. In this case, the predictor variable could not predict any more accurately than could the throw of dice. Both the fall of the dice and my judgment depend on numerous trivial and inconsequential circumstances that make them useless for prediction purposes.

Prediction is also not possible when the variable to be predicted has negligible reliability. Grades on a ten-minute test in a particular course have low reliability and may be almost unpredictable for this reason. The grade of the student on the test may depend on such factors as whether he had been sick or well on the previous day, whether he interpreted the question correctly or incorrectly, whether he attended or did not attend the lecture of a guest speaker who discussed a related topic, whether the instructor who grades the papers is tired or fresh when he comes to this particular student's paper, and an endless number of other factors. The grade on the particular test is, almost certainly, unreliable. Indeed, if the same quiz were given unexpectedly again a week later and if the papers were to be graded by a different instructor, there would, almost certainly, be only a very small correlation between the two sets of grades.

Such a measure would be virtually unpredictable. Now the reader may argue at this point that the illustration is trivial because nobody would ever want to predict a grade in a particular course; but many conditions that are not trivial and that one might want to predict have similar characteristics. For example, in a slum population, it may be virtually impossible to predict which of the youth will be convicted for minor or major crimes, because delinquency is widespread and chance factors determine which ones get caught. The condition to be predicted—conviction or nonconviction during a particular period of time—has virtually zero reliability and, hence, is unpredictable. In such a case, the selection of highly reliable measures as the potential predictors does not help the situation, for there is nothing sufficiently solid to predict to make a forecast possible.

The more commonly occurring problem is where both the variables selected as predictors and the measure, or measures, that one seeks to predict are of limited reliability. In such a case some degree of prediction is *possible* even though, of course, it may well happen that what we have selected as potential predictors do not predict at all under the circumstances involved. The reliability of both the predictors and the variable predicted sets a ceiling on the value of the correlation that could be found.

Efforts are always made in prediction studies to select variables that have as high reliability as can be found. Sometimes, however, the only measures available may have low reliability, and little can be done either to improve the measures or to obtain others with more desirable characteristics. Under such circumstances one has to accept the fact that limitations have been placed on the accuracy of any prediction that can be made.

Empiricism and Research on Problems
of Educational Prediction

Research on problems of predicting educational achievement has not usually been scientific in the sense in which the term has been used in this volume. Inevitably this has been so, for the urgent need for making accurate educational predictions has prompted those concerned with the problem to grasp whatever facts were available. In addition, in the partial solution of urgent problems that are complex in character, it is often much more feasible to try out a large number of possible solutions and see which will work rather than to develop a program of research along systematic and scientific lines. At least three types of empirical procedures have been adopted in this setting, and the merits of each need to be considered.

Method I. The miniature-situation approach. This is a procedure for developing methods of prediction that really involves no research at all, but simply requires the educator to reproduce a miniature and abbreviated situation in which a subject can be given, so to speak, a trial run. The experimenter hypothesizes that performance in the miniature situation will reflect quality of performance in the larger situation in which it is desired to predict behavior. Thus, in the development of algebra-prognosis tests, an attempt has been made to introduce into the test situation some of the learning activities that the pupils will have to face in his first course in algebra. Language-prognosis tests use a similar technique. One such test measures the ability of the student to learn a small amount of Esperanto. It has been shown that the ability to learn small amounts of this artificial tongue is related to the ability to learn large amounts of other languages.

This technique is generally a successful one. The major condition that may mitigate its use is that which occurs when learning in the early stages of an activity involves abilities different from those involved in learning in a later stage. Such changes in the determinants of behavior as learning progresses have been shown to occur in certain instances, but these changes have not been particularly striking and probably are not sufficient to prevent the use of a miniature learning situation for selecting pupils most likely to succeed. However this may be, activity directed toward the development of such a technique for a particular purpose cannot be said to make a contribution to scientific knowledge. The product is a technique that in no way adds to available organized knowledge.

From the point of view of developing guidance practices, the miniature learning situation does not result in a product that fits well into current procedures. It is clearly quite impractical for the guidance counselor to administer as many miniature learning situations as there are situations in which one may desire to predict behavior. The guidance worker, needs a short and comprehensive battery of tests that overlap as little as possible. Guidance batteries that are currently widely used do not include the miniature learning situation type of test.

Method II. The hit-or-miss approach. This method has already been discussed, and it is briefly mentioned here in order to contrast it with other methods. This approach to the problem of prediction involves the administration of a wide range of instruments in the hope that one will be found that predicts successfully. This statement is a little exaggerated, in that the investigator is unlikely to try out just *any* instrument; rather, he will select those that appear to have at least some connection with the phenomenon to be predicted. The technique finds support in the fact that it has had a long and fairly successful history of application. A strong point in its favor is that many a time an unpromising variable has turned out to be the best predictor. Once this has occurred, it is nearly always possible to find a good reason why it should be so. On the negative side, there are several points to be noted.

The method involves a great amount of work on the part of those administering the tests and on the part of those taking them. *Careful thinking through of the problem might result in the tryout of a much more limited battery of instruments, with less time lost by all.* This gain must be balanced against any loss that may result from unlikely variables turning out to be good predictors.

In addition, the variables likely to be selected are those that have some superficial relationship to the phenomenon that is to be predicted. If an analysis of the prediction problem is made in terms of current psychological knowledge, it is probable that only a few likely predictor variables will appear, but these may not have any relationship to the predicted variable obvious to the layman.

Method III. The scientist's approach to the problem of prediction. A third method involves the development of a theory concerning the nature of the phenomena to be predicted, and, on the basis of that theory, the derivation of methods hypothesized to predict.

A good example of the systematic development of a device for making predictions is found in Carroll's Modern Language Aptitude tests. The development of the Carroll tests is to be contrasted with the development of the language-aptitude tests, previously discussed in this chapter, in which the student was given the task of learning a small sample of an unfamiliar language. Carroll developed his test by first making an analysis of the skills required to learn a foreign language and came to the conclusion that such a learning task involved five distinct skills. For each of these he developed a test. The first test in the series involves what may be called auditory alertness; the second measures the ability to learn written symbols corresponding to particular sounds; the third involves spelling ability and, to some extent, the ability to associate sounds and symbols; the fourth measures sensitivity to grammatical construction; and the fifth part measures the ability to associate one word with another, an ability presumed to be related to vocabulary acquisition. The soundness of Carroll's analysis is shown by the fact that the test has been successful in predicting performance in foreign-language courses. The division of the test into a number of separate components is also of value in that the acquisition of a particular foreign language may be much more dependent on one component than on another.

The Modern Language test is an excellent example of the development of a device to be used for prediction through a systematic scientific analysis of the behavior to be predicted. So little has been done to develop prediction studies on the basis of this method that it is difficult to discuss the problems that it presents. The primary difficulty most certainly lies in the theory-construction phase itself.

Validity and the Design of Prediction Studies

In most modern prediction studies, the variables selected as potential predictors are those that have had a history of predicting well in related situations. Because there is hardly an aspect of human activity in which prediction studies have not already been undertaken in considerable numbers, no study need be carried out on a blind hit-or-miss basis. Generally, some kind of analysis such as Carroll undertook in preparing the Modern Language test will provide a basis for the selection of appropriate measuring devices; but from the several that are likely to be available, the ones with the best history of prediction should be chosen. Thus consideration must be given to the selection of instruments for which there is data showing that they can be expected to make valid predictions.

The research worker has to be extremely careful to avoid using measures merely because they have names that make them attractive for the purpose at hand. Numerous prediction studies have involved the use of measures described as providing assessments of *achievement motivation*. This term suggests that the measures should predict, for example, scores on achievement tests. What the users have often failed to note is that measures of achievement motivation, built on the basis of theory of motivation, can be expected to predict achievement only when the persons involved feel challenged by the task they are to perform. Measures of achievement motivation have construct validity, that is to say they fit into a system of ideas of how certain predictions can be made. If they are used within that system, then they will provide limited predictions. Whenever there is information available the research worker should attempt to determine whether a particular instrument has construct validity for making the kind of prediction that he wishes to make.

Conditions Necessary for Effective Prediction

In predicting performance in a college algebra course from, say, the college admissions battery taken six months earlier, much may happen between the time of the taking of the tests and the taking of the course. Some students during this interval may take additional work in mathematics to prepare them for college work in the same field, whereas others, who also need the additional work, do not. Such events will seriously upset the possibility of predicting performance in the college algebra course from the admissions test battery. The longer the interval between the prediction and the event to be predicted, the smaller are the chances of making a successful prediction.

Many prediction studies end in failure that could have been avoided if the researcher had considered the problem carefully in advance. In many such cases, a careful consideration of the problem in the first place would have led to the realization that the prediction was not a feasible one.

Consider the problem of predicting the number of teachers who will resign from a large school system during each year for the next ten years. This is no trivial problem, because the long-term training of teachers requires that candidates be trained to replace those resigning from the system as well as to take other positions that will have to be filled over the course of the years. Large numbers of resignations may leave gaps that cannot easily be filled unless there has been long-term planning.

The time when it is necessary to make the prediction of whether a given group of teachers will or will not resign is four or five years before resignations actually take place, because this is the time required for recruiting and training new teachers. This is a considerable span of years over which to make predictions, but many educational forecasts are made with a useful degree of accuracy over this period.

An immediate suggestion about how the prediction should be made is that data be obtained from the past and applied to the future. It certainly would be possible to obtain data on resignations over a long previous period, say twenty years, and to work out an average resignation rate. On the surface, this may appear to be a good method, until the data are closely examined and the discovery is made that most of the resignations occurred during a short period during the boom of the early sixties. The reason for this was that teachers then were offered wages in industry far above those that could be obtained within the educational system. However, even if such a period of high wages for ex-teachers did recur, school districts in the future might be willing to offer teachers a bonus or other financial incentive to stay on in the system—in which case the resignation rate might be held at a low and constant level. Insofar as the resignation rate depends on unpredictable economic conditions and international tensions, it is not predictable by any technique at present available. At least, economists and political scientists have not yet succeeded in predicting such events and conditions.

An alternative approach can be taken if the problem is redefined. In place of stating the problem as that of predicting the percentage of teachers likely to resign in a given year, it can be redefined as that of identifying those who are most likely to resist the temptation to resign. Stability could be given to a teaching body if it included only those who are likely to stay with the system indefinitely. It seems reasonable to assume that the personal characteristics of those who remain might be different from those who resign. One might suspect that those would stay who have a deeper interest in teaching and a more favorable attitude toward the activities it involves than those who would leave for economic reasons. (One might perhaps hypothesize that those who stay might tend to be less ambitious, and perhaps less intelligent, than those who leave.) Conceivably, a study could be designed to discover ways of identifying teachers who would not resign for economic reasons. At least some of the necessary conditions for practical predictions exist when the problem is stated in this way. However, it must be pointed out that the usefulness of a study of this kind might well be questioned. It would be hard to imagine an acceptable teacher-selection procedure that would permit the rejection of those who did not present characteristics making for long years of service. Indeed, such a procedure might well eliminate some of the ablest teachers—those who might come to provide leadership for the system. However, it must be pointed out that the problem of creating a stable body of teachers should be attacked realistically by making economic adjustments, for economic conditions are clearly a major determinant of resignations, and attempts to solve the problem by selection would not attack it at its roots.

From what has been said, it is clear that, for a phenomenon to be predictable, the determinants must exist in some well-identified and measurable form at the time when the prediction is made. If partial predictions are to be accepted, and they must be because perfect predictions cannot be made, then only partial determinants need exist in an identifiable form.

Another condition that should be established before a prediction study is undertaken is that the phenomenon to be predicted is relatively uniform in its causes; that is to say, that it generally has the same causes. An example of a condition that it has not been possible to predict with much success because of the multiplicity of possible causes is delinquency. It is obviously most desirable to predict which children are most likely to become delinquent, so that the clinical psychologist and social worker can get to work to prevent this from happening. The difficulty is that there are many major determinants of delinquency. Some delinquency is a product of lack of intellectual insight into what is happening. Other causes include the effects of associates, the home background, and various pathological psychological conditions, to mention but a few. Under these conditions there is no single effective way of identifying the potential delinquent, although some measures have been developed that provide rough overall predictions.

An additional important condition for prediction is that whatever is to be predicted must represent a well-defined phenomenon, and, if possible, a measurable variable. A much discussed variable such as teacher effectiveness does not meet these standards. On the other hand, if specific and well-defined aspects of teacher effectiveness are used in prediction studies, then there is danger that the researcher may be able to predict only the trivial. The discovery of a significant and well-defined variable to forecast is often the major difficulty in the development of a prediction study.

Research designed to evaluate the effectiveness of counseling frequently suffers from the fact that the condition to be predicted cannot be described in terms of a single variable. Although we may talk in generalities and point to, say, *adjustment* as the condition to be predicted, there are many ways in which a person may adjust, and these cannot be compared to one another easily, if at all. In the face of this difficulty, many quite ridiculous criteria of the success of counseling have been evolved. For example, in one study the success of the counseling procedure was evaluated in terms of whether the counselee returned for more. A somewhat better solution might be to classify those who come for counseling into a number of different categories in terms of the type of adjustment to be made or the problem to be solved. Within any one group, it may be possible to distribute success at making the desired adjustment along a single scale.

Finally, consideration must be given to the problem of using biographical data provided by the individual about his own past for the making of predictions. The use of such data is based mainly on the assumption that the exposure of the child to certain environmental conditions results in the development of particular attributes that later become determinants of behavior, such as job success. Difficulties in the use of such data arise because of the problem of identifying just what happened in the individual's past. There is· little difficulty in determining *what he himself thinks happened,* but this may be quite different from what actually happened. Also, what *he thinks happened* will probably change from time to time, whereas what actually happened will not change. For this reason, among others, the predictive value of biographical events as they are reported has been found to be small.

Fractionating Populations to Increase Accuracy of Predictions

A number of interesting cases have been found in which it has not been possible to make predictions for an entire group, but in which predictions could be made within a section of that group. For example, it has been found in studies of achievement motivation that in some situations this variable shows little relationship to performance when an entire group is involved. On the other hand, when it is possible to separate from the total group those who see the task to be performed as a challenge, a marked relationship exists between achievement motivation and performance within this small group. This is not surprising, because achievement motivation can hardly be expected to operate in situations in which the individual does not feel a need to do his best.

In almost every area of educational research, one can think of situations in which it is necessary to partition a population of events in order to establish relationships. Where relationships are to be found between the qualifications of teachers and the characteristics of the curriculum, one would expect different relationships in urban schools than in rural schools. Sometimes it may be necessary to separate boys from girls in order to make a meaningful prediction. Sometimes it may be necessary to separate cultural groups. In other cases, relationships may apply to only certain types of economic conditions. A careful thinking through of most studies is likely to reveal the possibility that some of the relationships expected are more likely to occur in certain sections of the population than in others. It is of considerable interest to determine whether such hypotheses are sound.

Some tests are designed to separate into distinct categories those for whom the test provides a valid score and those for whom the score is not valid. The separation is accomplished by means of a validating score generally derived by scoring certain special items in the test. Such scores are referred to as validating scores and these are generally designed to indicate whether the individual tested showed reasonable cooperation. These scores may also reflect other attributes that may invalidate a test score, such as a tendency to respond to personality inventory items with an excessive number of positive or negative responses. Some persons have a tendency to answer "Yes" to inventory types of items and others have a tendency to answer "No." Such tendencies are referred to as response sets. The identification of persons excessively influenced by such sets is important in prediction studies. The elimination of such persons from the population studied will often show that an instrument can be used for predicting the behavior of the remaining individuals.

Clustering of Variables to Increase Accuracy of Predictions

It happens frequently in educational research that numerous variables are included as potential predictors of a particular phenomenon. These predictors may show irregular but low correlations with the variable it is desired to predict. It would be possible, of course, to compute a combination of the variables that will *best* predict the particular independent variable. If this procedure were followed, a combination that maximized the prediction would provide what appeared to be an accurate prediction, but when the same combination of best predictors was applied to a new sample, the prediction would shrink substantially. This is the well-known phenomenon of *shrinkage* that has dealt a fatal blow to many studies that were promising on the surface. The problem of shrinkage is discussed in greater detail in a later section of this chapter devoted to the topic.

A second approach to the problem of building up predictions does not suffer from this hazard. It involves, first, the clustering of those predictor variables that belong together in terms of their intercorrelations. This can be accomplished by means of factor analysis or by the related method of cluster analysis. Variables that cluster are then combined in some way. Such composite variables can generally be expected to have the merit of having higher reliability than the relatively low-reliability elements of which they are composed. Thus, in place of having six different measures of the cultural level of the student's home—such as educational level of the father and the mother, number of books, intellectual level of the magazines purchased, and so on—a single measure can be derived by combining these.

In the clustering of such variables, a cluster is constituted of elements that belong together, not only statistically but also according to a rationale. Unless this is done, any prediction made from the cluster is unlikely to contribute systematically to knowledge; rather it is likely to represent only an odd but perhaps useful relationship.

Just as variables within the predictor group may be clustered and then combined in the hope of improving the accuracy with which predictions may be made, so too may groups of independent variables be clustered. For example, an investigator concerned with the prediction of teacher behavior might have observed a group of teachers for the frequency with which they perform various acts, such as raising their voices, threatening to punish, offering rewards, asking for suggestions, encouraging a pupil to pursue a matter further, offering help, and so on. The investigator would probably find that only the poorest predictions could be made of the extent to which a teacher manifested any of these categories of behavior. However, it is quite likely that a correlational analysis would show that some of these behaviors tended to cluster together. It would certainly be expected that all behaviors representing expressions of hostility would represent a cluster of correlated measures of behavior. When measures of all of these behaviors are added to form a measure that might be described as the tendency to manifest hostility—from what has been learned about such a variable from other sources—one might expect this characteristic of teacher behavior to be reasonably predictable from test scores.

Clinical Versus Statistical Prediction—A Problem in the
Validity of the Direct Observation of Behavior

In recent times, there has been considerable controversy concerning the relative merits of clinical predictions and so-called actuarial predictions. What is meant here by a *clinical prediction* is a judgment arrived at by a psychologist after considering a certain body of data. An *actuarial prediction* is made by combining quantitative data to derive a score, which is used to make a prediction. Clinical psychologists have generally maintained that it is possible to make more accurate predictions through the exercise of clinical judgment than could be made by the statistical treatment of data alone—at least insofar as it is treated by the methods at present in common use. The problem is an important one in the current connection, because it implies that the data processing method of the researcher is inferior to that of the machine.

Various approaches have been taken to the study of this problem. One has been to compare the actuarial prediction with the prediction of the clinician made on the basis of the same test scores.

P. E. Meehl (1954) has reviewed studies in which the accuracy of predictions made by clinicians using test scores are compared with the results achieved by statisticians using objective methods. The results seem to vary considerably from one study to another, depending on the nature of the condition to be predicted. In no clear-cut case did the clinicians predict more accurately than the psychometricians. One suspects that the psychometrician who has a well-developed procedure for predicting a particular type of event or condition will do better than the clinician, but if he does not have such a procedure, the clinician may possibly do better.

Just what can be concluded from the comparison of the statistician's predictions and the clinician's predictions made from the same data is difficult to understand. It would indeed be immensely surprising if a clinician could improve on a testing and statistical procedure that had been developed and refined over the years for making a specific type of prediction.

Conceivably the clinician is better at making predictions than the statistician in certain situations, but the statistician may be more accurate in others. If, for example, it were desired to predict what the author will be most likely to do next Sunday, test scores would be a very poor basis for making a prediction. However, what he is likely to do can easily be predicted from a knowledge of his habits. It would seem that, whenever the behavior to be predicted is based on well-established individual regularities of behavior, the clinician is almost certainly likely to do a better job than the statistician working with test scores. It is highly doubtful that a test could be made that could successfully identify the major habit patterns of the individual.

Tests are not well designed for predicting how a person will perform in particular situations of brief duration. Rather do they predict general characteristics of behavior over a period of time. It is generally much easier to predict how a student will achieve in courses over a four-year period than it is to predict how he will achieve in specific aspects of courses.

Problems of Multiple Prediction

So far in this chapter, consideration has been given to the problem of predicting a single criterion variable from one or more predictor variables. There are, however, more complex prediction situations that must also be given consideration here. A common problem of multiple prediction is that of validating vocational guidance batteries for predicting vocational success. It clearly would not be practical to develop data for predicting success in each and every occupation, for it may be presumed that occupations can be grouped together into categories that call for similar combinations of abilities. The same may be true for predicting success in vocational training programs from this same battery.

The basic question is how many categories should be used in the classification of vocational skills. No very satisfactory answer can be found, because for two training programs to be classified in different categories it would mean that persons exposed to both would have to show a performance in one that was quite unrelated to performance in the other. Such a fact is almost impossible to establish at the present time, because it is not feasible to submit the same individuals to two extended training programs one after the other. For this reason, certain indirect approaches to this problem have been proposed. One of these is to determine whether persons who successfully complete the one course of training can be differentiated in terms of a battery of aptitude tests administered prior to training from those who complete the other. If no such differentiation can be made, then the two programs are considered to belong to the same classification. This conclusion is based on the assumption that all relevant aptitudes have been measured, which may not be the case at all.

If occupations could be grouped into two broad categories, such as mechanical and clerical (obviously more categories would have to be involved), then the prediction problem would be that of finding some kind of combination of measures of aptitude that would best discriminate those successful in the one group of occupations from those successful in the other. An imaginary case of the scores of individuals on two aptitudes that discriminated between successful persons in the two groups of occupations is shown in Figure 5. The circles

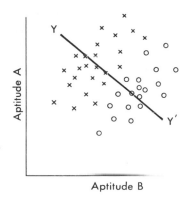

FIGURE 5. *Graphic illustration of discriminant function.*

represent individuals in the one occupation and the plus signs the individuals in the other. Neither aptitude alone provides a good discrimination between the two groups, but the line *YY'* represents a dimension that provides a very good discrimination. This function, when it is the best possible one, is referred to as a *discriminant function*. A person's score with respect to this function can be used to indicate whether he is more likely to belong to the one group or the other.

When more than two groups and many tests are involved, there may be more than one way in which it is possible to discriminate one group from another. In such a case there will be more than one discriminate function. This is illustrated in a study by D. V. Tiedeman, J. G. Bryan, and P. J. Rulon (1953). In this study scores on seventeen tests were obtained for airmen in eight different Air Force jobs. The problem was to determine the extent to which the test battery as a whole permitted the discrimination of the men in the different occupational groups. Two discriminant functions, each representing particular combinations of scores, showed some capacity for discriminating between the groups. One of these was a combination of scores that represented a variable differentiating mechanical and nonmechanical occupations. The other involved a differentiation in terms of the degree to which the occupation involved intellectual requirements. This illustration shows how more than one discriminant function may be found when many groups are involved.

It has often been considered that the discriminant-function procedure represents a desirable model for educational classification. When this is suggested, it is often forgotten that the mere fact that it is possible to discriminate between two groups does not mean that the basis for discrimination is necessarily one that can be used for future classification. An illustration may help in understanding this point. In a certain research organization with which the writer is familiar, nearly all the research workers are men and nearly all the clerical workers and laboratory assistants are women. From these facts it is clear that sex may be used to make an almost perfect discrimination between the research workers and the assistants, but it is also clear that it would be most hazardous to classify future applicants for jobs as research workers if they are male and as clerical workers and assistants if female. Discriminant functions may be such that they are based on characteristics wholly irrelevant for purposes of subsequent classification. Many occupational groups may be discriminated from other occupational groups by accidents of history. The mere fact that a variable discriminates is not a sufficient basis for using it for subsequent classification. It is a necessary but not a sufficient condition for use in classification.

Most of the problems of prediction that have been considered up to this point are likely to resolve themselves ultimately into problems of selection. Thus we may seek to establish methods of predicting the classroom behavior of the teacher; but the ultimate justification of such studies stems from the fact that they contribute to an organized body of knowledge that will improve methods of teacher selection and enable us to discriminate between teachers who behave in accordance with some prescribed pattern that is considered desirable and those who behave in some manner that is inconsistent with this pattern. The usefulness of prediction studies in their contribution to selection and related guidance procedures has fully justified the extensive effort that has been channeled into them.

Outcomes of Research on Prediction

The outcomes of research on the type of problems of prediction that have been considered in this chapter very largely represent contributions to the technology of education rather than contributions to an organized body of scientific knowledge. Nevertheless, when the outcomes of such studies are successful, they are likely to result in techniques for forecasting situations where it is very important to make accurate predictions. Tests for the selection of college students were developed through prediction studies of the type discussed here. Although these studies, which were extended over nearly a decade, did not result in any major contribution to knowledge, they did provide useful measures of certain aspects of scholastic aptitude. Nothing was discovered in these studies concerning how students learn.

Viewed from another light, it can be said that in such studies the relationship between a response in a test situation R_1 and a response in a learning situation R_2 is discovered. Such relationships R_1–R_2 represent a low-level type of law that does not involve any direct functional relationship between R_1 and R_2. Whatever relationship exists is based on a complex ramification of events. It is obscure relationships of this type that are unearthed and rendered useful by these kinds of prediction studies.

The Phenomenon of Shrinkage

It is necessary to discuss further at this point the phenomenon of shrinkage and to reintroduce the topic through a concrete example.

A researcher was interested in the personality traits that distinguished the most popular pupils from the least popular in the twelfth grade of a large high school. By means of a sociometric technique he was able to select two groups of one hundred pupils each. One group contained only pupils rated high by their peers in the matter of personal popularity, whereas the other included only pupils rated low. The researcher then administered a battery of sixty tests to both groups and computed the mean standard score of each group on each test. The five tests that gave "significant differences" between the two groups were then considered to be those that could be used to discriminate between the two groups. However, on data collected on different pupils the following year, the five tests failed to discriminate the most popular from the least popular pupils. This example illustrates the shrinkage phenomenon, but it needs to be interpreted in order to be understood.

What has happened is this: Suppose that data, the same as that described, had been collected one hundred times and that, on the average over the entire series, scores on Test X differed negligibly for the two groups. Even if this were so, it is highly probable that in some of these experiments there would be found substantial differences between the groups in their average scores on Test X. This is the kind of thing that may have happened in the study involving the administration of sixty tests to the two groups of one hundred pupils. The tests that showed "significant differences" between the groups just happened to show such differences on that particular occasion. Such differences were produced by what is called chance.

In the illustration given, it is probable that the five tests selected as the most discriminating were those that happened to show a particularly large difference between groups on that particular sample. For this reason one can expect shrinkage of these differences on later samples.

Just as differences in means may show shrinkage when an experiment is repeated, so too may other statistics show shrinkage when they are selected for extremes of magnitude and new data are collected. Suppose that it were desired to predict success in shorthand courses in high school. A large number of tests might be given to beginning students in the hope that some of these might be correlated with later shorthand grades. If the tests that *happened* to have the highest correlation with shorthand grades were chosen as those most suitable for selecting shorthand students, the experimenter might expect to be disappointed when the tests were actually used for that purpose. Correlations of these "high predictors" with shorthand grades might be expected to shrink on subsequent samples.

In order to make sure that we are not deceived by apparent predictions that later shrink to nothing, precautions have to be taken. The usual way to do this is to divide the population to be studied into two groups. On the first group all measures are applied in order to identify those most likely to be effective in making the desired prediction. The most promising measures are then applied to the second group to find out how far they can be relied on to make the same prediction in a new population. This procedure is called crossvalidation. All prediction studies should have built into them a crossvalidation procedure.

Nonlinear Relationships

Most prediction problems that are investigated by educational researchers are based on the assumption that the relationships between the variables involved are linear. A *linear relationship* is simply one in which equal increases in the predictor variable are accompanied by equal increases in the variable to be predicted. It is generally quite acceptable to assume that any relationships that may exist are linear, for rarely have nonlinear relationships been found in the educational field, even when they have been actively sought. This is hardly surprising, because most measuring instruments are constructed in the first place to be such that they have a linear relationship with certain criterion variables. Thus the approach usually taken to instrument construction results in the lack of curvilinear relationships between the instrument and other variables. In addition, those engaged in the study of individual differences have developed a wide range of statistical techniques based on the assumption that relationships are linear.

Some examples of curvilinear relationships are found in the study of the characteristics of those who belong to extremist political groups. The political position of individuals can be measured on a scale extending from the extreme political left to the extreme right. Now if one studies the relationship between political position on this scale and some personality characteristics, he finds that those individuals occupying the opposite extreme positions are very similar, but that they differ from those in the middle of the scale. For example, those at the either extreme tend to be rigid, but those who occupy the political middle tend to be more flexible. A curve showing the relationship between political position and rigidity is high to the political left, low in the middle, and then high again to the right. This is a curvilinear relationship.

Some Problems of Predicting Rare Events

Meehl (1955) has pointed out that even though a measure may have predictive value for a given purpose, it may still happen that fewer errors may be made by *not* using it than by using it. Until it is understood, this paradox appears to present a situation filled with contradictions. Consider the problem of identifying persons who will become involved in delinquencies during a given year. Suppose that a test has been developed, which, it has been demonstrated, has value in identifying future delinquents. Let us also suppose that this test was given to 10,000 high school children, and that two hundred were identified as likely to become delinquent. At the end of several years, it would be possible to determine which of those identified as probably delinquent actually were delinquent. A table similar to Table 3 could then be drawn up.

One additional statement must be made in order to interpret these

TABLE 3. Hypothetical data on the identification of those expected to be involved in delinquencies.

	NUMBER ACTUALLY INVOLVED IN DELINQUENCY	NUMBER NOT INVOLVED IN DELINQUENCY
Those predicted to be involved in delinquencies	30	170
Those predicted not to be involved in delinquencies	70	9730

data, namely that the delinquency rate for this group is ten per 1000. This is referred to as the *base rate*. With this fact in mind, the table indicates that the test does have some success in identifying those who become involved in delinquencies. However, by using the test on the group of 10,000, altogether 240 incorrect decisions were made (170 + 70). If no test had been given and if all of the group had been classified as nondelinquent, one would have expected only one hundred incorrect decisions to have been made; namely, all the cases that became delinquent. Thus fewer incorrect predictions are made by avoiding the use of the valid test than by using the test. Is it desirable to avoid the use of predictors where similar circumstances exist?

The answer to this is not a simple matter. Note that in Table 3 the test does identify correctly 30 of those later involved in delinquencies; but problems are created by the fact that it has erroneously identified as delinquent 170 cases who were not so. What has to be determined is whether the advantages gained by identifying the 30 delinquents outweigh the disadvantages of incorrectly identifying 170 as delinquent. If the testing requires an elaborate procedure and the help of many technicians, the losses may outweigh the gains. Also, financial and social problems may be introduced by identifying as potential delinquents those who are not.

The problem that has been discussed in this section becomes particularly acute as the base rate of the characteristic to be identified becomes very small. Attempts to identify rare talents, rare diseases, or any rare phenomena present situations such that selection devices are likely to provide a very much larger number of misclassifications than are provided by failure to use the instrument. This problem is most easily avoided when the base rate is near the 50 per cent mark. In addition, as the usefulness of the test for selection purposes is improved, the number of misclassifications is also reduced.

Summary

1. Studies designed to develop methods of prediction in education are of great practical significance but do not necessarily contribute to scientific knowledge.

2. There are three general approaches that can be taken to the problem of predicting educational achievement, which are as follows:
   a. The development of test situations that are miniatures of the learning situation in which it is desired to predict behavior
   b. The administration of a wide range of instruments in the hope that one will predict
   c. The development of a theory of prediction and the development of methods on the basis of that theory

3. An event can be predicted if all of the conditions that ultimately lead up to that event can be observed or measured at the time when the prediction is made.

4. A major difficulty in predicting behavior is that one does not know the precise nature of the situation in which behavior is to be predicted.

5. The event to be predicted should represent a well-defined phenomenon.

6. Most prediction studies of behavior are based on the assumption that personality consists of a complex of relatively enduring and permanent traits. Even though stable intellectual traits can be measured, the same cannot be said of the field of personality.

7. A major difficulty in conducting many types of prediction studies stems from the fact that the conditions necessary for research on the prediction problem simply do not exist. This is particularly true of most attempts to predict teacher effectiveness.

8. Sometimes it is feasible to make a successful prediction in one section of a population but not in another.

9. A common method of improving predictions is to combine variables that are related. Sometimes it is possible to cluster the criterion variables as well as the predictor variables.

10. Numerous studies have been made that attempt to contrast the relative success of the statistician and the clinician in making predictions from test scores. However, these studies do not compare the accuracy of the clinician in making predictions through clinical techniques with the accuracy of the statistician making similar or other predictions through psychometric techniques.

11. Many problems of prediction involve the determination of how

many predictors are to be used for classifying persons into a number of groups such as occupational groups, and also how many of the occupational groups form a reasonable system for the classification of occupations. Research is only beginning to explore such problems.

12. In most prediction studies, the phenomenon of shrinkage is likely to occur, and the studies should be designed so that it is possible to estimate the effect of shrinkage or to eliminate it.

13. One cannot always assume that the relationships between variables will necessarily be linear.

14. The fact that a variable has predictive value in a particular situation does not necessarily mean that it can be used profitably in that situation. Meehl's paradox occurs when the base rate for the occurrence of a particular event is low.

CHAPTER 12

‖I‖II‖II‖II‖III‖II‖IIII‖II‖III‖IIIII

Experimentation in Education

THE MEANING OF LABORATORY EXPERIMENTATION

Characteristics of Experiments

THERE are certain terms used in experimental research in the behavioral sciences with which the reader should be familiar. The person or other living organism whose behavior is studied in an investigation or experimental inquiry is referred to as the *subject*, or sometimes simply as S. In the literature of experimental psychology, S may stand equally well for a rat, a monkey, or a human being. It is an impersonal term denoting the living organism that is the center of the study. The person who conducts the investigation or manipulates the experimental conditions is the *experimenter*, a term commonly abbreviated as E.

The word *experiment* has many different meanings. Scientists of man's past have generally used it in a broad sense to cover explorations that cannot be considered to involve rigorous testing of hypotheses. Many of these experiments are explorations in which the scientist has no clear hypothesis but only the thought at the back of his mind: "I wonder what would happen if I did this?" Some important examples of this kind of experimentation can be found in current literature. For example, Hebb (1946) exposed chimpanzees to a number of different stimuli in order to determine the nature of those that evoke fear responses. Skinner tells the story that he became interested in the behavior of pigeons when, during the war, he was assigned space in an attic to undertake Government research, but delay in receiving the authorization to proceed led him to look for ways of occupying his time. The pigeons on the eves attracted his attention and, after capturing a few, he began to play with ways of teaching them tricks. Later, the work developed into rigorous and systematic methods for the study of the behavior of pigeons. These methods have produced an enormous technical literature of high quality. Much of the research that sparked the development of the physical sciences was of this character. The work of Michael Faraday at the Royal Institution, and his manipulations of wires and magnets and solutions, fits this pattern; so too does the work of Mendeleyev, who "experimented" with different ways of ordering the elements until they fell into the pattern of the periodic table. This kind of experimentation was successful in the hands of a Faraday or a Mendeleyev, but these were men who ranked among the greatest of their respective generations. Such exploratory activity without a clear goal in mind is rarely successful when undertaken by the inexperienced, let alone by those who lack the acme of creative genius. Yet the fact is that such activity has been characteristic of a majority of those who laid the foundation of the physical sciences. To the examples of Faraday and Mendeleyev one can add Cavendish who, upon burning hydrogen, discovered that the product was water; Magleigh, who conducted experiments on the polarization of light; Boyle, who mixed acids and alkalies to produce compounds with properties different from those of their original constituents; and numerous others. These exploratory demonstrations or experiments, as they have been called, form the very cornerstones of physics and chemistry.

Today, the exploration of a phenomenon and its description is commonly referred to as a *demonstration*, rather than as an experiment, although there is still no completely uniform usage. The very interesting demonstrations by Piaget and his associates of how children of different ages solve problems are referred to in his own writings as experiments, although American scientists would be more likely to describe them as demonstrations.

In this chapter consideration will be given to experimentation in the narrow sense of the term rather than in the broad meaning discussed in the previous paragraph. In its narrow meaning, *experimentation* refers to a situation in which some condition or conditions are deliberately varied in order that the effect of the variation can be studied. In classical experimentation, a single variable is studied; but in some of the more modern experimental designs the effect of several variables can be studied within the framework of a single experiment. The reason for restricting our discussion to this kind of experimentation and excluding the exploratory type of experiment is that the latter appears to be quite unsuited to the beginning research worker—unless he is a rare genius.

Just as there is no clear-cut line of demarcation between the carefully planned laboratory experiment and the demonstration or exploration, so too is there none between field studies and laboratory experiments. In a school that has a cooperative administration, one can divide third-grade pupils into several groups by random assignment. One can then determine the relationship between spelling ability and differing amounts of daily drill in spelling (given over, say, a two-month period). The researcher would have to arrange for the teacher in two or more groups to give, perhaps, five minutes a day of drill in spelling and for the other teachers to give about fifteen. In order to take into account the fact that teachers differ in their ability to teach, more than two teachers and more than two groups would have to be involved in such an experiment. In this case the school is used as a laboratory and a variable—the quantity of drill—is *manipulated*.

A very similar study might have been conducted on a field study basis without manipulating the variable quantity of drill. The scientist might have selected fifty classes approximately equal in spelling skill at the start of the third grade. He then might have obtained a measure of how much time was devoted to spelling drill in each one of the classes during a three-month period and, at the end of that time, he might have measured the spelling skill of each pupil in each class once more. Thus an estimation could be made of the relationship between spelling skill and drill, but the knowledge thus achieved would be much less certain than that derived from the experiment previously discussed. It is possible that those teachers who provided the greatest amount of spelling drill were those working in districts where parents were concerned about spelling and were giving their children help in this skill in the home. Thus, in the field study, classroom drill in spelling might be augmented by help in the home, and the observed gains might as easily be a product of that help as a product of drill conducted by the teacher. For reasons such as this, the laboratory type of study—wherever it can be carried out—is likely to yield more useful and more certain information than the field study.

The field study, in the latter illustration, can be viewed as being very similar to an experiment and, for this reason, has been referred to as a quasi experiment. The term *quasi experiment* has been widely used since its introduction to educational research by D. J. Campbell and J. C. Stanley (1963). The essential difference between a genuine experiment and a quasi experiment lies in the fact that, in the genuine experiment, the different conditions to which the different groups are exposed are assigned at random to the groups. On the other hand, in the quasi experiment the conditions are taken as they are found in naturally occurring situations. The difference may appear to be a small one, but it is actually immense. The genuine experiment, for logical reasons, necessarily yields more certain knowledge than the quasi experiment and, whenever possible, should be undertaken in preference to the quasi experiment.

Stanley (1966) makes a distinction between quasi experiments and pseudo experiments. He cites as examples of a pseudo experiment the early studies in which it was shown that pupils who studied Latin knew more about English than those who did not. The fact that the pupils taking Latin differed from those who did not take Latin, perhaps even before they entered school, was not taken into account; but it inevitably biases the outcome. Even if such differences prior to the study of Latin were taken into account, this would not overcome the fact that while the one group was studying Latin it was also probably enjoying cultural advantages to which the non-Latin group was not exposed. Although Stanley states that "we should distinguish sharply" (P. 83) between quasi-experimental and pseudo-experimental studies, there is a big grey area where the two overlap.

In the case of many studies one may wish to conduct in the classroom, great difficulties are encountered in manipulating the experimental variables involved. Although it is easy to ask two groups of teachers to teach by two different methods, many individual teachers may find it virtually impossible to play the classroom roles that a particular method calls for. Even when teachers are able to perform in accordance with the experimental conditions, the experimental results are often seriously affected by other uncontrolled aspects of the classroom situation. Suppose, for example, that one is interested in discovering some of the conditions related to the acquisition of foreign vocabulary. One might be interested in determining whether it is easier to associate a foreign word with either the corresponding English word, or with a picture of the object denoted by the word. One could invite teachers to cooperate in such a study with some teaching their pupils to associate foreign words with pictures and some teaching their pupils to associate foreign words with the corresponding English words. Even with the most cooperative group of teachers, the study conducted under classroom conditions would probably be a very unsatisfactory piece of research, for some teachers would provide more drill than others and some would make the drill more interesting. Also, teachers would differ in the extent to which the words acquired during drill periods were introduced at other times. A much better study could be undertaken if the children were taken from the classes for a few minutes each day and were exposed systematically to the learning of foreign vocabulary in a language they were not studying and under the two different conditions. If the study were conducted under naturally occurring conditions in the classroom, the existence of so many other irrelevant and influential events might prevent the outcomes from ever showing any significant differences between the two methods of learning. On the other hand, if the study were to be conducted in the laboratory, under well-controlled conditions, there would be much better opportunities for the effects of the two approaches to the learning of foreign vocabulary to show themselves, for they would not have to show themselves through a fog of other unrelated events.

There are those who raise the cry "Artificiality!" when the proposal is made that studies be conducted under the grossly simplified conditions of the typical laboratory experiment. This criticism should be evaluated in terms of the fact that most of our knowledge of the highly complex events of the physical world has been derived from the study of simplified events that the scientist has studied in the laboratory. The study of simplified phenomena under artificial conditions has been a highly successful technique in developing useful knowledge.

Of course, the laboratory itself introduces variables it may be desirable to control but that cannot be controlled easily. For instance, human subjects who are introduced into a laboratory come with certain expectations that may often influence the outcomes of experiments.

For example, many attempts have been made to study the effect of fear and anxiety on learning. In some studies this has been done by telling subjects that very high voltages are involved in the experiment that may be dangerous if the subject makes a mistake and pushes the wrong button. But one wonders how many subjects are ever influenced by such directions, for most of those who volunteer to help in these experiments know well that nothing is going to be done that will endanger their lives. This expectancy may keep them calm in a situation designed to make them fearful.

The term *experimental school* should receive comment at this time. Sometimes such schools are also called *laboratory schools*, but in actual fact they are not experimental in the sense in which the term is used here. Neither do they provide laboratory conditions—that is to say,

conditions under which carefully controlled experiments can be conducted. The term *experimental* in this context refers more to the *novel*
character of the curriculum and to the fact that something new is
being tried out rather than to experimentation in the technical sense
of the term. In this chapter, we are concerned with controlled experimentation in the laboratory sense rather than with the uncontrolled
study of curricular innovations.

The Need for a Cautious Approach to Experimentation

Experimentation is the most powerful method for deriving knowledge that has any certainty of validity; hence, it should be vigorously
pursued. Nevertheless, experimentation is one of the more difficult
of methods to pursue successfully. It is therefore necessary to consider
in detail all the common difficulties that experimental studies are
likely to encounter. This is likely to give the student the impression
that the difficulties of experimentation are so many and so widespread
that the new researcher should simply avoid experimental studies.
Such an inference should not be drawn; rather, the reader should take
the approach that once he is forewarned of the difficulties commonly
encountered, he is well equipped to design productive experimental
studies.

Even though it is commonly said that experimentation is the path
by which a science advances, this should not be taken to mean that
it is the only one. Most of the major figures who have advanced science
in the last hundred years have not been notable as experimentalists.
Einstein never carried out a major experiment, and neither did Darwin
or Freud. Although experimental workers have checked many of the
deductions of Einstein, these experiments followed rather than preceded major advances. To a considerable extent, experiments serve
to consolidate advances already made, rather than make advances in
and of themselves. Priestley's experimental studies of combustion
served to demonstrate to the scientific world what he already was sure
was true. Much classic experimentation serves the purpose of demonstrating to the world at large what the scientist already knows to be
the case. The moral to be drawn is perhaps summarized by the statement that although thought without experimentation may be productive, experimentation without thought is futile. In other words,
when the student embarks on an experiment, it is assumed that he is
checking some aspect of a well-thought-out theory, which may be
his own or somebody else's.

Let us now face squarely some of the major difficulties encountered in developing experimental studies, realizing that well-designed experiments can be carried out by the student who is aware of the common pitfalls.

CONCERNING DIFFICULTIES IN MANIPULATNG EXPERIMENTAL CONDITIONS

Some variables can be successfully and easily manipulated in experiments with human subjects, whereas others cannot. Most of the experimentation that has been undertaken in the field of education has involved the manipulation of learning conditions—perhaps because these are the most readily manipulated. Unfortunately, much of this work fails to meet the standards of good experimentation because in reading an account of the experiments one cannot determine just what was the nature of the variable manipulated. When one reads that one group of classes was taught by programmed methods and one group by traditional methods, one has little basis for inferring just how the two groups of classes differed in the learning conditions provided. They probably differed in numerous unspecified ways.

The first rule to follow in designing an experiment is to be sure one knows exactly how conditions are to be varied among the experimental groups. This is much more than a matter of attaching labels such as programmed or traditional. If such categories are to be used, then a clear set of specifications must be drawn up to establish just how these two sets of learning conditions are to differ. Such a set of specifications would have to indicate the characteristic behaviors of teachers and their interactions with pupils under these two conditions and also any other teaching events which distinguish one method from the other. In addition, some provision would have to be made to collect data in the classes in order to determine whether the conditions actually differed in the way in which they were supposed to differ in terms of the experimental design. But even if all this were done, the experiment would still not be worth undertaking as a scientific endeavor for it would involve a jumble of variables and no clear-cut conclusion could be drawn concerning the relationship of particular learning to the achievement of the pupils. Experiments that make significant contributions to knowledge involve the manipulation of much simpler conditions. Although the chapter on development gives consideration to some of the variables that can be profitably introduced into learning studies, consideration will be given here to the extent to which some of these variables represent manipulable conditions.

Conditions related to the presentation of information to the pupil. Some of these variables have been extensively studied in connection with the use of new educational media. For example, many studies have been undertaken that compare the relative effectiveness of visual and aural presentations of content. On the surface such studies appear to be easy, but they involve all kinds of difficulties. One can readily present information by means of movies or by lecture, but there are difficulties in insuring that the same amount of information is presented through the two media. Furthermore, the visual medium may present the information in pictorial form or in written form. If the written form is used, the outcomes of the experiment may be determined by the fact that reading rate is generally more rapid than speech—which gives an advantage to the visual presentation. A comparison of the effectiveness of different media may not make too much sense at this time. Perhaps a more important problem is that of determining the particular techniques that can be effectively used with each medium. In addition there are important problems to be studied concerning the value of transmitting information through more than one sensory channel. Many major projects that involve the development of movies for instructional purposes have implicitly assumed that the use of ears *and* the eyes together is better than the use of either alone and that both sensory channels should be used simultaneously. This assumption is probably unwarranted and suggests a whole area for research.

Extensive research has been undertaken in the area of audiovisual communication using both actual instructional materials and "artificial" materials developed especially for experimental purposes. When the author and some associates began to work in this area in the early sixties, they began their work by making a review of previous studies, most of which had involved classroom materials. Their conclusion was that such studies did not seem to be leading anywhere and, indeed, some seemed to be misleading. They concluded that the only productive approach to the scientific study and design of audiovisual materials was through laboratory research and embarked on a program of such studies. Some of the results of the latter program are reported in a publication by Travers, *et al.* (1966). These laboratory studies did seem to be leading toward the development of a set of principles that could be used in the design of audiovisual teaching materials, although previous research outside the laboratory had not led to such an outcome. Although the student of education may become fascinated with the possibility of conducting a laboratory study of some problem in this area, he should approach the project with caution. Most such studies require the use of laboratory equipment that is not typically available in colleges of education. Indeed, it is the absence of such equipment that has limited advances in knowledge in this important aspect of education.

Conditions related to feedback. Even though Thorndike stressed the importance of knowledge of results, this is still a neglected but promising area for research that permits the manipulation of important variables and also permits experimentation within the classroom. Research already indicates that the manner in which a teacher marks and comments on the papers of the students may make a substantial difference in their learning rate, but as yet relatively little is known about the value of various classes of reinforcement. Insofar as the feedback of information calls for behavior on the part of the teacher, difficulty may be experienced in exerting experimental control. However, feedback provided by written comments and by various ways of enabling a student to check on his answers when workbooks are used are clearly amenable to experimental study. Perhaps such studies are more easily carried out in classrooms run along traditional lines than in those with a more modern atmosphere. In the classroom run along more modern lines, much of the feedback is provided by peers in informal ways and little control can be exerted over it.

One of the conditions related to feedback that has produced interesting and consistent results is failure—a condition that has generally been demonstrated to have a depressing effect on intellectual processes. However, most of the studies of this problem have been laboratory studies, and much more needs to be learned about the effect of failure in a classroom situation.

Conditions related to classroom management. The experimentally minded educational research worker is likely to be tempted to manipulate conditions of classroom management. Studies that attempt to compare one condition of classroom management with another are generally referred to as *studies of teaching methods.* The experimenter simply does not have the control over this class of variable needed to undertake much in the way of systematic experimentation. The same thing may be said of experiments with administrative conditions. The administrator is not able to change or modify his pattern of administration at will. One might hazard the generalization that experiments in which humans are required to produce a change in their own behavior as the variable manipulated are not likely to be very good experiments if they are undertaken in classroom settings.

Some further consideration must be given to this problem. Suppose that a student desires to study the effect of certain aspects of teacher behavior, such as the number of rewarding statements, on specific aspects of pupil learning. Teachers may be quite willing to cooperate and to provide a specified amount of praise for pupil accomplishment, but some teachers will be much more convincing than others when they praise a pupil. If an experiment has been set up involving a group of teachers who administer much praise and a group who administer little praise, the experimenter can be sure—however well he has trained and rehearsed the teachers in their respective roles—that some teachers will deviate markedly from the prescribed course of action. Whenever behavior is the condition to be manipulated, we cannot expect to conduct experiments with clear-cut results. Even more complicated and unsatisfactory are experiments in which the cooperating teachers are personally involved in the outcome and hence are likely to be influenced in their behavior by their own desires. Most experimental demonstrations of the merits of new methods in education suffer from this limitation, particularly because they usually require teachers to adopt, for experimental purposes, methods that they believe to be unsound. What happens under such conditions is that the teaching methods with which the new methods are to be compared are presented in a way that can be described only as a caricature. The results of such studies obviously cannot demonstrate any useful principle.

There is a final matter to be considered in classroom experimentation, and that is what may be called the personal bias of the pupils. To some extent, pupils will behave in the way in which they believe they are expected to behave. If they know that the class, or the teacher, is being observed, they are likely to cooperate with the teacher, because cooperative behavior is considered most desirable for children. This pupil phenomenon is most pronounced, and even teachers who have serious problems in maintaining class control may have no trouble when they are being observed.

Conditions related to motivation. Although motivation is widely considered to be a major factor in determining rates of learning, not too much success has been achieved in establishing the conditions in the classroom that raise or lower motivation. McClelland, *et al.* (1953) based their work on the assumption that motivation can be aroused by the introduction of appropriate cues, such as telling a person that his performance on a particular task indicates his worth. Numerous studies have now been conducted in which such cues have been manipulated by the experimenter, but the results have often proven to be very difficult to reproduce. The student is cautioned against considering undertaking a study in this area because of the high probability of obtaining negative results. H. Heckhausen (1967) has provided a review of research in this area.

A particular cue that has been extensively used in experimental research on learning is threat. Sometimes the threat involves a physical consequence, as in research in which subjects are threatened with an electric shock. More often threat is designed to have psychological consequences, as when a subject is told that he is doing miserably or that "nearly everybody does better than you have done." In most of the research in this area, threat is introduced as a motivational cue and is designed to produce internal stress in the subject. The effect of threat and the resulting internal condition of stress vary from situation to situation and also, no doubt, with the characteristics of the subjects involved. Nevertheless, research in this area continues for it is important to find out more about the relationship of threat and stress to learning but there is the additional important educational problem of training individuals to meet stressful situations and handle them effectively.

Although threat and stress, which is the response to it, are an important area for research, the results of studies have not been particularly profitable. The products of experimentation in one laboratory can rarely be reproduced in another laboratory. So inconsistent are the results that often when the same experiment is reproduced in the same laboratory, the data may lead to opposite conclusions. The reasons for this were not apparent when researchers first embarked on experimentation in this area, and not all of them have yet been identified. However, there are some that seem to be sufficiently clearly recognized at this time to permit a brief discussion.

1. There is the difficulty, already mentioned that persons who visit a laboratory as subjects realize that no real harm will come to them, and that whatever threats they face will result in only transitory unpleasantness. On this account, whatever must be suffered by the subject may be accepted in much the same spirit as thrills and fears are accepted by those who visit the side shows at county fairs. The threats introduced by the laboratory situation may produce entirely different responses from those introduced by life situations.

2. It is possible that most of the stress situation that it is desired to reproduce in the laboratory are not those that result from single incidents; rather are they those resulting from conditions existing over a relatively long period of time. There is at least a little evidence that neurotic conditions derived from childhood experiences

are not the results of a single dramatic episode, but that they stem from recurrent situations that disrupt because of their frequency rather than because of their severity.

3. The experimenter is limited for ethical reasons to the manipulation of certain mild threats. One cannot assume that responses to mild threat are the same as those to severe threat except in degree. It is quite conceivable, and in some cases we know it to be a fact, that the response to severe threat is quite different from the response to mild threat.

4. In the laboratory situation the goals of the subject may be quite different from those in other situations where similar stresses operate. Unless some control can be exercised over these goals, the effect of stress on performance cannot be studied in any meaningful way, so the control of this aspect of the situation is crucial.

5. Experimenters are so limited in the stresses they can reasonably and ethically induce that serious questions may be raised about whether it is worth even attempting to experiment in this area, despite its obvious educational importance.

Finally, stress, threat, and related variables can probably be studied most easily in the classroom situation as it ordinarily occurs. It is not difficult to find classrooms where threat is frequently used and where the pupils live in a continuous state of tension. Such conditions probably represent much more severe threat and stress than the experimenter would ever dare introduce into any experimental situation.

On the Importance of the Availability
of Experimental Techniques

A student may decide to conduct an experiment on a significant problem before establishing whether suitable experimental techniques are available. This error is very common among graduate students. Because the development of experimental techniques is a painstaking endeavor often requiring long and sustained effort, such students are likely to find themselves engaged in a project requiring much more time than the thesis or dissertation ordinarily demands. The graduate student should choose an experimental research in an area in which well-worked-out techniques already exist.

The history of experimental studies shows that the development of an experimental technique for the study of an important problem has often sparked a long train of related studies. For example, when Ebbinghaus developed a series of experimental techniques involving the use of nonsense syllables, he made it possible to study problems of memory that had never been amenable to study before. The approaches he used are still the basis for much research. Even in those sciences that have had a longer period of rapid advance than has psychology, a single important technique may have had an equally significant long-term effect.

The student who is conducting his first research and who is intrigued by experimental approaches to problems would be wise to choose an area for study in which there are already well-developed laboratory techniques. Although his time would be well spent on the development of a new technique, such an enterprise is not generally considered appropriate for a dissertation or thesis.

The Trial Run

A student who reads an account of an experiment rarely realizes the laborious work that went into the design of the final experiment. The published account of the experiment omits reference to most of the false starts that were made and may, perhaps, fail to mention that the research worker initially was investigating a different problem, which he was forced to abandon because it did not prove to be amenable to study with the tools available. Also, at the start, the experimental scientist may have difficulty stating his problem in a form that permits a rigorous experiment to be undertaken. For example, L. C. Gilbert (1959) showed that in order for a printed word to be received and understood by the person who views it, a certain amount of time must be provided free of new stimuli. This is why reading fixations occur. Each fixation represents the time required to perceive the words around the fixation point. When the author became interested in this phenomenon, he began to ask questions about the effect of different words on the time required and whether it made a difference in the time involved if the words were familiar or relatively unfamiliar. This led to a redefinition of the problem in terms of information theory. The words carried information and, hence, the more information they carried the longer the processing time would probably have to be. But then he encountered problems in determining the amount of information transmitted by particular words or groups of words. This, in turn, led to abandoning the use of words for the purpose of studying information-processing time and individual differences in information-processing time. Other materials such as letters of the alphabet or digits were then used as experimental materials because they permitted the experimenter to estimate the quantity of information carried. Thus a perception problem ended up as an information-transmission problem and this, in turn, required the experimenter to turn to entirely different materials from those that he had originally intended to use.

One of the major functions of a trial run is to determine what is and what is not measurable in terms of available instruments or new instruments that it is feasible to develop. Quite commonly an experiment or investigation is planned, but attempts to execute part of it demonstrate that the suggested procedure could not possibly yield any results because of the crudeness of available measurement procedures. The need for such preliminary trial runs to establish the meaningfulness of results as well as the feasibility of obtaining measurements of adequate accuracy has not been properly recognized by educational researchers. It would be easy to point to large educational investigations that have been pursued over many years at a cost of hundreds of thousands of dollars and that have produced no results of any consequence; these investigations would never have taken place if a few preliminary studies had been conducted.

Laboratory Paradigms

Most experimental sciences advance knowledge about commonly observed phenomena by introducing into the laboratory simplified versions of these phenomena referred to as paradigms. Galileo wished to study the laws of falling bodies but found that their high speed under natural conditions made it almost impossible to study them, and also that natural bodies fell under such varied conditions that systematic study was difficult. For this reason he proposed to study bodies moving down an inclined plane. Such bodies move relatively slowly, and their laws of motion can be studied with relatively crude instruments. History has fully justified this practice, for the laws discovered have been found to be a sound basis for making inferences about bodies falling under free conditions. When Count Rumford observed that the boring of a cannon generated great heat, his inference, that the heat generated was proportional to the work expended, was one that could be tested only in a laboratory setting and with equipment other than cannon-boring machinery. Man's curiosity about lightning had to be satisfied almost entirely through the study of small quantities of electricity manifested by sparks in the laboratory. Cavendish could never have determined the density of the earth except through a laboratory technique that permitted him first to work out a value for the universal gravitational constant. The reduction of natural phenomena to laboratory-size paradigms has been almost universally the main basis of scientific progress.

When Galileo decided to study falling bodies by means of bodies moving down inclined planes, he had a logical and rational argument underlying this procedure. A simple mathematical function related events in the inclined-plane situation to events in the free-falling-body situation. In contrast, in the behavioral sciences in general and in the educational branch of these sciences in particular, such well-established relationships between the laboratory phenomenon and the out-of-the-laboratory phenomenon do not exist. Such relationships as do exist can be expressed in words that are vague in comparison to the mathematical relationships characteristically found in Newtonian physics. Because the relationships thus expressed in words are vague, the generalizations derived from such laboratory studies lack the certainty of applicability to other phenomena that is characteristic of Newtonian types of generalization.

This means that the procedure for applying the laboratory generalizations of the behavioral sciences must involve much more caution than is necessary in the physical sciences. This does not mean that the physical scientist is never wrong in his applications, for he is, but because of the rigorous nature of his deductions he is less likely to be wrong than is the behavioral scientist. The rationale of the physical scientist can be wrong, and it often fails to take into account factors that influence large-scale phenomena but do not influence events in the test tube. For this reason, large-scale manufacturing plants are sometimes failures although the small pilot plant was a success.

In spite of the risk that generalizations derived from laboratory experiments may not be applicable to real-life problems, many scientists believe that this should not deter us from experimentation with educational problems on a laboratory basis.

Apart from the obvious advantages of laboratory experimentation that have been discussed, there is the fact that many phenomena simply are not amenable to study under the conditions in which they are ordinarily observed. This does not mean that all educational phenomena can be studied with advantage under laboratory conditions, because many are not amenable to such investigations. For example, if the researcher were interested in the effect of neurotic behavior of the teacher on pupil behavior, he would not use a laboratory approach, because psychologists would generally hold the opinion that the main effect of the teacher's neurotic behavior is observed after pupils have been subjected to it over substantial periods of time. In the laboratory, we could not and would not expose individuals to neurotic behavior over several months or years. Such matters must be studied in educational situations as they occur.

Some Difficulties in Undertaking Experiments

A chapter on the conduct of experiments has to be written in a negative tone because there are numerous pitfalls to avoid and few positive rules to follow. The fact is that in the behavioral sciences even well-established research workers often conduct experiments that have to be resigned and redone later because the original version was shown to include a fundamental flaw. One can even trace the development of the design of some lines of experimentation over a period of fifty or more years and see the slow elimination of poor aspects of the design. Studies of concept learning, for example, have shown a gradual evolution of design that makes present-day procedures much more effective in providing clear answers to questions than were the early procedures of nearly half a century ago. Sometimes even prolonged effort does not eliminate all of the snags and snares in experimental procedures. For example, decades of experimental work have been involved in attempts to design an experiment to determine whether learning in a motor task can occur without reinforcement. Although some of the outstanding experimental psychologists have tackled this problem of design, it has not been solved. Whatever the design involved, some ingenious person always manages to suggest some subtle way in which reinforcement is occurring. Problems of experimental design are not readily solved, and some may be virtually insoluble.

Problems of design are studied not only by experimental scientists but also by mathematical statisticians, who view them from a rather different standpoint in terms of the logic they involve. The problems of experimental design studied by mathematical statisticians are considerably different from those considered in this chapter, for they revolve largely around the efficiency of experimental design. This concept of efficiency is related to the matter of planning experiments so that the maximum amount of information is obtained from a given number of observations. Problems of experimental design in this sense of the term will be given brief consideration in the chapter that follows, which is planned to make the student of education sensitive to such problems and to perhaps encourage him to study further.

It is important that the student also be sensitive to certain difficulties in experimentation in the behavioral sciences that are largely a product of the type of events studied. These difficulties are rarely discussed in books on experimental design because such works are usually written by statisticians who are unfamiliar with common flaws in the mechanics of actual experimentation. It requires experimentation in the field to become aware of these difficulties, which are not necessarily a product of the logic of the design.

In the pages that follow, flaws that the author has commonly observed in experimentation in education are discussed. Undoubtedly there are many others that occur with less frequency.

Deficiencies in design as a result of failure to include a control group. This is the most elementary of all deficiencies in experimental design. A principal wished to find out how much progress his fourth-graders made in social studies as a result of the curriculum offered. He was able to find a published test that seemed to measure the achievement of objectives of social studies stressed by the fourth-grade teachers, and he administered the test at both the beginning and the end of the school year. He was pleased to find that the group made as much progress as that shown by the norm group described in the manual for the test. What the principal did not know was that pupils who did not study material related to the content of the test made just as great a gain in score over the year as the pupils whose achievement was being evaluated. Experimental design always involves the establishment of conditions such that a comparison can be made between the effects of two or more conditions. Where the second condition is absent, the results become uninterpretable.

Deficiencies produced by the experimental procedure generating the results. This deficiency is somewhat similar to that previously discussed. One should make sure that the experimental procedure itself does not introduce increments in score that can be carelessly attributed to the experimental treatment. An example is necessary in order to illustrate this error in experimental design. P. B. Ballard (1913) performed a well-known experiment in which he assigned school children the task of learning poetry. At the end of the learning period, the children were asked to write out as much as they could remember of the poem. Next day Ballard returned to the school and asked the children to write out once more all they could remember of the poem. He was surprised to find that on the second occasion, the children were able to recall more of the poem than they had on the first occasion. This apparent increment in learning, after formal learning had supposedly ceased, became known as the *phenomenon of reminiscence,* and for forty years it was described in textbooks on education and learning as a genuine phenomenon. However, information now available indicates that reminiscence is probably a product of faulty experimental design. The error lies in the fact that the procedure used to measure retention immediately after the learning session is itself a learning experience, which increases the scores achieved on subsequent measures of retention. H. Ammons and A. L. Irion (1954) performed an experiment in which groups were given poetry to learn. Some were tested immediately after learning and also after an interval of time, whereas others were tested only after an interval of time. Only those groups that were tested immediately after learning showed the apparent phenomenon of reminiscence. The groups tested only after an interval of time produced average scores no greater than the average of the groups tested immediately after learning. This study suggests strongly that the supposed phenomenon of reminiscence is a product of faulty experimental design.

Various designs that can be used routinely have been suggested to take care of this hazard. One that has been suggested makes use of four experimental and control groups and can be used generally for determining the effect of a particular learning condition. The four groups used in this design, denoted by the letters A, B, C, and D, are exposed to four different schedules as follows:

Group A	learning experience,	test,	retest
Group B		test,	retest
Group C	learning experience,		retest
Group D			retest

Only Group A is administered the entire series of tests and learning experience. The remaining groups are administered only varying portions of the schedule. In this way the experimenter can determine whether some irrelevant aspect of the experiment is producing any increment from test to retest in Group A.

A similar design can be used when the experimenter is interested in a change in performance that can be attributed to a particular learning experience. Such a design would be applicable, for example, in the case where the research worker was interested in finding out whether a formal course in rapid-reading skills actually made a change in the reading skills of, say tenth-graders. The design would be as follows:

Group A	pretest,	reading instruction,	post-test
Group B	pretest,		post-test
Group C		reading instruction,	post-test
Group D			post-test

A gain from pretest to post-test scores might be found in Group A, and one might be tempted to jump to the conclusion that the gain could be attributed to the instruction given in reading. However, if Group B were to manifest a similar gain, then one might well suspect that it could be attributed only to the fact that the students learned from the pretest how to take such tests and this knowledge improved performance on the post-test. This conclusion would be confirmed further if Groups C and D showed lower post-test scores. Group D adds further information because it can indicate whether the post-test is particularly easy or difficult in comparison with the pretest and which, hence, may show gains in scores that are only artifacts.

Deficiencies produced by contamination of data. Many experimental designs give spurious results because of spurious elements. For example, a scientist was interested in discovering the abilities related to talent in a course in creative writing. As a part of his study, he administered a battery of tests of creativity to the students at the beginning of the semester and planned to study the relationship between these test scores and measures of the characteristics of their written products during the course. The tests were scored, and the researcher discussed these scores with the instructor in the course in order to obtain cues concerning the relationship of the tests to creative talent— but this was an unfortunate mistake. What it did was to open the possibility that the instructor's evaluations of the students' writing might be influenced by his knowledge of their creativity test scores. The data provided by the instructor concerning the students and their creative product was contaminated by his knowledge of their scores on the tests of creativity.

Contamination is one of the commonest of the errors of educational research design that render data uninterpretable. Such contamination is often difficult to identify and may pass unnoticed. One of many reasons why research plans should receive independent review is so that such factors can be identified.

The research worker's expectation of how data should appear may also contaminate the outcomes of research in many subtle ways. On one occasion, a graduate student was administering to subjects a complex perceptual task involving the use of complex equipment. After the task had been administered to two subjects, the graduate assistant looked at his data and found that they were far from what was expected. He soon noted that a switch that should have been turned on had been left in the off position. After he had remedied this defect in the procedure, the subjects began to behave according to expectation. Now the fact that he found an error in the procedure and remedied it was entirely to the good, but suppose the data from the first two subjects had been according to expectation. In the latter case the entire set of data might have been collected and interpreted as if they had been collected under the conditions that were supposed to exist in the experiment. What this means is that errors of procedure tend to be caught only when the data run contrary to expectation. The net effect of this is that experimenters tend to produce data that fit their expectations.

Deficiencies that result from making unwarranted assumptions about the nature of the scales used. The commonest examples in education of designs that manifest this error are those involving the use of growth scores. For example, a researcher set up the hypothesis that teachers who introduced into their classes rewarding comments (such as, "That's good, Billy") produced greater gains in pupil knowledge of social studies than those who did not. This study was to be conducted in sixth-grade classes in a large school system in which the teachers follow a rather rigidly prescribed social studies curriculum. The general plan of the study was to administer equated forms of a social studies test at the beginning and end of the sixth grade, and to correlate average gains in scores for each class with the observed frequency of rewarding comments occurring during visitation periods. If the researcher were not aware of the central defect of this design in the early stages of his work, it would probably become apparent in the later stages, when it becomes evident that some classes had greater knowledge at the beginning of the sixth grade than others had at the end. Even though some increased their average scores from, say, thirty to fifty correct items, others increased their average scores from fifty-five to seventy-five. These two increases are numerically equal and according to the design of the study should be treated as equal, but the equality of these two increments must be considered an unjustifiable assumption. As a matter of fact, there may be reasons for believing that the one increment is much more difficult to achieve than the other in terms of the time and effort required. Also, the two increments may differ qualitatively, in that the one may be achieved by bright students whereas the other is achieved by the dull. The two increments cannot be considered comparable, and studies assuming that they are should not be designed. Such studies will provide results that are uninterpretable.

Deficiencies that result when relevant variables are confounded with irrelevant variables. This is one of the more obvious errors of experimental design. The meaning of the term *confounded* can perhaps be best explained by means of an illustration. A researcher wished to study the effectiveness of flash cards in the teaching of reading. In order to do this, sixty first-grade pupils were given a reading readiness test. They were divided into two matched groups such that for each pupil in one group there was a corresponding pupil in the other group who had the same reading readiness score and who was of the same age and sex. Both groups used the same readers and workbooks, but the teacher of one group devoted time to the use of flash cards each day whereas the other teacher did not. At the end of six months the reading skills of both groups was measured, and the relative achievements of the two groups compared. However, this comparison was quite meaningless, because any advantages attained by one group over the other might as easily have been a product of differences in teachers as a product of differences in method (flash cards vs no flash cards). It could be said of this situation that differences in teachers were *confounded* with differences in method, so that any differences in the two groups could not be attributed to the one or the other. It is imperative that such confounding of the main conditions be avoided.

Various procedures could be adopted to remedy the technical defect in this experiment. One would be to use the same teacher for both groups, but this introduces another difficulty: the teacher may perhaps be in favor of using flash cards and his prejudice may influence the results in some subtle way. Another procedure is to have several different teachers use the one method in their classes and another different group of teachers use the alternative method. In this way differences in teachers could be expected to average out. Statistical methods exist that permit one to estimate the extent to which the resulting difference between the two methods of teaching can be considered to be reliable and not just a result of differences between the teachers involved.

Deficiencies resulting from sampling by groups and not by individuals. Somewhat related to the error described above is this sampling problem. Consider the spurious design involved in a study in which the effects of two methods of teaching reading were compared. In this study, the researcher selected from one school six second-grade classes that agreed to use Method A, and from another six second-grade classes that were to use Method B. The researcher drew the unjustified conclusion that the results showed that Method A was superior to Method B on the basis of the fact that, although both groups had closely similar initial scores on a reading test, the final scores for Group A were substantially larger than those for Group B. The conclusion was not justified because there might have been differences between the two schools other than those in teaching methods. Differences in socioeconomic level or social status of the two school populations might alone lead one to anticipate that differences in rate of learning to read would be found. What has happened in this experiment is that differences in treatment in which the researcher was interested have been confounded with other differences. This is similar to the deficiencies previously discussed, but it can be remedied without adding additional cases.

The basic defect in the design could have been remedied by the simple procedure of dividing the six classes in each school into two groups, one of which would have been exposed to Method A and the other to Method B. In this improved design, it would be possible to estimate differences between methods within each of the schools and to estimate the differences between schools regardless of method. Assigning individuals at random to treatments rather than groups to treatments will always avoid this flaw.

Deficiencies as a result of insufficient cases. One of the most elementary errors in experimental design results from failure to include a sufficient number of cases, but no simple rule can be given to guide the student in this respect. Part of the difficulty stems from the fact that when very small differences between groups exist (in relation to their internal variation), more cases are needed to demonstrate the difference than when relatively large differences are involved. Much also depends on the nature of the experimental design used, for some designs are much more sensitive than others in identifying small differences.

However, quantity can never make up for quality in the collection of data. The researcher is always better off with a few carefully made observations than with large quantities of observations made under varying conditions and of doubtful reproducibility.

If very large numbers of observations have to be made in order to obtain a reasonably accurate estimate of a difference, then it is doubtful whether a difference of that particular magnitude is large enough or consequential enough for the researcher to spend his time in further studies of the phenomenon. The author's own prejudice, which he follows in his work, is that if a difference between two treatments is not clearly apparent when each treatment is applied to fifty cases, then the phenomenon is one of small consequence. Certainly phenomena for investigation that provide for clear-cut results of the type sought can be found quite easily.

Deficiencies in design as a result of failure to take subject bias into account. In most situations, there is a tendency for human subjects to behave in a way that they feel is expected of them. Thus in a classic experiment in which a group was singled out for observation in a factory, it was found that any variation in the conditions of work produced an increase in output, which remained even after the original conditions were restored. Groups singled out for study in schools are likely to learn more than groups not thus identified. For this reason, in any educational experiment where there is an experimental group and a control, both groups should feel equally singled out, or better still, both groups should be unaware of the fact that they are participating in an experiment. For this reason, in experiments with drugs, one group receives the drug to be tested while the other receives a placebo that looks and tastes exactly like the drug. Both groups are kept in ignorance of the fact that some received the drug and some did not.

Deficiencies resulting from the views and attitudes of the experimenters influencing the experimental results. This looks like a simple pitfall to avoid, but experimenter behavior has been demonstrated to exert subtle influences on data. A series of experiments by Rosenthal and his associates have shown very clearly the insidious nature of this influence. Some of the early demonstrations of this phenomenon have been summarized by him (1963) in a form that may well interest the educational research worker. A more comprehensive report on the biasing effects exerted by experimenters has been published by him in book form (1966).

Rosenthal began with experiments involving rats as subjects and graduate students as experimenters. The student experimenters were told that each would be assigned a group of rats that were to learn to run a maze, or to solve other problems, and that some groups of rats were from "bright" strains and other groups from "dull" strains. The students were also given the most detailed directions for carrying out the experiment involving the training of the rats. Each student was then given his group of rats and told whether he was given a dull group or a bright group. Now, although each student experimenter carrying out the experiment was convinced that he was dealing with either a dull or bright group, all the rats came from the same colony and had been sorted into groups by random assignment with the anticipation that all groups would be about equal in learning ability. Indeed, the entire purpose of the experiment was to find out whether the students who thought they were running dull rats would produce significantly different data from those that thought they were running bright rats.

In the series of experiments conducted by Rosenthal, the general trend of the results was for the student experimenter running what he believed to be a bright group to produce data showing more rapid learning than was found in the case of the rats dubbed as dull. The experimenter's expectation that his animals would produce superior performance somehow resulted in superior performance. The converse was true in the case of the experimenters who believed that their rats were dull.

Rosenthal has also conducted other experiments in which the experimenters used human subjects. In this case, the subjects were required to perform a rating task on photographic portraits, and different experimenters had different expectations about how these ratings should turn out. Here again, experimenters showed a tendency for their subjects to produce ratings according to the experimenter's expectations. The results are not quite as simple as this statement implies, for the effect was not always entirely clear.

Now the question may well be asked about how experimenters do actually influence data. The problem is quite a puzzling one, particularly in the case of experimentation with rats, where the student experimenters were working under supervision and did follow a rigid routine. Some observations indicate that those who believed their rats were bright tended to handle the animals more gently and, in fact, were generally more kindly in the way they treated them. In the case of the human subjects, the experimenter probably introduced subtle reinforcements such as a slight smile or a slight nod of the head when the human subject rated a portrait according to expectation. Such subtle reinforcements could conceivably occur without either the subject or the experimenter being aware of them.

The subtle influences of the experimenter on the outcome of an experiment can best be reduced by utilizing, as far as possible, completely mechanized forms of collecting data. Directions can be given by means of a tape recorder and all of the events during the experiment can be completely controlled with equipment. During the last few decades excellent equipment has been developed for doing almost anything that experimenters want to do. However, when experiments are conducted in schools, with whole classes and their teachers used as complete experimental units, the problem is more difficult. One would certainly expect that teachers who knew the purposes of the experiment would, inevitably, bias the results. For this reason, the teacher and the pupils should be kept in the dark concerning what is being studied, although this does not entirely solve the problem. Rumors concerning the purpose of a school experiment may influence the behavior of some of the teachers and bias the results. One suspects that if a teacher merely believes that a particular method of teaching is a superior one that this same teacher will produce superior results when using it.

Deficiencies as a result of planning studies in which rare events form the crucial aspects of the data. An experimental design is not likely to be feasible if it is built around a rare type of event. An example from outside the field of education provides an illustration of a type of problem familiar to the reader. During the early days of the development of antipoliomyelitis serums, experiments were carried out in an attempt to determine the value of various experimental serums. In some of the first experiments, approximately 20,000 pupils were randomly assigned to two groups. One group was given the experimental serum while the other was administered a placebo. At the end of the season, when the incidence of polio in the general population had fallen to its lowest ebb, the number of cases of polio in the two groups was counted. In such an experiment, it might have been found that in the innoculated group there had occurred six cases and in the placebo group ten cases. Now, although this difference is numerically large, it can be accounted for in terms of the differences one might expect if many samples of 10,000 cases each had been administered the placebo. In the conduct of such research, it soon became quite obvious that what appeared to be large samples were inadequate for the purposes at hand; and it was necessary, as the reader will remember, ultimately to use samples of as many as 300,000 cases in both the experimental and the control group.

Again, suppose it were planned to introduce a safety program into the elementary schools of a small city. It might be proposed that steps be taken to evaluate the effectiveness of the program by excluding half the elementary schools from it and then by comparing the traffic-accident figures for these schools during a semester with those for the schools that had the safety program. The weakness of the design is that too few children are likely to be involved in traffic accidents for the comparison to be statistically meaningful.

Deficiencies in design resulting from the experimental procedure itself affecting the conditions to be observed. A serious difficulty in educational research results from the fact that the process to be observed is often changed beyond all recognition by the mere process of observation. The description and recording of events within the classroom presents this problem in an acute form. We can no longer accept the notion, based on wishful thinking, that the introduction of an observer into the classroom does not affect events therein, for clearly it does. Indeed, some have suggested that it just may not be possible to study the events in the classroom under the conditions that ordinarily prevail. They have likened the situation to the Heisenberg principle in physics, which states that the position and the velocity of certain particles cannot both be determined at the same time. These difficulties of conducting classroom studies seem to be insuperable at the present time, but it must not be assumed that they do not exist.

THE DESIGN OF TRANSFER OF TRAINING STUDIES

Most areas of research have their own special experimental designs. For example, research on the study of transfer of training has evolved distinct designs to handle the investigation of the problems involved. Most transfer experiments involve two learning tasks commonly designated *Task 1* and *Task 2*. The general purpose of such an experiment is to determine the effect of learning one of the tasks on the learning or retention of the other task. Two basic experimental designs are involved; these are known as the *retroaction* and the *proaction* designs.

The problem of generalization of learning, or transfer of training as it has been commonly called, is—from the educational standpoint—one of the most important areas of learning and development that can be investigated. If school learning were conceived to be the accumulations of isolated items of information, the expected consequences of education would be extremely limited. Fortunately this is not the case, for school learning is conceived largely as the learning of techniques, skills, principles, and methods that can be applied to a vast range of problems outside the school. This is possible because the solutions to some problems learned in school can be generalized to certain other problems outside school.

The retroaction design involves the following experimental procedure:

Transfer Group: performs Task 1—performs Task 2—performs Task 1
Control Group: performs Task 1—rests or performs some unrelated
                  task—performs Task 2

This is referred to as the retroaction design since the backward effect of Task 2 on the retention of Task 1 is studied. In this design there is always a problem raised concerning what to do with the control group while the transfer group is performing Task 2. Just to allow them to rest is not satisfactory because this may give the control group some advantage over the transfer group. On the other hand, to engage the control group in some supposedly irrelevant task might conceivably raise or lower their subsequent performance on Task 2.

The proaction design is rather different and can be represented in the following way:

Transfer Group: performs Task 1—performs Task 2
Control Group: rests or engages in irrelevant activity—performs
Task 2

In this design the purpose is to determine if the performance of Task 1 facilitates or interferes with the *subsequent* performance of Task 2. The task may be either a learning activity or merely a measure of performance at a particular level of learning. In most transfer experiments both tasks involve a learning activity.

Research on transfer at the beginning of this century typically involved learning situations similar to those that occur in schools, but the trend in recent times has been to use greatly simplified learning situations that bear only a remote resemblance to school learning. Although the early studies were directed toward the determination of the amount of transfer from one school subject to another, more recent research has been aimed at the development of a theory of transfer. Thorndike's theory of transfer, known as the *identical elements theory,* held sway for over a quarter of a century. The inadequacies of this theory are now quite apparent. The problem is that of finding a substitute theory that can be of value in the designing of curricula and training programs.

Some Final Points

The preceding sections of this chapter emphasize the negative side of experimentation—what not to do; but mere avoidance of pitfalls does not insure that the resulting experiment will be even mediocre in value. In the literature can be found reports of study after study that are flawless in technique of design but otherwise completely inconsequential. Ingenious experimentation of the type that builds a science of behavior owes its contribution to the fact that it is built on a sound theory and that the idea could be developed experimentally under available circumstances. These two conditions need to be discussed further here.

A sound idea for experimentation in the behavioral sciences must find its roots in the current tide of organized ideas that constitute the present state of the art. Many ideas that appear sound from the view-point of the layman may not be sound from the point of view of current knowledge. The layman will always protest this statement, as he always has, for it is inevitable that he will conceive of himself as an authority on problems of education. This conflict between lay opinion and scientific opinion is not new and has occurred in fields other than the psychological. The layman's emphatic belief that the earth was flat or that it was the center of the universe are illustrations of common sense being wrong while the scientist was right. Today it is not uncommon for the student of education to base the ideas about which he wants to experiment on lay opinion as well as on his professional background. This is a real handicap, but it is hard indeed for a person who has spent the first twenty or thirty years of his life thinking in terms of the layman's conception of behavior to change and to think in terms of the scientist's conception. Early habits of thought are probably never entirely discarded.

Many experimentalists have pointed out that the careful surveillance of the collection of data is vital for successful scientific research. This is not just a matter of watching to see that the experimental procedure is carried out with care. Incidental observations made during the course of an experiment may often provide valuable data. One does not have to go far to find discoveries of the utmost importance that have been made as a result of incidental observation during the course of some other investigation. A classic example is the discovery by Fleming that led to the discovery of penicillin. Fleming noted that staphylococci died in certain dishes that had become contaminated from outside sources. Although many research workers would have written off this phenomenon as an experimental nuisance, Fleming saw that it suggested a means of destroying staphylococci causing infections. Roentgen's discovery of X-rays was also the result of an incidental observation made during the course of an inquiry into the nature of certain kinds of radiation.

One cannot tell the experimentalist what to look for, but only that he should be forever vigilant. When he sees something of particular interest he would be well advised to stop and investigate. Many scientists have said that a research worker is fully justified in dropping everything in order to explore an unusual event that has caught his attention. Even though systematic investigation is most desirable, it does not mean that the scientist should be compulsive about following his plans through to the end and shutting out all distracting phenomena.

A final word of encouragement. Finally, the student is again urged not to be overwhelmed by the difficulties of experimentation. Rather, he should feel that he is now familiar with the major difficulties commonly encountered and that he is now in a position to plan well-designed studies. Because most flaws in experiments arise simply because the novice in research is unaware of their existence, the reader at this point should feel prepared to try his hand at designing experimental studies. The great value that this approach offers to the development of a science of behavior in educational situations is a factor that should urge him to use experimental methods whenever they are feasible. The more ambitious doctoral student may well deliberately choose these most powerful of all methods of collecting information.

Summary

1. Some experiments are essentially demonstrations. Some represent explorations conducted by the scientist without knowing quite what to expect. In recent times the tendency has been to reserve the term *experimentation* for those inquiries in which a study is made of the effect of manipulating one or more variables.

2. Just as there is no clear line of demarcation between demonstrations and systematic attempts to study the effect of manipulating a particular condition, so too is there no rigid line between field studies and experiments.

3. Although the term *experiment* is used with a diversity of meanings in educational circles, the chapter is concerned with a narrow interpretation of the concept. The term *experimental school* does not refer to any phase of experimentation as it is considered here. An experiment, as considered here, involves the manipulation of one or more conditions and the study of the effect of changing conditions.

4. In recent years the distinction has been made between genuine experiments or true experiments and quasi experiments. What has been referred to here as a well-conducted field study is, essentially, what others have called a quasi experiment. The ill-planned field study has been appropriately named a pseudo experiment. The genuine experiment has far greater potential for producing knowledge than does the quasi experiment, although much research has to be undertaken through the latter type of inquiry.

5. There are many difficulties involved in the manipulation of conditions in educational experiments. An error of past generations of educational experimentalists has been the attempt to manipulate complex conditions such as progressive and traditional approaches to

education. Experiments involving such complexes of variables do not generally produce results of value. Of the various conditions that are likely to be manipulated in classroom experiments, those related to classroom management present the greatest difficulties.

6. Laboratory studies are usually simplified versions of the phenomenon in which the scientist is interested. This approach can be justified in terms of the immense success it has achieved in the past. However, it may be much more difficult to generalize from laboratory studies in the behavioral sciences than from studies in the physical sciences.

7. There are certain common deficiencies in the design of experiments, which recur with such frequency that they should be familiar to all who undertake research in education. These are deficiencies resulting from:

a. The failure to include a control group when one is needed
b. The experimental procedure itself generating a variable
c. The contamination of the data
d. The making of unwarranted assumptions about the nature of the scales used
e. The confounding of irrelevant variables with relevant variables
f. Sampling by groups and not by individuals
g. The failure to include a sufficient number of observations to provide the precision needed
h. The tendency of subjects to favor one outcome rather than another
i. The human observer being biased in the making of his observation because he knows which subject or group has been exposed to which particular treatment
j. The failure of the experimenter to recognize that he is dealing with a rare type of event
k. The experimental procedure itself affecting the conditions to be observed

8. Special areas of research have evolved particular designs that are suitable for studying the problems involved. One such area is that of transfer of training that has slowly evolved two basic designs for experimental studies.

9. Sound experiments are based on sound scientific theories. The mere fact that a design is statistically sound does not mean that it is being used in a significant experiment.

||||||||||||||||||||||||||||||||||

CHAPTER 13

Problems of
Research Design

IN THE preceding chapter the practical problems of experimentation, with particular reference to the feasibility of undertaking various types of experimentation were discussed. In this chapter the logic of design will be discussed, but the reader should keep in mind that designs that are methodologically sound from the statistical and logical viewpoint can be applied to trivial problems and can even be based on assumptions inconsistent with those that the use of the particular data require.

Terminology of Design

In order to understand research design, it is necessary to understand certain terms that are commonly used in the discussion of designs. The knowledge derived from a research is generally derived from a *sample* of a *universe*. The sample might be all the eighth-graders in Chicago whose birthday falls on the first day of any month, and the universe might be all eighth-graders in Chicago at the present time.

The researcher is sometimes interested in the effect of the presence or absence of some conditions on behavior, such as the effect of drill on spelling achievement, or the effect of knowledge of results or lack of knowledge of results on computational skill. Differences in the conditions in which the researcher is interested are referred to as differences in *treatment*. In the simplest type of educational study, differences between the presence or absence of a particular condition are

299

studied, and this would represent a comparison between two levels (presence or absence) of a particular treatment. In more complicated experiments, many different treatments may be involved and the interaction of these treatments may be studied. For example, one might study formal drill versus no formal drill in the teaching of mathematics, and the teaching might be undertaken by either extrovert or introvert teachers. Extrovert teachers might be more successful with drill methods than with nondrill methods, and the reverse might be true of introvert teachers. Designs that permit the estimation of the effect of each treatment can be adopted within a single study.

Sometimes the research worker is concerned with the characteristics of the individuals involved in a study, especially in relation to some aspect of performance. Thus in studies of the results of different teaching methods, the researcher may wish to take into account pupil differences in ability because he may believe that some methods are better for bright pupils and others better for the dull. The characteristics of the population studied that are taken into account in a design are referred to as the *population characteristics*. These may be physical characteristics or psychological characteristics such as are measured by tests. They may also be derived from the person's background and represent the experiences to which he has been exposed.

It is not the purpose of this book to familiarize the student with the statistical problems underlying advanced designs and their merits. Such matters are well taken care of in textbooks devoted to such problems.

There is some division of opinion among those engaged in educational research concerning the utility of complex designs that take into account a large number of different variables, except in areas where much knowledge has already been acquired. Those who design studies involving numerous variables claim that this is necessary if useful results are to be achieved. The argument is that many variables are involved in most behavioral phenomena, and hence these should be taken into account in any study that is planned. On the other side of the argument it is claimed that the research worker usually does not know what these variables are, and guesswork rather than sound theory is likely to be the basis for including those that are included. Only rarely do elaborate designs give the impression of being firmly rooted in theory. Skinner (1956), who has participated in this controversy, has pointed out that most of the important facts of science were discovered long before complex designs had ever been invented. In addition, it is true that important facts in the behavioral sciences continue to be brought out by workers in educational research using the simplest type of experimental designs. Many fine studies may illustrate the use of complex designs, but it seems likely that simple designs will serve a useful purpose for many years to come.

Functions of Statistical Method

It would be inappropriate in this book to provide any extended discussion of statistical methods, because these require intensive study on the part of the student of education who is preparing himself to engage in educational research. The student will always be limited both by what he knows and by what is known in the field of statistics in the planning and execution of studies.

Statistics serve a number of different functions. First, they commonly serve the purpose of summarizing data. A mean is calculated for this kind of purpose. A state department of education will indicate the *mean* cost per pupil of elementary education in the state. The presentation of the *mean* cost in the superintendent's report saves the report from being cluttered with data from every school or from every school district. The mean is used as a descriptive statistic. Although the use of descriptive statistics seems to be a simple and straightforward procedure, there is a great amount of mathematical work on the problem of the choice of suitable statistics for summarizing data. Some statistical procedures for summarizing data are very complex. For example, factor analysis is a very elaborate procedure that sometimes permits one to summarize the information provided by a very large number of test scores on each pupil in a form that involves only a few scores. The calculation of the mean is a method of summarizing data that almost anyone can apply, but factor analysis can be applied only by those who have sufficient scientific sophistication.

Procedures that just summarize data have become progressively less and less acceptable as the core of doctoral dissertations in education and in the behavioral sciences. Part of the reason for this is that the procedures can be mechanically applied, but it is generally agreed that a thesis or dissertation should require the student to solve a problem at least partly by concentrated personal effort and reflection. There is little educational value in grinding out a study by mechanical means.

A second purpose of statistical methodology concerns the justifiability of inferences made from data, or, in other words, the confidence that can be placed in particular inferences. The testing of hypotheses involves the application of statistical devices known as tests of significance. These tests enable one to estimate the confidence that can be placed in various inferences from the data. Tests of significance vary in the degree to which they are efficient. Some do not make proper use of all the information provided by the data, whereas others do. Most tests of significance are based on assumptions that have to be satisfied if the application of the test of significance is to be fully justified. A test of significance may require, for example, that the events studied be distributed in the form of a particular kind of bell-shaped distribution known as the normal distribution, but very few measures show a distribution very close to this form. Usually we know only that the conditions required by most tests of significance are only partially satisfied, but some comfort can be found in the fact that, in the case of most tests of significance, studies have shown that considerable departures from the assumptions called for can be made before the statistical test becomes substantially biased.

The graduate student of education is most likely to be mainly involved in statistics that serve the second major purpose; namely, the testing of hypotheses. Through such methods a science of behavior in educational situations is likely to be produced.

General Characteristics of a Well-Designed Experiment

First, it is necessary that the data of the experiment be free from bias. In testing the relative efficacy of two methods of teaching reading, it is not sufficient to choose two groups of schools that appear to be equal and to assign one method to one set of schools and the other method to the other set. Suppose these two sets of schools were the Southside Schools and the Westside Schools, and that the researcher decided to assign reading Method A to the former and reading Method B to the latter. In making this decision, he may have been influenced by certain quite unconscious biases. For example, he may have been convinced in his own mind that Method A was superior to Method B. He might also have given his prejudice weight in deciding to assign Method B to the Southside Schools, forgetting that previous test results showed that their pupils were generally slower learners than pupils in the Westside Schools. In such an event, the conditions of assigning teaching methods to schools were such that the data resulting from the experiment would inevitably show a bias in favor of Method A. It is just this kind of bias that a well-designed experiment is designed to avoid. This is accomplished by eliminating the influence of personal choice in the assignment of treatments to schools. If it were administratively necessary to treat each set of schools as a block, then the reading methods could be assigned to the schools by tossing a coin. However, to treat each set of schools as a block would be highly unsatisfactory. What is needed is to assign the methods to each pupil by use of a table of random numbers or by some other means free of personal bias. Some specific instances of introducing bias into data were discussed in the preceding chapter.

Sometimes in the collection of data, bias is introduced by the fact that treatments are assigned on the basis of conditions over which the experimenter had no control. For example, the author was at one time confronted with the problem of determining the effect of the use of diagnostic reading tests within a school system where some schools used these tests and others did not. Those that used the tests made some effort to interpret the profile of scores attained by each pupil and to plan a program of work designed to overcome the deficiencies thus revealed. It was suggested by the school authorities that a simple method of studying the problem might be to measure the reading proficiency of pupils in the two sets of schools, and to determine whether the pupils in schools that used the diagnostic tests were superior in reading to the pupils who did not have the supposed advantages of the diagnostic tests and the related remedial training program. However, the results from such a study would almost certainly be biased. In the situation under consideration, it could be shown that the pupils in the schools using diagnostic tests came from more favorable home backgrounds than those in the other schools. This in itself would probably produce differences in level of reading in the two sets of schools and make the results of the proposed study uninterpretable.

This would probably not have been the only source of bias in that study. The schools in which the diagnostic tests had been introduced might have had better trained facilities than the other group of schools, and this superiority would have reflected itself in teaching and in the resulting level of reading skill. Perhaps this discussion may not only illustrate the problem of eliminating bias but also point up the advantages of an experimental method in which treatments are assigned to cases by a bias-free method.

Secondly, the experiment must be designed in such a way that it is possible to determine the magnitude of the differences that might be the result of sampling alone. This can be stated in another way; namely, that the experimental data must yield an estimate of error. This condition could be overlooked in most of the experimentation conducted by the physicist or chemist, because in such experiments errors of measurement are extremely small and data tend clearly to support or reject the hypothesis under consideration. It is only when the experimenter enters fields where errors begin to be large in comparison with differences between treatments that the concept of estimating error becomes a matter of prime importance. Many experiments of great significance were performed before the statisticians' concept of estimating error was introduced, but the scientists who undertook those experiments were not oblivious to the idea. They relied on their knowledge of errors of measurement that their equipment and materials involved.

There are some excellent experiments in psychological literature where no systematic effort has been made to estimate error. The early studies of learning conducted by Ebbinghaus involved no such attempt; but here again, the results were so clear-cut that the experimenter's knowledge told him that the errors were extremely small compared with experimental effects.

Thirdly, the experimental design must insure that there is sufficient precision for the data to be able to provide answers to the questions that are asked. In an experiment known to the author, students of education in their sophomore year were divided into two groups. One group was given extensive opportunity to visit school classrooms, whereas the other devoted an equivalent amount of time to additional academic work. It was hypothesized that those who had the school experiences early in their course would be able to profit more from the academic work and would be able to see its implications for classroom practice more clearly. The criterion for the success of this procedure was to be found in terms of the effectiveness of the student's performance in practice teaching. The experimenter was careful to divide the twenty-four sophomores by random assignment to the classroom visitation and the academic work groups, and fortunately all twenty-four stayed with the program long enough to complete student teaching. The students were rated during student teaching by the regular classroom teachers to whom they were assigned, on the basis of their over-all effectiveness as well as on more specific aspects of performance. For the purposes of this study, the over-all rating of performance was used and an attempt was made to determine the significance of the difference in the rated performance of the two groups that had been exposed to different educational treatments. As one might expect, the results were negative, because the difference between treatments was small compared with the size of the error involved in making the ratings. The experiment lacked the precision to answer the question that was asked.

What can be done to increase the precision of such an experiment? One answer, but perhaps not the most satisfactory, is to increase the number of observations. As observations are added to the original experiment, a more and more precise and stable estimate can be made of the difference as a result of treatments. In the present case, additional observations could be added by dividing the sophomores year after year into two groups and providing the differential training for each pair of groups.

But this is not the only method by which the precision of an experiment can be increased. It is the one that should be used as a last resort and only after other means of increasing precision have been exhausted. The main alternative involves the removal of known sources of error. Thus, in the study of student teaching that has been described, if one could obtain a more reliable measure of student teaching than the ratings used, a main source of error would be reduced. However, one might not be able to find a more satisfactory measure than that provided by ratings. Another source of error is the variation shown by the students in their teaching performance, for many different reasons. Some may have problems in the classroom because they feel insecure. If the two groups exposed to the two training methods before student teaching could be selected to make the groups as uniform as possible, with respect to characteristics that influence performance in student teaching, then another source of error would also be reduced.

Traditional experimentation in the physical sciences involved the manipulation of a single factor at a time. Indeed, textbooks on experimental procedures that are more than twenty-five years old stress this aspect as an essential feature of the experimental method. Largely through the initial work of R. A. Fisher and the later work of his students and associates, the concept has been developed of varying more than one factor at a time. The advantages of such multifactor experiments are numerous. First, they answer several questions within the framework of a single experiment. Secondly, each observation may contribute data to the answering of every question with almost as much precision as if the experiment as a whole had been designed for answering a single question. Thirdly, through the multifactor experiment it is possible to answer questions concerning the effect of one factor on the other. This is a matter that was not easily investigated before Fisher developed his techniques, although the problem was familiar to many scientists. It thus may be possible to demonstrate that under certain conditions of work, incentives interact with the student's level of motivation, and thus it happens that the well-motivated student is the one who responds to the incentives for learning held out by the teacher. These interaction effects are probably extremely important in the behavioral sciences, although scientists are likely to remain preoccupied with more straightforward and less complex effects for the present.

Controls in Experimental Design

The design of research is closely associated with the use of what are called *experimental controls*. Although well-designed experiments and other forms of research have been undertaken for many hundreds of years, the use of the term by scientists goes back for only about one hundred years. E. G. Boring (1954), who has studied the history of the concept of control in experimentation, finds three common uses of the term, which have added confusion to writings on scientific methodology because they have been used interchangeably.

First, the term *control* is used to refer to a restraint on experimental conditions. Thus in the administration of a test to determine whether children who have had certain diseases suffer a hearing loss, it may be considered desirable to conduct the tests in a soundproof room so that extraneous noises do not interfere with the results obtained by some pupils and not by others. Extraneous sounds are *controlled* so that the resulting conditions will be as uniform as possible.

Secondly, the experimenter exercises control over the variable that he is manipulating. In determining auditory acuity, sounds are presented that vary in loudness and pitch. It is important to control the pitch of the sound because some persons may have a hearing loss only for sounds of a certain pitch. It is known, for example, that as individuals grow older they begin to manifest a hearing loss for sounds of high pitch. Thus the experimenter *controls* the pitch as well as the loudness of the sound that is presented as a stimulus.

Thirdly, there is a sense in which the scientist refers to *control groups* or *control experiments*. Boring introduces this meaning of the term by referring to Mill's method of experimental inquiry. Mill's first method is the Method of Agreement, which states that if A is followed by *a,* then presumably A is the cause of *a*. The word *presumably* is used advisedly, because it is obvious that A is not necessarily the cause of *a* even if it always has preceded it. In my home, eggs are always served after grapefruit at the breakfast table, but nobody would claim that the grapefruit causes the eggs. In Mill's second method, it is postulated that if A is always followed by *a*, and if the absence of A is always followed by the absence of a, then A can be asserted to be the cause of a. This method is an extension of the first, and it involves the introduction of the *control* consisting of *the absence of A.* It represents a very common method of educational experimentation. For example, it can be shown that children who have certain speech defects improve if they are given remedial speech treatment and do not improve if such remedial work is withheld. If studies of this problem had demonstrated *only* that those who had remedial work improved, it would still leave open the possibility that improvement was not because of the treatment but because of the passage of time and various unidentified influences. However, by showing that the withholding of treatment is associated with an absence of improvement, the experiment is enormously strengthened and the conclusion that the treatment produces improvement is justified. The use of control groups is of crucial importance.

The extent to which controls (in the third meaning of the term) need to be introduced is always a matter of judgment. If a teacher of calculus administers a pretest to his students to determine how much they know about the subject matter of his course and then administers a final examination, and if the content of both tests relates only to the course in calculus, it may be inferred that substantial increases in scores from the pretest to the final examination may be attributed to learning in the course. Indeed, if this mathematics professor were to introduce a control group that took both examinations but that received no training in calculus, his colleagues would probably speak of him as being unreasonably overcautious and too free in wasting the time of his students. On the other hand, the psychology professor who also gives a pretest and a final examination may well wonder whether increases in scores are a result of learning in his course. In this case, the increase may be a result of general reading, discussions with other students, and related materials learned in courses in biology, sociology, and other subjects that overlap with psychology. It would be necessary to include a control group in the latter case in order to improve the possibility of attributing above-chance scores on the final examination to the content of the course.

The student should also be aware of the possibility that a pretest may, in itself, be a learning situation. Although little knowledge of a field may be acquired through taking a test, the student may become familiar with the form of an examination and this in turn may facilitate the answering of questions on subsequent tests. Pupils learn test taking skills even if they learn nothing else.

*The Function of Replication in Relation to the
Problem of Estimating Error*

In the behavioral sciences, a single experiment in which a measurement is made on one subject exposed to experimental treatment and the same measurement is made on a control subject cannot yield meaningful results. The design of experiments that can achieve this end and that can be used to derive useful generalizations requires the introduction of what are known as replications.

The term *replication* is frequently used with reference to experimental designs, and it refers to the making of additional observations comparing two or more treatments. Some replication is obviously necessary if there is to be any experiment at all. This can be explained by an example.

Suppose that it is desired to determine the effect of a second-grade workbook on the development of skills. A very unsophisticated experimenter might start with two beginning second-graders of the same age and with equal reading skill. One of these two pupils might be given a particular workbook to use during the semester, while the other would not. At the end of the semester, both pupils would be again tested, and let us say the pupil who had had the workbook made the higher score. Just what can be concluded from such an experiment?

The answer to this question is that no conclusion of any value can be drawn. If two pupils have equal scores on a reading test at the beginning of a semester, they will probably have different scores by the end of the semester—as a matter of fact, they will very probably have different scores if they are retested only a day later. The latter effect illustrates the fact that there are errors of measurement. Thus the pupil who achieved the higher score might have achieved this score without the use of a workbook. Also the child who had the workbook might also have had certain advantages, such as a parent who worked with him on his reading difficulties. All of these uncontrolled sources of variation in final test scores are collectively referred to as *experimental errors*. In order to estimate their magnitude, it is necessary to replicate the treatments (with and without workbook) with additional cases.

This matter can be considered from another point of view. If the score of the pupil in the one group is X_1 and the score of the pupil in the other group is X'_1, then the single difference $X_1 - X'_1$ cannot be evaluated for its significance because there is no standard with which it can be compared. If a second pair of cases is added to the data, a second comparison $X_2 - X'_2$ may be computed, but the added data also enable us to begin making an estimate of variability within each group through the comparisons of X_1 with X_2 and X'_1 with X'_2. As pairs of cases are added, it becomes more and more possible to evaluate differences between groups, because the data enable us to estimate what differences would be expected if both members of each pair were drawn from the same group.

The question is inevitably asked at this point concerning the number of replications that should be included in the design. This is not an easy question to answer. Sometimes it is possible to compute the number of replications that are needed to attain a particular level of precision. There is also a second procedure, which is particularly applicable to research in the behavioral sciences, where data are collected not at one time but in a series of separate sessions. When this is done, replications can be added until the desired precision is reached; that is to say, until conclusions can be drawn with a definite degree of risk that they are wrong. A procedure known as *sequential analysis* may be used at any given stage in the collection of data to determine how many additional replications are needed in order to obtain the desired degree of precision.

Replication is necessary in order that the variability of subjects exposed to a particular treatment may be estimated. However, the multiplication of observations may serve an additional purpose if more is done than merely adding cases randomly selected in pairs from the same populations. In the case of a study comparing two reading methods, it would be desirable to draw samples exposed to both methods from different intellectual levels, and perhaps too from schools in different socioeconomic neighborhoods. If such a plan of investigation were pursued, it might then be possible to determine whether one method was superior to the other, not only for children in general but for children at different intellectual levels and for children from different socioeconomic backgrounds. An interaction might be found between method and intellectual level—that one method was better with the brighter children and one with the duller. If the design is properly planned so that it includes other factors, much more information can be derived from a single inquiry than if all replications represent only the addition of randomly selected observations from the same population.

More information will be supplied by a single pair of observations if factors other than that which is being studied (differences in teaching method) are controlled, but control is important only insofar as it affects the variable in which we are interested; that is to say, in the example under consideration—reading achievement. The procedure of matching one member of each pair with the opposite pair on one or more relevant variables can be adopted. If pairs could be matched absolutely on all relevant variables, and if our measure of reading achievement involved no error, the remaining difference between pairs would be attributable entirely to differences in reading method. This situation is, of course, a limiting condition that can never be actually achieved. Usually we do not know what all the relevant variables for matching the pairs should be, and many that can be identified cannot be measured.

There is, of course, no certainty that even in an experiment where subjects are carefully paired for exposure to the two treatments there may still be differences between the groups thus selected for study. This is why it is necessary to obtain an independent measure of experimental error. All that can be done is to assign subjects to the two treatments in such a way that there is equal probability of the subjects in the two groups being affected by these uncontrolled conditions.

Matching procedures increase the precision of experimentation; that is to say, they increase the amount of information that can be derived from a particular number of cases. Thus experiments with matched cases can be undertaken with a smaller number of subjects than when assignment is by a random procedure. Nevertheless, there are often serious difficulties in the matching of groups. Often relevant data are not available. Often there are not a sufficient number of subjects to permit the careful matching of several groups. This is clearly shown by the fact that educational literature is remarkably devoid of studies that have involved the use of carefully matched groups.

There is also a criticism of matching procedures arising from the fact that matching has often been accomplished only after large numbers of cases have been collected in both the experimental and the control groups. When this is done, it usually results in the very uneconomic procedure of discarding subjects, which means that time and energy are lost. Such loss of data is not a necessary part of a matching technique, for if only carefully matched subjects are used in an experiment that is tedious to undertake, it may be possible to reduce materially the time spent in experimentation.

An approximation to the effects of matching can also be achieved through a number of different statistical procedures. When the latter are adopted, the two groups that have received different instruction may be considered to differ on their final performance on a reading test, partly because the two methods of instruction produce different effects and partly because the pupils in the two groups differ with respect to other important characteristics (on which they would have been matched in the methods previously discussed). If measures are available of these other variables influencing the reading scores, then statistical methods can be employed to determine the difference in the performance of the groups exposed to the two reading methods attributed to these other variables and, hence, the difference that can be attributed to instructional procedures. The use of these statistical procedures is generally preferable to the use of matching procedures because they permit the utilization of all the data available.

Sources of Error

A basic problem in the design of research is the estimation of error. Without such an estimate, the results of a study cannot be interpreted. Little has been said about the sources of such errors, so a brief consideration of this matter is now appropriate.

A convenient classification of error is provided by E. F. Lindquist (1953). He divides sources of error into three types according to whether they are associated with *subjects, groups,* or *replications.* He refers to these three types of errors as S errors, G errors, and R errors, after the first letters in the words *subjects, groups,* and *replications.* These errors can be illustrated by a simple example. Suppose that sixty first-graders were to be used in an experiment to determine the relative effectiveness of two methods of teaching reading, and that they were divided at random into six equal groups. It is possible that one of these groups might have more than its share of bright pupils, and as a result that group would have an advantage in learning to read regardless of the method used. This source of error, which is entirely the result of chance factors determining which pupils are to be exposed to each method, is referred to as an S-type error. However, even if the groups are perfectly matched, it is possible that one group might have advantages over the other group during the experiment itself. For example, it might happen that the one group had had a better teacher than the other. The errors introduced through such uncontrolled events are referred to as G-type errors, because they are attributable to differences in conditions to which the two groups are exposed. If the same experiment were repeated in another school, it is possible that the method of teaching reading found most effective in the first school might be least effective in the second school, and this phenomenon might be a genuine one. It is certainly conceivable that a method of teaching reading that is highly effective for teaching children from literary homes might be a poor method for teaching children in impoverished neighborhoods. Such differences between replications are referred to by Lindquist as R-type errors. Such an effect as that discussed could also be referred to as an interaction of socioeconomic background and teaching method. It is desirable to design studies so that errors resulting from all of these sources are reduced to a minimum.

Factorial Designs

Up to this point, our discussion has been limited to simple, classical designs that are based mainly on the concept that an experiment is performed by keeping all factors constant except one. The essential principle that R. A. Fisher introduced to revolutionize experimental design was the concept that more than one factor could be varied within the structure of a single experiment. Such an experiment involving many factors may contain all the information and provide the same precision as a series of independent experiments involving each of the factors singly, and it will provide savings in effort and work on the part of the experimenter. An additional advantage of the multi-factor design is that it may permit the estimation of the effect of the interaction of the variables.

The concept of interaction is a relatively advanced one in the history of the experimental sciences, and it has become particularly useful in the biological and social sciences. It has become a key concept in the biological sciences largely through the study of chemicals in the form of fertilizers and drugs. In the use of fertilizers, the interaction phenomenon is dramatic in effect. Nitrogen alone added to a deficient soil may produce little effect on growth, and the same may be true when phosphorus alone is added. However, when both are added the effect on plant growth may be remarkable. Under these conditions, it would be said that the variance of plant growth because of nitrogen alone, or of phosphorus alone, would be negligible; but variance because of the *interaction* effect of nitrogen and phosphorus would be large. Other well-known and important interaction effects are found in pharmacology, where the combined effects of Drugs X and Y are found to be greater than what one would expect to find from the effects of the two drugs administered separately. This effect is known as the *synergic effect,* and it is extensively illustrated by the well-known procedure of compounding several drugs into a single dose of medicine.

In the behavioral sciences, it is not possible to point to clear-cut and well-recognized phenomena that illustrate the interaction effect, possibly because such interaction phenomena are not usually studied in most experiments. One reason for this is that it is only rarely possible to provide a rationale on the basis of which they can be studied. It is easy to see why plants do not grow in a deficient soil even if either nitrogen or phosphorus is added, for plants need both of these elements in an available form, and one can well understand why it is that both added together produce results greater than would be expected from the effect of each separately. Other interactions in the biological sciences are fully in accord with expectation, but in the behavioral sciences one is much less certain of what to expect. Perhaps at this point it may be well to pause and consider some cases in educational research where one may expect to find interaction effects.

One such situation is presented by the relationship of teachers to the type of curriculum in terms of which they can most effectively work. It has been suspected for a long time that the teacher who presents what has been called an "authoritarian" personality has great difficulty in working within the framework of a school program in which pupil initiative is encouraged. It is alleged that such teachers work most effectively within a traditional type of curriculum, where nearly all activity is initiated, controlled, and directed by the teacher. Such a situation does at least call for habit systems that are consistent with those one might expect to find in the so-called authoritarian personality. On the other hand, the teacher who feels secure in a classroom situation and who does not find activity initiated by the pupils threatening, might be most effective in a situation where there was no need to control every movement of the pupils and where he could function more as a counselor and guide than as a dictator. As far as the author is aware, it has never been demonstrated that there is this type of interaction between teacher and teaching program, yet it is reasonable to suppose that such an interaction may be crucial. If such a study could be undertaken, it should provide data important for the selection of teachers.

Consider the comparison of the two methods of teaching reading, in which there are two methods said to represent Factor A in the study, two socioeconomic levels representing Factor B, and two ability levels representing Factor C. Information might be obtained from this experiment concerning each of the following:

The effect of A on reading achievement
   "   "   " B "   "   "
   "   "   " C "   "   "
The interaction effect of A and B on reading achievement
   "   "   "   " A " C "   "   "
   "   "   "   " B " C "   "   "
The interaction effect of A, B, and C on reading achievement

The "interaction effect" of A and B refers to the effect of combining those two factors over and above the effect of the two factors alone. Thus if there are three factors (A, B, and C) there would be a minimum of 2^3 observations that would have to be made in order that each one of these effects could be evaluated, because each level of A would have to be combined with each level of B and each level of C. In actual practice, there would have to be a replication of the eight observations in order to increase the precision of the experiment to the point where it could yield useful information.

Testing of Hypotheses

All that has been said in this chapter up to this point is based on the assumption that the experimenter has in mind certain clear-cut hypotheses to test. The methods of experimental design that have been discussed are such that they assist the experimenter in testing his hypotheses with the minimum amount of data for a given degree of precision, and sometimes they permit the formulation of generalizations that cover a wider range of circumstances than would be possible if the classical type of experimental design were used. It is common to formulate hypothesis in a form known as the *null hypothesis*. In this form the hypothesis states that no difference is expected. Thus, if an experiment were to be carried out involving two methods of teaching reading, and reading skill was measured by a test at the end of the training period, the null hypothesis would state that the two groups would not differ. If a difference were found between the mean scores of the two groups, the next step would be to determine by appropriate statistical methods the probability that such a difference or a larger difference would occur by chance. If the chances are found to be quite small that such a difference or a larger difference would occur by chance, the null hypothesis is rejected. Because the testing of the hypothesis from the data involves the determination of the probability that such a difference or greater would occur by chance, there is a certain logic in stating all hypotheses in the null form. In the sense described, it is possible to test the null hypothesis, and if the chances are extremely small that the difference (or a larger difference) would have occurred by chance, we may be willing to accept the alternative possibility that the difference was a product of differences in treatment. The latter hypothesis cannot be proven in terms of the data, but it does become more and more plausible as the null hypothesis becomes less and less plausible.

There is also a somewhat different approach to the matter of stating what we expect to find and evaluating our expectancies in terms of the data. In place of stating that we expect no difference (the null hypothesis), and of rejecting or accepting this expectancy or hypothesis in terms of the data, we may ask a question of this type: "If the data shows that there is a numerical difference between the treatments, then with what degree of confidence can we consider that difference to represent a real difference between the treatments and not just the consequence of random errors?" In asking this kind of question, we are not expecting an answer in a form where a decision is made to accept a difference as a genuine difference or to definitely reject the notion that the difference represents something other than the operation of error factors. On the contrary, we expect only to find out whether the chances are high or low that an equal or larger difference would be found if the experiment were replicated. The answer to our question indicates the confidence that can be placed in the particular difference or in statements that we may make about it. In a particular experiment, the answer to our question might be "There is one chance in a thousand that a difference as large as or larger than the one found would occur by chance." If the data provided this answer, then one would be highly confident that the difference found was not just the product of chance circumstances.

The analysis of variance and related statistical techniques that are outside the scope of this book are the techniques used for testing hypotheses, and they always provide an estimate of the probability that a particular difference could have occurred as a result of variations produced by chance circumstances. The probability value that must be reached before it is decided to reject the null hypothesis is a matter of judgment, but it will depend on the consequences of making an error. In this connection, two types of error have been distinguished and have become known as *errors of the first kind* and *errors of the second kind*.

In an experiment comparing the effect of two methods of teaching reading, the results might be presented in the form of the statement,

"The probability that the observed difference or a greater difference would occur as a result of chance variations alone is 0.1." This means that if the two treatments had no differential effect, the results of sampling would produce a difference this size or greater in 10 per cent of all experiments. The experimenter might say to himself that this probability is small, and hence it is reasonable to conclude that the observed difference is generated, not by chance variations in the sample drawn, but by differences in treatment. If more thorough experiments were carried out later, substantial evidence might be collected to show that this conclusion was wrong. If this were the case, the experimenter would have made an *error of the first kind.* In this type of error, the null hypothesis stating that there is no difference between treatments is rejected when it should be accepted.

Errors of the second kind are exactly the opposite type of error. They represent the case where the experimenter accepts the null hypothesis when he should not have done so. It is not possible to say that these errors are more or less serious than errors of the first type, because everything in this respect depends on the circumstances. Fortunately, in education, the result of committing either type of error is not likely to be catastrophic, but in experimentation in other fields an error of either type may on occasion result in the loss of human life. In the interpretation of experimental results, it is important to keep in mind the consequences of each one of these types of errors. If the penalties involved in committing one of these types of error are heavy, caution must be taken in arriving at a conclusion that may make these penalties take effect.

Design in Relation to the Question Asked

The care that needs to be exercised in relating the design to the question asked is well illustrated in a study by D. M. Medley, *et al.* (1955), which was developed to illustrate some of the problems that this may involve. The research made use of data from an earlier study in which two observers made four visits apiece to each of four classroom teachers. From these observations, a climate index was derived for each visit to each classroom. Three major questions that might be asked of these data are stated as follows:

1. Did the two observers ". . . detect differences among the four teachers' behaviors on the four particular occasions on which they were visited with respect to the . . . climate index?"

2. Is it reasonable to hypothesize on the basis of the data that, if other observers visited other teachers on other occasions, differences between teachers other than chance differences would be found?
3. If the two observers were assigned to observe other teachers in the population of teachers from which the four were drawn, would other than chance differences in the climate index be found?

The analysis involved in these three cases is considerably different. The particular question to be asked in this case depends much on what are the experimenter's future plans and what he intends to do with the results.

The first question is a rather trivial one. It is of interest only if we wish to know whether the same observers visiting the same teachers on different occasions would still be able to observe differences between those teachers. The answer tells us absolutely nothing about the differences that might be found if other teachers or other observers were used.

The second question leads to a much more useful answer, if it can be answered. The experimenter is likely to be interested in predicting what would happen if other observers were used with other teachers. In order to answer this question the four teachers must be considered as a sample of a population of teachers from which other teacher samples could be drawn, and the observers as a sample of a population of observers from which other observers might be drawn. We are interested in generalizing from our observers and teachers to other observers and other teachers. If the results of the study are to be used, this type of generalization is necessary.

The answer to the third question is particularly useful if the study under discussion has been conducted as a preliminary to a more extended study using the same two observers. It indicates something about the results to be expected from these two observers.

Sampling and Problems of Generalization in the Design of Studies

The design of experimental studies and investigations in the behavioral sciences, as in the biological sciences, is intimately connected with the problem of sampling. The intention of the author cannot be to provide the student with an adequate background in theory of sampling; it can be only that of making the student sensitive to some of the problems in the area so that he can turn to more comprehensive works to learn about the details of their solution—at least insofar as these problems have a solution.

In the testing of almost any hypothesis by statistical means, an assumption is made that the observations recorded represent a sample drawn from a defined universe by methods that do not introduce bias. A universe from which a sample is drawn consists of all those cases that might be included in the sample. Universe is a technical term and is used in a technical sense. Some of the factors that introduce bias into the drawing of a sample were already considered in the chapter on survey techniques, with particular reference to the problem of identifying a limited number of persons who are to be interviewed from an unidentified universe of persons. In this chapter, the more general problem of obtaining samples of specified universes will be discussed.

Suppose that the director of research in a large school system decided to survey the reading abilities of children who had passed their ninth birthday but who had not yet reached the age of nine years and six months. In this school system, a few less than 10,000 school children fell within this age range and these were distributed among twenty-five schools. It was clear that the director of research could not test all of these children on the particular test to be used. Therefore he decided to test a sample and to use statistical methods for making inferences concerning the total population from the scores derived from the sample. A member of the board of education immediately suggested that it would be administratively convenient to limit the testing to pupils in a single school, since these pupils could then be tested together in a single session. The director was quick to point out that it was a well-established fact that one could not justifiably make inferences from the reading performance in a particular school to the reading performance in all schools, because average scores on the particular test in earlier years had been shown to fluctuate substantially from school to school.

Thus it is clear that the accuracy of the inference made from a sample to a universe will depend on the way in which the sample is selected. The suggestion of the member of the school board lacks merit because it introduces bias into the sample for the sake of administrative convenience. Whatever sampling procedure is used, it is absolutely essential that it not include any systematic bias. The simplest method of obtaining a sample from a population is that of obtaining a random sample, which is simply a sample in which every case in the population has equal chance of being included. By definition, the sample deliberately derived from one school could not be considered a "random" sample because cases from other schools would have no chance of being included in it. One way of obtaining such a sample would be to obtain a list of all such children, number them consecutively, and then select from this list by means of a table of random numbers. Such tables can be obtained from libraries. In using such a table, it would be appropriate to start by taking the first four digits and selecting the child who had the number corresponding to these four digits. The investigator would then take the next four digits and select the child whose number corresponded to these digits, and so forth. Thus each child in the population identified would have equal opportunity for being included in the sample to be studied.

In this simple type of inquiry, it is presumed that the director of research is interested in estimating the mean reading score of the defined population from the sample. In the case of the random sample that has no systematic bias, the best estimate of the population mean is the sample mean. It is of course expected that there will be a difference e (e for error) between the sample mean and the universe mean, but because the method of drawing the sample introduces no systematic bias, if the inquiry were repeated with new samples one would expect e to be negative as often as positive.

In this very simple inquiry, much can be done to reduce the value of e to a minimum. If the investigation is efficiently designed, it will be possible to obtain an unbiased sample such that e is smaller than it would be with a random sample of the type discussed. In essence, what is done is to take steps to insure that the sample is as far as possible *representative* of the universe sampled with respect to important characteristics that are related to reading. For instance, it is known that girls show a tendency to be better readers than grade-school boys of the same age. Hence it would be desirable to insure that the sample included the same proportion of boys and girls as was included in the universe under consideration. Because neighborhood is also related to reading skill, it would also be desirable to insure that the schools were represented in the sample in proportion to the actual enrollment of the particular age group under study. Thus the sample would be stratified, and by making the sample more and more closely representative of the population, the tendency would be for the error term e to be steadily reduced.

Let us now consider a slightly more complicated problem of design in order to illustrate the relationship of problems of design to problems of sampling. Suppose that the director of research had been asked to evaluate a remedial reading program. In this program, approximately one hundred children in the elementary grades were given special remedial training in reading each year. The problem may be stated in this way: "If the reading skills of the pupils are measured at the end of the year of special remedial training, what is the probability that a random sample of children, similarly selected but without training, would perform as well or better than the trained sample?" It is therefore necessary to estimate the reading characteristics (mean and standard deviation) of the universe from which the remedial reading group was a sample, for the time at which the remedial group finished its special training.

The director of research would do well to start by identifying the universe to be sampled. One way of doing this might be to administer a reading test to all grade-school children at the beginning of the year. In each grade (or possibly in each age group), the lowest 10 per cent or 5 per cent might be considered to be the population eligible for remedial training in reading. Another method of identifying the universe might be to define it in terms of the cases recommended by teachers, but this method is likely to provide a highly variable population from year to year. Therefore, let us assume that the director of research identified his universe in terms of a cutoff on a distribution of test scores. His next step would be to select a sample to be given remedial training, and, at the same time, to select a second sample that would also be followed up but would be given no remedial training. The latter sample, referred to as a *control sample*, would be used for estimating the reading skills at the end of the year of the universe of pupils who did not receive special training. The data would then permit a comparison of the reading skills of the group receiving special training with the group not so trained.

In all sound experimental design, it is important to start by defining the universe to be studied and then to establish methods for sampling that will maximize the information supplied. All too often the reverse procedure is undertaken. The author is aware of a book that describes the behavior of four cases of reading difficulty. These four cases are presented without any inkling of the nature of the population of which they may be considered to be a sample. The reader is thus left wondering about the inferences that can reasonably be made from the data provided by the sample of four. On the other hand, if it were known that these cases were every tenth case admitted to a reading clinic for eight- to twelve-year-old children in a large city public school system, it might have been possible to make certain inferences from the data about other children admitted to the reading clinic. One should not make inferences about typical children in classrooms from data derived from special clinic cases, and neither should inferences in the reverse direction be made. If the children sampled are drawn at random from public school classes in a particular city, then the data derived from them can be used for making inferences about children in public school classes in the same city.

Perhaps the commonest single error in educational research is to study a number of cases and then seek a population of which the cases could reasonably be considered to be a sample. When such a population is believed to be found, an attempt is then made to draw inferences about that population from what is known about the cases studied. This procedure is quite unjustified as a basis of inferences.

The Error of Sampling One Universe and Generalizing to Another

Although consideration has been given to the cardinal sin in experimentation of failing to identify the universe sampled, a still more grievous sin is commonly committed by those who attempt to utilize and to apply research results. This is the error involved when a specific and well-defined universe is sampled and the results are generalized to quite different universes. Writers in the area of mental health seem to specialize in this error. They find, for example, that the children who come to a particular clinic and are examined there display an inability to do schoolwork under pressure and have to be given reassurances of the teacher's support if they are to learn effectively. In numerous writings such data or similar data have been taken as a basis for inferring that optimum classroom conditions for typical school children involve warm supportive behavior on the part of the teacher. Of course, the conclusion may be right even though it is based on an invalid inference. The error is obvious but rarely pointed out. Here, the behavior of children sampled from a clinic population has been studied. The scientist may make inferences about the clinic population from the behavior of the sample, but there is no basis for making inferences about other populations of children such as normal school populations. Although this example of false inference is commonly found in the writings of clinical psychologists and psychiatrists, a similar error is made by writers on education who specialize in areas other than the clinical. It is a very easy error to make. The student of education should be particularly on his guard when he comes to writing the last chapter of his thesis—the place where he can bring out the full implications of his study for education. At that point he had better ask himself to identify carefully the population to which his results

may be reasonably generalized and the assumptions that underlie
that generalization.

Individual Differences and Block Design

Research designs of the block type, which originated in the work
of R. A. Fisher, are unsatisfactory in the way they handle the matter
of individual differences. This can be explained by means of an example. Suppose that a study were being conducted to estimate the extent
to which differences in pupil satisfaction in differen᠁ classes could be
associated with teacher differences. In this study four high school
teachers, who were each teaching four different classes of thirty pupils,
were selected. Two of these teachers were judged to be the most
intelligent in the particular school, and two were judged to be the
least intelligent. The pupils in each class were also divided into the
fifteen more intelligent and the fifteen less intelligent in terms of a
well-known intelligence test. The experimenter had in mind the hypothesis that the ablest students derived satisfaction from the ablest
teachers but not from the least able teachers, and that the reverse was
true in the case of the least able students. Now the experimenter in
this case was undoubtedly thinking in terms of a continuous distribution of the intelligence of teachers, and probably assumed that what
happens in the case of the two extreme groups of teachers can be
used as a basis of generalization to intermediate groups.

However, such a generalization is often not justified. The relationships established with extreme groups may not represent two points
on a linear continuum. The responses of pupils to the intermediate
teachers may be quite different from what it might be expected to be
on the basis of that assumption. This situation can be remedied to
some extent by including intermediate groupings, but the inclusion
of more groupings adds greatly to the complexity of the design.

Brunswick's Representative Design

Particular attention to the problem of generalizing from experimental results has been paid by E. Brunswick (1947). This writer
points out that thinking in psychology is still influenced largely by
classical experimental design, in which an aspect of some phenomenon
is isolated and then studied under laboratory conditions. Thus in
psychophysics, the aspect of the phenomenon of visual acuity that has

been most closely studied is the ability to perceive two closely situated points of light as distinct points. The separation that such points must have before they are perceived as separate by a particular individual would be considered a measure of the visual acuity of that individual. In further classical types of experimentation with this problem, the relationships of numerous conditions to visual acuity, as thus defined, have been studied.

Brunswick points out that these designs have one central weakness that has been disregarded. Even though they are usually planned with the purpose of including a sample of cases representative of a particular population or subpopulation, they fail to sample the variety of conditions to which it may be desired to generalize the results. In a great number of psychological experiments, the results found under one set of conditions may not be reproducible under other conditions. Indeed, it sometimes happens that one laboratory is unable to reproduce the results of another laboratory. Even in a simple experiment in which visual acuity is to be measured and studied by means of two points of light, it is doubtful whether the results are satisfactorily generalizable to other situations. If the purpose is to obtain results that can be generalized to other situations, the results may be disappointing. A person who has relatively low visual acuity in the laboratory situation may do surprisingly well in other situations, for it is known that visual acuity is related to the general nature of the visual field, the intensity of surrounding illumination, the wavelength of the light involved, the state of adaptation of the eye, and so forth. What Brunswick suggests is that we sample these conditions systematically in order to obtain results that, by and large, are applicable to these varied conditions.

Brunswick developed at least one example of a representative design that involved a problem of size constancy.[1] In this design, size constancy was measured under a great many different conditions, such as in a closed space like a room, outside the building, under different illuminations, and so on. The purpose was to derive principles that could be applied under these varied conditions. Similar types of representative design are extremely difficult to undertake on matters of educational interest. For example, it would be valuable to be able to measure the expressed attitude of white children toward Negro children under varied conditions in order to predict related behavior under

---

[1] Size constancy is the tendency to see objects as being of a given size even though the distance between the object and the observer varies. Thus, a Cadillac appears to be a big car even though it is viewed at a distance of several hundred feet.

those conditions. Although the researcher might want to do this, the probability is that he would be able to measure such an attitude only under classroom conditions, and this would provide inadequate information for predicting what expressions and other evidences of attitude would occur under other conditions. Representative designs in the attitudinal area are rarely feasible.

The acute reader at this point may well ask why it is that a "representative" design is suggested. Would it not be simpler to list the extraneous variables that might affect the outcomes of an experiment and then incorporate them in a design of the Fisherian type? When this can be done, it is of course the recommended procedure, but in research in the behavioral sciences the conditions that affect a particular phenomenon are usually so numerous that it is not feasible to incorporate them in a block design, for an unwieldy number of blocks would be involved. In most cases, it would also appear that these incidental conditions, though numerous, each contribute only a small effect—probably too small to produce significant results in a feasible design. In this type of situation, Brunswick suggests that a systematic effort be made to obtain representative samples of these conditions.

Brunswick's position leads one to understand why a single study, conducted in an educational setting, so often has little to offer the practitioner in other settings. School studies have to be repeated under varied circumstances and with consistent results before they can provide knowledge that has any widespread application. Sometimes the argument is put forward that a study, yielding positive findings, undertaken in one setting can be used as a basis for practice in another similar setting. This assumes that we already know what makes two settings similar or different; but the fact is that we do not. Too often an educational research has been repeated in two different locales that are judged to represent similar circumstances, and the results have been completely dissimilar. Circumstances obviously existed that produced the difference in results and yet the nature of these circumstances was not at all apparent. If a great amount of knowledge were available concerning the influence of various conditions on the outcome of education, there would not be the great need for educational research.

The concept of representative sampling that Brunswick has developed has come in for much criticism. One criticism that the reader will probably already have considered is that major advances have already been made in many areas in the behavioral sciences without resorting to the elaborate procedures Brunswick's system demands.

The psychology of learning is an example. Most of the important facts and principles of human learning that are discussed in typical textbooks were derived from laboratory experiments. For example, the principle that knowledge of results is an important condition for learning was derived from a consideration of learning as it occurs in the laboratory and was demonstrated with simple laboratory experiments. Yet it seems to have wide application in the field of teaching.

A second criticism is that it results in the production of probabilistic laws—that is to say, laws that state only that there is a certain probability of a certain event happening as a result of a given set of conditions. Because Brunswick's system permits prediction over a wide range of situations, it is inevitably limited in the accuracy it can achieve. On the other hand, the more traditional approaches, because they aim ultimately at establishing *all* of the determinants of a particular event, have the aim of perfect prediction.

SUMMARY

1. Courses in experimental design provide the student with a limited range of techniques for planning studies. However, a well-planned study in terms of the statistical design can still deal with a trivial problem.

2. Statistical methods serve two main purposes: one of these is the testing of hypotheses; the other is the summarization of data.

3. Well-designed studies have certain characteristics: they are free from bias, which may be introduced in various ways, some of which are not easily discerned. They must provide some satisfactory way of estimating error. They must insure sufficient precision to provide answers to the questions that are asked. The design must also be such that it yields as much information as possible from the number of observations that are made.

4. The term *control* is used in a number of distinct senses. It can refer to the control of conditions that may interfere with the outcome of a study; it can refer to the control of the crucial variable that is being studied; or it can refer to the use of control groups or control observations.

5. Replication is introduced in order to increase the precision of a study; that is to say, to increase the accuracy with which the main effects and interactions can be estimated.

6. An alternative to replication for the purposes of increasing the precision of a study is to control some of the sources of error. The

traditional method of doing this was by a matching procedure, which has now largely been replaced by statistical methods.

7. The multifactor design is becoming more and more commonly used. Not only does this design permit the estimation of the effect of more than one variable, but it also permits the estimation of the effects produced by the interaction of these factors.

8. The outcome of an experiment may be a statement rejecting or accepting the particular hypothesis under consideration, or it may be a statement of the confidence that can be placed in accepting a particular hypothesis.

9. A distinction has been made between errors involving the rejection of a hypothesis that should be accepted and the acceptance of a hypothesis that should be rejected.

10. Good designs begin with the asking of very precise questions. All too often at the completion of an experiment the experimenter finds that a much more trivial question was answered than the question he wanted answered. He may want results that can be generalized to other observers and other teachers but may find that his results cannot be generalized beyond the particular observers and teachers used.

11. The experimenter usually wants to be able to generalize his results to a larger population than that studied. In order to be able to do this he must be careful to draw his subjects from a specified population. The results of a study involving children who happened to be playing outside the laboratory can, probably, be generalized only to other children who happen to be playing outside the same laboratory. The results probably cannot be generalized to children playing outside other laboratories. Particular care should be taken to avoid conducting an experiment on one population and generalizing the results to another population.

12. Block designs of the kind originated by R. A. Fisher are not particularly satisfactory for the study of problems of individual differences.

13. Brunswick has pointed out that results of experiments should be generalized only to situations similar to those in which they were undertaken. If one wishes to generalize to numerous different situations, then the experiment should be conducted in a sample of those situations.

|||||||||||||||||||||||||||||||||||||||||||||

CHAPTER 14

Studies of Development

SOME PROBLEMS IN THE STUDY OF GROWTH AND DEVELOPMENT

Basic Research Problems

STUDIES of development, unlike most of those that have been considered up to this point, are concerned primarily with time trends; that is to say, with changes that occur as a function of time. Survey studies and prediction studies are occasionally concerned with time trends, but their techniques are not primarily directed toward the study of such phenomena. This chapter on developmental studies is included for two reasons. First, there are difficulties inherent in the conduct of such studies, which the student of education should recognize. Secondly, studies of development are of such far-reaching consequences for education that research of this type must assume a place of great importance in the future even if it did not in the past. The central task of education is that of producing development.

Some of the most important problems of education involve time trends, for education itself is concerned with personal change and with the control of learning as it occurs in the pupil. Even though the classroom teacher is mainly concerned with change over a relatively short period of time, such as a semester or a school year, administrators and those concerned with policy making at a high level are concerned with change over a much longer period, such as a decade or a lifetime.

Classroom examinations given at the end of a semester are limited studies of development in which increments in an area of intellectual skill are studied over a short period of time, perhaps without recognizing that change may not be permanent but will undergo a period of waning as well as waxing as time goes by. The latter type of problem has become of increasing importance as educators have extended their interest in educational problems from the childhood years to the entire life span. Studies of the intellectual functions in the later years are largely studies of decline.

The early studies of development tended to ignore the fact that development may be highly influenced by environmental circumstances. The pioneer studies of Arnold Gesell and Jean Piaget and their immediate associates were designed to provide descriptions of the pattern of development of behavior that was assumed to occur under all circumstances. Although the pattern was believed to occur in all children, most of the early writers conceded that it could be accelerated or slowed up by environmental circumstances. However, little attention was paid to what those circumstances might be.

Developmental studies can be quantitative or qualitative. Pioneer studies, such as those by Gesell on the development of motor and perceptual skills in young babies and those by Jean Piaget and his associates on the higher mental processes, have been essentially qualitative and descriptive in nature. Both have attempted to describe the nature of certain changes that occur in children as they grow. Little attempt has been made to measure changes in these studies, but rather the purpose has been that of description. Perhaps it is necessary to begin developmental studies at the descriptive level, for then the investigator is able to obtain a "feel" for what is important to measure and what is trivial. Until the researcher knows which variables are of genuine importance, he is not really in a position to conduct quantitative studies.

Qualitative descriptive studies are for the expert and not the beginner. He should engage in attempts to test clearly stated hypotheses through techniques that involve measurement—that is to say through quantitative techniques. The beginner who attempts qualitative studies is likely to become involved in two sources of difficulties.

First, the observation and description of behavior at various age levels permit the observer to see what he wants to see—and even the best observers tend to some extent to see what they want to see. Secondly, the observer faced with the innumerable events that constitute the flow of behavior is likely to be bewildered by the richness of the material. He may be overwhelmed with the abundance of fact and, as a result, he may direct his efforts to recording masses of material that he does not know how to handle.

Measurement of Growth and Development

When a young child is taken regularly to a pediatrician, he will be weighed and his height measured. The change in these measures from one visit to the next are taken to indicate the extent of growth and development. A failure to achieve an appropriate amount of change in height or weight during a substantial period, such as a year, will result in the physician initiating a search for the cause. In order to obtain the measure of growth, the physician simply subtracts the height measured at one visit from the height measured at the next visit. The difference in the two measures provides a measure of growth in height, and the pediatrician can perform a similar subtraction and obtain a measure of growth in weight. The formula for obtaining growth scores in this way appears simple and straightforward; but when psychologists began to apply a similar formula to psychological data they immediately encountered difficulties. Problems arose because the errors of measurement in psychological data are very large in comparison with the errors in measuring weight by means of a scale in a doctor's office. (Note that the balanced beam scale of the doctor's office is perhaps ten times more precise than the common bathroom scale.)

Now consider a situation in which the height of children is measured, but under conditions that produce errors of measurement comparable to those found in psychological measurement. Let us suppose that we give an observer the task of judging the height of children. Each child is brought into an empty room and is asked to stand against a plain white wall at a place shown by a marker on the floor. Six feet to the right of the child, a scale is marked off on the wall in feet from the floor. The observer who sits in the middle of the room faces the child, but he can observe the scale by turning his head slightly to the right. His task is to judge the height of each child to the nearest inch. Let us suppose that he does this on one hundred boys who are all within a month of their fifth birthday, and that he repeats the procedure immediately and then again two years later.

Now let us consider the two measures taken one after the other. They would, almost certainly, be correlated—that is to say the children who were judged as short the first time would tend to be judged as short the second time; but, because the procedure involves judgment, and judgment involves rather large errors, the correlation between the two measures would be far from perfect. We would also probably find that the average height of the children based on the first measurement would be very near to that obtained by averaging the second measurement. If it were not for error, the two averages based on the two sets of measures would be equal, because the children would not have had time to grow a measurable amount during the morning when the two sets of measurements were made.

Because the children did not have time to grow appreciably during the course of the morning, the difference in the estimated height of the child when he was first judged and his estimated height when he was judged a second time represents an error of measurement. By examining these differences, one can identify some of the ways in which errors of measurement can influence measures of growth when the two measures are separated by sufficient time to permit an appreciable amount of growth to occur.

The differences between the first measure and the second measure for the two immediately successive measures show certain important features that surprise the newcomer to educational research. Those who are judged tallest when first measured tend to be judged smaller on the second occasion. Those that are judged as smallest in height tend to be judged as taller. It is as if the tall ones shrunk and the small ones grew. This phenomenon is only a reflection of the way in which errors are made by the person doing the judging and is not attributable to either shrinkage or rapid growth on the part of the children. A similar kind of phenomenon would be found if the children were given a psychological test on two successive days. Those who scored highest on the first occasion would tend to slip to a lower score on the second occasion and those who obtained the lowest scores would tend to score higher next day.

How does this systematic lowering and increasing of measures occur as a result of the way in which errors of measurement are made? What happens is this: Let us suppose that the six tallest children in the group all have a true height of 48 inches. The person doing the judging does not judge all the children to be 48 inches in height because he nearly always introduces some error into his judgments. However, his errors are sometimes positive and sometimes negative and are distributed at random. His actual judgments of the heights of the children are 46, 46, 48, 49, 49, and 50 inches. In this way three of the children are judged to be taller and three shorter than they actually are. Now when the three tallest have their heights judged a second time, the chances are that they will tend to be judged as shorter, for only through chance was their height overestimated. The probability is that next time the height of some of those whose height was overestimated on the first occasion would be underestimated on the second occasion. Thus, when the tallest are judged a second time, the estimates of height tend to be lower. For a similar reason, those at the lower end of the scale tend to be judged as taller on the second occasion.

Now this tendency for those at the top to *appear* to shrink and those at the lower end to shoot up has certain important consequences when dealing with growth measurements. If one were to calculate a correlation between the initial height of the children the first time they were measured and correlate this with the apparent change in height from the first to the second measurement, one would find a negative correlation. Even when there is time between the first and second measurement for growth to actually occur, there is a tendency for the initial measure to be correlated negatively with the measure of growth found by subtracting the first measure from the second. What this implies is that the measure derived by subtracting the second measure from the first does not give a very satisfactory measure of growth.

Now let us return to the data on judged height. The reader will recall that three judgments were made, the first two merely giving us some understanding of the effects of errors of measurement. Now let us consider the growth scores for the two-year period derived by subtracting the first judgment of height from the judgment of height made two years later. We would almost certainly find a small and negative correlation between the initial height of each child and the growth score represented by his increase in height. If we did not know that this was an artifact of the measurement procedure, we might be led to the erroneous conclusion that the short children tended to grow the most and the tallest children tended to grow the least. Because this effect would vanish as errors were reduced in our measurement procedure, the conclusion, although true under the particular conditions of measurement, is both trivial and inconsequential. Indeed we may want to adjust our data so that this effect, as a result of errors of measurement, will not influence our statistical analysis. As a matter of fact, if this adjustment is not made, the results of any statistical analysis will be thoroughly misleading. Indeed, the unadjusted data and the adjusted data may lead to opposite conclusions, a fact that should caution the beginning research worker to be extremely cautious in working with growth and development data.

Various methods have been proposed for adjusting growth scores representing the difference between two measures made at different times. The reader concerned with this problem should consult a volume by C. W. Harris (1963) that presents not only methods of adjusting scores but also provides some excellent references to studies in which different methods of adjustment have been used.

The problem just considered is not the only one that causes difficulties in the interpretation of growth scores. Another is rooted in the fact that psychological measures do not generally represent scales in which the units of measurement can be said to be equal. In the study of growth and development, this limitation of most psychological measures produces very substantial difficulties when studies of development are undertaken. For example, suppose that a test of achievement were administered to sixth-grade pupils at the beginning and at the end of the school year. One pupil shows an increase in score from 35 to 45, whereas another raises his score from 85 to 95. Both of the increments were ten points. But let us ignore the fact, at this time, that if these scores were adjusted in the manner already discussed they might not be equal. A teacher familiar with the test and the curriculum might affirm that much more work was required for a pupil to raise his score from 85 to 95 than from 35 to 45. What the teacher is saying is that the test does not consist of a scale of equal units. At the lower end of the scale each point is judged to represent a rather small increment in knowledge compared with the units at the high end of the scale. Unless one has a scale in which the units in different parts of the scale can be demonstrated to be in some way equal (as they can in the case of a 36-inch yardstick), one cannot reasonably compare the amount of growth measured in one part of the scale with an increment in growth measured in another part. A way out of this difficulty, which is not likely to be very practical, is to conduct growth studies with groups whose members have very nearly the same initial scores. Any growth that then takes place is always in approximately the same region of the scale.

Finally, the point must be made that all scores measuring *change*, which are derived from typical psychological measuring instruments, must be suspected of having very low reliability. The fact is that the reliability of most measures of change, as for example a measure of change in IQ over a year, must be considered to be almost worthless for research purposes. This is one of the reasons why growth in IQ over one year shows only a very small relationship with growth during the subsequent year. Thorndike (1966), who has considered this problem, estimates that such growth scores have reliabilities between 0.1 and 0.3. These low reliabilities render the growth scores almost useless for research.

STUDIES OF DEVELOPMENT OVER LONG
PORTIONS OF THE LIFE SPAN

Some Traditional Approaches

Long-term studies of development may follow either one of two rather distinct patterns. In one type of study, an attempt is made to follow a group as it grows and moves forward through life, and every attempt is made to retain contact with all members of the original group. This is the longitudinal method of approach. It is the hard way of conducting developmental studies. In the second type of study, no attempt is made to follow a whole group; instead, individuals at each one of several age levels are selected for study. This can be referred to as the *cross-sectional approach*. It has the obvious advantage of permitting the researcher to complete his developmental studies without waiting for individuals to grow up. This second technique has a long history. Its beginnings go back to the days of Francis Galton, who made the first systematic attempt to trace the growth and decline of human abilities. A brief review of one of his classic studies will be used here to reveal some of the weaknesses of the approach.

Galton's efforts to measure human characteristics and to trace their course of development not only represent pioneer attempts in scientific measurement but are also the first to cover the life span. The collection of data for these studies was made possible by the unusual circumstances presented by an international exhibition held at Earls Court, London, in 1884. Galton was invited to set up a booth at this exhibition, and he seized on the opportunity of using it as a means of collecting data about a sample of persons whose ages spread across the entire life span. With this end in view, he set up a number of tests that covered such varied phenomena as height, speed of movement, the ability to make simple judgments such as those involved in bisecting a line or judging its perpendicularity, strength of grip, visual acuity, and so forth. The population on whom such measures were made consisted of those individuals who happened to visit the booth—people of the sort who typically visit exhibitions, some in almost every age group, but a preponderance of those in the younger groups.

Galton tabulated the data in order to arrive at a general impression of the curve of each of the abilities measured, and for more than a generation his data remained unique in the field. A curve derived from such data is presented in Figure 6.

A straightforward interpretation of data such as those presented

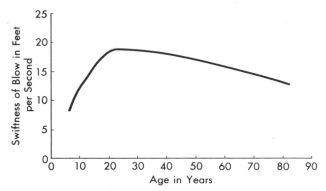

FIGURE 6.   *Data illustrating changes with age. Relationship between age and swiftness of blow.* (Data collected by Francis Galton in 1884 and later reported by H. A. Ruger and B. Stoessinger 1927.)

in the figure just considered is not as sound as it might appear on the surface. The curve cannot be considered to represent the typical growth and decline that an individual might be expected to follow. The reasons for this must now be given consideration.

1. The older group in a population is always a selected sample of what was once a much larger population. A group born in 1970 will lose some of its members through death by 1980, and death is not an event that strikes at random. One can be quite sure that those who survive over the decade will be different in many respects from those who die. Among other things, the survivors will probably be living, for the most part, in more favorable economic circumstances than those who die. There will also probably be some selection for intelligence, in that the more intelligent will be more able to cope with the hazards of daily life. At the other end of the age scale there may well be selective survival for personality attributes that make for quiet and sober living. Thus, in plotting the average of a given characteristic for each age group over the life span, one is plotting data for groups that are selectively changed at each age level. The data may be considerably different from those that would be obtained if the same group were measured at regular intervals through the years. On this account alone, the cross-sectional method of obtaining developmental data must be considered highly unsatisfactory except for the crudest purposes.

2. If the cross-sectional method is adopted in a particular community, the results may be distorted by selective migration. For example, the author knows of a community on the northern border of the United States where in recent years there has been a tendency

for the better-educated members of the young adult group to move south to the larger industrial centers. This migration has not affected either those in the upper grades of school or those in more advanced years. If an intelligence test were given to every member of this community and the average score for each age group were plotted against age, the result would be a curve that would show a rise up to about the age of twenty, then a decline, followed by another rise in the region of the early thirties. A graph of this kind could not possibly be considered to represent the rise and decline of intelligence in this population, because other conditions are operating to determine the shape of the curve.

3. Even if the problems that have just been discussed exist only in minimal amounts, there is another difficulty in the interpretation of data derived from the cross-sectional approach that must be considered. In the case of the individual there is doubt whether it is reasonable to expect that development occurs in the manner depicted by the smooth graphs resulting from the type of data collected by Galton. Functions such as height may show periods of acceleration and depression, which result from disease or particularly unfavorable or favorable circumstances in the child's environment as well as from changes in glandular functions. These important individual irregularities in developmental functions are obscured by the cross-sectional approach.

The longitudinal method of studying development is not without its difficulties. However, these are not related to the interpretation of the data but to the process of collecting them.

First, there is the obvious difficulty involved in waiting year after year for the data to accumulate. This difficulty is not necessarily insuperable, for many long-term studies have been made that require researchers to follow cases over a decade or more. W. Olson (1949), for example, was able to follow the development of children on numerous variables as they progressed through school. He was not only able to plot individual curves for various functions, but he was also able to interrelate the different functions and to demonstrate that changes in development rate are related to many differing conditions. In addition, Olson was able to demonstrate a certain parallelism in the development of different functions, and he put forward the hypothesis that all development variables are functionally interrelated.

Secondly, there is the problem of attrition. It is not uncommon for a researcher involved in, say, a ten-year study to find that fewer than one-third of his cases remain by the end of that period. If funds for travel are available, it may be possible to follow those who have left the community, but this is an expensive process. In planning follow-up studies, the researcher would do well to choose a community in which a highly stable population, without much emigration, is known to exist. Whatever procedure is adopted, attrition adds immensely to the cost of the study, if only because this factor makes it necessary to start with far more cases than are to be included in the completed study.

Thirdly, there is the difficulty of sustaining the interest and cooperation of the subjects in the study. This is not too much of a problem when the subjects are "captive," as they are in experimental schools run by universities and colleges, but it is a problem when the subjects must be contacted at their homes and brought into the laboratory for study. Under such conditions, it may be desirable to reward the subjects with a knowledge of their performance and perhaps with money, too, if any is available. With adults, an effort may be made to keep the group informed of the purposes and progress of the study, but this attempt to stimulate interest will probably have appeal only to the brighter elements in the group.

The points raised here should indicate to the reader the time, money, and effort that are required for the successful completion of a longitudinal study of development.

A final point to be made is that a study could be designed in which the cross-sectional and the longitudinal approaches were combined. In such a study, the cross-sectional approach might be used as a preliminary check on hypotheses and those which were consistent with the data could then be rechecked in a longitudinal study.

Looking Backward: An Approach to Long-Term Developmental Studies

There are limited possibilities for conducting developmental studies by searching in the records for data that have already been collected on individuals. For example, many school systems administer intelligence tests at regular intervals through perhaps as many as twelve grades. The researcher may look back through the records of the system and trace the development of particular individuals who have passed through it. With these data and a little patience, it may be possible to trace their subsequent development and hence to have a record that covers two or more decades.

A major difficulty in following this procedure stems from the fact that school records rarely contain the material in which the researcher is interested. Also, school records in the matter of tests are far from being the reliable sources of information that one would like them to be. Too often, the records show the entry of an intelligence quotient without giving any indication of the test on which it is based. It is well known that intelligence quotients based on different tests are not comparable; hence such data must be considered to be largely uninterpretable. The professional staff of schools should not be blamed for this situation, because they often are fully aware of its existence but unable to remedy it because of lack of the clerical help needed for the keeping of adequate records.

When data are available that adequately document the tests given as well as the scores, another problem arises. This is a result of the fact that different tests are often given at different times in the school program. If these data are to be used, it is necessary to convert the various test scores to a common base. The data for doing this may or may not be available. At best, such converted scores are far from being as satisfactory as scores based on comparable tests. The conversion process itself tends to weaken the data because it involves the use of constants that are only imperfectly estimated.

The use of previously collected data is one type of developmental study that involves looking backward. Another type of study that requires the subjects involved to look backwards in their lives is illustrated in the work of D. R. Miller and G. E. Swanson (1958). These investigators were initially impressed with earlier studies that had demonstrated that some social and economic groups manifest a higher incidence of certain mental diseases than did other groups. For example, the lower socioeconomic groups produce more than their fair share of schizophrenics. Now, although this is an important empirical finding, it does not indicate *why* this relationship exists. Miller and Swanson set themselves the task of investigating this and similar relationships for the purpose of determining the variables in the background of the individual that have important effects on certain aspects of later personality.

The general procedure adopted was that of identifying a sample of subjects to be studied, obtaining information about the child-rearing practices to which they had been exposed early in life, and then determining the response of each to a number of situations in which conflicts of motives had been aroused. In order to limit the number of variables operating, the selection of subjects was narrowed by confining the group to white Protestant boys who had been born north of the Mason-Dixon line. Additional restrictions included were that they had to be within one year of the average grade of boys of their age, emotionally stable, above average in intelligence, and from stock that did not come from northwest Europe. Those from broken homes were also eliminated. The application of all of these criteria resulted in retention for the study of only 1 per cent of the boys available. The extreme care exercised over the selection of subjects should emphasize to the reader the importance of this phase of a well-planned series of studies.

The mothers of all the boys included in the study were interviewed. In order to determine the way in which the boys responded to conflict situations, projective tests related to such conflicts were administered. These tests were all of the story-completion type and were designed to determine the way in which the individual responds to a situation involving a conflict of motives. The tests were also administered after the individuals had been exposed to a realistic situation in which the same conflict of motives was likely to occur.

The technique employed by these investigators is likely to be a productive one, and some of the relationships discovered are of considerable interest, even though they should not necessarily be accepted at face value. For example, they found very definite relationships between the type of maternal discipline exercised and the way in which the subject expressed aggression. However, maternal discipline is not related to the severity of guilt feelings or to the development of defenses against these feelings. Time of weaning was found to be related to severity of guilt about death wishes (wishing someone were dead), about stealing, and about disobedience.

A major difficulty in the interpretation of the results of this series of studies stems from the possibility that the background conditions studied may not be the ones that are really producing long-term effects on behavior. It is possible, for example, that age of weaning may be related to a whole host of important attitudes on the part of the mother. These attitudes, in turn, may have important consequences on child development. Thus it may be that attitudes rather than time of weaning are producing the particular effects. The chief strength of the studies stems from the fact that the results fit rather well a widely held theory of the Freudian type.

The technique is essentially an historical one. An attempt is made to reconstruct past events on the basis of documents and reports. Such reconstructions are always difficult to undertake, particularly when they involve the human memory over a span of many years. Historians, who have learned to exercise great caution in the use of evidence, might well discard as useless the kind of evidence psychologists sometimes use in developmental studies when they try to reconstruct what happened in a particular home twenty years earlier.

Newer Approaches

The Study of Conditions Related to Development. As scientists have become aware of the inadequacy of the concept that development follows a fixed pattern, attempts have been made to study the effect of modifications of the environment on the developmental pattern. Such studies can be made by two different procedures. Suppose that one were interested in studying the effect of lack of interaction with adults during early childhood on the subsequent social behavior of the school-age child. One way to go about such a study would be to find groups of children who, through circumstances, had little contact with adults and to compare their subsequent behavior with that of children who had had relatively high amounts of interaction with adults. The socially deprived group would probably be composed of children from foundling homes and orphanages, while children raised in typical homes (and whose mothers did not work outside the home) would constitute the high social-interaction group. An immediate difficulty stems from the fact that the two groups differ not only with respect to the amount of social interaction with adults, but also with respect to other important factors that may affect the results of the study. The foundling group is likely to come from genetically inferior stock. Many of the foundling children will have suffered from serious malnutrition and exposure prior to admission. In the foundling home they are likely to lack intellectual as well as social stimulation. These factors may well account for any subsequent social difficulties that such children display, and the lack of interaction with adults in the foundling home may be only a minor factor in the total picture. Similar difficulties are likely to plague all research workers who attempt to study long-term development through the study of selected groups.

A second approach is to manipulate experimentally the conditions which one may desire to study. One of the most famous examples of this procedure is found in the work of M. G. McGraw (1935, 1943), who conducted studies of development on twins. In these studies one twin was given special training in a skill, such as stair-climbing, whereas the other twin was deprived of both the training and the opportunity to acquire the skill until the age at which the skill typically appears. In technical terms, one would say that in these studies the condition experimentally manipulated was training. The results of McGraw's experiments on training conditions in relation to development are well known. The effect of the special training on the course of the development of the skill was negligible. Once he was given the opportunity to learn, the twin that had had no special training rapidly acquired the skill and caught up with his specially trained twin. Deferred training was much more efficient than training spread out over a very extended period which began at much earlier age levels.

The general results are mentioned because from them emerged a number of educational doctrines that represented unjustified generalizations from limited scientific data. The general conclusion that tended to be drawn from such studies was that learning should be postponed until maturation reached the point at which learning could occur rapidly and efficiently. This conclusion does not follow from the data provided by studies such as those of McGraw. Indeed, the results have to be interpreted today in a way entirely different from that in which they were originally interpreted. Consider, for example, the case of twins, one of whom was trained in stair-climbing while the other was not. The assumption is made that the one not given special training did not have relevant learning experiences, but such was almost certainly not the case. A young child who had never seen a staircase would still have had extensive opportunity to learn the components of the skill of stair-climbing. Merely pulling himself to his feet and then climbing on a chair would involve all the component skills involved in stair-climbing. Thus, the twin given special training in stair-climbing may have had only a negligibly greater amount of experience than the other twin. Much of what were considered to be the effects of maturation in such experiments were more probably the results of learning by daily experience and bear a close resemblance to what Hebb has referred to as "early learning." Of course, some of the skills involved in such developmental studies are motor functions closely allied with inborn mechanisms in the nervous system that would minimize the effect of special intensive early training.

A review by W. Fowler (1962) serves to point out that the generalization from early developmental studies that emphasizes the role of maturation was an unjustified conclusion. He marshals ample evidence to show that in the area of conceptual and perceptual development early training may have dramatic results in producing precociousness. Many of the studies he cites, which describe effective training in the first few years of life, need to be repeated. For example, he cites a study by H. P. Davidson (1931) in which children in the three- to five-year-old range were given training in reading ten to fifteen minutes a day with remarkable results. Although many of these children were of average ability (as measured by an intelligence test), they made substantial progress and two of the three-year-olds completed the equivalent of a first-grade program and were well on the way to becoming fluent readers. Such studies need to be repeated for, if they are reproducible, they have enormously important implications for the planning of education. A perusal of other sections of Fowler's review will reveal many other exciting studies which need to be reproduced and which could well form the basis for a thesis or dissertation.

Although variables related to the development of intellectual and motor skills can be manipulated and controlled by the experimenter, there are some conditions that cannot. The relationship of the mother to the child is considered to be of the greatest importance to the development of personality, but mothers often cannot be trained or persuaded to handle their children in particular ways for the sake of a scientific inquiry. For this reason, many studies relating important environmental conditions, such as child-rearing practices, to personality development of the child must be undertaken by other means. In such a case, the study has to be conducted by finding parents who display different child-rearing practices and then relating these practices to the characteristics of the children. R. R. Sears, *et al.* (1957) provide an example of such a procedure. In this study an investigation was made of both the child-rearing practices and the behavior of the children, and some effort was made to relate the two. Such a procedure is not as sound as the experimental approach and is likely to yield less information. To illustrate this problem it may be pointed out that child-rearing practices are to some extent related to social class; hence one cannot be sure that a particular effect on the child is the result of child-rearing practices, as such, or whether it is a result of some other aspect of social class. Experimental procedures avoid this difficulty in those cases in which they can be applied.

Research on the Development of Individual Differences. In recent years a new type of study has appeared designed to throw light on the development of individual differences. Textbooks on educational psychology published as far back as the first decade of this century noted the fact that there is great uniformity of behavior at the beginning of human life. As the child grows, there is a constant increase in the amount of differentiated behavior that appears, and individuals show an ever-increasing range of differences in the responses they manifest to a given situation. L. L. Thurstone was so much impressed with this fact that he proposed that a convenient zero of intelligence might be established at that point at which individual differences vanish.

Most measures of intellectual ability indicate a tendency for individual differences to increase as age increases. Some caution should be exercised in the interpretation of this fact, because the change in the spread of scores may be as much a product of the measuring instrument as it is of the function that is being measured. Instruments available for measuring intellectual skills may be such that they do not measure individual differences adequately at the lower levels. In other words, individual differences at all age levels may be identical. This interpretation is generally not considered acceptable, for it does not fit the common observation that young babies show little in the way of individual differences, their repertoire of behavior being limited to a small number of responses that all (or very nearly all) babies show.

A new approach to this problem has been taken in recent years through the extension of factor-analytic methods to this area. The reader is undoubtedly familiar with the fact that most batteries of aptitude tests that are administered to adults can be considered to measure a limited number of factors: the verbal factor, the numerical factor, the deductive reasoning factor, and so forth. It has been postulated by many workers that tests given in the lower grades do not manifest the existence of a series of underlying traits represented by these factors, but, rather, that they appear to demonstrate only the existence of a single general intelligence factor. The differentiation of behavior that occurs as education progresses is accompanied by the appearance of the distinct abilities that are measured by typical aptitude batteries. The procedure for studying this problem has been to administer batteries of similar tests at various age levels. The batteries used must be such that the tests differ in difficulty but not in content. Thus an arithmetic reasoning test would be one in which the problems at all levels involve reasoning with quantities, but differed from level to level in the complexity of the reasoning process involved. The computations involved should be of the same order of simplicity at all levels, because the computation aspect measures a factor different from that measured by the reasoning aspect. After such batteries have been administered to a series of different age groups, factor-analytic procedures are applied in order to determine whether the same underlying structure of abilities appears at the different age levels. Although the evidence derived from such studies remains somewhat ambiguous, it does nevertheless tend to support the hypothesis that factors emerge in the structure of human ability as the individual grows up.

Such studies are not without weakness. One of their very unsatisfactory features is that they do not give any indication at all about what causes the emergence of various factors in the structure of human ability. For example, some of the abilities related to the understanding of spatial relationships emerge late and cannot be recognized as clearly identified and distinct abilities until the late teens. Whether the emergence of this ability is dependent on the kinds of experiences some teen-agers have remains an open question. Studies of the aptitude test factors that appear at particular ages tell us nothing that will be useful in controlling their emergence or in, perhaps, facilitating their emergence.

Studies of Perceptual Development. Certain striking lines of research that appear to raise questions about current educational practices will be mentioned here briefly to suggest to the student avenues which he may wish to explore further.

First, brief consideration must be given to the work of Donald Hebb on perceptual development and sensory deprivation. Hebb has demonstrated, with data derived from both human and subhuman subjects, that normal intellectual and emotional development is highly dependent on exposure of the organism to appropriate stimulation during the period of growth. Deprivation of opportunities to use the sense of vision in both men and animals, for example, results in an inability to undertake the simplest visual perceptual tasks—such as shape and form recognition—even though the eyes may be in perfect functioning condition.

The dramatic effects that early perceptual experiences of humans and subhumans have been shown to have on the effectiveness of their subsequent performance have stimulated related research on children. The current trend in this research is to design special preschool or elementary school experiences that will foster intellectual development. One major project of this character is being financed by the U. S. Office of Education and is being coordinated by J. McV. Hunt. Other projects are exploring the effect of intellectual stimulation during the first year of life on the pattern of development. A project in the latter direction has been undertaken by Ira Gordon at the University of Florida. Participating mothers have been trained in appropriate ways to stimulate their babies, who have later been compared with a control group not thus stimulated. There is also some research in progress on the effect of the perceptual stimulation of foundling infants who tend to live in an environment where there is little else than a set of white walls and a white ceiling. The introduction of perceptual variation into his environment can be expected to produce in the foundling infant intellectual behavior similar to that of children raised in more typical surroundings. Certainly, research in this area has been invigorated by the early experimental results derived mainly from research on animals, indicating that problem-solving ability is far from fixed but is subject to extensive modification through appropriate early experiences. The concept that intelligence is flexible does not mean that individual differences will be eliminated when all children have appropriate early experiences. Individual differences might then be as large as they ever were before, and perhaps even larger; but the whole intellectual level of society might be raised. Individual differences in the intelligence of children still appear even when the children are all raised in cognitively rich environments.

Evidence is accumulating that appropriate early training in children of preschool age may well make it possible for the child to master many skills years before they are ordinarily mastered at present. An interesting overview of such educational possibilities is provided by Fowler (1962), who has accumulated evidence that precocity is often the result of early and extensive perceptual training.

A second important area of research, related to that which has just been considered, is the tracing of the development of self-perceptions and perceptions of others. Those involved in elementary education have been particularly interested in studies related to the development of a concept of the self and the extent to which this concept influences achievement. There is also the additional research problem of determining the conditions that influence the development of a concept of self. One speculation is that the child acquires his self concept largely through listening to adults talk about him. The basic idea is that when a child hears an adult say "You are a bad boy," he begins to incorporate within himself the idea that he is a bad boy. If he hears a similar statement enough times from enough people then he may develop a concept of himself as a bad person. However, this is speculation and much research is needed to find out how self concepts develop.

The establishment of any relationship that may exist between the self concept of a child and his school achievement presents difficulties that have not yet been solved. The fact that one can demonstrate that children who have learning difficulties also tend to have inadequacies in their self concepts cannot be taken to mean that a poor concept of the self results in ineffective learning. The reverse may be true; the child who achieves poorly may, as a result, view himself as an inadequate person. R. C. Wylie (1961) concludes that research on problems of the self-concept is plagued by difficulties that make it impossible to interpret the data. Wylie's book provides a good account of what all these difficulties are and a source that anyone undertaking research on related problems should consult.

Research on how perceptions of others develop has great importance for education. For example, teachers must have correct perceptions of each of their pupils if they are to play a helpful role in the classroom. One of the functions of teacher training is to develop skill in forming such perceptions. A summary of what research has discovered in this area is provided by H. C. Smith (1966), whose book also reviews the difficulties that such research encounters.

A third research frontier having implications for education is the study of the relationship between the individual's needs and values and his capacity to perceive. Although this area presents a series of fascinating problems, the research worker is likely to encounter many pitfalls. An informative illustration is provided by the early researches, which supposedly showed that anxiety-producing words (*punishment, illegitimate, accuse,* and the like) were less easily recognized than words that do not produce anxiety. Later research showed that the main reason for this was that anxiety-producing words are less common and less frequently encountered than words that do not produce anxiety. The next step was for research workers to prepare lists of anxiety-producing and nonanxiety-producing words that appear with equal frequency in print. The technical difficulties such research involves are considerable, and the beginner must be sure to familiarize himself thoroughly with what has already been accomplished before designing his own study.

A fourth important area of research on perceptual development, which has been of particular interest to persons in education, is the study of the way in which the human is able to represent within himself the important features of the outside world. This problem has long been the focus of research for Piaget and his associates at Geneva and has, more recently, become a major research theme at the Center for Cognitive Studies at Harvard University. Jerome Bruner, the director of the latter center, spent considerable time in Europe where he had direct contact with the Geneva group, a contact that did much to shape his later work. Bruner (1966), following the lead of Piaget, points out that there are three ways in which a person can be said to have knowledge of, for example, a simple skill such as that of frying an egg: (1) He can know the skill in the sense that he can actually perform the task of frying an egg. (2) He can know how to do it, in another sense, in that he can have an image or an internal picture of what the skill involves. (3) He can be said to know how to fry an egg if he can describe in ordinary language or in other symbolic form how to fry an egg. These are three distinct and different ways of knowing. Piaget, and Bruner following him, take the position that the development of the child in a modern society shows a progression from information stored in terms of actions tendencies; to information stored as images; and, finally, to the stage in which information is stored in a coded form as a system of symbols. The extent to which progress is made in this sequence of development determines to some extent the capability of the individual to deal with the complexities of the world.

Research in this area has many facets. Much can be learned by studying the limitations that each of these modes of representation of the external world places on the individual. For example, if the external world is represented only by action systems, then the person is capable only of handling a limited number of immediate situations, but would have little capacity for giving consideration to situations that were not physically present. Once he can think in terms of images, some capacity for dealing with absent situations is possible; but the ultimate in flexibility is achieved when the external world is represented internally by a language.

In recent years, much of the research on human development has centered on the development of language. Such studies have included the analysis of the syntactical structures used by children of different ages and the emergence of the use of particular classes of words. This area of inquiry has shown a high degree of sophistication in the research techniques used and shows the impact of linguistics, epistemology, formal logic, cultural anthropology, philology, and psychology. An educational-research worker interested in entering this area would do well to read the first two chapters of Bruner's (1966) book to find out how much he may have to know in order to do acceptable research.

STUDIES OF DEVELOPMENT AND CHANGE OVER SHORT PERIODS OF TIME

A great many studies have been undertaken that attempt to measure development over relatively short periods of time—perhaps as short as a few months. These studies of development are particularly significant for education because of the emphasis that they place on learning phenomena such as occur in schools. Such studies relate measures of development to environmental conditions and learning conditions on the one hand, and to pupil characteristics on the other. They are designed to find out who learns what and under which conditions. In such studies, learning is conceived in the broadest sense. Not only are skills such as reading considered to be learned, but so too are thinking, judgment-making, and decision-making skills. Characteristics of personality are also presumed to be learned and subjected to the influence of the school environment; hence, developmental studies of such characteristics as they emerge under different conditions constitute an important field for educational-research workers.

Short-Term Studies of Intellectual Development

Of all the branches of psychology, the one that has shown the most sophisticated development in terms of theory construction is that of learning. Since the turn of the century many of the greatest leaders in psychology have devoted their efforts to the construction of theories of learning. With this historical fact in mind one might well expect that, of all educational research, the area having the most adequate theoretical basis would be that of classroom studies of learning.

In the early part of the century this was so. The research developed by Thorndike was closely tied to his theoretical conception of the learner. Within this framework, educational research became focused on the problem of finding the most efficient classroom situations that would produce in the learner bonds between particular situations and particular responses. When dissatisfaction with this theoretical position began to appear, no satisfactory substitute for guiding research emerged. The theoreticians of the next generation, such as Hull (1943), tended to produce statements of theory that had few implications for learning in as complicated a situation as the classroom. Indeed, such theories were mainly of value as a guide to further laboratory research. Some scientists, such as Skinner, took the position that the science of psychology had not developed to the point where abstract concepts could be introduced and suggested that scientists should stay as closely as possible to the facts.

In the immediate post-Thorndike era of 1940–1960, experimental psychologists tended to remain close to their laboratories and showed little interest in problems of education. At the same time, the educational-research workers became engaged in classroom research that had few ties with the ideas being explored in the laboratory. The comprehensive theories of learning of the psychologist seemed to provide little help for those attempting to solve practical problems of education. This situation is now changing, for there is now emerging a new kind of theorist with whom the applied-research worker can more easily work.

Somewhere between the scientist who develops a comprehensive theory of learning and the scientist who rejects theory construction at this stage of scientific development is the research worker who attempts to develop very limited theories in restricted areas of behavior. Such limited theories of learning have been developed by Benton Underwood in the area of associative verbal learning; by Bruner and his associates in concept learning; by David Ausubel in meaningful verbal learning; by D. E. Berlyne in the area of curiosity; by Albert Bandura in social learning; and by many others in varied limited fields of enquiry. The trend in learning research is to tie studies to these limited theories and to explore the conditions under which they apply. The work within these limited areas also provides the research worker with useful research techniques for approaching practical problems. For example, Bandura and his associates have developed numerous simple procedures that can be applied by the novice in research for studying the conditions that influence the social learnings of children. These techniques have opened up whole new avenues of research that could be explored with profit by numerous research workers, and without any of them running out of new problems to explore. The student of education who wishes to conduct a study of learning might well begin by studying one of these limited theories and then finding himself a problem that falls within its scope.

Studies conducted within these limited theoretical systems may involve development and change over periods as long as several months or over just a few minutes during a laboratory experiment. The area among those named that has proven particularly attractive to both graduate students and faculty in schools of education is that of concept learning. The classic research presentation that stimulated much of the current interest in concept learning is that of Bruner, J. J. Goodnow, and G. A. Austin (1956). The argument presented by these writers is that man is able to cope with his very complex environment because he is able to group together and categorize events and discriminate these from other events or other categories of events. Thus man has classified colors into a few categories that are given names such as *red, yellow, blue,* and so forth. Thousands of colors that can be discriminated from one another can be classified under this simple system of names. A category is simply a class of events that are all treated as if they were equivalent. Much of human learning consists of acquiring the ability to discriminate between what should be included and what should not be included in particular categories, such as *dog, cat,* and so forth. According to this theory, when a person is able to discriminate between events that should belong and events that should not belong in a particular category, he has achieved *concept attainment.* The studies by Bruner, *et al.* are concerned with the conditions related to concept attainment.

In order to develop further the presentation of this type of theoretical development, consider the case of a child who is learning to discriminate between those moving objects that adults categorize as *dogs* and those moving objects that are categorized as other than *dogs.* On seeing a moving object, the child makes a tentative prediction or *decision* whether or not the object is a dog. The decision is found to be correct or incorrect when he names the object and an adult indicates approval or disapproval. This is the *validation* of the decision. The consequence of a decision is referred to as the *payoff.* The decision and the test of the decision provide potential information concerning the attributes that can be considered as predictable of belonging to the category *dog.* As this information accumulates, it progressively limits the possibilities of what is to be included in the category. The child might go about this by first attempting to make the discrimination in terms of color and by calling all moving *brown* objects *dogs.* This would be referred to as a *strategy.* In other words, the sequence of decisions through which information is acquired is called a strategy or a sequence of strategies. The strategies adopted depend on the requirements of the problem situation, and they are retained or changed as they are successful or unsuccessful.

Concept learning can be viewed from many different points of view. A position that has become popular in recent years is to view it as an information-processing operation. This view was presented in detail in a work by Hunt (1962) whose thinking has been much influenced by the analogy between thought and the operation of computers. A volume by Klausmeier and Harris (1966) provides extensive discussion of recent research on concept learning and the implications it provides for teaching.

Short-Term Studies of Personality Development

Studies of the development of interests and attitudes have had a long history. Thurstone, who developed the first well-designed attitude scales, also initiated research on the role of various pupil experiences in the development of attitudes. Throughout the thirties large numbers of studies relating attitude changes to educational experiences appeared in the literature. Such studies showed again and again that curricular materials designed to change attitudes did so in terms of responses to verbal attitude scales. There is as yet little evidence to show that the changes in attitudes measured by these scales are associated with corresponding changes in other phases of behavior. In recent years there have been some attempts to remedy this basic defect through the introduction of disguised attitude scales, which are designed in such a way that the person taking them is unaware of the purposes for which they are given. Scales of this type must still be considered to be experimental in character, and the relationship between behavior on such scales and behavior in other areas still needs to be established. There is also another question that must be raised about such studies: "Are the changes produced just changes in superficial characteristics that have little deep value for the child?" Changing a child's expressed attitude toward a racial minority by showing him a film may mean only that for a little while he will repeat the sentiments expressed in the film rather than those he has heard elsewhere.

Numerous theories have been developed concerning the conditions that are most effective in producing attitude change. The application of these theories to problems of changing attitudes through education needs to be explored. A volume by C. A. Insko (1967) reflects the wealth of theoretical developments that there are in this field, but it also brings out the great gap that can exist between theory and practice.

An important area of educational research related to the short-term development of personality is that of counseling and guidance. Evidence that guidance services provide effective modifiers of behavior has been difficult to find. When the author (1948) reviewed studies related to this problem, he could find no substantial evidence that guidance and counseling procedures had measureable effects on personality. Some years later, when Carl Rogers and William Stephenson began to apply a technique known as Q-methodology, some evidence began to accumulate that measureable personality changes could be attributed to counseling. However, this approach, like most others that have been attempted, has come in for a considerable amount of criticism. Research in this area is obviously very difficult to undertake and many false starts have had to be made.

Some of the more indirect approaches to the problems involved appear to have been productive when the more direct approaches have failed. C. B. Truax and R. R. Carkhuff (1967) have reviewed a great amount of research around the periphery of the counseling area that is highly suggestive of what the conditions of effective counseling are. For example, they point out that numerous studies have shown that the warm, sympathetic, and genuine person is more likely to produce learning in a teaching situation than the person who is cold and aloof. Perhaps the same is true of effective counseling. These same writers have also brought together a substantial amount of evidence concerning the characteristics of both clients and therapists that are associated with effective therapy. Nevertheless, the whole area presents problems that research has not yet been particularly successful in solving. The novice in research is warned that he may become involved in deep difficulties if he becomes engaged in work on such problems.

Even though research on problems of guidance advances slowly, the development of new techniques for providing clients with occupational and other information are developing rapidly. IBM is developing a system similar to computer-assisted instruction that will enable persons to obtain immediate and up-to-date information about occupations and their requirements. Studies evaluating these new procedures will have to be undertaken.

Finally, mention must be made of the successful demonstrations that have been given of social learning through the use of reinforcement and through the presentation of models of behavior that an observing child may emulate. The book by Bandura and Walters (1963) reviews much of the research literature in this area and is a good point of departure for a person interested in embarking on a research project.

RESEARCH ON DEVELOPMENT IN THE ADULT YEARS

Although most developmental studies related to formal training and learning have been undertaken with children of school age, some interest has also been shown in problems of adult learning. This is an important and worthwhile area for fruitful studies and one which has been influenced by many preconceived notions, as is illustrated by the commonly heard statement, "I am too old to learn."

Pioneer studies in the field of adult learning and in the problems of teaching adults were conducted by Thorndike (1928). His general findings were that the older adult in his fifties has about as much capacity to learn as the youngster leaving high school. But there ap-

pear to be differences in motivation: the older adult expects to learn
too much in too short a time and becomes impatient with the slow-
ness of his pace; the younger adult is much more accepting of the
fact that learning is slow. Such motivational differences have not been
adequately investigated as yet, but they are important from many
standpoints. An understanding of these differences would have direct
application to the rehabilitation of the adult who must train for a new
job because disease prevents him from pursuing his old one or because
a changing industrial economy has eliminated his occupation. Research
in this area would also have many other important practical applications.

Considerable interest has been manifested in research into changes
in intellectual functions and personality characteristics in the later
years of life. These problems of education, counseling, and recreation
provide a new and intriguing field for research, although perhaps it
must be said that they have attracted the sentimentalists rather than
the mature and established research workers. The poor quality of
much that has been done in this area in the last twenty years is probably accounted for by this fact.

A central problem of considerable scientific and educational interest that has been studied in this area is that of the extent to which
different abilities show decline during adulthood. Empirical studies
of the decline of abilities are extremely difficult to undertake for
reasons that have already been discussed, such as differential mortality
among different ability groups. There are also problems in testing
older individuals, for such persons may be very poorly motivated in
the testing situation and may fail to show any enthusiasm for finding
out their abilities. Insofar as this is so, the decline in measured ability
may be at least partly a function of declining motivation. Just what
abilities should be measured in the older adult in order to appraise
his continued capacity to make a contribution to a community is also
problematic. In the case of the young, it is common to study development in terms of those abilities that are known to be related to educability in the academic sense of the term. But one does not know
whether these same abilities are related to the educability of the older
adult. The problems in this area represent an important field of educational research, but one that should be approached with the greatest
caution, for the difficulties involved in making genuine advances are
immense.

A related problem is the determination of the age at which man
reaches his peak performance in particular activities. The importance
of this problem to education becomes clear when it is pointed out

that education should be planned so that the years of maximum ability are not those primarily occupied with course work. This may be the case at present, for the tendency is for the doctoral degree to be completed in the late twenties—although in many areas the period of maximum performance may well be the early twenties. The subject is not without problems from a research viewpoint. The usual techniques have involved the determination of the average age at which the great men of history produced their finest works, although one cannot deduce from the evidence that this age truly represents a peak of performance of the nervous system. Perhaps this peak of performance is mainly a product of the cultural conditions under which the persons involved happen to work.

Summary

1. Studies of development involve time trends—that is to say, research on changes in the organization of behavior in relation to the passage of time. The early developmental studies were attempts to describe the changes that take place during the years of growth, and little attention was paid to the conditions under which development occurred. In addition, research has been hampered by the technical difficulties involved in using growth scores.

2. Research on development over the period of growth has generally been undertaken in the tradition of the biologist and has assumed that the pattern is uniform for all members of the species. However, more recent research has tended to break from this tradition.

3. Long-term studies of development can be undertaken either through a cross-sectional approach or the longitudinal approach. The latter approach has immense advantages. The early research of Francis Galton, although a greater pioneer effort, reflects all the problems that the cross-sectional approach encounters.

4. Longitudinal studies are rarely undertaken because of the extended time that they involve. However, other difficulties are also encountered and not the least of these is that of keeping track of the persons to be studied. In addition to losses from the sample through families moving to other communities, without leaving an address behind them, are the losses from death. None of these losses are random. Hence, the final population studied may differ in fundamental respects from the initial population.

5. Longitudinal studies can be undertaken by inquiring into the history of a group of individuals and by relating their background

to their present characteristics. Such studies incur all of the difficulties that are encountered in the undertaking of historical studies.

6. Newer approaches have placed an emphasis on the direct study of the conditions related to development. Sometimes these conditions can be experimentally manipulated and controlled and genuine experiments on development can be undertaken. Often, the research worker has to adopt the alternative procedure of studying children who have been exposed to differing conditions. Although early research in this area tended to emphasize the role of maturation in development, the more recent studies have tended to emphasize the effect of learning. Another approach is that of studying the emergence of individual differences and the conditions that are related to their development. Studies of perceptual development have been particularly productive in that they have shed light on some of the effects of deprivation on intellectual functioning. Piaget has done much to construct a theoretical basis for such studies and provides a picture of development that has formed the basis of a large volume of research.

7. Research on pupil learning in school generally represents an attempt to study development over a short period of time. Such studies have become progressively more influenced by learning theory as the latter has developed and become more explicit. Particularly influential in this respect in recent years has been the influence of reinforcement concepts on the planning of learning. Although considerable effort has been devoted to the study of the effect of the self concept on learning, the methodological difficulties involved in such research has limited any findings.

8. The study of concept learning has produced extensive knowledge with important implications for education. This is an area of expanding research that has derived its theoretical basis from many different sources.

9. Short-term studies of the development of nonintellectual attributes of the learner have most commonly been focused on the acquisition of attitudes. The latter are considered to be extremely complex phenomena with cognitive, affective, and action components. Most studies have been concerned only with the affective components, which may bear little relation to action systems. Studies of the effect of guidance and counseling also represent short-term developmental studies concerned mainly with noncognitive components of behavior.

10. Studies of development in the adult years are of consequence for the planning of adult education.

||||||||||||||||||||||||||||||||||||

CHAPTER 15

Data-Processing and Reporting

MECHANICS OF DATA HANDLING

Data-Processing

T HE plan for the processing of data should be made at the time when the study is designed. By this is meant the time when the final plan is evolved. Of course, some preliminary studies have to be undertaken to insure that the enterprise is feasible. This is a more important matter than it may seem to be on the surface, and perhaps its importance may be brought home by citing an example.

A student once approached the author with a proposed study of the effectiveness of two methods of teaching typing. The design of the experiment was a familiar one, with several pairs of matched groups assigned to the two methods. At regular intervals throughout the training program tests were to be taken by the students. These tests would require rather prolonged periods of typing, lasting for as much as an hour each. The experiment was to be conducted over two semesters. During the conference with the student on this matter, a rapid computation was made of the volume of data to be collected and the time it would take to derive the scores that would be subjected to analysis. As nearly as could be determined, the work would have taken about six months of the student's full-time attention. Also, the data would have consisted of sheets of typing and were such that it hardly seemed possible to design a device that would result in the

355

quick scoring of the material. It would have been an unreasonable use of the student's time to spend six months in clerical work, since this period could be much better spent in training related to his professional goals.

Various devices may be used to facilitate the derivation of scores from the raw data. One of these is a stencil scoring device. Unless it is absolutely essential, never conduct research in such a way that the answers to a test are marked in a booklet. A separate answer sheet is a compact method of recording raw data. If the scores are to be converted to standard scores, then it is sometimes convenient to print the conversion table right on the answer sheet. If possible, the researcher should avoid having scores recorded on both sides of the answer sheet, because it is inconvenient to transcribe these scores onto rosters. Sometimes the separate answer sheet should not be used. Whenever speeded tasks of simple functions are involved, the task of finding the appropriate place on the answer sheet and marking it may contribute more to the variability of the score than the function it is desired to measure. In such cases, it is obviously desirable to avoid the use of a separate recording system. What can be done in such a case is to print the problem right on the answer sheet above or beside the place where the answer is to be recorded.

An alternative to the answer sheet is a version of the IBM punched card. Such cards are familiar enough to the reader through their several common uses—as checks, as bills, and so forth. They can be printed so that they have spaces on them similar to those found on answer sheets. The cards are then marked with a soft pencil, just as would be answer sheets, but of course they cannot be scored with the usual test-scoring machine. Instead, they are run through a machine that converts the marks to punched holes. A computer can then be used to derive scores for each card.

Test-scoring machines can be adapted to the analysis of all kinds of data. At the present time the common type of scoring machine is one built by IBM. This machine not only scores but also is fitted with an item-counter device. This device permits the counting of the number of answer sheets that are marked in a particular position. It is thus possible to run a number of answer sheets through the machine and to determine the number that chose the first answer to the first problem, the second answer to the first problem, and so forth.

Other organizations have also constructed test scoring machines for special purposes. Testcor, a Minneapolis organization, was one of the first to develop a special machine for the high-speed scoring of the *Strong Vocational Interest Blank* and then branched out into machines especially adapted for the scoring of other instruments. Many other organizations now offer special scoring services. The graduate student interested in obtaining the services of one of these organizations would do well to consult the university counseling center in order to obtain advice on which service to use.

Some ingenious investigators have used a plan to reduce the clerical work involved in the handling of data, but one that is not endorsed here. The procedure is simply that of requiring the subjects to undertake the clerical work. Where responses are to be coded, the subjects perform the coding; where the tests are to be scored, the subjects score the tests. This is an undesirable practice, for two reasons. First, it introduces sources of error variance over which the researcher may have no control. This is to some extent true even when a simplifying device such as an answer sheet is used. At least some error is introduced through errors in marking the answer sheet, but this becomes particularly pronounced when a speeded function is involved. If a complicated recording procedure is used, substantial errors may be introduced by the process. Secondly, a problem of ethics is involved. The researcher may have some justification in asking for the time of persons for the purpose of advancing knowledge, but he must respect their time and ask them to do only what is essential. The researcher should not be guilty of exploitation. Of course the issue does not arise if the subjects are paid, except that it may be much more efficient to employ a few well-supervised, trained clerks than a large number of untrained persons.

What to do about missing values is a particularly perplexing problem to which there is no completely satisfactory solution. In studies involving the analysis of correlation coefficients, a missing value in a table of raw data is of little concern. It does not matter much whether the coefficients in a table are based on slightly different numbers of cases. In factor analysis and in many other mathematical methods that are used for structuring data, slight variations in the number of cases from coefficient to coefficient are of little consequence.

On the other hand, when block designs are being used as the basis for an experiment or as a basis of any other type of research, the problem of missing values becomes acute, because the computational methods that have been developed and that form the basis of tests of significance require the use of all cell entries. If certain cells are disregarded, the net result is to introduce an unknown amount of bias into the test of significance. There is no point in applying a test under these conditions, since it will not yield any kind of answer to the question posed.

At one time it was commonly suggested that mean values be substituted for the values of missing observations. The argument was that the measures were presumed to be normally distributed, and in such a case the class interval that includes the mean includes also the most frequently occurring values. Thus the insertion of the mean is an attempt to substitute the most probable value for the missing one.

Another approach is to compute expected values for those missing from the other values provided by the data. Through the computation of regression equations, it may be possible to provide a solution to this problem. However, this procedure is likely to produce more internal consistency in the resulting data than they would otherwise have. It will also bias tests of significance to an unknown degree. This problem has been worked on, and solutions that attempt to eliminate bias in tests of significance have been developed for many of the commoner block designs.

Another problem that sometimes arises is that of whether to discard certain observations that for one reason or another fall far outside the range of the other observations. Such discards must not be made after a preliminary inspection of the data has shown that the discarding of certain observations would make the data more in accordance with expectation. Discarding *must* take place before the significance of the data has been examined, for if this rule is not rigorously observed, the tests of significance that are applied will probably be biased. On the other hand, if this practice is observed, there is no reason why the researcher should not set up rules for discarding observations. These rules must apply to all observations, never only to certain groups. An example may illustrate this point.

An example of the effective discarding of data is found in a recent study involving four different methods of teaching the principle of refraction from physics. Four methods of instruction were used, one involved an actual demonstration; two involved the use of diagrams; and another provided a lecture without a demonstration or diagrams. Each of several classes in three schools were divided into four groups and each group was exposed to one of the teaching methods. A cursory examination of the data revealed that the children in one of the schools were showing no learning on the task regardless of the instructional method used. In addition, evidence showed that the children in this particular school did not perform significantly better on a test of their ability to apply the principle of refraction than a control group of children who took the test but who were given no instruction. On this basis *all* the data from the school where the children did not learn were discarded. This involved discarding equal numbers of cases from each method of instruction. What this procedure accomplished was to reduce the experimental error and to make the relative effectiveness of the different methods of instruction more apparent.

An important point to note is that the data could be discarded without biasing the results; in this case because data were dropped from all four experimental instructional procedures. One could not discard data involving only one method of instruction in one school without biasing the results. For example, discarding one small group of students exposed to the demonstration of the phenomenon of refraction, because that particular group did not do very well, would have had the effect of making that method appear more effective than it really was.

The researcher should always be on guard lest the procedure established for discarding observations does not by some means affect tests of significance that are later applied. This can happen in many ways, but the basic effect is always produced by there being a greater number of discards in one group than in another.

Observations can be recorded on rosters or on cards with numbered spaces. The author's preference is for the latter system, because it provides greater flexibility and facilitates certain operations with data, such as the separation of groups of cases on which it is desired to conduct special studies. The roster method of recording is highly inflexible, and even the correction of errors on rosters may present difficulties.

It is particularly important to check the accuracy with which all entries are made. The procedure is such a simple one that it often gives the false impression that it is just not possible to make errors on such a straightforward copying task. One very common type of error is the transposition of digits, such as occurs when a number is correctly read as 51 but incorrectly recorded as 15. Another source of error is the recording of digits in incorrect boxes on the cards or on the roster. All recordings must be checked with the most scrupulous care in order to catch such errors, for they may seriously affect the conclusions drawn from the data.

The processing of data presents certain problems that must now be considered. The scientist should *know* his own data. Unless there is a close personal contact between the researcher and his data, many important findings will never be made. Limitations may remain unnoticed unless close contact with the data is maintained throughout the processing procedure. For these reasons, there is at least some wisdom in performing a part of the data-processing by hand methods. This is no problem in the case of the student who is conducting research to fulfill the requirement for a master's degree, because the quantity of data is relatively small, and in any case it is probable that he will process all his data himself.

The student should be warned against the incorrect use of information derived from data. One such use is found in the researcher who gets to know his data well in order that he may derive from them hypotheses to be tested later by means of statistical tests. It should be remembered that statistical tests of hypotheses are not designed to test hypotheses derived from the data themselves. If such tests are applied to these hypotheses, they will produce answers that are biased.

The problem is perhaps better understood by considering an actual example. A research worker studying differences between delinquents and nondelinquents finds negligible differences between the two groups in all of the variables where he had planned to test the difference. However, a close scrutiny of the data reveals that the blue-eyed children who were unusually tall for their age showed a high incidence of delinquency, and this is advanced as one of the major conclusions of the study. The error made by the research worker in this case is that if one were to compare the two groups on a large number of characteristics, some combination of characteristics would be found that just happened to differentiate the two groups. There would be no reason for believing that the results would be repeated in a new sample.

What the student should do is to list, during the planning stages of the study, all of the *reasonable* hypotheses that he proposes to study. His data should be collected for the purpose of testing these hypotheses and no others. All subsequently developed hypotheses squeezed out of the data would be subject to the criticism that they are not firmly rooted in the theory on which the study is based, and any apparent positive results would probably be the result of chance peculiarities of the particular sample.

Processing Qualitative Data

Much of the data collected in educational research is qualitative and presents special difficulties when it is to be processed. In the early stages of acquiring information about a phenomenon, no attempt can be made to process carefully the facts that are collected. Freud's classic observations on the behavior of disturbed patients are examples of qualitative data collected and examined for the purpose of developing hypotheses, and the conclusions that he drew guided the research work of subsequent generations of psychologists. Early explorations are usually made in this way, but ultimately such observations must be analyzed systematically. The mere inspection of data without the aid of systematic analysis is a hazardous process, and there is always danger that the researcher will dream into his data elements he wishes to see there but that do not really exist. For this reason every effort must be made to reduce such data to a form in which they can be analyzed by appropriate methods. In this way personal prejudice can be eliminated from the interpretation of the material.

As a first step in the analysis of qualitative data, it is necessary to code the facts that are involved. This means simply that a number must be assigned to each class of fact. Thus, if the cumulative records of children are to be studied, it may have been determined that perhaps eighty items of information are to be coded. Those concerned with the coding operation might be asked to code all items of information on a sheet, a section of which might be as follows:

42. Progress through school   0 — never held back a grade
                                        1 = held back one grade
                                        2 = held back two or more grades

43. Speech   1 = no speech difficulties reported
                                        2 = speech difficulties but no action taken
                                        3 = speech difficulties and remedial work started

Through such a code sheet the qualitative information obtained in the cumulative record is converted into a set of numbers, which are then used for the analysis. Sometimes the numbers are entered directly onto the code sheet, if it is quite brief. If the code sheet is long, the code numbers are often entered on a separate sheet or card. The code numbers on the cards can then be punched into other cards if the data are to be analyzed by machine, or the cards can be sorted by hand if a hand analysis is to be made.

Any set of rules established for the purpose of quantifying qualitative material should be tried out by submitting the material to different coders in order to determine whether the rules can be applied with consistency by different workers. This tryout helps to establish the error resulting from differences in the judgment of different persons.

The tryout may also result in the development of met'ods that elimi-nate these discrepancies. The reliability of such procedures should al-ways be given in the report of the study, unless the procedures are such that it is clearly evident that *careful* independent workers can produce independent results. This might be true where the entire proc-ess of quantification required only the counting of the number of words written in documents produced by subjects.

Errors are commonly made in clerical procedures that involve the coding of data. These are usually referred to as errors of carelessness, but in actual fact they are probably caused not so much by the failure of the clerk to be conscientious as by the immensely boring nature of much of this work. The upshot is that it is essential for all clerical work of this kind to be rechecked independently by another clerk. It may not be necessary to lay down the standard that only perfect agreement is to be accepted, because this may be unrealistic; but some standard should be established. Scores that do not agree within one point, or two, or three—or whatever is considered reasonable—must be rede-termined, preferably by another person. Clerks must work indepen-dently, otherwise this check would be quite meaningless.

WRITING THE REPORT

Even though the author imagines Heaven as a place where one can do research without ever having to write a report, the requirements of this world are that research has to be described in writing. For many research workers, the preparation of the report is a particularly burden-some task. Here are some points to keep in mind in undertaking this task.

First, the report should be written in a uniform style throughout. Table headings, footnotes, and appendix material should follow a con-sistent format. Editorial assistance is very helpful in producing such consistency. Many graduate schools recommend manuals to follow in the writing of theses and the student should familiarize himself with the style requirements of his school. He will probably have to set him-self a few rules to follow. For example, some use the word *data* as a plural noun as it is in the Latin from which it is derived, but some newer writers prefer to consider *data* as a singular noun. A number of rules to follow in such respects should be noted.

Secondly, a scientific report must be written in clear and concise terms; there is little place in it for personal animosities, anecdotes, dis-plays of wit, and the like. Recently, there appeared a report of a very interesting research project that was ruined by the overwhelming intrusion of the research scientist's personal whims, his hostilities toward colleagues, stories of personal experiences that had no relevance to the topic, and other inconsequential material. The reader of such a report reacts much like a teacher who has read through a pupil's term paper that would have been outstanding were it not for an inexcusable boner in the last paragraph. His first impulse is to give the student a failing grade, but later, after his emotional reaction has subsided, he may change the grade to a C or even a B. Much the same is likely to be true of a reader of a research report who finds it spoiled by a display of personal prejudice and irrelevant humor. This does not mean that the report has to be written in a dull pedantic style. Enthusiasm can still appear between the lines while the report as a whole is conveying the spirit of adventure. But the report should be a presentation of research, not a presentation of the personality of the author, although the latter inevitably shows through.

Thirdly, the tone of the report should be one of appropriate modesty. The scientist is a humble person who realizes that even the labor of a lifetime is likely to add but a small increment to man's knowledge of his environment. In writing a research report it is easy to let one's enthusiasm lead to an overemphasis of the importance of the findings. The scientist is rarely in a position to evaluate the significance of his findings in the total picture of knowledge. Only through subsequent history can such an evaluation be made.

It is common for a dissertation to be written in at least two forms. The initial form presents the material to an examining committee. The second form is a condensed version that presents the material for publication. The initial version, like any other piece of writing, must be written with the nature of the specific audience in mind. It is to the student's advantage that he know personally those who constitute this audience and be able to write specifically for them. To some extent, he should write with their expectations in mind. If one of them is likely to ask the student to relate his findings to some particular theory, then he should be sure to do this.

In the case of writing for formal publication, the problem is much more difficult. The student would do well to start by reading articles in the journal that is being considered as a place of publication. From this overview, he should arrive at judgments concerning the nature, length, and organization of the articles that the editors favor. Editors, like any other people, have personal preferences, and these must be taken into account because they may be the deciding factors in determining acceptance or rejection of the student's product.

Over-all Format of the Report

The research report is a record of what the researcher did. Like all good records of history, it should permit the reader to reconstruct what happened and without distortion. The research report typically follows a time sequence, beginning with an account of previous work followed by a description of the research undertaken, and ending with ideas for future studies. There are many ways of providing a documentary record concerning what happened in a particular study, but the following outline represents a plan of presentation commonly found in research literature:

1. *Introduction*
    A. The problem
    B. Previous research
    C. Theoretical implications of previous research
    D. Relation of present research to the theoretical position stated in C
    E. Specific hypotheses to be tested
2. *Procedures*
    A. General procedure adopted in the research
    B. Equipment and other types of instruments used
    C. Directions given to subjects
    D. Selection of subjects and their characteristics
3. *Results*
    A. A summary of the data
    B. Tests of significance
    C. The testing of the hypotheses outlined in 1
    D. Conclusions
4. *Implications*
    A. Implications of the research in relation to the theoretical position previously taken
    B. Implications for further research
    C. Practical implications (if any)

Introductory Sections of the Report

The introductory sections usually begin with a statement of the problem. In the reporting of most research studies, at least the general nature of the problem to be investigated should be outlined in the very first paragraph of the report. The statement may not be in a full and precise form at this stage, because it may first be necessary to introduce the reader to a number of terms and concepts before the problem can be accurately set forth; nevertheless, there should be a statement of the problem, even if only in a general form.

The introduction must also provide an appropriate theoretical orientation for the reader. This may involve a history of the problem and a review of related studies. In some cases, the theoretical framework of the problem may be so familiar to those who are likely to read the article that it may be quite unnecessary to state it except in general terms. For example, a student working on the problem of reinforced learning would obviously not review reinforcement theory, which has been described fully in so many other sources. On the other hand, if the research is concerned with a theory with which the reader is unlikely to be familiar, it is essential that the theory and its background be outlined in the introductory section. If the theory is the researcher's own, it is desirable that it be fully presented in terms of the procedures described in earlier chapters of this book.

In the preparation and execution of a research, extensive work is often undertaken on the review of previous studies in the area. If it is done by a senior research worker with broad experience in the field, this may constitute a major contribution in itself. When substantial effort has been devoted to this phase of the undertaking, it is possible that a separate article may ultimately be prepared and published to cover the outcomes of this activity. Such publications may form an immensely valuable contribution to the professional literature.

The review of the literature should lead up to the full and complete statement of the problem. If the introduction gives or implies the statement of a theory, as it should, the problem should be stated as a deduction or consequence of the theory. Earlier in the introduction, the student should have defined all the terms needed for understanding both the theory and the statement of the problem. By the end of the introductory section, the reader should be fully prepared for understanding the explanation in subsequent sections of how the problem was solved.

Description of the Procedure

The vital importance of the section that describes the procedure or method is often not appreciated by the novice in scientific research. The criterion of a well-written description of the procedure or method used is whether it provides sufficient detail for another researcher to reproduce the study. Too often the experimenter writes up his work only to find that insufficient detail is given for another even to begin to reproduce it. In the behavioral sciences, the writer faces real difficulties in deciding what are and what are not the important details to report in describing his procedure. It is clearly quite impossible to detail all of the conditions related to the undertaking of a study. For example, in describing an experiment, is it relevant to report that the experimenter was a woman, or that she was a blonde, or that she was born in Germany? The author knows of one study in which it was relevant that the experimenter was a woman, and the results probably could not be reproduced without a control over that factor. However, he does not know whether any experiment has been reported in which it was relevant that the experimenter was blonde or was born in Germany. In any event, if a factor is important in one study it does not mean that it would necessarily be important in another study. The decision has to be made in each case concerning what is to be reported and what is to be omitted. The fact that this decision must be based largely on judgment reflects our lack of knowledge about behavioral phenomena.

The description of procedures should include a reproduction of verbal directions given to the subjects. If these are lengthy, they can be relegated to an appendix, or a footnote can indicate where a complete set can be obtained. Minor differences in wording may have substantial effects on the outcomes of a study. Unfortunately, matters of intonation and emphasis cannot be accurately described, although these may have substantial effects on the results.

The description of apparatus is likely to be unsatisfactory unless the greatest care is taken. Because it is not usually possible to publish a blueprint, it is necessary to specify the essential details. However, the experimenter sometimes may not know what are the essential details. This statement may need some explanation.

The author was concerned some time ago with the replication of an experiment that involved apparatus. The piece of equipment specified was the Harvard tachistoscope, which is widely used in psychological laboratories and is readily available. The object to be viewed through the tachistoscope was illustrated in the original article, and this was easily reproduced by a draftsman. However, after some work with the equipment, it became evident that a crucial feature of the entire arrangement was the size of the object presented. This had not been specified in the original article, but the results could be reproduced only when the object was a certain size. The original experimenter had been unaware that this was an essential aspect of his experiment and had failed to report it. Unless there is a great deal of replication with variation, the experimenter is likely to be unaware of the essential characteristics of his apparatus.

One advantage of using standard apparatus can be seen when the problem of description arises. It simplifies matters greatly to be able to report that a Hunter Timer or a Brush Model 392 amplifier was used, because this equipment can be duplicated by other experimenters. The home-grown type of equipment needs careful description.

Sometimes the research worker calibrates apparatus, in which case it is necessary to describe the method and technique used in calibration. Sometimes the equipment used in calibration is as complicated as the apparatus itself.

A common omission in studies of educational behavior is a failure to indicate just who was included and who was excluded from the study. This is the matter of specifying the sample that was included, or perhaps one should say what universe was sampled in selecting subjects for study. There is the same need for specifying the universe that is sampled when the objects are inanimate as when they are living. The student will realize that unless the researcher knows how his sample is drawn, he will not know to what his results can be generalized.

Reporting the Results and Stating the Conclusions

The results of a scientific study should usually be presented in a table for which there is some explanatory material; but, since many studies in education do not approach ideal standards, this method of reporting cannot always be attained. A distinction should be made between the results of the study and the interpretation of the results. By "results" is usually meant the summarized data and the test that is applied to determine whether they are or are not consistent with the hypothesis they were designed to test. In educational research some test of significance must usually be applied to the data in order to test the hypothesis. It is usual to describe this test in the results section of the report. The results section should also describe any special and unexpected events that occurred during experimentation, as when subjects were unable to complete the schedule because of illness or other causes. The treatment of missing values should also be discussed in the results section.

As far as possible, the table or tables presenting the results of a study should be self-explanatory and should not require extended reading of the text in order to understand them. On the other hand, the material in the text should point out the important aspects of the data and draw attention to the relevance of the results.

Just how much tabular data should be presented is always a matter of judgment. As a general rule, only those statistics that are crucial to the testing of a hypothesis should be presented. Detailed raw data rarely can find a place in a research report, except where they are of such unusual interest that their reproduction is definitely in the interest of science.

A common error in the presentation of results is the division of the results into too many separate tables. Many research reports can be improved by the consolidation of tables into larger units.

Some comment should be made on the problem of what to do with experiments that do not yield anything that can ordinarily be reported as results. Reference is made here not to experiments that yield negative results, which can usually be reported by the procedures discussed, but to experiments that are prevented, by some technical hitch, from being carried through to their proper conclusion. These abortive efforts are not entirely useless in the information they provide. Indeed, if the problems they raise are never discussed in the literature, others will attempt similar experiments and end in similar difficulties. The difficulty of reporting such efforts stems from the understandable unwillingness of editors to accept articles about them. To the author, the way out of this dilemma is to report the results of abortive experiments in the introductory section of a report of a further experiment that was successful. One may preface a successful experiment with an account of the various avenues and approaches that were explored before it could be undertaken. Such an account can be brief, but it should be sufficient to warn others about the limitations of the alternatives that were explored.

This does not mean, of course, that weaknesses in the approach revealed during the course of the study should not be noted. Sometimes it is necessary and desirable to admit that the main knowledge derived from an experiment is how to design a more conclusive study. It also happens quite frequently that a study designed as a crucial and conclusive experiment turns out to be, on further examination, ambiguous in its results because of the various ways in which they can be interpreted.

A common error is made in drawing conclusions from research results. This error is seen in cases where an investigator collects data that reject a hypothesis. Under such circumstances, some investigators are inclined to turn around and seek reasons why the experiment was really not a crucial test of the issue it was designed to settle. The situation indicates either that the investigator had become too attached personally to his own ideas or that the test of their validity was inadequate in the first place. If the latter were the case, the question can be raised as to why the experiment was ever conducted. If the experimenter changed his mind during the research and began to question its utility, then he should have stopped his work and certainly not published his results.

Writing the Implications and Discussion Section

The creative research worker will inevitably speculate on the implications of his study that extend beyond his immediate purposes. He will also want to communicate his thoughts on such matters to a wider public. True, nobody is ever likely to treasure these thoughts as much as their creator; nevertheless some may be useful to other research workers, and a few may even be real gems. The section of the report dealing with implications can be used quite appropriately for setting forth these thoughts.

It is important that the section on implications be more than a splurge of personal notions. Whatever ideas are presented must be set forth in a well-organized form. Sometimes it is convenient to organize them around a few areas for which the implications have special importance. For example, in one study of mechanical problem solving with which the author is familiar, the implications were organized around two topics; namely, the selection of mechanical trouble-shooters and the training of trouble-shooters. Good organization will develop in the reader of the report a better appreciation of the importance of the writer's ideas than will a poorly organized section.

Brevity in the implications section is also a very desirable characteristic. Most readers have only limited appetite for the speculations of others. A lengthy section may produce boredom and lead to the rejection of even the good ideas that are presented. Even though a discursive style can, at times, be extremely useful for driving home a point, a certain degree of crisp conciseness should be aimed for here, as in other parts of the written report.

The section on implications is also the section in which it is appropriate to give some indication of the future direction of the program of research of which the report represents a part. Perhaps it is a good idea to remind the reader again that if research is to be profitable, it must be programmatic. A research report should end, therefore, not with a note of finality, but with some indications of the unfinished business that should be the next preoccupation of the researcher.

If the report has been introduced with the presentation of a theory that the research is designed to extend or modify, then the final section may well restate the theory in the light of the findings. This process may involve such radical changes in the original formulation that what is virtually a new theory has to be stated. Whenever the research results in the restatement of a theory, it follows that the research report should indicate how changes in the theory should modify current practices.

Use of Diagrams, Tables, and Figures

A common error in the writing of technical reports is the failure to use diagrams effectively. The author can remember more than one instance when he had to wade through ten or more pages describing a complicated piece of apparatus when a simple diagram and a page of description would have sufficed. The author also suspects that some readers are quite unable to translate verbal descriptions into visualizations of the equipment described. The medium used for communicating should be appropriate to the material to be communicated.

If diagrams of apparatus are given, and they are necessary if any apparatus has been used in the study, it is most desirable that they be prepared by an artist. This is not necessarily as expensive a procedure as it sounds. If an artist is provided with a good sketch, he is likely to produce a finished diagram with considerable speed. The author has had many such made for approximately ten dollars each.

The artist or draftsman will have to be informed of the size to which a diagram will be reduced on publication. Usually, he will draw it on a larger scale and his drawing will be reduced photographically.

Figures and graphs should be presented in such a way that they are self-explanatory. The headings and captions to figures and graphs should provide all the explanation needed. Discussion of what the table or graph demonstrates in relation to the hypotheses can be appropriately included in the text.

Other Points on Organizing the Research Report

When a research report is of such a length that it requires organization into chapters, provide the reader with certain devices that will enable him to keep track of the argument and to find his way around in the mass of material. This can be done in several ways.

1. It is desirable to provide chapter summaries. These should help the reader to organize his thoughts by going over the highlights of what he has read and the conclusions and arguments presented. The summary should be strictly that; it should not include new material that happened to occur to the researcher after the report was written. It can be organized into a series of numbered paragraphs, and these should be written in a concise form.

2. A system of paragraph and section headings should be adopted. Indeed, some writers like to begin by preparing a list of headings and then writing the sections and paragraphs in any order, working at any one time on those where they feel that their thinking has reached the point of maturity and where an organized statement can be put down on paper. Some writers prefer to use a system of major headings and minor headings, in addition to chapter headings, but this can be done only where the material lends itself to this type of organization.

3. A good table of contents is a most desirable guide for the reader. Where paragraph and section headings are used, these should be listed in the table of contents.

4. Brief mention must be made of style of writing in the report. Anyone who tries to advise another on questions of style is treading on uncertain ground. When one sees how often literary critics have been wrong in predicting the acceptability of the works of writers, one realizes how unreasonably prejudiced one may be in one's preferences for style. Also, a person's style is dear to his heart, and suggestions that it be changed or even that it be criticized may arouse ire. Therefore the author, acting with a certain sense of self-preservation, will at this time point out only certain common features of technical writing that detract from its value in communication.

There is the error of using too difficult a vocabulary level. A writer should not select a word just because it is appropriate and because *he* knows the meaning of it. A necessary condition for the use of the word is that the reader also know its meaning. When unfamiliar words are introduced, the writer must remember that the reader will have to learn them. It is not sufficient that they be formally defined once and then used. This is like asking a person to learn a word by exposing him to it once. What one has to do in writing is to give the reader as much opportunity as is feasible to learn new terms. These must be not only defined but also used in contexts where their sense can be inferred from the general meaning of the sentence. The writer who introduces several unfamiliar terms and then fails to provide the reader with a learning experience is likely to find that most of his public does not read beyond the introduction.

A few technical writers have acquired the reputation of writing in a language familiar only to themselves. Such writers may have been careful to define their terms, but because these terms have not acquired general usage, readers have never learned them and much of the writing that uses this language is never carefully read. Hence, much of it is lost. For this reason, the reader should realize that new terms should be coined only when it is absolutely necessary to do so.

Although abbreviations are widely used in contemporary technical writing, the opening paragraphs of an article should not overwhelm the reader with a flood of new symbols he must master to comprehend the rest. Do not write paragraphs such as the following:

The words from the basic list were divided into high difficulty (HD) and low difficulty (LD). In addition, they were also divided into emotion arousing (EA) and neutral (N) categories. The responses of the subjects were classified as correctly recalled words (CR), or incorrectly recalled words (IR), or no word given (NW).

Only the most determined reader will go through such a paragraph and then proceed to the rest of the article. The argument for the use of such a system of abbreviations is that it saves space, but the amount of space saved is generally negligible.

Just as unfamiliar words should not be used except where they are essential, so too is it desirable to avoid passing references to obscure theories with which the reader may not be familiar. If such a little-known theory must be mentioned, it is desirable to introduce it by presenting its main features. Such brief descriptions can be appropriately introduced as a part of the text. The nineteenth-century practice of using lengthy and elaborate footnotes to explain any obscure point in the text is one that has become less and less frequently used in scientific literature.

Some repetition is necessary in most writing, and the old adage applies that the teacher should start by telling his audience what he is going to say, then he should say it, and finally he should say what he has said. A report, as much as a lecture, is a learning experience for the audience and a teaching experience for the writer. Thus systematic repetition of the type described by the adage is a desirable feature of written presentation.

A frequent error of style, particularly common in the literature of educational research, is that of writing out in extended detail facts that have been presented in a table in concise form. Here is an example of this from a mythical report:

The table under consideration shows the percentage of correct answers to the arithmetic problems given by various categories of college students. It can be seen that freshmen, sophomores, juniors, and seniors obtained on the average 32, 34, 43, and 44 per cent of the problems correct. When the same group of freshmen is divided according to whether they came from Type A, Type B, or Type C schools, the percentages are 29, 31, and 33. The corresponding figures for the sophomore group are 31, 32, 36; for the junior group, 41, 42, 45; and for the senior group, 43, 44, 45.

Drivel of this kind fulfills only the purpose of confusing the reader, who would have understood the data perfectly well had he been left to examine a well-constructed table. By contrast, a writer does well to point out the highlights of a table and also any important features that might otherwise escape notice.

A similar stylistic fault is seen when a writer is attempting to explain a mathematical operation that he has performed on data and does this by giving an extended account of the arithmetic involved instead of providing a brief account of the algebra or of the general purpose of the operation. An example of this kind of error of presentation follows:

The totals for each one of the horizontal rows were squared and from the sum of these values was subtracted the square of the grand total divided by 500. The result of this operation was then divided by 6 and the dividend was entered in Table X. A similar arithmetical operation was then performed with the totals of the vertical rows, etc.

What the writer should have done was to state that he performed an analysis of variance according to customary procedures. If he wanted to explain further what he was doing, a brief algebraic explanation would have sufficed.

Final Publication

Most theses and dissertations do not achieve publication beyond that provided by microfilm services or the reproduction of a summary in *Dissertation Abstracts*. This is usually not because the findings do not merit publication, but because the author does not take the necessary steps to incorporate his findings in the professional literature. Most doctoral dissertations from a well-established graduate school contain enough of consequence to provide at least one publication, and some may yield several. They would not have been accepted in partial fulfillment of the requirements for a degree if this had not been so. True, a dissertation of no consequence occasionally slips by through some misunderstanding, as when everybody involved had become committed to accepting it before its worth had been properly evaluated, but such cases are exceptions. Failure to publish the results of a doctoral project is almost always the result of the student's not taking the steps necessary to achieve this goal. Often it is because of lack of motivation: the achievement of the doctoral degree represents the achievement of a personal goal, and publication has little to offer to the student. In addition, he may have already revised his product so many times that any further revision is seen as a most distasteful and repulsive task. However, the doctoral student, although aware of these blocks and impediments, should recognize that he has to consider more than personal gain in deciding whether or not to publish. He also must consider that in the preparation of his dissertation he has occupied much professional time on the part of a faculty, and that he can repay this debt to society by making his findings part of the body of professional knowledge represented by published literature. If he does not do this, much of his time and the time of others will be lost, and later students may repeat his work without ever knowing that they are merely repeating what has already been done. Master's degree students have a lesser responsibility in this respect.

The most desirable place of publication is the professional journal that specializes in the field in which the student has worked. Many such journals publish without charge except for special materials such as tables and cuts. Less desirable as places of publication are those journals that require the authors to defray the cost. It is inevitable that the free-publication journals should be able to select the best contributions.

Most journal editors will provide considerable help in shaping an article so that it presents its material in the most effective way. Suggestions by editors concerning the revision of manuscripts should be given careful consideration. In such matters, the editor's experience is likely to provide a sounder basis of action than is that of the neophyte in the field. Editors are deeply concerned with making their journals into the best publications they can possibly produce. They can achieve this goal only with the cooperation of authors.

New Methods of Distributing Technical Information

Twenty years ago it was a relatively simple matter to publish long articles that included substantial quantities of tabular material, but today lengthy scientific documents are extremely difficult to publish. This change is partly the result of the large increase in publication costs that has taken place over the period. However, an additional factor is the expansion of research in the behavioral and educational sciences, with the result that most journals receive many times as much material as they ever have space to publish. One partial solution for this problem is for journals to provide additional sections in which material can be published at the expense of the author. A few writers have been attracted by this proposition, and especially by the fact that it results in immediate publication and the usual long delay is eliminated. Nevertheless, the expenses of such early publication are high and beyond the economic circumstances of most young research workers, even if they are fortunate enough to have their article accepted.

Those who have thought about the problem of providing publication facilities, and hence of the problem of distributing scientific information, agree that traditional journal sources will become progressively even less adequate than they are at present. New methods of distributing scientific information must be found, and some are in the process of being developed.

One approach has been to provide locations where materials supplementary to short publications can be deposited and remain available to interested users. For example, tables of data and detailed analyses are far too expensive to publish in regular journals, but journal editors may arrange to have them deposited with the American Society of Information Science (formerly the American Documentation Institute) where copies can be obtained for a small charge. Another approach is that of publishing only abstracts for general distribution, but providing a copy of the complete paper to a limited group of interested specialists who purchase the papers on a subscription basis. Still another approach is the development of government sponsored depositories of information that provide catalogs of the information available and copies of the documents at a nominal charge.

The rapidly developing information sciences are likely to evolve many new and highly original methods of information distribution during the next few years. These will influence the way in which the graduate student goes about reviewing the literature relevant to a problem, the format of the thesis or dissertation, and the way in which the knowledge discovered by the graduate student is disseminated.

SUMMARY

1. The plan for the processing of the data should be drawn up at the time the study is designed.

2. Data should be collected in a form convenient for processing.

3. If apparatus is used that records the desired data mechanically, it should be arranged so that it delivers data in a concise and manageable form.

4. Procedures for quantifying data should be written out in detail and should be given a trial run prior to actual use in the study. The reliability of these procedures should be reported if they involve judgment.

5. The problem of handling missing values should be discussed with a statistician if it arises. The discarding of observations may seriously bias the outcomes of a study unless the research worker knows how to handle this problem.

6. Clerical work should be checked for accuracy, because inaccuracies may introduce large errors.

7. The research worker must avoid the error of deriving hypotheses from the data and then testing the hypotheses from the same data.

8. The introductory sections of the report should always contain a clear and concise statement of the purposes of the research. These sections should also outline the background of the problem and the theory on which it is based. They may sometimes form the basis of an article for journal publication.

9. The section of the report that describes the procedure should be sufficiently detailed to permit reproduction of the study. This is not the easy matter that it may appear to be on the surface.

10. The results section of the report should contain statistical summaries and reductions of the data rather than the raw data. The conclusions drawn from the study should be clearly related to the hypotheses that were stated in the introductory sections.

11. The final section on implications should discuss the problem, "Where do we go from here?" The writer of such a section should avoid the temptation to throw in many wild ideas. The section should be a well-organized presentation of thoughts and concepts that emerge from the study.

12. Diagrams and tables should as far as possible be self-explanatory. Often they are appropriate substitutes for lengthy discussion.

13. The student should seek to publish at least an abbreviated ac-

count of his study so that the results are made available to the profession.

14. Many new methods of information storage and distribution are appearing. These will undoubtedly influence the way in which information contained in theses and dissertations is distributed.

‖‖‖‖‖‖‖‖‖‖‖‖‖‖‖‖‖‖‖‖‖‖‖‖‖‖‖‖

CHAPTER 16

Some Problems of Conducting Historical Research

Historical Research and Case History Research

RESEARCH conducted by historians has differed from research conducted by the majority of scientists in so many fundamental ways that a chapter on the subject almost seems out of place in this volume. Nevertheless, its inclusion is justified on three grounds. First, many theses written by students in schools of education are historical in character. Secondly, a review of research literature is in itself an historical study, for the reviewer is attempting to reconstruct what was done and what happened in the past. Thirdly, the last few decades have seen a rapprochement between historical research and research in such areas as anthropology, sociology, and psychology. The Social Science Research Council has made persistent efforts to bring together scholars in history, anthropology, sociology, and related disciplines so that each can profit from the knowledge of technique and method acquired by the others.

An example of this rapprochement is found in a Social Science Research Council Report by L. Gottschalk, *et al.* (1945) in which the knowledge of a historian, a sociologist, and an anthropologist is pooled to provide a more complete understanding of the use of the personal document in research. Psychologists have also conducted inquiries on the fringe of historical research. For example, the writings of Allport

(1942) on the use of personal documents in research has had some impact on students of historical method.

Historical research is concerned with man's past, and although it has as its aim the reconstruction of the past, such a reconstruction can never be fully achieved. The problem of the historian is similar to that of psychologists working with case history material who seek to reconstruct from such material the nature of the person to whom it pertains. The information is always fragmentary and the reconstruction provides a sketch rather than a finished portrait. Different students of a case history may arrive at different reconstructions from the same evidence, but the student of personal case histories sometimes has an advantage over the historian in that he may go out and study his case further and validate through the collection of additional evidence the reconstruction he has built. The clinical psychologist typically does this. From the evidence he collects about a case, he attempts to reconstruct the person. Then he validates his reconstruction by further observing the person. The historian cannot look to the future to validate his reconstructions of the past.

But history is not just any reconstruction of the past as A. Nevins (1963) reminds us. In order to be designated as history, it must reflect the spirit of critical inquiry that aims to achieve a faithful representation of past events. The historian aims to write history that is in some sense true, but much that is written about the past is notorious for deliberate distortions. Nevins points out that presidential campaign speeches reviewing events of the past four years are not examples of the writing of history, for they do not reflect the historian's dedication to the spirit of scholarly inquiry. A Commissioner of Education, appearing before a congressional committee in order to support a request for funds, may "review the progress" of the last year, but with no stretch of the imagination could his report be construed as being history of educational progress during the year. Both the Commissioner and the members of the congressional committee know that the report is biased and selective in the presentation of content. The report of the Commissioner can be considered a document for the historian to examine to extract from it whatever truth is there, but it is not history.

The Historian's Use of Documents

Reconstruction of the past, which is called history, is based on inferences made from documents. The term *document* is used here in a broader scnse than it is used in daily living. A document is an impression left by a human being on a physical object. The impression may be made with ink on a piece of paper, with a sculptor's chisel on a piece of stone, with the artist's brush on canvas, with the potter's hand on soft clay, and in any other way in which a human may leave a trace of his activity. This conception of a document is derived from the writings of Gottschalk (1945), who makes no distinction between written impressions and other impressions. In any case, the latter distinction is not easily made, for primitive written communications are pictorial, and every object on which the human hand has left an impression tells a story.

Documents are derived from *sources*. A particular observer is an example of a source; he may be the source of many documents. A newspaper is another example of a source. However, the word source also has another meaning in that a document is commonly referred to as a source of information.

That sound inferences about a culture can be made from objects is so obvious that the point hardly needs to be pressed further. If a visitor from another planet were able to procure some of the common objects used by modern civilization but died on the return trip home, the objects themselves would permit the inhabitants of the other planet to go far toward reconstructing a picture of our civilization. Take, for example, a good quality kitchen knife. The fact that it contained high-grade steel would indicate that the civilization from which it was derived had an advanced technology in the processing of metals and had probably made substantial scientific discoveries. The name of the manufacturer on the knife would indicate a knowledge of writing and the widespread use of writing and printing in daily life. The plastic handle would provide further cues concerning the scientific and technical development of the culture. Additional inferences from other objects in the collection would not only provide some verification of the inferences made from the knife, but would also add to the reconstruction.

The reconstruction of the past is undertaken in terms of a set of written symbols. The assumption is that the words of history bear a well-defined relationship to past events, much as an equation of a physicist bears a relation to the processes occurring in an experiment. One important difference is that the physicist can always reproduce the process in order to check whether his formula actually corresponds to real events. The historian has much greater difficulty in doing this. In an earlier chapter the use of models in the development of science was discussed. In a sense, history is a model of certain events of the past.

The thinking habits of most people are such that they have difficulty in thinking of written history as merely an attempt to build a verbal model of past events. One can understand why this is so. To read a chapter by a great historian of high literary talent is to have a vivid experience of living in the past with a feeling for the reality of the past much as one has a sense of the reality of the present. The compelling reality of the image of history imparted to us is an illusion conjured up through the literary and research skills of the historian. The reality of history is illusory, for one cannot know the past in the way in which one can know the present. One cannot know it in the way in which it was known to those that lived it. Written history is only an attempt to provide, through the use of words and symbols, some representation of what are inferred to be events that actually took place. How close a relationship exists between the written symbols and the actual events is always a matter for conjecture. Language itself, with its many limitations, probably has only limited capacity for representing the events as they actually happened.

The problems of selecting, examining, and making inferences from documents are the problems of historical method. They present essentially the same difficulties that are encountered in making inferences from psychological tests and other materials, but they have the added difficulty that there is often no direct way of validating the inference. When one considers that trained psychologists have been relatively unsuccessful in making predictions about individuals even from very extensive case histories, one may well wonder whether the historian is likely to be more successful in reconstructing history from the documents available.

Choice of a Subject

Every historical study begins with the choice of a subject. This may seem to be an easy decision to make, but the fact is that it is not and there is considerable controversy among historians concerning the criteria to use in the selection of a topic. Gottschalk (1951) suggests that four questions should be asked in identifying a topic:

1. Where do the events take place?
2. Who are the persons involved?
3. When do the events occur?
4. What kinds of human activity are involved?

Other prescriptions exist for defining historical topics. One of these is to define the topic in terms of some important idea or set of beliefs. One school of historians has taken the position that history is the history of important ideas and if it is not this, then it lacks significance. Thomas Carlyle thought that history was simply a collection of biographies.

The scope of a topic can be varied by varying the scope of any one of the four categories: the geographical area involved can be increased or decreased; more or fewer persons can be included in the topic; the time span involved can be increased or decreased; and the human activity category can be broadened or narrowed.

In a sense, historical studies can only begin with a very rough determination of what is to be the topic involved. Because in the beginning stage the research worker does not yet know the scope his topic may acquire after all the facts have been assembled, he can only indicate in a rough way the scope of the projected research. As he studies the sources available to him, he may find that the proposed topic involves so many and complex events that he must limit its scope. He may also find that the area is an impoverished one and that a broadening of the scope of the study is desirable.

Historical dissertations and theses in the area of education are commonly biographical studies, perhaps because these are more readily undertaken than other forms of historical inquiry. Yet there seems to be a particular need, in education, for the historical study of important ideas that have influenced both the schools and public policies related to them. So often education has moved through cycles of ideas only to return, ultimately, to the starting point. A better understanding of the history of ideas in education would prevent much activity that has been called "rediscovering the wheel." So often a great new educational program is little more than one that had been in vogue thirty years previously. For example, the new emphasis on developing creativity through education is really a revival of a similar emphasis displayed during the thirties when the Progressive Education Association attempted to encourage creative activity on the part of pupils. The activities involved in such creativity training today are essentially the same as those that were advocated thirty or more years ago. The numerous individualized teaching programs that are claimed, by some, to represent a new great advance are extraordinarily like those developed at Winnetka many decades ago. The present vogue for Initial Teaching Alphabets (ITA) is a revival of an unsuccessful movement of a century ago; and it is highly doubtful whether the present special reading alphabets are any better than those that were tried out in whole school systems in the 1800s. Those who play leadership roles in education need to be far more sensitive to the history of education than they have been in the past. Research on the history of ideas in education has a very valuable function to perform.

Selection of Sources

Historical studies usually begin with a delimitation of the general category of events that is to be reconstructed. The next step is the establishment of sources from which inferences can be made concerning the nature of the events. A common classification of sources is into *primary* and *secondary*. A primary source is one which has had some direct physical relationship to the events that are being reconstructed. A person who observes directly an event would be classified as a primary source, and so, too, would a photograph or sound recording of the event. A reproduction of such a photograph would also be considered as a primary source. The writings of a person whose life is being reconstructed as a history would be considered a primary source even if he wrote about himself in the third person, as certain writers have done. Secondary sources are those that do not bear a direct physical relationship to the event that is the object of study. They are related to the event through some intermediate process. Thus, if the historian is interested in the life of a character whom we will designate X, he may have to use documents produced by Z who never knew X personally. Z may have derived his information about X through an interview with Y, a close personal friend of X. In such a case both Y and Z introduce distortions, hence Z as a secondary source is necessarily a poorer source of information than Y. If the chain involved in the transmittal of information is lengthened from $X—Y—Z$ to a chain of four elements, the adequacy of the information is again decreased. Psychologists have conducted experiments on the transmittal of information by this kind of human chain and have found that substantial distortions may occur in very short chains, even to the extent that the information transmitted loses all its original characteristics.

Many sources include both primary and secondary elements that the person conducting historical research, or research involving the use of personal documents, may have to sort out. Many biographies have been written by close personal friends of the principal character involved. The biography will be a mixture of information derived by direct observation and material obtained by the writer from other sources. Often there is no way of determining which parts of a source are primary and which are secondary, although this may be a vital issue in determining the inferences to be made from the material.

Criteria of the Validity of Inferences and Reconstructions

The scientist uses many different criteria to determine the validity of the ideas he develops. One criterion may be called an *internal* criterion—whether the idea fits with other ideas derived from different sources. The wave theory of light derived from a study of lens phenomena and interference phenomena does not fit with the quantum theory of light derived from such phenomena as the photoelectric effect. Both conceptions of light must be inadequate—they are incompatible with one another, although each is compatible with the evidence on which it is based. Inferences made from different sources about the same historical event must be compatible and fit together if they are to be considered valid. This type of validation procedure used by the historian closely resembles that used by the scientist. But the scientist has another method of validating his inferences; namely, by making predictions on the basis of the inferences and determining whether such predictions are correct. The historian is not able to use the latter approach to validate his inferences.

A difficulty that the historian faces when he attempts to validate his inferences is that this process always involves a considerable degree of personal judgment and subjectivity. The scientist attempts to overcome this difficulty by using measuring devices and laboratory procedures which eliminate, as much as possible, the factor of judgment. For example, by inference from data, Einstein developed an equation relating mass to energy. This inference could be validated by finding situations in which there was a conversion of mass to energy and *measuring* the amount of energy produced by a given loss of mass. There is very little guesswork involved in this kind of validation. There is much greater difficulty in validating the inference that a Supreme Court justice held a particular personal view with respect to a particular issue, although to hold such a view was in conflict with a decision he had endorsed. Indirect information may *indicate* that his personal views were in conflict with the position, but how much evidence does one have to have, in this case, to substantiate the hypothesis? The answer is strictly a matter of opinion, a matter that makes the task of the historian a particularly difficult one.

Although agreement among sources and the criterion of internal consistency is commonly used, it cannot always be justifiably applied.

The psychologist is, in this respect, in a much better position than the historian, for very rarely in psychological work can the criterion of internal consistency not be applied. In contrast, the historian often encounters instances in which much evidence appears on the surface to point in one direction, but the inference is wrong. Consider, for example, the documents left in Germany after the end of the Nazi regime. Document upon document takes the position that the difficulties of Germany were manufactured by the Jews. Clearly, the position is nonsense and although the documents show consistency, the criterion of consistency cannot be applied.

Evaluation of Written Documents

Before a written document can be used as a basis for making inferences, its worth for the purpose must be evaluated. This is generally done from two distinct points of view. First, an appraisal must be made of the authenticity of the source. Secondly, if the authorship can be established, the characteristics of the author must be weighed in order to determine whether the document he produced can be considered a sound source of information. Each of these presents problems in evaluation that must be considered separately.

The evaluation of authenticity. Sometimes a problem of authenticity will arise in the research that students of education are likely to undertake, although less often than in other kinds of historical research. For example, if a student were to make an analysis of the content of speeches made by superintendents during a given period of time in order to study the educational policies of the period, he would be faced with the problem of determining how many of the superintendents used ghostwriters. The same problem arises in the case of correspondence, for it is very common for an official letter to be composed by a person other than the signer. Autobiographies are also commonly written by ghostwriters and throughout history there have been persons who earned their livings by such writing.

The historian is plagued by the fact that the details of many documents are incorrect and, unless checked, may give rise to incorrect inferences. Barzun (1957) gives an interesting example of how an incorrect date on a letter might lead to incorrect inferences. He cites the case of a letter written by Berlioz to his publisher about the preparation of an index for a book. According to the letter, it was written from Paris on Thursday, June 23. No year was indicated. Establishing the date of the letter presents an interesting problem. Barzun points out that other sources indicate that Berlioz lived in Paris from July 1849 until April 1856 and hence a reference to the calendar should indicate in which one of these years June 23 fell on a Thursday. The calendar indicates that the year would have been 1853, but Barzun then goes on to point out that the year could not have been 1853 for at that time Berlioz did not have any manuscript in the final stages of completion. The year must have been 1852 and the day Wednesday rather than Thursday, June 23. The evidence indicates that Berlioz made an error in noting the day of the week.

The evaluation of the writer as a transmitter of information. The authors of documents may represent excellent sources of information or worthless sources. A number of characteristics are commonly considered in making evaluations of writers.

1. Was the writer a trained or untrained observer of the particular event? If a biologist recorded that he observed the Loch Ness monster, greater credibility would be given the report than if a person not trained in biological observation had reported it. Related to this is the matter of the expertness of the observer. The biologist in this case is not only a trained observer but also an expert on animal life. More credence is given to the observations of experts than those of amateurs.

2. What was the relationship of the observer to the event? The closer the writer was to the event recorded, the greater the value of the source. Persons who arrive *after* an event has taken place or who were some distance from it are not in a position to provide reports to which great significance can be attached. An accident report of a principal who arrived on the scene after the incident occurred is likely to be worth less than that of a teacher who saw it happen.

3. To what extent was the writer under pressure to distort? There are many cases in which educational documents must be considered as almost certainly representing a distorted picture of what happened. A school board that meets behind closed doors and then releases for publication a report of the deliberations is likely to produce a distorted statement of what occurred. The statement is likely to be designed to please the public and the personnel of the school system. Again, in a public session of a school board, a newspaper reporter is likely to give greater stress to those aspects of the proceedings that might be of political interest to his particular newspaper.

4. What was the intent of the writer of the document? This is related to the previous item, but covers a greater range of circumstances. Documents may be written for many different purposes: to inform, to remind the writer (as in the case of a personal memorandum), to command (as in the case of a directive), to produce a

particular effect on a particular reader or on a group of readers, or sometimes even to unburden the mind of the writer (as is sometimes the case with personal correspondence). The intent of the writer of the document, if it can be determined, should have a powerful influence on the evaluation of a document as historical evidence.

5. To what extent was the writer an expert at recording the particular events? The well-trained newspaper reporter is much more likely to provide an accurate report than the casual tourist who happened to observe the same event. Untrained observers in schools may report entirely erroneous impressions. Many critics of the public schools have not been inside one since they left school and base their criticism on anecdotes brought back by their own children. Such children would be considered to lack expertness in recording events that occurred.

6. Were the habits of the author of the document such that they might interfere with the accurate recording of events? This is an interesting problem. A good writer is not necessarily a good reporter. The writer with literary talent may be unable to control the temptation to embellish. The opportunity to display a clever turn of phrase or an apt analogy may interfere with precise reporting. The talented writer is also often imaginative and creative and experiences difficulty in discriminating between what actually happened and what he imagines happened.

7. Was the author of the document of such a nature that he might omit important materials or distort others in order to avoid being sued for libel? Every writer will yield to some extent to this, but the bold will still report more than the timid and with less distortion. Even though this point is an important one, advice cannot be offered that will help the historian distinguish the bold writer from the timid one.

A source of considerable controversy has long been whether historians should approach the study of a document with ideas of what they are looking for, or whether the approach should be with an open mind. To approach a document with an hypothesis concerning what the document can show has, in the past, been regarded by the majority of historians as leading to a biasing of the process of observation. However, Allen Johnson (1965), a noted historian, has pointed out that, if scientists had restricted their activities to observing without hypothesizing, the sciences would have never developed. He goes on to argue that historians typically have hypotheses, hidden vaguely at the back of their minds, whenever they scan a document. Were this not so, most historical documents would be sterile and perhaps even trivial documents. Imagine a social worker reviewing a case history, a common form of historical document, without any hypotheses concerning the kind of person that the case history described. The reviewer of such a case history would, almost certainly, begin to attempt to visualize the person involved after reading only the first few sentences, checking this mental reconstruction with the material that followed. Such a mental image of the person involved represents, in its early stages of development, a set of hypotheses. The historian, dealing not with case histories but with other forms of documents, can hardly be expected to review all of the material without ever forming hypotheses concerning the nature of that which is being described. He must also be extremely careful to avoid allowing his hypotheses to color the appearance of the facts.

Cause and Effect Relationships

Just as the behavioral scientist generally avoids referring to Event A as being caused by Even B, so too is the historian very cautious in his use of the concept of cause. No historian would want to discuss the *cause* of war or the *cause* of depressions. Both are highly complex events with complex relationships to other events. Only the physicist dealing with very simple isolated laboratory phenomena can use the word *cause* without running into difficulties. A physicist can appropriately say that a given force causes a given acceleration in a given mass. He can make such statements because he is dealing with an isolated phenomenon. The historian is never in such an enviable position.

The historical research worker must accept the fact that he is not dealing with clear-cut cases of cause and effect and must avoid such notions in his writing. It is very easy to make such a statement as "John Dewey's experiences with the experimental school he founded in Chicago caused him to recast his views on education." Such a statement is quite inaccurate because, although Dewey's experiences in connection with the Chicago school were extremely important to him in the development of his ideas, they were only one set of circumstances among many others from which his later conception of education finally emerged. The historian generally deals with chains of related events, but he cannot say that one event in the chain was caused by the previous event in the chain. A student might undertake an historical study of the changing role of the school faculty in establishing educational policies during the last twenty-five years. In undertaking such a project, the research worker would realize that many conditions and circumstances have been responsible for the changing role of the school faculty in this respect, but he cannot identify clear-cut cause-and-effect relationships. The change that has taken place is a result of many factors and the influence of a particular factor cannot be accurately assessed. In addition, there are events and conditions that have had some influence but that have not been identified. For a discussion of this problem, the reader is referred to Barzun (1957).

Synthesis of Information

If the preparation of a history were merely the digging out of facts, the task would be a simple one. But we have already seen that the study of documents often raises puzzling problems of what is fact, and that judgment is always involved in determining the extent to which the inferences made have a high probability of being correct. These processes present difficulties enough, but even more difficult is the step involved in using the facts and inferences to build an organized account of the events that the history is to cover. This process of putting together a history after the basic research on sources is completed is referred to as the *process of synthesis*. How this should be done is a matter of controversy.

One cannot clearly separate the search for documents and their examination and study from their synthesis into a coherent work. The synthesis of historical material is closely related to the whole problem of making inferences from historical data. Consider, for example, a history focused on the life of a central character. If it included only the objective facts—what the person had been observed to do or had left some record of having done—it would be a dull and lifeless history, lacking any unifying ideas. In order to avoid producing such a cold, lifeless, and objective history, the writer may infer from the data that the person was motivated throughout life by certain powerful and enduring motives. What would be a life of Thomas Jefferson if one could not see in it dedication to the achievement of certain values? What would be a life of Galileo if one could not see in it his devotion to the pursuit of truth and his imperviousness to the social pressures of the times? The historian generally infers from his data that there are underlying characteristics that give unity to the personality he is studying. But, as every psychologist knows, there are substantial hazards involved in making such inferences, and two persons studying the same historical character may not infer the same underlying motives or other basic characteristics.

Because psychologists cannot agree on a list of fundamental motives or underlying personality traits, the historian must choose a system he prefers for the description of behavior. Typically, he chooses a popular conception of personality organization rather than a technical one. One is unlikely to find a biography of Napoleon written in terms of how he was *conditioned* to manifest power-seeking behavior; neither is one likely to find one written in terms of psychoanalytic concepts. True, a few historians have attempted to describe their human subjects in terms of psychoanalytic concepts, but these are notable exceptions and are regarded as bold experiments rather than as orthodox treatments. Perhaps the two major reasons why interpretations of behavior undertaken by historians follow popular conceptions of personality structure are that historians are most familiar with this conception of personality and that history is written for a consumer and the popular conception of personality is the only one that the consumer is likely to understand. Synthesis of conceptions of historical characters in terms of popular conceptions of behavior will continue to be made.

The point emphasized here is that the historical reconstruction of human behavior can be undertaken in many different ways. Historians aim to reconstruct real persons with motives, values, fears, inner conflicts, struggles with their consciences, hates, loves, and the wealth of internal processes that make man more than a mere empty frame. This procedure involves many assumptions about human nature that research may ultimately show to be unsound.

Although the historian is limited in his interpretation of historical characters by his own conceptions of psychology and behavior, he is also limited by the inevitable fact that he must interpret the past in the light of contemporary thought. He may attempt to build a verbal model of the past, but the model is always a product of contemporary thought. A history written today reflects events of today as well as events of the past. The mind of man can mirror the past, but the image may be distorted by the very shape of the surface. Our picture of the schoolrooms of the Middle Ages is colored by what we know about our schools today.

Even at a much simpler level of synthesis than the one just considered there are difficulties involved in putting together what are ordinarily considered to be the facts of history. Consider, for example, two items about the French revolutionary Georges Jacques Danton:

(1) Danton said, "I always act in accordance with the eternal laws of Justice," and (2) Danton was a man of violent and extreme views. The two items differ in their derivation: One has been reproduced from a document whereas the other has been inferred from many separate documents. Now consider the problem of putting these two "facts" together. One might write any one of the following statements:

Although Danton was a man of extreme and violent views, he said, "I always act in accordance with the eternal laws of Justice."

Danton said, "I always act in accordance with the eternal laws of Justice," but he was a man of violent and extreme views.

Although Danton said, "I always act in accordance with the eternal laws of Justice," he was a man of violent and extreme views.

Even though Danton was a man of violent and extreme views, he said, "I always act in accordance with the eternal laws of Justice."

Words such as *although* and *but* can introduce meanings that may take history beyond the realm of reasonable inference.

Written history may, in several different ways, go beyond the facts. There is some agreement among professional historians concerning what can be legitimately added and what can not, but there is far from complete agreement. For example, historians would object to including in a written history a dialogue that, almost certainly, never took place, even though the dialogue might bring out and describe precisely some political issues that played a leading role in the political events under consideration. Even though the reported conversation might not distort history and might provide literary color, it would not represent an acceptable product of historical inquiry. Yet history that is written strictly in terms of established facts is an uninteresting and drab affair. Nevins (1963) discusses this problem by citing a vivid account of General Braddock's advance upon the French and Indian forces over the rugged terrain of Pennsylvania. The account provides a vivid picture of the ruggedness of the mountain wilderness and the problems of moving heavy equipment over bolders and treestumps and rivulets and gorges; and yet the description also gives a picture of the beauty, as well as the inhospitableness of this desolate region. Nevins points out that none of the documents on which the account is based mentions any of these specific details about the landscape, but an account of Braddock's march that omitted any mention of them would be lifeless. They were all an inherent part of the trek of Braddock's army, and a faithful reconstruction of history requires that the historian resurrect in his imagination the setting that made it what it was.

There is a third sense in which the historian adds to the facts and that is through an attempt to derive lessons, or generalizations, from the past. Gottschalk (1963) points out that historians cannot help using generalizations. Any sentence beginning with the words, "The Romans . . ." inevitably involves a generalization about Romans. The issue among historians is not whether generalizations should be used, but whether generalizations of history drawn from the study of one civilization can be applied to an understanding of other civilizations. Are there broad lessons to be learned from history? Can the broad lessons of history, if there are such lessons, be applied to the solution of contemporary human problems? These are questions of the greatest importance, but historians have not agreed on their answers.

Quantitative Methods in Historical Studies

Many attempts have been made to apply the quantitative methods of the scientist to the solution of historical problems. So far the impact of these methods has not been extensive, and much research in history, like much research in anthropology, must remain on a qualitative level. Most of the quantitative methods that have been developed are applications of content analysis.

Some of the earliest efforts to apply quantitative methods involve the use of word counts. Writers typically use particular words at their own frequency rates. A word that has a high usage rate by one writer may have a low usage rate by another. The usage rates of different words can be studied to throw light on the authenticity of the source of a document. Word-usage rates can also be used as a basis for inferring inner emotional states, such as anxiety.

A second and related type of analysis has been developed by McClelland (1961) in an attempt to illuminate the motives operating in individuals in different cultures at particular times in history. McClelland argues that, if the writing appearing in a culture reflects strivings after excellence and provides what he terms "achievement need imagery," the culture may be considered as one with high achievement need. If such an inference can be made, it opens the way to the study of the social conditions that lead to high achievement need in the population. It also opens the way to the study of history in terms of a modern psychological theory of personality. McClelland's approach involves a very careful quantitative analysis of written documents in order to obtain measures of the extent to which a particular culture at a particular time manifests achievement need. The approach to history is a novel one, but it has been met with considerable skepticism by professional historians who claim that the same understanding of history can be achieved by much simpler means and without a quantitative analysis of written materials. (See, for example, Gottschalk, *et al.* (1963).)

During World War II elaborate and careful attempts were made to make analyses of the public speeches made by Nazi officials for the purpose of identifying possible underlying conflicts within the Nazi party. In addition, some attempt was also made to use such content analyses for the purpose of inferring probable next moves on the part of the enemy.

This brief discussion of the introduction of quantitative methods into historical research may stimulate some readers to explore the possibility of applying such methods to the analysis of educational documents. For example, what motives have been stressed in elementary school readers over the last century? How have these motives changed, and how are the changes related to cultural change during this period? These are but a few of the problems that might be worth investigation.

History as the Study of Nomothetic or
Ideographic Phenomena

In Chapter 3 the distinction is made between nomothetic laws, which apply to all persons, and ideographic laws, which reflect the individual's unique history and which, hence, do not apply to others who have had different life histories. Allport (1961) has stressed this distinction in his writings and a parallel distinction is made by historians. Just as some psychologists emphasize the unique characteristics of each individual person, so too do some historians stress the uniqueness of each historical sequence of events.

The issue is as unsettled in the study of history as it is in the study of psychology. In both disciplines there are those who emphasize the nomothetic qualities of their subject matter and those who emphasize the ideographic. Arnold Toynbee, for example, has taken a nomothetic approach to history. He has attempted to show that within a group of twenty distinct cultures common trends are found, much as there are, to some degree, common trends in the psychological development of all children, even though each child has unique characteristics that distinguish him from other children. Certain historians emphasize the unique development of each and every culture.

The issue is one mainly of theoretical interest and has relevance to the issue of the extent to which the historian can predict the future turn of events, or may be able to do so one day. Contemporary historians, good scholars that they are, make few claims that historical trends are so well established that the future of a civilization can be predicted. Hopes of being able to make such predictions go far beyond expectations reasonable at this time, but there is another important relation that historical research has to future events.

Although historians may not be able to predict the future of a civilization, the study of history does affect the future by influencing the decisions of those who participate in government. Such persons as Roosevelt and Churchill have had a deep and scholarly interest in history, and their knowledge must influence their decisions. At least, some of the grossest follies of mankind may not be repeated, although perhaps this is setting our hopes too high. In the same spirit, those responsible for the establishment of educational policy are influenced by their knowledge of the history of education. The amateur reformers in the field of education would probably drop most of their plans for the remodeling of public education if they had a better understanding of the failures of the past.

Use of Case Histories: A Special Problem
in Historical Research

The teacher, the counselor, the social worker, the research worker using biographical data, and the historian share in common the task of reconstructing case histories in the course of their professional work. Although the historian writing a biography of some famous contemporary and the social worker writing a case history for presentation to a court are not likely to think of themselves engaged in the same activity, both are attempting to reconstruct what happened in the life of a particular individual. In addition, both are trying to be objective; both are attempting to collect information on what actually happened and to distinguish this from what was rumored to have happened; and both are attempting to fit together fragmentary pieces of evidence into a total picture. Even though the style of the product of the historian and the social worker differ substantially, both encounter similar problems of method in going about their respective tasks. The research worker who uses biographical data comes perhaps closer to the historian, not only in how he goes about his task, but also in the product that emerges from the research.

In the traditional type of biographical study, biographies are examined on an intuitive basis much as the clinician examines a patient. An example of this type of approach is manifested by Anne Roe in her studies of creative talent. The purpose of the examination of the biographies in this case is to determine whether the group of creative individuals show any common characteristics running through their lives. In the case of Anne Roe's studies the attempt seems to have had some success, and the results have been confirmed by other sources of evidence. Nevertheless, the success of this method in the case of some studies does not mean that it is always successful. The truth seems to be that the method has many dangers, and unsuccessful applications tend to be overlooked.

A major danger is illustrated by the early biographical studies of neurotic patients. In these it was shown again and again that such individuals often had been exposed to traumatic experiences. The conclusion was erroneously drawn that traumatic incidents in childhood produce neurotic behavior in adult life. This conclusion is not justified, for when the background of well-adjusted individuals is also examined, it is found that this group, too, shows a similar incidence of traumatic events. A related error was made at one time as a result of investigations on the family background of psychotic patients. It was found that such patients had a large number of relatives who were "queer" in some way. It is not reasonable to conclude on this basis that psychoses are inherited, because further investigation shows that so-called normal individuals also have numerous relatives who are commonly described as "queer." The reader will recognize that the way to prevent such erroneous conclusions is to introduce a group of "normals," whose background is also examined. The introduction of a control group is really necessary in order that any conclusions at all may be reached.

The collection of biographical data involves the same care and rigorous controls that have to be introduced in the collection of any historical data. Biographical data, collected through an interview with the person whose life history is being reconstructed, provides only the most limited data and often data of rather doubtful validity. The fact is that individuals are often brought into contact with a case worker because they cannot see themselves objectively and because they grossly misinterpret the actions of others toward themselves. These conditions that bring them into contact with the case worker are just the conditions that make them poor sources of historical data. Other sources of evidence have to be introduced in order to be able to select out those facts that dovetail together and separate them from those that display inconsistencies across different sources of information. However, biographical data about living persons is not readily obtained from their contemporaries. One cannot ask questions about another person easily unless one has some good reason such as that of obtaining an employment record. Society does not bestow on the research worker any particular right to collect information about a person from those who have known him. Yet without such information a case history is a document of very limited value.

The information presented by autobiographies or derived from interviews is difficult to treat in any scientific study because of its diffuse nature and because of the multiplicity and variety of the events that it may cover. These characteristics force on the investigator the intuitive approach that must be taken in examining such material. The intuitive approach involves the interpretation of the material, but an interpretative process invariably introduces error. In order to avoid such errors, inventories have been developed for recording biographical information.

In the typical biographical inventory, a standard series of questions is asked about a person's background. The questions are answered by choosing one of a number of alternatives. Typical questions are the following:

In what type of community did you spend most of your time before entering school?
1. In the country
2. In a town with less than 5000 inhabitants
3. In a town with 5000 to 10,000 inhabitants
4. In a town with 10,000 to 50,000 inhabitants
5. In a town with more than 50,000 inhabitants

Which group of school subjects did you prefer when you were in high school?
1. English, speech
2. Social studies, history, geography
3. Science, mathematics
4. Music, art
5. Athletics

Biographical information collected in the form illustrated here has had a long history of practical use and also some history of having played a useful part in research. Many have regarded it with skepticism, but the fact that it has had a long history of practical utility in the selection of various classes of employees has forced researchers to give it serious consideration. It is of interest to note that the first really successful use of the biographical inventory was in connection with the selection of salesmen, particularly life insurance salesmen. Such devices remain, even today, the main instruments that are used for this purpose. Of course, such devices were not developed on the basis of any particularly sophisticated psychological theory of selling. The point stressed here is that this work of practical importance demonstrated that biographical information collected in this form could be used for making predictions, and probably with more success than biographical information collected in narrative form. Of particular significance is the fact that biographical items related to factual material had considerable predictive significance, whereas those related to opinions and attitudes tended to be of doubtful value.

During World War II, some success was achieved in the use of biographical information blanks for the prediction of performance in flying training, and there were even indications that such devices could be used for predicting aerial combat leadership. These inventories were much more sophisticated than earlier devices in the theory on which they were based, and this sophistication has been shown in work that has been undertaken since that time. A major development incorporated into more recent biographical information blanks has been an attempt to group items in such a way that they measure a number of distinct and separate influences in a person's background, or even a series of relatively independent traits that may emerge from such backgrounds. There has also been considerable interest in attempts to predict variables other than occupational success. For example, there have been many studies in which biographical information has been used to predict reaction to stress, and predictions of sufficient accuracy to be used have been achieved.

The clinician has never been particularly in sympathy with this approach to the matter of using biographical information. He has tended to believe that the very uniformity of the material included in a biographical information blank is a disadvantage. He points out that the unique event is often a crucial factor in the life of an individual, and the unique event would be missed by any standard inventory. The clinician has not proved his case in this matter, and the success achieved with biographical inventories may perhaps make him stop and ponder.

Summary

1. The methods of historical research and those of the scientist have certain common characteristics and attempts have been made to bring together historians and social scientists to find unity among their methods.

2. Historical research attempts to provide a verbal reconstruction of man's past. Written history attempts to provide a verbal model of the past much as an equation of a physicist is a model of physical phenomena.

3. History is reconstructed from a study of documents, defined as objects on which man has left an impression. Inferences are made from these documents. Historical method deals with the problems of selecting, examining and making inferences from documents.

4. Historical research begins with the choice of a subject, which may be narrowed or broadened in scope as the inquiry is pursued.

5. Sources of historical information are generally categorized as *primary* or *secondary*, according to their proximity to the event about which they are considered to be sources of information.

6. The historian is limited in the procedures he can use in validating inferences made from documents. He is unable to use the scientist's criterion of making and checking predictions of future events on the basis of the inference. To some extent he may be able to validate an inference by checking with other sources and documents. However, he must use caution in the application of this method because consistency alone is not a sufficient condition for the validity of an inference.

7. Written documents must be carefully evaluated before inferences are made from them. The historian must evaluate the authenticity of a document. He must also evaluate the standing of the writer as a transmitter of information, the extent to which the writer was trained to observe the phenomenon he describes, the relationship of the writer to the event, the extent to which there were pressures on him that might have led to distortion, his intent, his expertness, his habits, and the legal system of the culture within which the document was produced, as well as other factors.

8. The concept of cause should be used with caution in the writing of history. The historian typically deals with chains of related events in which causal relationships are generally complex and not clearly identifiable.

9. The end stage of historical research is a synthesis of the infor-

mation and inferences that have been thus derived. A synthesis of history, like the process of making historical inferences, generally makes assumptions about human nature within a framework of psychological theory. The choice of a theory of behavior is crucial to the writing of a history and should be explicitly stated.

10. Quantitative methods are slowly influencing historical studies. The main influences in this respect are the methods derived from content analysis.

11. Controversy exists whether history should be considered the study of nomothetic or ideographic phenomena.

12. Case history material is essentially historical material. The development of a case history involves the reconstruction of the life of an individual from fragmentary evidence. In order that the reconstruction have some validity, varied documents and sources should be consulted. Material should be retained insofar as it is supported from different sources and rejected when different sources lead to inconsistent conclusions.

‖‖‖‖‖‖‖‖‖‖‖‖‖‖‖‖‖‖‖‖‖‖‖‖‖‖‖‖‖

CHAPTER 17

Applications of
Computers to Education

EVERY educational research worker today has to have some knowledge of computers in order to plan his work effectively. A general knowledge of what computers can do is important because many research approaches to problems have been made feasible through the availability of these devices. The educational-research worker needs to know something about computers for another reason: He will often be called upon to advise on the installation of computers in school systems.

The conception of a modern computer was first developed by Charles Babbage (1792–1871) who was able to persuade the British government to support an effort to develop one over a ten-year period. Babbage's machine, which he referred to as his analytic machine, was a tremendously ambitious venture, but it ended in failure largely because the art of machine construction in his day was not sufficiently advanced to perform the functions that he specified should be performed. He did manage to produce a small "differencing" machine that could solve some simple problems in the application of calculus, but this device was far short of the highly elaborate machine of which he had dreamed. Indeed, the "analytic" machine he planned to produce would have had a storage capacity not far short of that of a modern computer and an extraordinary capability for performing complex numerical operations. Relics of the components of his machine, exhibited today in the London Science Museum, are reminders of the great dream Babbage had, but his failure was a product of his excessive ambition. Had he been willing to settle for more modest goals, large computers might have come much earlier than they actually did.

Babbage's dream was that of a digital computer; that is to say, it was a plan for a machine that would deal with numbers and perform arithmetical operations with them. Many subsequent computers were built that did not handle numbers; they handled quantities. These latter computers are referred to as *analog* computers. A digital computer adds one number to another and finds the sum, but an analog computer adds, say, one voltage to another voltage, and finds the sum of the two voltages. The difference between the two kinds of computers is that between a counter, which can register only whole numbers, and a voltmeter, from which voltage can be read within certain limits of accuracy. Analog computers are typically built for specific purposes such as solving particular kinds of equations. For example, many analog computers were built prior to World War II and were designed specifically for solving systems of simultaneous equations. Problems that can be solved on analog computers can be solved on digital computers.

The digital computer can be adapted to handle symbols other than digits and thus has the potential for becoming a general-symbol manipulator and, ultimately, a universal problem-solving machine. For example, Euclidean geometry can be so coded that the axioms, and rules for making deductions from them, can be stored in a digital computer. The computer can then be programmed to produce the proofs of certain propositions; that is to say, it can originate proofs of Euclidean theorems. The fact that such manipulations of symbols can be performed has encouraged some to believe that the computer will ultimately become the universal problem solver. Hunt (1962), indeed, has suggested that the ultimate in universal problem solvers would be a machine capable of continuously redesigning itself with improvements.

Thus, the emerging modern conception of a computer is of a machine that manipulates symbols, much as man manipulates symbols in his thinking, rather than a machine that is limited to arithmetical operations. A machine, conceived in this way, has the potential for making decisions on the basis of data in accordance with the rules in terms of which it is designed to operate.

Description of Computers

All computers involve four essential systems of components. These are, (1) the input-output system, (2) the storage system, (3) the processing system, and (4) the control system.

The input-output system is exactly what the name implies, namely, the mechanism through which information is transmitted to the machine and the mechanism through which the products of the work of the machine are removed. The input can be undertaken through various different avenues. Some machines take in information through the familiar IBM card. Others use a continuous tape that has the information stored on it either in the form of punched holes or on a surface that is magnetized in small spots. The small magnetized spots take the place of holes. Input through tape is generally much faster than input through cards. The output is generally on magnetic tape that can be fed into auxiliary equipment where it is converted into a printed form. Modern printers operating from magnetic tape work at very high speeds printing more than six hundred lines per minute. The reader can well imagine the speed when he realizes that such a machine prints out at a speed of ten or more lines per second. Inputs and outputs may be in the form of numbers or alphabetical material. Outputs may also be in a number of other forms. Sometimes the output is so arranged that it will plot the points of a graph on a cathode ray screen, which is essentially the same device as a television picture tube. There are also arrangements whereby the output can be made to plot a graph on a sheet of paper.

In many situations the outputs of the computer are stored electromagnetically on disks. The advantage of disk storage is that one can obtain very quick access to the information thus stored. If a bank were to keep a record of all of its accounts in disk storage an employee could obtain within a fraction of a second a statement of the balance in any one of thousands of accounts. If the information about the accounts were stored on tape, a search for a particular account would involve running an entire tape through a scanning device—a matter that might take anything from minutes to hours depending on the number of accounts involved. In contrast, information can be obtained from disk storage very expeditiously.

Every computer has an internal storage system for retaining (1) the data that are to be worked on and (2) the directions that tell the machine what to do to the data. The latter set of directions is referred to as the *program*. A major problem in the development of computers was the development of a storage that had sufficient capacity to solve complicated problems. The mechanical storage of information on counters, which Babbage used on his early calculating machines, is of little use for this purpose.

Modern storage systems within computers are of two general types. First, there is core storage. This is a system that has the advantage of providing very rapid access to the information stored in any storage unit. The limitation of the system is that it is bulky and, hence, its capacity is likely to be limited in size. Secondly, there is a system of internal storage that permits a much larger capacity in a smaller space, namely, disk storage—the same system that can be used for storing information outside the computer. The disadvantage of disk storage is that it does not provide instantaneous access to the information stored. The amount of time involved in the retrieval of information is only a very small fraction of a second, but these small fractions add up when thousands or millions of retrievals have to be made in handling a single problem. Each item of information is stored in a particular location in the storage system and each location has an *address*. The addresses are simply numbers that indicate particular storage locations. Thus, the address represented by the number 292 represents a particular location where information is stored. A program might direct the machine to go to location 292 and read the information stored there before performing some operation on it. When the computer reads information from a storage location, the information is not erased. Only when new information is placed in a storage location is the original information stored there erased.

The processing unit generally consists of one or more registers in which information is placed and in which operations are performed on the information. For example, the machine may be directed to take whatever number is stored in 292 and place it in the register of the processing unit. A second command to the machine may call for the removal of the number stored in memory location 396 and to add to it the number from location 292, which has already been entered in the register. The register now contains the sum of the two numbers. A third command may call for the removal of the sum in the register and the storage of the sum in memory location 896. The register in which such operations are performed is commonly referred to as the *accumulator*.

Finally, every computer has a control unit that interprets the program of instructions and arranges for their execution. The control unit takes commands from the stored program in numerical order and keeps track of which command is being worked on at a particular time. As soon as one command is executed, the machine moves to the next appropriate command. Hence the control unit goes through the cycle of obtaining a command, interpreting it, executing it, and then reading a new command.

A program may also require a machine to make certain decisions and to undertake work in terms of the results of those decisions. At a certain point the machine may be instructed to apply a test of significance, such as a test for the significance of the difference between two means. If the difference between the means is significant beyond a certain level, then certain additional tests are applied; but if the difference does not surpass the particular level, then the work is terminated. In order for a computer to make such decisions and to take appropriate actions, the details of how the decisions are made have to be spelled out precisely and in detail in the program.

Communication with the Computer

Computers are machines that do exactly what they are told with great rapidity and high precision. They can provide answers to problems only when given precise instructions in a form they can understand. Communication with computers is possible because of the existence of languages that have been specially designed for this purpose. Ordinary English is so thoroughly ambiguous and imprecise that it could not be used as a language for communicating with computers; it has been necessary, therefore, to invent languages that have vastly greater precision. These languages generally involve the common mathematical symbols, such as plus and equals, and also many common English words such as, SUM, DO, GO TO, READ INPUT, WRITE OUTPUT, and END. An example of a program is shown in Figure 7.

In order to function, a computer requires a sequence of commands referred to as a program. This set of commands is written in a programming language but, from the point of view of the machine (with no apologies for the implied anthropomorphism), this is a shorthand kind of language that has to be translated into detailed directions before it can be actually used for controlling the operation of the machine. For example, in a program language one might write a simple arithmetic statement of the form $R = A/B$. In order for the machine to find R from the quotient of A divided by B, a series of more detailed directions must be written. The machine must be instructed to take the quantity A from storage; then take the quantity B from storage and divide it into A; and then store the quotient in the storage location assigned for R. If the program writer had to write out all the details implied in his statement $R = A/B$ a great amount of time would be occupied in preparing a program for the calculation of even a simple function. He is saved this time by having a program language that permits him to write a brief statement. There is then a simple way of converting his brief shorthand statement into the

```
      DIMENSION SX(23),SXQ(23),VAR(23),XM(23),T(23,23),X(23)
C     N IS THE NUMBER OF VARIABLES
   11 READ 7,N
    7 FORMAT (12)
      DO 2 I=1,N
      SX(I)=0
    2 SXQ(I)= 0
      TX =0
C     X(I) THE VARIABLES THAT ARE READ IN
    5 READ 1,(X(I),I= 1,N)
1     FORMAT(3F2. 0)
998   IF(X(1)-99. )3,10,3
    3 DO 4 I=1,N
C     SX(I) IS THE SUMMATION OF X
      SX(I)=SX(I)+X(I)
C     SXQ(I) THE SUMMATION OF X SQUARED
    4 SXQ(I)=SXQ(I)+X(I)*X(I)
C     TX IS THE SIZE OF SAMPLE
      TX=TX+1.
      GO TO 5
   10 DO 6 I=1,N
C     VAR(I) IS THE VARIANCE DIVIDED BY THE SIZE OF THE SAMPLE
      VAR(I)= (TX*SXQ(I)-SX(I)*SX(I))/(TX*TX*(TX-1. ))
    6 XM(I)= SX(I)/TX
C     MEAN OF X(I)
      DO 16 I=1,N
      DO 16 J= 1,N
C     T(I,J)= (X(I) MEAN-X(J) MEAN) DIV BY SQ RT OF (VAR(I)/N+VAR(J)/N)
   16 T(I,J)=(XM(I)-XM(J))/SQRT (VAR(I)+VAR(J))
      PUNCH 8,TX
C     NO. OF DATA CARDS
    8 FORMAT (F8. 2,2X,5HCARDS)
      PUNCH 19
   19 FORMAT (5HMEANS)
C     HEADING CARD-MEANS
      PUNCH 18, (XM(I),I= 1,N)
   18 FORMAT (F7. 2,15F5. 2)
      PUNCH 20
C     HEADING CARD SIG. DIFF. BETWEEN MEAN
   20 FORMAT(24HSIG. DIFF. BETWEEN MEANS)
      PUNCH 88, ((T(I,J),J= 1,N),I=1,N)
88    FORMAT(8F10. 5)
      GO TO 11
      END
```

FIGURE 7. *Illustration of a program written in FORTRAN.*

detailed instructions required by the computer. The conversion of the shorthand statement to computer longhand is undertaken by means of a device known as a *compiler*. The statements written in the programming language are expanded by this device into detailed instructions. Sometimes this may involve a very large expansion indeed. A statement calling for a square root, or a sine, or a logarithm can easily be expanded into a set of more than fifty steps.

A program may contain a number of what are referred to as subroutines. For example, a routine for the extraction of square roots can be stored to be available whenever needed. The existence of such subroutines can greatly simplify the preparation of instructions because, in place of a long set of instructions needed for calculating square roots each time a square root is needed, a single command can be used calling for the subroutine.

Many different program languages have been invented for special purposes. For example, Cobol is a language that is particularly well suited for handling many kinds of business problems. The letters in Cobol stand for *Common Business Oriented Language*. Many other languages have been developed for special purposes. Fortran (*Formula Translator*), one of the first programming languages to be developed, has particular advantages in handling mathematical quantities and is probably the most widely used computer language at the present time. An attempt has been made to establish through an international committee a uniform international programming language; however, although the specifications for such a language have been drawn up, there are few signs that such a language is likely to be adopted very soon. The student who takes a short course in a programming language in America today is more likely to be trained in Fortran than in any other language, perhaps because equipment using that language is widely available. Figure 7 gives an example of a Fortran program.

The programming languages suitable for handling numerical data and the solution of algebraic problems are not generally suitable, without modification, for handling other forms of symbols such as those that are used in logic. When a programmer wishes to have a computer undertake logical derivations or manipulate symbols according to some set of rules other than those involved in arithmetic, he must use language that has been specifically built or adapted for that purpose. An adaptation of Fortran for this purpose has the exotic name of Lisp (signifying *List Processor*). This language is useful for instructing computers to play games such as bridge and chess and has important applications in the study of certain problems in the behavioral sciences.

The reader is referred to elementary texts on computers (B. F. Green, 1963) and to the manuals put out by computer manufacturers if he wishes to gain further familiarity with computer languages. Specific references of the latter kind will not be given here because the manuals are revised so frequently that the references would be obsolete before they appeared in print. Such manuals provide an introduction to the syntax of the language and a classification of the statements that can be made in it. The reader should realize that syntactical rules of a programming language are far more rigid than those governing the use of common language. In a programming language the omission of a comma might jeopardize the utility of the entire program. For this reason, new programs invariably contain "bugs," and the procedure universally called debugging typically takes more time than the writing of the program itself. A check system is commonly introduced into a new program in order to facilitate the debugging procedure. Learning to write programs is an incomparably good exercise in the precise use of language.

For most applications of computers new programs do not have to be written. The reason for this is that a very large number of programs have been written in the past and most of these have been stored in libraries. Major computer centers not only have such program libraries but they also have program catalogs covering programs available in other centers. Programs are typically written in a general form that permit them to be applied to a range of problems, rather than just to the specific problem for which they were originally written. Thus, a program for computing correlations might, perhaps, have been originally written for computing all the correlations between, say, twenty-five variables; but the program could also be applied to problems involving the intercorrelations of one hundred variables or more, the limit being set by the storage capacity of the computer. A program for analysis of variance will not specify that it was designed for, say, a two-way classification problem; it will indicate that it is for an N-way classification problem. The program is a general procedure for solving a class of problems.

Often new programs can be readily adapted for new purposes. Indeed, when a program is not available, a first step taken by a programmer is likely to be that of searching for a program that can be readily adapted to the purpose at hand. The doctoral student in colleges of education is very unlikely to have new programs prepared or have old programs adapted for his purpose, because programs are available for almost every statistical manipulation he is likely to encounter.

Some Points for Graduate Students Using Computer Services

The enormous speed of computers, in comparison with desk calculators, makes them highly economic for performing statistical analyses. For example, a statistical analysis that might require six weeks of the work of a person operating a desk calculator might well be executed on a computer in less than one minute. High-speed computers will perform as many as 15,000,000 operations in a minute of time. Under such circumstances, a computer, for which the charge time is $300 per hour, may still perform extraordinarily large amounts of work for less than $25. With such facilities now almost universally available, doctoral students can embark on studies they could not have undertaken at all only a few years ago, simply because of the prohibitive cost of analyzing the data. Also, if computers are available, one can also include in the analysis procedures that have little likelihood of yielding results, yet which are of interest and useful for providing cues for further studies.

Despite all the virtues of the high-speed computer, the desk calculator still holds its own. Indeed, there are more desk calculators in existence today than ever before. One reason is that there are still many researches where it is less trouble to analyze the data on a desk calculator than it is to arrange for the computer work. For example, analyses of variance involving experiments with small samples are so readily computed by hand that they might as well be. In addition, after data has been processed by computer, the research worker may want to perform additional analyses, which are readily calculated from the statistics that the computer has already provided. Often a substantial amount of hand calculation follows an analysis on a computer.

The research worker should not be tempted to ask for computer help merely because he would not know how to undertake the analysis himself. He must also be cautious in handing over data to a computer without examining it carefully himself. There is much to be said for a researcher knowing his data well. Sometimes an examination of the data will indicate that a proposed analysis cannot be appropriately undertaken. A simple analysis involving means and standard deviations is often profitably undertaken before the data is sent away for more sophisticated analyses.

A check should be undertaken of the statistical analysis that is returned from the computer because, although computers virtually do not make mistakes, programmers sometimes do. The author can recall an occasion when a large table of correlations appeared to be providing results inconsistent with all expectations. The hand calculation of a few of the correlations indicated that those produced by the computer were incorrect. What had happened was that the program used to arrange them for the print-out had an error in it and they had been printed in an incorrect order. In such operations, the possibilities of human error are always large. Some kind of independent spot-check is mandatory.

Applications of Computers

A new and increasing use of computers in the field of education is for record keeping. Many schools are moving toward a plan where there will be a record-keeping center to serve many schools and, probably, many school systems. The advantages of such a system are great, not only for the research worker, but for the teacher and administrator. The fact that all the files on a pupil are kept centrally does not mean that the teacher will not have access to them. Indeed, data systems exist that permit the teacher to obtain full and complete data on a pupil by the pressing of a button. Methods of providing recorded data on television screens could permit the teacher to have literally at her fingertips a large amount of data on each and every pupil in her class. The problems of the central storage of data and the provision of means whereby the teacher can have almost immediate access to these records have been solved, but much further from a solution are the problems of getting the teacher to use the information available in the making of decisions. Experience with information systems in business has tended to show that executives who have access to the fullest information for the making of decisions do not tend to use more than a small fraction of the information available. Many supervisors suspect that much the same is true of teachers. Decisions tend to be made in spite of the data rather than on the basis of the data. In order to plan information systems much more needs to be known about the habits of teachers in handling information. Studies need also be undertaken of methods of improving the teacher's use of information.

One suspects that the major use of computers in education will be in relation to such administrative tasks as room assignments in high schools; preparing payrolls and payroll records; keeping teacher personnel records and preparing simple studies related to problems of teacher personnel; keeping inventories of books and materials used by students; and similar housekeeping functions.

Computers have an additional application in helping to arrive at decisions on the basis of information. This application virtually lets the computer make the decision. For example, a physician can collect data on a person's heart by means of an electrocardiograph and other devices. He can then feed the data into a computer and receive back a diagnosis. The computer has been programmed to make the diagnosis from data collected on a large number of heart patients whose diagnosis had been clearly established. Now, in the case of certain heart ailments, it can be shown that a computer will make better use of data than the physician and provide a more accurate diagnosis than he is able to provide. One suspects that there are many other problems encountered by professional people where similar aid in problem solving by computers might be beneficial. The day may come when the reading specialist can provide a computer with extensive data collected on a child who is a reading problem and have the computer not only provide the diagnosis of the source of the difficulty but also recommend procedures for handling it. Computers, unlike humans, can function completely rationally and do not jump to conclusions before the data have been fully examined.

Because the computer can be made to behave completely rationally, it is sometimes thought of as representing an artificial intelligence. Those who have viewed computers from this point of view have been impressed with the fact that computers can demonstrate completely rational sequences of operations with much less irrelevant action than can the human. In a sense, man has been able to create a thinking machine that overcomes the deficiencies in thinking that he has, at last, come to recognize in himself. Man can program such a machine to think the way he knows he should think rather than the way he does actually think. The general use of such problem solvers will encounter obstacles, for man has a way of wanting to solve his own problems rather than having them solved for him.

The conception of the computer as an artificial intelligence has led also to a new approach to the study of human thinking and problem solving. This approach is known as simulation. Even though a computer may behave completely rationally, man does not. One may ask what has to be introduced into the function of a computer as an artificial intelligence in order to make it behave like a human problem solver. By programming computers so that they are only partly rational in their behavior, scientists hope to achieve some understanding of how man thinks. It is argued that if a computer were programmed to behave like a human problem solver then the working of the computer might provide some clues concerning the functioning of the human intellect. Substantial effort has been devoted to this approach to the study of human problem solving, but the time is too early to say whether it will be profitable. A book of collected writings on this topic edited by H. Borko (1962) indicates the vigor of this scientific field. Nevertheless, the fact seems clear that it is much easier to program a machine so that it behaves completely rationally than to program it so that it behaves like a human.

A relatively new application of computers is to use them as a component in teaching machines. In one of the most sophisticated of such existing systems, the computer controlling the teaching machine is located at Endicott, New York, but the stations where the students are located can be any place in the country. The computer provides information to the student with a problem for him to solve. The student types out his answer, which is transmitted to the computer where it is evaluated for correctness. The student then receives an evaluation. The student can also ask the computer for further information, but he is limited both in the words he can use and in the syntactical structures of his questions. Any extensive use of such a system for teaching would almost require that the student acquire skill in the use of a language for communicating with the machine. The Endicott computer is programmed for the teaching of quite complex subject matter, but other computers have been designed for teaching simpler skills such as spelling. For example, the *University of Pittsburgh Research and Development Center* has used its own computer for instructing children in the lower elementary grades in spelling. The device asks a child to spell a word through its recorded speech unit. The child then attempts to spell out the word on a typewriter keyboard and the letters he selects appear on a screen. When he makes a mistake he is told to try again. If he does not succeed, he is then shown the correct spelling. Later, the machine returns to the same word and the pupil has another chance to spell it.

There may well be times and places where such devices can be profitably used. Because gadgetry in our society has high status, work on computers as components of teaching machines has received extensive support. However, one's enthusiasm for gadgetry should not deter him from soberly considering that more might have been achieved by devoting the same money to the improvement of printed material. Guttenberg, with his printing press, still has no rival as an educational innovator.

SUMMARY

1. The first conception of the modern computer was developed in the last century by Charles Babbage, but mechanical and electronic design had not then developed to the point where a machine with the capability envisaged could be developed.

2. Computers are either digital or analog. The practical analog computer came first but it is being rapidly replaced by the digital computer. The digital computer can be adapted to more and different purposes than the analog computer and has, hence, greater flexibility.

3. All computers involve four essential systems, namely, (1) the input-output system, (2) the storage system, (3) the processing system, and (4) the control system.

4. Instructions to a computer have to be given through the medium of statements written in a computer language. The choice of a language depends on the purpose involved. Some computer languages are much better for some purposes than for others. The statements written in the computer language represent general commands to the machine. These general commands have to be translated into detailed step-by-step procedures that will tell the machine exactly what to do. The translation of the general commands into detailed instructions is undertaken entirely by machine.

5. Most programs call for a number of subroutines that are already stored in the computer. A common subroutine used in statistical analysis is that for calculating a square root.

6. Computer centers have libraries of programs from which one can draw a program suitable for any commonly used statistical technique. Very rarely will the graduate student of education need to have a program especially written for handling his particular problem. The latter will happen only if he decides to use some very new or unusual technique of analysis. The programs available can often be adapted for new purposes.

7. Substantial quantities of work can be undertaken by computers for a very moderate fee. However, the computer should not be used simply because the student does not know how to do the work himself, for he should be in a position to check the work of the computer by a spot-checking procedure.

8. The major impacts of the computer in the field of education are for record keeping, scheduling, and accounting.

9. Because the computer is capable of rational performance, some have viewed the device as representing an artificial intelligence. Considerable thought has been given to the problem of extending the capability of the computer so that it can become a universal problem solver.

10. Experiments have been conducted with computers to explore their usefulness as devices for controlling teaching situations. Although this new exploration is an interesting one, there is little evidence as yet that it will solve major educational problems.

‖‖‖‖‖‖‖‖‖‖‖‖‖‖‖‖‖‖‖‖‖‖‖‖‖‖‖‖‖‖‖‖‖‖‖‖‖‖

CHAPTER 18

Some Final Considerations

I N THIS book, an attempt has been made to familiarize the student with some of the methods that can be adapted or that already have been adapted to the purposes of educational research. If this presentation has left the impression that a knowledge of techniques placed at the command of a shrewd analytic intellect represents the essential ingredient of successful research, the author is guilty of misrepresentation. This final chapter has been written to impress the reader with the importance of other factors in a successful research enterprise. To some extent, this chapter must be speculative, for very little is known concerning the personal and environmental conditions that are necessary for the production of creative research.

Ability, Productivity, and Some Reasons
for Lack of Productivity

The conditions necessary for high-level creative work have been identified to only a limited degree. At present there is much speculation concerning this matter—and a little research, much of which is stimulated by the worthy hope that it will be found that a democratic type of organization is most favorable to the creative process. Certainly it will be many decades before sufficient information will have been acquired about this problem to advise the student concerning the environment he should seek out if he is to be creative in his research. Perhaps different students will have widely different requirements in this respect. However, there would be some agreement among graduate school faculties that certain students who seem to have all the intellectual skills necessary for creative talent often fail to produce original research, and that lack of productivity often has its roots in certain common causes that must be given brief consideration here. The student who is aware of some of these conditions may find means of avoiding them.

First, there is the problem of excessive ambition. Every graduate school is familiar with the student who cannot find a problem worthy of his consideration. He sees his fellow graduate students as persons willing to study trivia that are beneath his dignity. He is likely to spend time disparaging the efforts of his associates. It is most desirable not to be this type of student. Until a person has accomplished much in research, he is not in a position to criticize the simple-mindedness of his associates. Only accomplishment in research brings with it the right to criticize, except for the few who have established themselves as recognized critical reviewers. The behavior of the graduate student who is hypercritical of others is usually interpreted to be a symptom of defensiveness and of feelings of inadequacy. The student should be aware of this, and perhaps this awareness will help him avoid this error.

The foregoing remarks need to be qualified. Often the overambitious graduate student has the greatest potential as a creative research worker. The student who is content to study some commonplace problem that can be solved by routine methods is probably concerned mainly with obtaining his doctoral degree and then leaving research forever. He has neither the ambition nor the creative talent for a career in research, which takes high ambition and a willingness to undertake a search for knowledge as a pursuit worthwhile in itself. Perhaps, also, a successful scientific career requires a certain impermeability to criticism and a tendency to pursue courses of action that others think are unproductive.

The author also suspects that the graduate student who is most capable of generating novel research ideas is the one who is often least able to evaluate such ideas critically. This is hardly surprising, for critical abilities seem in themselves to inhibit the free flow of ideas. Those who have ideas may be expected to have many poor ones as well as many good ones, and they need help in sorting them into one category or the other. Such students need the help of faculty advisers who recognize worthwhile and researchable ideas and who praise the student for them. Too often such students are met with a barrage of criticism directed toward their poor ideas and do not receive credit for their imaginative talent.

Another source of lack of productivity is found when the researcher feels satisfied with his results only if they show high consistency with expectation. Part of this tendency is, no doubt, a fear of criticism. To present clear-cut results that can have only one possible interpretation places the scientist in a position beyond reproach and beyond criticism, but few experiments ever yield results of this kind. Most scientists in the behavioral area must be content with results that show some accordance with expectation but involve at least some small suspicion that the results could have arisen by chance. Difficulty in tolerating the ambiguity that such results provide has prevented many students from finishing well-conceived studies. Many completed studies remain unpublished for this same reason. This problem, insofar as it arises in a graduate school of education, is probably best handled through encouragement given by the faculty.

An interesting problem in this connection is posed by the work of Mendel, who, it will be remembered, counted the frequency with which smooth peas and wrinkled peas appeared in certain hybrids. Statisticians who have examined his results state that they manifest a much closer agreement with the frequencies that would be expected on the basis of his theory than are ordinarily encountered. Some have suspected that the Abbé may have seen that his results showed some departure from theoretical expectation and, fearing that his work might be rejected by the scientific body, made some adjustments in his data. Of course this is just a hypothesis, for we cannot possibly know with any certainty whether he did or did not tamper with his data. The moral to be learned is perhaps that even if Mendel did adjust his data, the theory that it was designed to substantiate was rejected by one of the world's leading scientific societies, and thirty years passed before it was accepted.

Another difficulty that seems to arise in the case of some research workers and that chronically limits their productivity is failure to communicate with others during the early planning stages of the inquiry. Such communication, with the resulting exchange of ideas, seems to be an important factor in the development of the research worker. It permits both the critical review of research ideas as well as the development of these ideas to the point where they are research-able. True, there are some workers who communicate little with their associates and yet produce research of real value, but such workers are generally persons who would be considered to be of the highest capability, even by graduate school standards. Most graduate students require substantial interaction with their associates as a part of their education and as a part of the process of evolving a researchable problem.

Difficulties of communication often permeate the entire research process. Some students show evidence of being able to conduct a well-designed experiment even though they do not seem able to describe it to others at the time or to write a presentable account of what they have done at a later date. Perhaps the administrative solution to the difficulties of such students might be to team them with some of their more communicative associates who are less adept as experimentalists. Graduate schools may have some difficulty in accepting such a solution.

Importance of the Social Atmosphere in Creative Work

Historians agree that creative work has been produced in quantity by mankind only at certain times in history. For reasons that are largely unknown, these periods of creativity have usually followed great wars. The social climate seems to be an essential factor in releasing creative talents, for one may assume that the available talent is the same from generation to generation.

It is doubtful whether graduate schools of education have been particularly successful in providing a social environment congenial to the development of creative talent. Schools of education, like most graduate schools, are designed for students who are willing to conform to a mass of rules and regulations, who take and pass required courses regardless of whether or not they consider them worthwhile, and who are willing to develop a dissertation about a problem of interest to the faculty. As Benjamin Bloom and his associates have shown at the University of Chicago, the college professor is interested in developing students similar to himself. There is nothing wrong with this—except for the fact that there is now considerable evidence that the creative person tends to be a nonconformist and is somewhat insensitive to the demands of the community in which he lives. Nonconformist students have always had their problems. One is reminded at this point that Oxford University was founded by a group of students from the University of Paris who did not like the way in which the latter institution was run.

Perhaps the nonconformist student who has never regarded himself as such may, by reading this, recognize the source of some of his difficulties and benefit by this insight. It is the writer's fond hope that some faculty members who read this may as a result develop softened attitudes toward students who find that bearing with the rules and regulations of a graduate school is distasteful. A sympathetic attitude toward the oddities that go along with creative talent would do much to generate in schools of education an atmosphere in which original research can thrive.

Another major difficulty in generating an atmosphere sympathetic toward research stems from the fact that few members of most schools of education faculties engage in research and thus do not regard it as an activity about which they can speak with enthusiasm. The young research worker should probably be developed in an environment where research is pursued with an excitement that can almost be described as breathless anticipation. This is not the kind of atmosphere found in most schools of education, though it does exist in a few. This situation has not been remedied by the development of bureaus of educational research, few of which conduct work that might be described as original research or research as it is discussed in this book. Most of these bureaus devote their efforts to rendering advisory services or to conducting surveys at a rather superficial level. They have an important public relations role, and if they do not contribute to new knowledge, they do at least facilitate the dissemination of the old. They provide an atmosphere that probably encourages the development of the administrator, but none has acquired a reputation for developing research workers.

The limited scope of such bureaus and institutes has been unfortunate. Although they may have provided service to local communities, they have contributed but little to the development of educational research as a branch of endeavor in the behavioral sciences.

An alternative avenue for the development of educational research has been provided in recent years through the research and development centers that have been financed by the Federal government. These centers are typically located on campuses, but not in colleges of education. This form of organization permits them to make use of all the resources of the university to which they are attached. In addition, their location outside of the college of education protects them from being overloaded with service functions, as have the bureaus of educational research. The independence of the new centers from service functions has also helped them to provide an atmosphere in which research can flourish. The bureau of educational research has all too often become a place where the Dean could dump practical problems that school administrators in the area asked for help in solving, and the work atmosphere thus produced has not been conducive to research. The research and development centers, although working closely with the related college of education, have been able to protect the scientists in them from being pressed into service to handle matters that the local school districts should probably handle for themselves.

Prolonged and Sustained Effort in Creative Work

A major difficulty faced by the graduate student in producing research that might be called original is that this requires prolonged and enduring effort. One can be misled in this matter by the well-known fact that many important ideas have come to famous scientists at times when they were thinking about something else. This is a rather typical phenomenon among high-level scientists. However, what should not be missed in this matter is that these important ideas did not appear in individuals who had never sought to discover them. In every case, they appeared in individuals who had struggled long to find a solution, and it happened that the solution came at a moment when they were concerned with other matters. There seems no doubt that the creative person spends extended periods of great conscious effort when all of his energies are devoted to the solution of a problem; indeed his energies may be so completely channeled that he appears to have almost a detachment from the other aspects of life, even to the point where associates may consider him to be callous or thoughtless. The absent-mindedness of the intellectual is just one symptom of this deep preoccupation. In this milieu of thoughtfulness the important ideas emerge, though often at a moment when the mind has turned to other things.

The graduate student, however talented he may be, is rarely able to devote his entire energies to the solution of a single problem. He has to be preoccupied with course work and with somewhat prosaic matters such as language requirements. It is probably for this reason that even the brilliant doctoral student rarely produces a brilliant doctoral dissertation. Conditions conducive to work of this quality are not provided for the graduate student.

What has been said up to this point fails to bring out the distinction between what may be termed *creative research* and routine investigation. Most master's theses and doctoral dissertations fall into the latter category. They are designed to test some fairly obvious hypothesis. They may be considered to develop, as it were, a territory that has already been well explored, but they are valuable, for it is the well-developed territory that yields riches. The graduate student as a researcher is a developer rather than an explorer. If he makes discoveries, they are minor if not a little prosaic. It is the explorer who makes the major discoveries, and for him too are reserved the special excitements of high adventure, the despairs of failure, and occasionally the thrill of genuine discovery. The developer's life is somewhat more tranquil and decidedly less venturesome. He knows a great deal about the territory in which he is operating. He knows with some certainty what will be the outcome of his labors. In contrast, the explorer is searching for something that he does not yet know except in the vaguest way, and like Columbus, he ultimately may not recognize what he finds. The reader will clearly recognize that this book is directed toward the developer rather than the explorer.

B. Ghiselin (1954) has described this aspect of the creative process in a way that is particularly appropriate. He refers to the creative person as one who is struggling to realize the unrealized, who wants to accomplish something still beyond anything he can as yet conceive but which is there in its vaguest outline at the periphery of consciousness. The creative person may spend a lifetime in struggling to find a medium through which he can realize this objective of peripheral awareness. Many never find it.

The characteristics of the research worker that have been noted in this chapter present a problem in the matter of developing educational research. The problem is generated by the fact that many schools of education require their faculty to have had public school teaching experience. This tends to select persons who are unlikely to have much of the disposition that one might hope to see in the researcher. A person who has a real interest in theoretical problems or in such abstract matters as represent the very roots of research can hardly be expected to show a deep interest in the activities of classroom management as a possible lifetime pursuit. The outstanding research worker, with his ability to detach himself from his environment, might even be considered a poor risk as a teacher in the public schools. Schools of education should come to realize that the talents required by personnel who operate schools are probably quite different from those required in research.

The argument has often been advanced that, in order to understand educational phenomena, the research worker must have direct experience with teaching in the classroom. The argument is so sufficiently persuasive that to occupy many research positions in education one is still required to have had experience teaching in the public schools. However, the argument finds little support in the behavioral and social sciences. The objective and detached attitude of the anthropologist, who has no personal involvement in the habits of the primitive peoples he is observing, permits him to interpret his data with a cold clarity he could not display if he had been raised by the same primitive tribe. One does not benefit in the study of criminology by having had a background in crime. Personal experience in the classroom may give one an emotional involvement in educational affairs that makes it difficult, if not impossible, to perceive them objectively. The training of the research worker requires that he have long and extended experience with the events of the world that he intends to investigate, but not personal involvement in those events.

Educational Research Organizations Sponsored by the Federal Government

Mention has already been made of the fact that the Federal government has, in recent years, supported a number of research centers in universities. Each of these centers has tended to have some specialized purpose and has adopted a research program directed toward its particular goal. Each center is supposedly engaged in three activities that are described as research, development, and dissemination. The original notion underlying the plan for the centers was that progress would proceed through research being undertaken in the center. Progress, in turn, would lead to the development of new educational techniques and procedures, and these would then be made available to the schools through activities involving the dissemination of information. The formula for advancement of research-development-dissemination is a bureaucratic conception of how progress in education should take place. The formula has a certain plausibility to it, but the history of progress provides little evidence that any simple procedure of this kind is likely to work. After reading this book, the student should not have much difficulty in pointing out some of the reasons why the formula is probably an unsound one.

Nevertheless, the research and development centers are places where some of the better educational research is being conducted at the present time. These organizations are also excellent training grounds for future research workers. The graduate student interested in developing his research skills and in devoting his life to research would do well to consider obtaining a part-time job in a center where he can serve as an apprentice to a well-established research scientist. The skills of the research worker are learned largely through such an apprenticeship. Books and coursework provide only a sketchy background on which actual sophistication in research can be built through other experiences. In selecting a center in which to apply for an assistantship, the graduate student should first find out which one of the various centers is concerned with problems in harmony with his own interests.

In addition to the university-located centers, a number of regional laboratories have also been developed. The functions of these organizations are still obscure. Functions will probably arise out of the experience gained in the first ten years of their operation. The claim is that they are to help schools apply the knowledge that has been gained through research, but nobody seems to be willing to define what this knowledge is that should be applied. Whether there is, or is not, a body of knowledge that can be applied to the immediate solution of educational problems is a matter about which there is controversy. Some of the speakers for the present educational policies speak as if there were a tremendous storehouse of immediately applicable knowledge, but many scientists take the position that the amount of available organized knowledge that can have direct impact on education is very limited indeed. Others have proposed that extensive Federal spending, and the work of the regional laboratories, be directed toward "innovation." By this is generally meant a change in the school or in its program that looks promising but that really is not backed by any extensive knowledge. The hope underlying the policy of innovation is that some of the changes thus produced will turn out to be effective. Trying out new practices and seeing which ones work is the opposite of the rational procedure of first advancing knowledge and then basing educational reform on the knowledge thus derived. It is a policy of impatience. It is a little like kicking a machine that will not work and hoping that some component will, thereby, be shaken into place. It is based on a faith entirely different from that expressed in this book.

The Future of Educational Research

One of the few statements that one can make with confidence about the future of educational research is that there will be an increasing demand for trained personnel. As a career area, educational research is likely to offer exceptional opportunities, and particularly to those who can undertake work at a sophisticated level. Other aspects of the future remain hidden in the clouds of unresolved issues.

A major issue that still remains to be resolved pertains to the question of who should control the funds for educational research and make the decisions concerning how they are to be spent. In the

years since the late fifties, when extensive funds for educational research first were made available, a number of different solutions have
been tried. In the early days of Federal support the plan adopted was
to delegate decisions to committees of research workers from the
academic world, a practice that the academic world endorsed. Very
much the same policy was adopted by large foundations. However,
in the case of the Federal government, the delegation of responsibility
to the academic scientist soon led to conflict. The scientist urged the
support of basic research related to education and showed little interest in sponsoring research on pressing problems of local school
systems. The government was more interested in research that offered
promise of immediate impact. The scientist was more likely to suggest
supporting research on how an impoverished environment depresses
intellectual functioning rather than research on the development of
a curriculum for disadvantaged children. The scientist would argue
that a first step has to be an understanding of what happens to the
intellect of the disadvantaged child and, only after understanding has
been achieved, can one design an effective curriculum for these children. Government departments have tended to take the position that
an elected administration has to show results for the money spent
during a term of office, and the only way to do this is to attack practical problems directly. The conflict between political interests and
scientific interests represents the major conflict in the matter of the
control of funds for educational research. The conflict exists, to a great
extent, because the Federal support of research on a large scale is a
relatively new kind of governmental phenomenon and the details of
how control shall be exercised over the funds involved have still to
be worked out. There is no simple formula for solving this kind of
problem, but the solution will have to grow out of many decades of
experience. A final point must also be made in this connection. It is
not only the Federal government that is caught in this conflict about
problems of control. Some foundations that have supported educational research are also caught in the problem of deciding whether to
have research policies established for them by external committees of
competent research workers or whether to delegate these responsi-
bilities to their own bureaucracies.

Another major unresolved issue is the role that colleges of education are to play in the development of educational research and the
training of research workers. Although these institutions can point to
a glorious history in the names of E. L. Thorndike and C. H. Judd,
they do not present a glamorous present. The number of colleges of
education that have a distinguished research program is still very

small, and the growth of research on education outside of these colleges has given them a declining role in this respect on the national scene. Many factors have contributed to this trend including the predominant interest of professors of education in philosophical rather than scientific problems; the appointment of deans from the area of educational administration, where interests are mainly in immediate practical problems; and the appointment of faculty with the dispositions of teachers rather than the dispositions of research workers. None of these factors reflect in any way on the competence of the faculty and administration of colleges of education, but they are facts of history that help explain why research is not a flourishing enterprise in schools of education. A change will not come readily, but it must come if research is to become an integral part of the educational enterprise.

The Application of Research

Few, if any, would dispute the view that research on problems related to education should ultimately lead to some kind of application. The expectations of the research worker are that sound applications are not going to come rapidly, but the legislator commonly hopes for dramatic applications in a short time, and preferably before the next election. Some legislators even take the position that only research having direct and immediate applications to educational problems should be undertaken at all, but scientists argue that only very basic research is going to have extensive impact. The nature of application is a problem to which we will finally turn here.

A first and most immediate impact of science on practical affairs is that it provides a precise language that can be used for discussing natural phenomena. For example, not only is it vastly more precise to speak of electrical storms than to say that the great god Thor is wielding his mighty hammer, but also a recognition of the nature of lightning leads to measures that can prevent damage from lightning. The first and simplest kind of application involves an improvement in the precision with which one can talk about frequently occurring, but important, happenings. This kind of impact of research on education has taken place and continues to take place. It was a real step forward when a teacher no longer commented that Jimmy did not have the moral fortitude to direct his attention diligently to his studies, but said, instead, that Jimmy had symptoms of brain damage. At least the latter kind of statement shows that thinking is on the road toward a solution, whereas the statement about moral fortitude indicates not only vagueness of thought but also a philosophy that has long been unsuccessful in solving educational problems.

A second and related application of research occurs when knowledge changes the general theory of what happens in education and how changes in pupils take place. Once research had shown that the mastery of complex subject matter had little value in disciplining the mind, the tendency was to think of such subject matter in terms of the other values it might have. If the study of Latin had little value in providing broad training of the mind, then it might be regarded as having cultural values for the few who might wish to enjoy the literature of antiquity. The main impact of this change of thinking was probably on the advice given in academic counseling situations where Latin came to be regarded as food for the scholar rather than as remedial work for the scatterbrained. In addition, the development of scientific concepts may give those involved in the planning of education insight into what areas of reform energies can be most profitably directed. So long as educators thought that the mind could be trained by presenting the pupil with very difficult assignments, the task of finding suitable mind-taxing exercises was a major one for teachers. Once this doctrine was disposed of, teachers were free to engage in the solution of more significant problems. Research changes our ways of thinking about problems and, as this happens, the activities of curriculum planners and others are changed in subtle ways. These changes in thinking are often difficult to identify, except over long periods of time.

A third kind of application is found when research justifies rule-of-thumb procedures that have long been practiced. An example is found in research on punishment, which has shown it to be an ineffective procedure for controlling learning or controlling behavior. Teachers and professors of education have long argued that punishment should not be used, although their arguments have often had a different basis than the concept that punishment is inefficient. Research that justifies current practice is useful in ending controversy, but it also often serves the purpose of providing a foundation for research leading to more powerful forms of application.

A fourth form of application is that in which a body of research indicates clearly that certain new practices should be adopted. This kind of application does not generally happen until research has advanced to a sophisticated level, although there are some instances where a relatively new branch of science has been able to produce innovation in practice. A few such research-derived innovations can be pointed to in education. For example, Thorndike was one of the first to point out that words differed in the extent to which they were understood and that the difficulty level of words, thus defined, was dependent on the frequency with which the words had been encountered. Thorndike then went on to suggest that the difficulty level of words could be measured by counting the frequency with which they occurred in common literature. He then proposed that these measures could be used for selecting words for elementary school readers and children's literature. In one of the first major applications of psychology to the curriculum, Thorndike adjusted the vocabulary level of many of the children's literary classics in order to make them more comprehensible for children.

Despite the early success of Thorndike in making far-reaching changes in the printed materials produced for children, the number of direct and sweeping applications of research has been relatively few. Perhaps later research workers have not been able to bring to the solution of problems a comparable genius, but perhaps the number of possible direct and sweeping applications may not be great.

Single researches rarely, if ever, have direct applications to the field of practical affairs. Indeed, the results of single researches should be held in question until the research has been repeated in other laboratories. The reason for this is that findings are sometimes dependent on the existence of the particular conditions that occurred locally in the place where the research was originally undertaken. For this reason, a *single* study, however great the practical implications of the study may seem to be, can be considered to provide only suggestive results. The time when the results of research can be most legitimately applied is when many studies are involved and there is no doubt that the results can be replicated by different investigators working in different places. When the results of different studies fit together, knowledge is provided that has substance and solidity that the results of a single study never have. This is the kind of knowledge that research should seek to develop and that practical people should attempt to apply.

An illustration of an organized body of knowledge with potential applications is that involving the effect of environmental deprivation during development. Knowledge concerning this problem has come from such diverse sources as the effect of blindfolding rats during the developmental stage; the effect of social deprivation during infancy on the subsequent behavior of primates; and the effects of serious cultural deprivation on the psychological development of the human child. The findings fit together extremely well and, ultimately, will provide an important basis for some aspects of educational planning. The reason they do not have any extensive immediate application is that they strongly suggest that what is needed are organized programs of education for the underprivileged during the first few years of life. Because such programs do not yet exist, the research findings cannot be applied. Educational programs for the early years for the under-privileged will ultimately come into existence and, when they do, the results of research will play an important part in their design. The problem of applying educational research is much more than a prob-lem of grabbing research findings and applying them immediately to the solution of educational problems.

A final application of research is in providing a basis for further research. This is the application about which there is much complaint among legislators who have the impractical dream of seeing every research enterprise producing results that immediately influence edu-cation. Yet the fact is that the accumulation of knowledge to the point where applications of consequence can be made demands that much of research be part of a chain of inquiries that result in the organized accumulation of knowledge. At least this has been the pattern of research and development in the physical sciences where, for example, a chain of research studies on laser beams over twenty years has resulted in eventual applications to laser communication systems, methods for boring holes in diamonds, and surgical tech-niques for repairing detached retinas. Although the need for political impact may attempt to pressure scientists in shortening the long chain of research events that lead to eventual application, there just may not be any short-cut methods except in a very few instances.

A final point to make is that much of the knowledge that can be acquired, which has important implications for educational change, may not be applicable without the exercise of political power. Scien-tists lack this power. For example, even though research may show that the way to overcome the effects of cultural deprivation in children raised in slum areas is to provide them with an educational program beginning with the first year of life and extending to adulthood, it seems quite clear at the time of writing that funds are not going to be made available to finance such a program. However clear-cut the results of research in this area may be, they cannot be applied without the exercise of political power—the crucial factor in application. Much of the knowledge available at this time cannot be employed to produce a more effective educational system simply because those who have political power are not going to use it to produce the expensive changes that are suggested. In time, the teaching profession may well gain the political power necessary for bringing about needed changes that research findings indicate and support.

References

Allport, Gordon W. *Pattern and Growth in Personality.* New York: Holt, Rinehart & Winston, Inc., 1961.

—————. *The Use of Personal Documents in Psychological Science.* New York: Social Science Research Council, Bulletin No. 49, 1942.

Ammons, Helen, and Arthur L. Irion. "A Note on the Ballard Reminiscence Phenomenon," *Journal of Experimental Psychology,* XLVII (1954), 184–186.

Ausubel, D. P. *The Psychology of Meaningful Verbal Learning.* New York: Grune and Stratton, 1963.

Backstrom, C. H., and G. D. Hursh. *Survey Research.* Evanston, Ill.: Northwestern University Press, 1963.

Bales, R. F., and H. Gerbrands. "The Interaction Recorder, an Apparatus and Check List for Sequential Content Analysis of Social Interaction," *Human Relations,* 1 (1948), 456–463.

Ballard, P. B. "Obliviscence and Reminiscence," *British Journal of Psychology, Monographs Supplement,* 1, No. 2 (1913).

Bandura, A., and R. A. Walters. *Social Learning and Personality Development.* New York: Holt, Rinehart and Winston, Inc., 1963.

Barzun, J., and H. F. Graff. *The Modern Researcher.* New York: Harcourt, Brace & World, Inc., 1957.

Bellack, A. A. *The Language of the Classroom.* New York: Cooperative Research Project No. 2023, Teachers College, Columbia University, 1965.

Berelson, Bernard. *Content Analysis.* New York: The Free Press of Glencoe, Inc., 1952.

Bergmann, Gustav. *Philosophy of Science.* Madison, Wis.: University of Wisconsin Press, 1957.

Bloom, Benjamin S. (ed.) *A Taxonomy of Educational Objectives.* New York: Longmans, Green & Co., Inc., 1956.

427

Boring, Edwin G. "Intelligence as the Tests Test It," *New Republic*, XXXV, No. 444 (1923), 35–37.

———. "The Nature and History of Experimental Control," *American Journal of Psychology*, LXVII (1954), 573–589.

Borko, Harold. *Computer Applications in the Behavioral Sciences*. New York: Prentice-Hall, 1962.

Broadbent, D. E. *Perception and Communication*. London, England: Pergamon Press, Inc., 1958.

Bruner, Jerome S., Jacqueline J. Goodnow, and George A. Austin. *A Study of Thinking*. New York: John Wiley & Sons, Inc., 1956.

Bruner, J. S., R. R. Olver, P. M. Greenfield, *et al. Studies in Cognitive Growth*. New York: John Wiley & Sons, Inc., 1966.

Brunswick, Egon. *Systematic and Representative Design of Psychological Experiments*. Berkeley: University of California Syllabus Series, No. 304, 1947.

Burke, Arvid J. *Documentation in Education*, fifth ed. New York: Teachers College Press, Teachers College, Columbia University, 1966.

Campbell, D. T., and J. C. Stanley. "Experimental and Quasi-Experimental Designs for Research on Teaching," in Gage, N. L. (ed.), *Handbook of Research on Teaching*. Chicago: Rand McNally Company, 1963.

Campbell, Norman. *What Is Science?* New York: Dover Publications, Inc., 1952.

Campbell, Roald F., and James M. Lipham (eds.) *Administrative Theory As a Guide to Action*. Chicago: Midwest Administration Center, 1960.

Cantril, Hadley, *Gauging Public Opinion*. Princeton, N. J.: Princeton University Press, 1947.

Chapanis, A. "Men, Machines, and Models," *American Psychologist*, XVI (1961), 113–131.

Coats, W. D. *Investigation and Simulation of the Relationships Among Selected Classroom Variables*. Cooperative Research Project No. 6-8330, 1966.

Cogan, M. L. *Pupil Survey*. Copyright ©, 1953, by the President and Fellows of Harvard College.

———. "The Behavior of Teachers and the Productive Behavior of Their Pupils," *Journal of Experimental Education*, XXVII (1958), 89–124.

Conant, James B. *On Understanding Science*. New Haven, Conn.: Yale University Press, 1946.

Coombs, Clyde H. *Theory of Data*. New York: John Wiley & Sons, Inc. 1964.

Cronbach, Lee J. "Coefficient Alpha and the Internal Structure of Tests," *Psychometrika*, XVI (1951), 297–334.

Dale, Edgar, and Gerhard Eichholz. *Children's Knowledge of Words*. Columbus: Bureau of Educational Research, Ohio State University, 1960.

————, and Jeanne Chall. "A Formula for Predicting Readability," *Educational Research Bulletin*, XXVII (1948), 11–20 and 37–54.

Davidson, H. P. "An Experimental Study of Bright, Average and Dull Children at the Four-Year Mental Level," *Genetic Psychology Monographs*, IX (1931), 119–289.

Davis, F. B. *Item Analysis Data: Their Interpretation, Computation, and Use in Test Construction*. Cambridge, Mass.: Graduate School of Education, Harvard University, 1946.

Dewey, John. *How We Think*. Boston: D. C. Heath & Company, 1910.

Dollard, John, and Neal E. Miller. *Personality and Psychotherapy*. New York: McGraw-Hill Book Company, Inc., 1950.

Evaluative Criteria. Washington, D. C.: National Study of Secondary School Evaluation, 1950.

Evaluative Criteria. Washington, D. C.: Cooperative Study of Secondary School Standards, 1960.

Evaluative Criteria for Junior High Schools. Washington, D. C.: National Study of Secondary School Standards, 1963.

Flanagan, J. C., *et al*. *Project Talent: The American High School Student*. Pittsburgh: University of Pittsburgh, 1964.

Flanders, N. "Analyzing Teacher Behavior as a Part of the Teaching Learning Process," *Educational Leadership*, XIX (1961–62), 173–180.

————. *Teacher Influence, Pupil Attitudes, and Achievement*. Prepublication manuscript of a proposed research monograph for the U. S. Office of Education, Ann Arbor, Mich., 1962.

Flesch, Rudolf. *How To Test Readability*. New York: Harper & Row, Publishers, 1951.

Fowler, H. *Curiosity and Exploratory Behavior*. New York: The Macmillan Company, 1965.

Fowler, W. "Cognitive Learning in Infancy and Early Childhood," *Psychological Bulletin*, LIX (1962), 116–152.

French, Elizabeth. *Development of a Measure of Complex Motivation*. Research Report AFPTRC-TN-56-48. Air Force Personnel and Training Research Center, Lackland Air Force Base, Texas, 1956. (Available from Armed Services Technical Information Agency Document Service Center, Dayton 2, Ohio.)

————. "Motivation as a Variable in Work-Partner Selection," *Journal of Abnormal and Social Psychology*, LIII (1956), 96–99.

Gage, N. L. (ed.). *Handbook of Research on Teaching*. Chicago: Rand McNally Company, 1963.

Gagné, Robert M. *The Conditions of Learning*. New York: Holt, Rinehart and Winston, 1965.

Gardner, John W. *Excellence, Can We Be Equal and Excellent Too?* New York: Harper and Row, 1961.

Gerlach, V. S., R. E. Schutz, R. L. Baker, and G. E. Mazer. "Effect of Variations in Test Directions on Originality of Test Response," *Journal of Educational Psychology*, LV (1964), 79–83.

Getzels, J. W. "The Question-Answer Process: A Conceptualization and Some Derived Hypotheses for Empirical Examination," *Public Opinion Quarterly*, VIII (1954), 79–91.

———, and E. G. Guba. "Social Behavior and the Administrative Process," *School Review*, LXV (1957), 423–441.

Gewirtz, J. L., and D. M. Baer. "The Effect of Brief Social Deprivation on Behaviors for a Social Reinforcer," *Journal of Abnormal and Social Psychology*, LVI (1958), 49–56(a).

———, and D. M. Baer. "Deprivation and Satiation of Social Reinforcers as Drive Conditions," *Journal of Abnormal and Social Psychology*, LVII (1958), 165–172(b).

Ghiselin, Brewster. *The Creative Process*. Berkeley: University of California Press, 1954.

Gilbert, Luther C. "Speed of Processing Visual Stimuli and Its Relation to Reading," *Journal of Educational Psychology*, LV (1959), 8–14.

Good, Carter V. *Dictionary of Education*. New York: McGraw-Hill Book Company, Inc., 1959.

Goodman, Frederick, L. "Application of Information Retrieval Principles to Education," *Proceedings, American Documentation Institute*, 1 (1963), 51–52.

Gordon, I. J. *Studying the Child in School*. New York: John Wiley and Sons, Inc., 1966.

Gottschalk, L. (ed.). *Generalization in the Writing of History*. Chicago: University of Chicago Press, 1963.

Gottschalk, L. *Understanding History*. New York: Alfred A. Knopf, Inc., 1951.

———, C. Kluckhohn, and R. Angell. *The Use of Personal Documents in History, Anthropology, and Sociology*. New York: Social Science Research Council, Bulletin 53, 1945.

Gray, W. S., and B. E. Leary. *What Makes a Book Readable?* Chicago: University of Chicago Press, 1935.

Green, B. F. *Digital Computers in Research: An Introduction for Behavioral and Social Scientists*. New York: McGraw-Hill Book Company, Inc., 1963.

Gregersen, Gayle F., and R. M. W. Travers. "A Study of the Child's Concept of the Teacher," *Journal of Educational Research*, 1968, 61 (in press).

Guba, E. G. "Research in Internal Administration," in Roald F. Campbell, and James M. Lipham (eds.), *Administration Theory as a Guide to Action*. Chicago: Midwest Administration Center, University of Chicago, 1960.

Guilford, J. P. *Psychometric Methods,* 2nd ed. New York: McGraw-Hill Book Company, Inc., 1954.

Halpin, A. W. *Theory and Research in Administration.* New York: The Macmillan Company, 1966.

Harris, Chester W. (ed.) *Problems in Measuring Change.* Madison: University of Wisconsin Press, 1963.

Hauck, Mathew, and Stanley Steinkamp. *Survey Reliability and Interviewer Competence.* Urbana: University of Illinois, 1964.

Hebb, D. O. "On the Nature of Fear," *Psychological Review,* LIII (1946), 259–276.

Heckhausen, Heinz. *The Anatomy of Achievement Motivation.* New York: Academic Press, 1967.

Heil, L. M., and C. Washburne. "Brooklyn College Research in Teacher Effectiveness," *Journal of Educational Research,* LV (1962), 347–351.

Heilprin, Lawrence H., and Frederick L. Goodman. "Analogy Between Information Retrieval and Education," *American Documentation,* XVI (1965), 163–169.

Hemphill, J. K., D. E. Griffiths, and N. Frederiksen. *Administrative Performance and Personality.* New York: Teachers College, Bureau of Publications, Columbia University, 1962.

Horst, Paul. *Psychological Measurement and Prediction.* Belmont, California: Wadsworth Publishing Company, 1966.

Hughes, M. M., and associates. *Development of the Means for Assessment of the Quality of Teaching in Elementary Schools.* Salt Lake City: University of Utah Press, 1959.

Hull, C. L. *Principles of Behavior.* New York: Appleton-Century-Crofts, Inc., 1943.

Humphreys, L. G. "Clinical Versus Actuarial Prediction," *Proceedings of the 1955 Invitational Conference on Testing Problems.* Princeton, N. J.: Educational Testing Service, 1956, 129–135.

———. "The Organization of Human Abilities," *American Psychologist,* XVII (1962), 475–483.

Hunt, E. B. *Concept Learning: An Information Processing Problem.* New York: John Wiley & Sons, Inc., 1962.

Insko, Chester A. *Theories of Attitude Change.* New York: Appleton-Century-Crofts, 1967.

Johnson, Allen. *The Historian and Historical Evidence.* Port Washington, New York: Kennikat Press, 1965.

Klare, G. R. *The Measurement of Readability.* Ames: Iowa State University Press, 1963.

Klausmeier, H. J., and C. W. Harris (eds.). *Analyses of Concept Learning.* New York: Academic Press, 1966.

Krathwohl, D. R., B. S. Bloom, and B. B. Musia. *Taxonomy of Educational Objectives, Handbook II: Affective Domain.* New York: David McKay, 1964.

Lindquist, E. F. *Design and Analysis of Experiments in Psychology and Education.* Boston: Houghton Mifflin Company, 1953.

Loevinger, Jane. "Objective Tests As Instruments of Psychological Theory," *Psychological Reports,* Monograph Supplement 9, 111 (1957), 635–694.

————, Goldine Gleser, and P. H. DuBois. "Maximizing the Discriminating Power of a Multiple Score Test," *Psychometrika,* XVIII (1953), 309–317.

Lorge, Irving. "Predicting Readability," *Teachers College Record,* XLV (1944), 404–419.

Lubin, Ardie, and Hobart G. Osborn. "A Theory of Pattern Analysis for the Prediction of a Quantitative Criterion," *Psychometrika,* XXII (1957), 63–73.

Mackie, Robert R., and Paul R. Christensen. "Translation and Application of Psychological Research," *Technical Report 716-1,* January, 1967. Human Factors Research Incorporated, Santa Barbara, California.

McCall, W. A., and J. P. Herring. *Comprehensive Curriculum Test.* New York: Teachers College, Bureau of Publications, Columbia University, 1941.

————, J. P. Herring, and J. J. Loftus. *School Practices Questionnaire.* New York: Laidlaw Brothers, 1937.

McClelland, D. C. *The Achieving Society.* Princeton, N. J.: D. Van Nostrand Co., Inc., 1961.

————, J. W. Atkinson, R. A. Clark, and E. L. Lowell. *The Achievement Motive.* New York: Appleton-Century-Crofts, Inc., 1953.

McGraw, M. G. *Growth, a Study of Johnny and Jimmy.* New York: Appleton-Century-Crofts, Inc., 1935.

————. *The Neuromuscular Maturation of the Human Infant.* New York: Columbia University Press, 1943.

McVey, William E. *Standards for the Accreditation of Secondary Schools.* Chicago: University of Chicago Press, 1942.

McPherson, Joseph H. *Predicting the Accuracy of Oral Reporting in Group Situations.* Air Force Personnel and Training Research Center, Lackland Air Force Base, Texas, Research Bulletin 54-13, 1954.

Medley, Donald M., and H. E. Mitzel. "A Technique for Measuring Classroom Behavior," *Journal of Educational Psychology,* IL (1958), 86–92.

————, and A. A. Klein. "Measuring Classroom Behavior," *Elementary School Journal,* LVII (1956–1957), 315–319.

————, Harold E. Mitzel, and Arthur N. Doi. *Analysis of Variance Models and Their Use in a Three-Way Design Without Replication.* New York:

N. Y. City Division of Teacher Education, Board of Higher Education, Research Report, No. 29, 1955.

Meehl, Paul E. *Clinical Versus Statistical Prediction: A Theoretical Analysis and a Review of the Evidence.* Minneapolis: University of Minnesota Press, 1954.

————, and K. MacCorquodale. "On a Distinction Between Hypothetical Constructs and Intervening Variables," *Psychological Review,* LV (1948), 95–142.

————, and Albert Rosen. "Antecedent Probability and Efficiency of Psychometric Signs, Patterns, or Cutting Scores," *Psychological Bulletin,* LII (1955), 194–216.

Mill, J. S. *A System of Logic, Ratiocinative and Deductive.* New York: Longmans, Green & Co., Inc., 1930.

Miller, D. R., and G. E. Swanson. *The Changing American Parent.* New York: John Wiley & Sons, Inc., 1958.

Mitzel, Harold E., and William Rabinowitz. *Assessing Social-Emotional Climate in the Classroom By Withall's Technique. Psychological Monographs,* No. 368. Washington, D. C.: American Psychological Association, 1953.

Morsh, Joseph E. *Systematic Observation of Instructor Behavior.* Air Force Personnel and Training Research Center, Lackland Air Force Base, Texas, 1955.

————, George Burgess, and Paul N. Smith. *Student Achievement as a Measure of Instructor Effectiveness.* Bulletin No. TN 55-12. Air Force Personnel and Training Research Center, Lackland Air Force Base, Texas, 1955.

Nevins, Allen. *The Gateway to History.* Chicago: Quadrangle Books, 1963.

Noble, C. E. "Selective Learning," in E. A. Bilodeau (ed.), *Acquisition of Skill.* New York: Academic Press, 1966.

Olson, Willard C. *Child Development.* Boston: D. C. Heath & Company, 1949.

Overing, R. L. R., and R. M. W. Travers. "Effect upon Transfer of Variations in Training Conditions," *Journal of Educational Psychology,* LVII (1966), 179–188.

Parten, Mildred B. *Surveys, Polls, and Samples, Practical Procedures.* New York: Harper & Row, Publishers, 1950.

Payne, S. L. "Interviewer Memory Faults," *Public Opinion Quarterly,* XIII (1949), 684–685.

Perkins, H. V. "A Procedure for Assessing the Classroom Behavior of Students and Teachers," *American Educational Research Journal,* 1 (1964), 249–260.

Platt, John R. "Strong Inference," *Science* CIVL (1964), 347–353.

Pool, Ithiel de Sola (ed.). *Trends in Content Analysis.* Urbana, Ill.: University of Illinois Press, 1959.

Rabinowitz, W., and R. M. W. Travers. "A Drawing Technique for Studying Certain Outcomes of Teacher Education," *Journal of Educational Psychology,* 1955, 46, 257–273.

Reeves, Pamela W., A. J. Goldwyn, Jessica S. Melton, and Allen Kent. *The Library of Tomorrow.* (Report of USOE Cooperative Research Project No. 1298). Cleveland: Western Reserve University, 1962.

———, A. J. Goldwyn, J. A. Melton, and A. Kent. *The Library of Tomorrow—Today.* Cleveland, Ohio: Center for Documentation and Communication Research, Western Reserve University, 1963.

Revised Manual of Accrediting. Commission on Institutions of Higher Education, North Central Association of Schools and Colleges, 1941.

Rosenthal, Robert. *Experimenter Effects in Behavioral Research.* New York: Appleton-Century-Crofts, Inc., 1966.

———. "On the Social Psychology of the Psychological Experiment," *American Scientist,* LI (1963), 268–283.

Ruger, Henry A., and Brencke Stoessinger. "On Growth of Certain Characteristics in Man," *Annals of Eugenics,* II (1927), 76–110.

Ryans, D. G. *Characteristics of Teachers.* Washington, D. C.: American Council on Education, 1960.

Scherer, G. A., and M. Wertheimer. *A Psycholinguistic Experiment in Foreign-Language Teaching.* New York: McGraw-Hill Book Company, Inc., 1964.

Sears, R. R., E. E. Maccoby, and H. Levin. *Patterns of Child Rearing.* Evanston, Ill.: Row, Peterson, and Company, 1957.

Seeman, Julius, and Nathaniel J. Raskin. "Research Perspectives in Client Centered Therapy," in O. H. Mowrer (ed.), *Theory and Research in Psychotherapy.* New York: The Ronald Press Company, 1951.

Skinner, B. F. "A Case History in Scientific Method," *American Psychologist,* XI (1956), 221–233.

Smith, B. O., and M. O. Meux. *A Study of the Logic of Teaching.* Urbana, Ill.: Bureau of Educational Research, 1965.

Smith, Henry C. *Sensitivity to People.* New York: McGraw-Hill Book Company, Inc., 1966.

Standards for Educational and Psychological Tests and Manuals. Washington, D. C.: American Psychological Association, 1966.

Stanley, Julian C. "Analysis of Variance Principles Applied to the Grading of Essay Tests," *Journal of Experimental Education,* XXX (1962), 279–283.

Stanley, J. C. "A Common Class of Pseudo-Experiments," *American Educational Research Journal,* III (1966), 79–87.

Stevens, S. S. "On the Theory of Scales of Measurement," *Science*, CIII (1946), 677–680.

Thelen, H. A. *Dynamics of Groups at Work*. Chicago: University of Chicago Press, 1954.

Thorndike E. L. *Adult Learning*. New York: The Macmillan Company, 1928.

———, and I. Lorge. *The Teacher's Word Book of 30,000 Words*. New York: Teachers College, Columbia University, 1944.

Thorndike, Robert L. "Intellectual Status and Intellectual Growth," *Journal of Educational Psychology*, LVII (1966), 121–127.

Tiedeman, David V., Joseph G. Bryan, and Philip J. Rulon. *The Utility of the Airman Classification Battery for Assignment of Airmen to Eight Air Force Specialties*. Cambridge, Mass.: Educational Research Corporation, 1953.

Tomkins, S. S. *The Thematic Apperception Test: Theory and Techniques of Interpretations*. New York: Grune and Stratton, Inc., 1947.

Travers, R. M. W. *Essentials of Learning*, 2nd ed. New York: The Macmillan Company, 1967.

———. "The Evaluation of the Outcomes of Guidance," *Educational and Psychological Measurement*, XVIII (1948), 325–333.

———. *Studies Related to the Design of Audiovisual Teaching Materials*, Final Report, U. S. Department of Health, Education, and Welfare, Office of Education Contract No. 3-20-003, 1966.

———. "Toward Taking the Fun Out of Building A Theory of Instruction," *Teachers College Record*, LXIIX (1966), 49–60.

Truax, Charles B., and Robert R. Carkhuff. *Toward Effective Counseling and Therapy*. Chicago: Aldine Publishing Company, 1967.

Tuddenham, Read D., and Margaret M. Snyder. *Physical Growth of California Boys and Girls from Birth to Eighteen Years. Publications in Child Development*, 1, No. 2, Berkeley: University of California Press, 1954.

Underwood, B. J., and R. W. Schulz. *Meaningfulness and Verbal Learning*. Philadelphia: L. B. Lippincott Co., 1960.

Wallace, David. "A Case For and Against Mail Questionnaires," *Public Opinion Quarterly*, XVIII (1954), 40–52.

Wallen, N., and R. M. W. Travers. *Measured Needs of Teachers and Their Behavior in the Classroom*. Final Report, U. S. Office of Education Contract No. 444 (8029), 1961.

Webb, Eugene J., Donald T. Campbell, Richard D. Schwartz, and Lee Sechrest. *Unobtrusive Measures: Nonreactive Research in the Social Sciences*. Chicago: Rand McNally Company, 1966.

White, R. K., and R. Lippitt. *Autocracy and Democracy*. New York: Harper & Row, Publishers, 1960.

Withall, John. "The Development of a Technique for the Measurement of Social Emotional Climate in the Classroom," *Journal of Experimental Education*, XVII (1949), 347–361.

Wylie, R. C. *The Self-Concept*. Lincoln, Neb.: University of Nebraska Press, 1961.

Zook, George F., and M. E. Haggerty. *The Evaluation of Higher Institutions*. Chicago: University of Chicago Press, 1936.

————. *Principles of Accrediting Higher Institutions*. Chicago: University of Chicago Press, 1935.

Indexes

Index

of Names

Index

of Subjects